Studies in Penal Theory and Penal Ethics

Series Editor: Professor Andrew von Hirsch

Volumes Published in this Series

Criminal Deterrence and Sentencing Severity

By Andrew von Hirsch, Anthony Bottoms,
Elizabeth Burney, Per-Olof Wikstrom

Ethical and Social Perspectives on Situational Crime Prevention

Edited by Andrew von Hirsch, David Garland and Alison Wakefield

Restorative Justice and Criminal Justice:
Competing or Reconcilable Paradigms?

Edited by Andrew von Hirsch, Julian Roberts,
Anthony Bottoms, Kent Roach and Mara Schiff

Restorative Justice and Criminal Justice

Competing or Reconcilable Paradigms?

Edited by

ANDREW VON HIRSCH
JULIAN V. ROBERTS
ANTHONY BOTTOMS

and

KENT ROACH
MARA SCHIFF

·HART·
PUBLISHING

HART PUBLISHING
OXFORD AND PORTLAND, OREGON
2003

Published in North America (US and Canada) by
Hart Publishing
c/o International Specialized Book Services
5804 NE Hassalo Street
Portland, Oregon
97213-3644
USA

Hart Publishing is a specialist legal publisher based in Oxford, England.
To order further copies of this book or to request a list of other publications
please write to:

Hart Publishing, Salters Boatyard, Folly Bridge,
Abingdon Rd, Oxford, OX1 4LB
Telephone: +44 (0) 1865 245533 Fax: +44 (0) 1865 794882
email: mail@hartpub.co.uk
WEBSITE: http//:www.hartpub.co.uk

British Library Cataloguing in Publication Data

Data Available

ISBN 1-84113-273-X (hardback)

Typeset by SNP Best-set Typesetter Ltd., Hong Kong
Printed and bound in Great Britain by
Biddles Ltd, *www.biddles.co.uk*

Preface

Over the past decade, Restorative Justice has emerged as a potent alternative paradigm in criminal justice. Several jurisdictions have witnessed a proliferation of programmes and policies that are guided by restorative principles. Some countries have introduced statutory reforms to advance restorative considerations in sentencing.

The aims of Restorative Justice have been variously—and at times ambitiously—described, and their precise meaning remains somewhat unclear. This volume seeks to clarify the aims and principles of Restorative Justice. As well, it seeks to explore the sometimes difficult relationship between Restorative Justice and more traditional models of justice. Some authorities have suggested that they exist in opposition; others propose overlapping goals.

The chapters fall into one of two categories. Some essays explore Restorative Justice and the use of theory, while others examine the impact of Restorative Justice at a more practical level. This examination includes experiences in several Western countries.

The chapters in this volume began as presentations at two seminars. The first was held at Fitzwilliam College, Cambridge in October 2000, and the second at the Faculty of Law, University of Toronto in May, 2001. We are most grateful to all participants attending the two seminars. Their insights made all the seminars richer and the resulting chapters have benefited greatly from participants' comments. We are grateful to the following organisations for their support of these seminars:

Centre for Penal Theory and Penal Ethics at the University of Cambridge; the Law Foundation of Ontario; the Law Commission of Canada; the Social Sciences and Humanities Research Council of Canada; the Faculty of Law and the Centre of Criminology at the University of Toronto, and the Connaught Fund at the University of Toronto.

Finally, we would like to thank Hannah Young for her support of the volume and Helen Griffiths for her tireless work in editing the chapters and preparing the manuscript for publication.

A.v.H., Cambridge
J.R., Ottawa
A.E.B., Cambridge
K.R., Toronto
M.S., Florida

April 2002

Contents

Notes on Contributors

Andrew Ashworth, DCL, FBA, QC is Vinerian Professor of English Law in the University of Oxford. Recent books include *Sentencing and Criminal Justice* (3rd edn 2000) and *Human Rights, Serious Crime and Criminal Procedure* (2002), and he has contributed an article to the special issue of the *British Journal of Criminology* on restorative justice (July 2002).

Sir Anthony Bottoms, FBA is Wolfson Professor of Criminology at the University of Cambridge. He has written extensively on criminological theory.

John Braithwaite is a Professor in the Research School of Social Sciences at the Australian National University and Chair of RegNet, the Regulatory Institutions Network. Recent books are *Restorative Justice and Responsive Regulations, Shame Management Through Reintegration* (with E Ahmed, N Harris and V Braithwaite) and *Restorative Justice and Family Violence* (edited with H Strang).

Kathleen Daly is an Associate Professor in Criminology and Criminal Justice at Griffith University. During 1998–99, she directed a major research project on restorative justice in South Australia; and in 2001–03, she is directing a second project on the race and gender politics of new justice practices in Australia, New Zealand, the United States, and Canada.

Jim Dignan, LLB MA is Professor of Criminology and Restorative Justice at the Centre for Criminological and Legal Research, University of Sheffield and has written on a variety of theoretical, practical and policy-issues relating to the development of restorative justice.

Antony Duff was educated at Oxford, and is a Professor of Philosophy at the University of Stirling, where he has taught since 1970. He has published *Trials and Punishments* (Cambridge University Press, 1986), *Intention, Agency and Criminal Liability* (Blackwell, 1990), *Criminal Attempts* (Oxford University Press, 1996), and *Punishment, Communication, and Community* (Oxford University Press, 2001). He has held a British Academy Research Readership (1989–91) and now holds a Leverhulme Major Research Fellowship (2002–05).

Carolyn Hoyle is a University Lecturer in Criminology and Director of the MSc Criminology and Criminal Justice at the Centre for Criminological Research, University of Oxford. Publications include *Negotiating Domestic Violence* (Oxford University Press, Oxford Clarendon Series, 1998), and *New Visions of Crime Victims* (Hart Publishing, 2002) co-edited with Richard Young.

Barbara Hudson is a Professor in the Lancashire Law School, University of Central Lancashire. She teaches and researches in criminology, penology and socio-legal studies and is the author of several books and articles on criminal justice topics. Publications include *Justice through Punishment* (Macmillan, 1987) and *Understanding Justice* (Open University Press, 1996). She is currently completing a book *Justice in the Risk Society*, to be published by Sage.

Leena Kurki is a Finnish lawyer and criminologist who lives in St. Paul, Minnesota. Her research interests include restorative justice, international standards for sentencing, and racial disparities in the criminal justice system.

Allison Morris was, until recently, Professor of Criminology and Director of the Institute of Criminology, at Victoria University of Wellington, New Zealand. She is now an independent researcher and is currently writing up the second New Zealand National Survey of Crime Victims and is involved in evaluations of family group conferences for young offenders and of restorative justice conferences for adult offenders.

Gabrielle Maxwell is Director of the Crime and Justice Research Centre at Victoria University of Wellington, New Zealand. Publications include: *Family Victims and Culture: Youth Justice in New Zealand* (Department of Social Welfare, Wellington, 1993); *Understanding Reoffending* (Victoria University, 1999; and *Restorative Justice for Juveniles: Conferences, Mediation and Circles* (Hart Publishing, 2001) all with Allison Morris.

Kent Roach is a Professor of Law and Criminology at the University of Toronto. He is the author of several books including *Due Process and Victims' Rights: The New Law and Politics of Criminal Justice* (1999) and *Criminal Law* 2nd edn (2000). He has also written several articles on sentencing and restorative justice and has been involved in the litigation of sentencing issues.

Julian Roberts is Professor of Criminology at the University of Ottawa. His most recent publications include *Penal Populism and Public Opinion* (with L Stalans, D Indermaur and M Hough) (Oxford University Press, 2002) and *Changing Attitudes to Punishment* (with M Hough) (Willan Publishing, 2002).

Paul Roberts is Reader in Criminal Justice at the University of Nottingham School of Law. He teaches postgraduate courses on the philosophical, international and comparative dimensions of criminal justice, and is Programme Convenor of the School's LLM in Criminal Justice and LLM in International Criminal Justice and Armed Conflict.

Mara Schiff is an Associate Professor of Criminology and Criminal Justice and Florida Atlantic University. She is co-editor of *Restorative Community Justice:*

Repairing Harm and Transforming Communities (with Gordon Bazemore) and recently completed a major research project examining restorative conferencing for youth in the United States.

Joanna Shapland is Professor of Criminal Justice and Director of the Institute for the Study of the Legal Profession, University of Sheffield, UK. She is co-editor of the *International Review of Victimology* and is currently leading the evaluation of the English restorative justice initiatives funded by the Home Office.

Clifford Shearing is a Professor in the Research School of Social Sciences at the Australian National University and a co-director of Security 21: The National Centre for Security and Justice within RegNet, the Regulatory Institutions Network. He is also a Professor at the School of Government at the University of the Western Cape. His research and policy work explores developments in governance.

Daniel W Van Ness is Executive Director of the International Centre for Justice and Reconciliation, a programme of Prison Fellowship International. His most recent book is *Restoring Justice* (2nd edn), co-authored with Karen Strong. He is an Adjunct Professor at Pepperdine University School of Law in California and at Hangdon Global University in the Republic of Korea.

Andrew von Hirsch LLD, is Honorary Professor of Penal Theory and Penal Law at the University of Cambridge, and is Director of the Centre for Penal Theory and Penal Ethics at the Institute of Criminology, Cambridge. He has written extensively on punishment and criminal sentencing theory.

Lode Walgrave is a Professor of Criminology at the Katholieke Universiteit Leuven (Belgium) and co-ordinator of the International Network for Research on Restorative Justice for Juveniles. He is, with Gordon Bazemore, editor of *Restorative Justice for Juveniles* (Criminal Justice Press, 1999). He has recently published several articles and book chapters on the relation of restorative justice with the state and the law.

Richard Young is Assistant Director of the Centre for Criminological Research, University of Oxford. Recent publications include *Criminal Justice* (2nd edn) (Butterworths) with A Sanders, and *New Vision of Crime Victims* (Hart Publishing), co-edited with C Hoyle.

1

Principles of Restorative Justice

John Braithwaite

Restorative justice, conceived as an intellectual tradition or as an approach to political practice, involves radical transformation. On this radical view restorative justice is not simply a way of reforming the criminal justice system, it is a way of transforming the entire legal system, our family lives, our conduct in the workplace, our practice of politics. Its vision is of a holistic change in the way we do justice in the world (Zehr, 1995; Van Ness and Strong, 1997). This essay seeks to explain the principles of such holistic restorative justice at two levels. First, it considers holism at the meta level of what sort of theory is required. Are we looking for a jurisprudence of restorative justice, a criminology of restorative justice, or what? I argue for an ambitious long-term project of integrating explanatory and normative theories of restorative justice and explain how this differs from the projects of those attracted to competing intellectual traditions. Second, specific suggestions are advanced for values against which the accomplishments and disasters of restorative justice might be evaluated. More importantly, I seek to develop a methodology for progressively elaborating restorative justice values at the same time as we do empirical research that illuminates the implications of such value framing.

Restorative justice is about struggling against injustice in the most restorative way we can manage. So conceived, it targets injustice reduction; to see the goal simply as crime reduction impoverishes its mission. It aspires to offer practical guidance on how we can lead the good life as democratic citizens by struggling against injustice. It says we must conduct that struggle while seeking to dissuade hasty resort to punitive rectification or other forms of stigmatising response. Injustice and precipitate recourse to punitive rectification of it together help explain a great number of the deepest evils of contemporary life—war, terrorism, our (in)justice system—particularly its prison system, poverty, racism, sexism. All of these evils are at the same time instances of injustice and causes of it; poverty is itself unjust and a cause of countless other injustices. The social movement for restorative justice is important because it provides a fresh practical programme for combating injustice and stigmatisation. The programme is grounded in moral intuitions of considerable resonance for most people because they have a long history, particularly in the spirituality of the world's great religions.

Unlike many of the contributors to this volume, I do not see restorative justice embracing retribution, another intuition of great resonance and history. I part company with those who see punishment as a respectful way of raising our children, of dealing with criminals or with nations we disagree with. Compared with restorative dialogue, even non-restorative dialogue, punishment is less respectful. That is not to say we should never resort to it. But when we do it should be on consequentialist grounds—because there is no alternative way of resisting injustice. We should then do so as respectfully as we can, but without deluding ourselves that hitting or confining can be inherently respectful.

I. INSTITUTIONALISING CONSENSUS ON LIMITS

That said, I agree with many of the reasons my colleagues in this volume advance for retribution or just deserts as applied to criminal offenders. All the contributors here are reductionists on punishment. That means that I have much more in common with them than with the political leaders of the nations from which they come, perhaps with the noble exception of Leena Kurki's homeland of Finland, whose leaders seem admirably reductionist. While I submit that the persuasive and the right way to convince political leaders to be reductionists is to show them the terrible consequences prisons have for peoples' lives, I concede there is a story about how deontologists can be persuasive about reductionism.[1] All writers in this collection believe that unbreachable upper limits should be placed on the punishment that can be imposed for each type of crime, whether that punishment is imposed by a court or a restorative justice process. Moreover, they all believe that there should be substantial limits, so that severe punishments (such as any use of imprisonment) should be permissible only for serious crimes. They would all agree that longer terms of imprisonment to incapacitate repeat property offenders breach the kind of upper limits they favour. Many of them believe in these limits on desert grounds. I derive the need for their unbreachability from a republican philosophy of what justice requires—pursuit of non-domination (Braithwaite and Pettit, 1990; Pettit, 1997). The nub of this argument is that, by definition, citizens cannot enjoy a republican form of freedom in a society where they are insecure or uncertain about the limits on state coercive power and few limits of this kind could be more fundamental than precise limits on the length of prison terms.

There has been a long-running argument between, for example, Philip Pettit and myself on one side and Andrew von Hirsch and Andrew Ashworth on the other as to who has a philosophy that most robustly ties down the assurance that under no circumstance can it be viewed as morally right to breach those upper

---

[1] Deontologists believe in honouring certain constraints regardless of the consequences of doing so. Consequentialists, in contrast, seek to maximise certain good consequences. Some consequentialists, however, argue it is possible to give sound consequentialist justification for certain constraints.

constraints. They accuse us of being vulnerable to a moral imperative to breach them, when doing so would reduce the amount of domination in the world (von Hirsch, 1993). We deny this, advancing a conception of non-domination that implies a consequentialist justification for tying our hands against ever breaching certain constraints. We can also be correctly accused of advocating breach of what many retributivists view as proper lower constraints by advocating mercy as a value for those who 'deserve' punishment. We retort that when we more often grant mercy in cases where the retributivist must punish, then the retributivist will more often breach *upper* constraints because by punishing more often in a system prone to error the retributivist will more often make the error of punishing the innocent. We accuse retributivists of slipping in and out of conceiving just deserts, hard treatment, or censure as a good consequence, leaving them vulnerable to the conclusion that in some circumstances breaching an upper constraint is morally required to assure that desert or censure is not escaped.[2] Moreover, we say that if crime prevention is a general justifying aim of a criminal justice system, how can it be coherent to honour constraints that defeat the realisation of that overarching aim? They reply that it makes all the sense in the world to justify the existence of a system in a different manner from the way you make it work.

The point I want to advance is that we can disagree passionately on whose philosophy is more invulnerable to breach of upper constraints on punishment while agreeing that the politically important thing is to institutionalise laws and regulatory mechanisms that work to forbid the breach of (reduced) upper constraints.[3] That requires respectful acknowledgement that both sides are intellectually serious about upper constraints and politically serious about working together to enforce them against judges and restorative justice processes. The important shared project is about how to make the regulatory mechanisms work. How do we fund youth advocacy groups to advise young people of their rights, to blow the whistle when a restorative justice conference imposes an outcome that is more punitive than a court would impose? How do we censure judges for overruling restorative justice outcomes as insufficiently punitive?

II. DEMOCRATIC PRAGMATISM

Here a feature of restorative justice of some importance is its democratic pragmatism. There is no blueprint for how an ideal restorative justice system should work.

---

[2] For example, if proportionate censure is conceived as what we are constrained to honour deontologically and hard treatment is conceived as necessary to achieve censure, then we are reasoning consequentially not about censure but about hard treatment as a means of securing censure. To that extent we are no less vulnerable to breaching hard treatment limits in pursuit of our obligation to censure than is a utilitarian in his pursuit of hard treatment to achieve the goal of crime prevention.

[3] Here I assume that deontologists are willing to be consequentialist about making enforcement work to assure that upper constraints are honoured. Of course, that enforcement action must itself honour proper limits. At each level of this regress the republican theorist believes she can design a regulatory strategy which is maximally effective (at the first level for preventing the injustice, at the second

There are restorative values we discuss below. They inform a vision of a direction for reform. As is clear from the presentations of others in this volume, there can be considerable common ground with desert theorists about a wide variety of reforms that move in the same direction—upper constraints and human rights constraints and shifts from punitive to restorative practices. Those who insist on coalitions only with folk who share their philosophy fail to bring about change. One needs a theory of the good, and a theory of how you move from the bad to the good working with colleagues who share only parts of your vision of the good. One of the exciting things about restorative justice as an intellectual tradition is that it may be slowly developing a sophisticated theory of transition. For a consequentialist, one of the virtues of incremental transition is that it enables experimentation, innovation combined with evaluation. Empirical research conducted by a number of the contributors to this volume has refined in various ways how we should think of the good and bad consequences at issue with restorative justice. So restorative justice at the moment is an adventure of research and development, where the research is proving tremendously encouraging in some ways, discouraging in others. As we use empirical experience to repair this leaky ship at sea, we should be careful about being too sure about a plan for the voyage. Rather we should see ourselves as in a process of Research and Development toward one.

In the R & D process, we should be wary of the Russian capitalism fallacy. Research on the movement of Russia from communism to capitalism finds it to be a disaster; people are poorer under capitalism than under communism. The fallacy is to induce from this research, as some Russian patriots do, that communism is superior to capitalism. The sad thing about Russia is that it had devoted impressive intellectual energies to analysing the transition from capitalism to communism but had done little serious thinking about how to execute the transition from communism to capitalism. There are moments in transitions where you get the worst of both worlds. What is needed is a theory of transition that is

---

level for preventing breach of the constraint) while honouring appropriate limits. The retributive deontologist is pessimistic about this capability at the first level but seems to be an optimist at the second level. If one is a retributive deontologist at the first level, one must consider whether to also be a retributive deontologist at the second level. That is, do we impose a punishment proportionate to their wrongdoing on a person who has breached proper limits on punishment—be that person a judge, police officer, parent or citizen? What the consequentialist should do is regulate such conduct with the regulatory strategy best designed for achieving the good consequence of honouring the sentencing constraint, combating judicial corruption, regulating community stigmatisation or corporal punishment of offenders that exceeds acceptable limits. If the deontologist says no, what we must do is give the non-compliant judge or citizen the punishment she deserves, then the deontologist has done a worse job of honouring the first constraint than the consequentialist. On the other hand, the retributive deontologist might say, 'I am only constrained to dispense just deserts when enforcing the law against injustice. When enforcing the law which regulates this law enforcement I will be a consequentialist who seeks to maximise the honouring of proportionality constraints'. This second answer is the one the pragmatic consequentialist hopes for. Still the consequentialist must ask: 'What then will be your consequentialist theory in this second order enforcement task? How will it be secured against breach of proper constraints? And what is the reason you choose to regulate primary rule-breakers deontologically while regulating the regulation of rule-breaking (by judges, police, parents or citizens in a conference) consequentially?'

realistic about the persistence of the worst features of the old regime. People who persist in their belief in these terrible features need to be given some democratic space in which they can learn some of the merits of the alternative. This is very much the way restorative justice approaches the punitiveness of many people in restorative justice processes. There is no need to despair if a lot of people are highly punitive in restorative justice processes (Daly, this volume); it would be astounding if this did not happen. Reason for despair would be if restorative justice failed to help more of them become less punitive over time.

Citizen empowerment, I wish to argue, should be a higher-order value of restorative justice than, for example, non-punitiveness. Genuine empowerment means that the punitiveness of punitive people is not ruled out of order. Restorative justice allows punitive outcomes so long as they do not exceed upper constraints imposed by the law nor abuse fundamental human rights. The evidence is at the same time that restorative justice conferences help people to become less punitive (Braithwaite, 2002: chapter 3). This is what I mean by the democratic pragmatism of the restorative justice approach to transition. The analogy to electoral democracy is strong. Democrats do not resort to arms if a democratic electoral process leads to the election of an anti-democratic government. Rather they prefer to work towards the next election; meantime they try to mobilise constitutional constraints against anti-democratic shifts the elected tyrants seek to bring about.

The next section develops a little further the rudiments of why it makes sense to work toward a broad theory of restorative justice to inform how to struggle against all forms of injustice restoratively. The section deals with how the properties of such a theory will be different from the theories that emanate from extant theoretical traditions. Then in the following section we consider what are restorative values and how these should be prioritised.

III. THINKING THEORETICALLY ABOUT RESTORATIVE JUSTICE

My approach to the theory of restorative justice is to seek to develop explanatory and normative theories that inform each other. Explanatory theories are ordered sets of propositions about the way the world is, normative theories are ordered sets of propositions about the way the world ought to be. Elsewhere, with Christine Parker and Philip Pettit, I have attempted to argue, using restorative justice as an example, that the effort to integrate explanatory and normative theory gives promise of simultaneously improving both theories—increasing explanatory and normative power (Braithwaite and Parker, 1999; Braithwaite and Pettit, 2000). What we aspire to is the development and testing of explanatory theories of how to prevent injustice, normative theories of what it means to prevent injustice and how we ought to do so.

Such an aspiration is frustrated by a variety of more dominant intellectual traditions that will be briefly considered in turn. If there were an award for the intellectual tradition least likely to nourish an integrated theory of restorative justice, the *philosophy of punishment* would surely be a contender. The philosophy of punishment is oriented to questions like: When should we punish? What is the right punishment? By this it means state punishment, mostly displaying a puzzling lack of interest in when it is appropriate for state versus non-state actors to do the punishing. The deepest problem with this tradition is that the answer to the question 'What is the right punishment?' will almost always be the wrong solution to the problem.

Jurisprudence is a broader tradition that considers a range of other remedies to a problem beyond punishment, though still mostly remedies at the level of state law. The trouble with jurisprudence from my perspective is that it is not interested in explanatory theory nor in testing empirical claims. Jurimetrics, the closest field of empirical study, has surprisingly little to do with jurisprudence. Jurisprudence is dominated by the discipline of philosophy which, according to millennial critics, had one of its weaker centuries in the twentieth. One reason suggested for this has been its retreat from the world of explaining social phenomena. This is one of the things that distinguishes great normative philosophers of previous centuries whose thought had an impact on historical events—like Mill, Bentham, Smith, Locke, Cicero, Aristotle—from the greatest philosophers of the twentieth century. The explanatory Smith of *The Wealth of Nations* is connected to the normative Smith of *The Theory of Moral Sentiments*. Contemporary economists read one and not the other; philosophers the reverse, to the mutual impoverishment of both disciplines.

Criminology is the contemporary discipline most systematically engaged with explanatory theory about injustice. Not only is it impoverished by substantial neglect of normative theory, it also tends to narrow the kind of injustice we are concerned about to crime. For any form of serious injustice, defining it as a crime and reacting to it in some way appropriate to that definition is only one of many options for countering the injustice. Regulation is a more fruitful research field because it does not assume crime to be the most productive or just way of viewing an injustice, nor does it assume that criminalisation will have relevance to its explanation. The most consequential questions about how to regulate injustice do not arise in the context of deciding how to deal with a criminal case that is being processed by the criminal justice system. They are questions about whether the injustice would be better addressed by a family, by providing economic incentives for just behaviour, by just speech, as opposed to criminalisation. A central claim about the importance of restorative justice is that it provides a method, a forum and a set of relevant values for making these more important judgements.

My prescription for restorative justice therefore is that it should not only be wary of these traditions, but actively liberate itself from their narrow strictures of evaluation. That said, the richest resources for restorative justice to draw upon in its own way are within these traditions. Criminal law jurisprudence, for example, has made a uniquely important contribution to our thinking about human rights precisely because of its obsession with punishment. It forbids punishing in certain ways or beyond a certain level without the guarantee of specified procedural safe-guards. So when citizens decide they would like to inflict a certain punishment on one of their number the court can step in and say: 'Yes, you can confiscate your son's access to the family car because he has been driving dangerously', or 'No, you cannot decide to imprison him'. If the dangerous driving is so terrible that this might be warranted, the allegations must first be proven to constitute a crime and then the crime must be demonstrated to be of a seriousness that allows the possibility of a prison sentence.

While there is a set of propositions that we are seeking to advance toward the building of normative and explanatory theories of regulating injustice restora-tively, there is also a need to nest under these general theoretical aspirations a plethora of more specific theories. For example, how to prevent violence as a form of injustice requires many different specific theories. Family violence in indige-nous communities demands a different theory from juvenile street violence. How to prevent violence between nations requires a different kind of theory from school bullying. For all these kinds of violence, however, there may be some recurrent explanations that account for violence in terms of failure of dialogue, in terms of domination, stigmatisation, disrespect begetting disrespect, unacknowledged shame, techniques that neutralise taboos against violence, and so on. It also seems that there is a meaningful sense in which constraints need to be properly applied to the regulation of all kinds of violence. Fundamental human rights as defined by the UN human rights instruments apply across all these areas of violence, though there is variation in which rights are more salient for different types of violence. For interpersonal criminal violence upper limits on prison terms that can be imposed are crucial. With violence between nations, the imperative limits are quite different—non-use of nuclear or biological weapons, no indiscriminate bombing of civilians, the Geneva Convention. And the institutions for regulating them are different—the UN Security Council, the European Union and NATO in Europe, shaming by NGOs like Amnesty and Human Rights Watch, and in future the International Criminal Court. The checks and balances against exceeding limits are quite different, but the claim that checks and balances can have explanatory power and should have normative force is a general claim. For a republican normative theorist, there is also a general assertion about who the regulatory community should be who exercises checks and balances against breaches of limits. It should be whichever community will be most effective at securing freedom as non-domination by making the checks and balances work in a decent way.

IV. VALUES

With values against which restorative justice should be evaluated, there are some general ones—like accountability—that must apply to restorative justice in all domains. But nested under the general values are more specific values that must be equally central in each specific regulatory context. So in regulating school bullying, the educational development of children is a core value that must be protected in whatever decisions are made in a restorative justice process. In healing a civil war fought over religious differences, religious tolerance may be the more central value to be advanced by the settlement. Some critics of restorative justice see it as a problem that restorative justice theorists put forward a confusion of values. Just as in an instance of armed conflict between states it seems obvious that there are a lot of values at stake, so in a case of street violence it also seems true that there will be many values at issue. Philip Pettit and I have argued that these competing values can be balanced and rendered commensurable for purposes of practical reasoning by evaluating their priority according to how they contribute to advancing dominion or freedom as non-domination. But this is an overly abstract criterion for operationalisation in empirical studies of whether values are realised and for giving practical guidance to practitioners.

Heather Strang and I have argued that restorative justice ought to pass a restorative process test as well as a restorative values test (Braithwaite and Strang, 2000). Here I reformulate restorative processes as procedural values of restorative justice. Strictly they are according to Rokeach's (1968) leading formulation of the values concept. Rokeach distinguishes values that are ways of behaving (eg fairness, a procedural value) from values which are desirable end states of existence or goals in life (eg peace, happiness). When a great deal is at risk for the alleged perpetrator of injustice—for example, imprisonment—procedural values rise in importance compared to outcome values. When less is at risk, procedural assurance can be more minimal. So when a parent does no more than issue an informal warning to a child over a minor act of violence directed against a sibling, it may not be necessary to have all stakeholders in the room. Indeed the warning may be issued on the run while the family meal is being cooked. In contrast, if there is any prospect that the child might be removed from his family and placed in a state institution as a result of the violence, all family members, including grandparents and other extended family and loved ones who would be affected by the removal, should have their say on the alternatives. While procedural requirements for the 'corridor conferencing' (Morrison, 2001) a teacher does with students on the run may be minimal, we would still want to put a lot of effort into seeking to persuade teachers of the virtues of other restorative values in respect of corridor conferencing. The same applies to our efforts to heal victims of a crime or tort where the wrongdoer is not known.

Elsewhere, I have collected my preliminary suggestions for restorative values into three groups (Braithwaite, forthcoming). The first group comprises the values that take priority when there is any serious sanction or other infringement of freedom at risk. These are the fundamental procedural safeguards. In the context of liberty being threatened in any significant way, if no other values are realised, these must be. They are:

Constraining Values
— Non-domination

— Empowerment
— Honouring legally specific upper limits on sanctions
— Respectful listening
— Equal concern for all stakeholders
— Accountability, appealability
— Respect for the fundamental human rights specified in the Universal Declaration of Human Rights, the International Covenant on Economic, Social and Cultural Rights, the International Covenant on Civil and Political Rights and its Second Optional Protocol, the United Nations Declaration on the Elimination of Violence Against Women and the Declaration of Basic Principles of Justice for Victims of Crime and Abuse of Power.

Non-domination[4]: We do see a lot of domination in restorative processes, as in all spheres of social interaction. But a programme is not restorative if it fails to be active in preventing domination. Any attempt by a participant at a conference to silence or dominate another participant must be countered. This does not mean the conference convenor has to intervene. On the contrary, it is better if other stakeholders are given the space to speak up against dominating speech. But if domination persists and the stakeholders are afraid to confront it, then the convenor must confront it. Preferably gently: 'I think some of us would like to hear what Jane has to say in her own words.'

Often it is rather late for confronting domination once the restorative process is under way. Power imbalance is a structural phenomenon. It follows that restorative processes must be structured so as to minimise power imbalance. Young offenders must not be led into a situation where they are upbraided by a 'roomful of adults' (Haines, 1998). There must be adults who see themselves as having a responsibility to be advocates for the child, adults who will speak up. If this is not accomplished, a conference or circle can always be adjourned and reconvened with effective supporters of the child in the room. Similarly, we cannot tolerate the scenario of a dominating group of family violence offenders and their patriarchal defenders intimidating women and children who are victims into frightened silence. When risks of power imbalance are most acute our standards should expect of us a lot of preparatory work to restore balance both backstage and frontstage during the process. Organised advocacy groups have a particularly important role when power imbalances are most acute. These include women's and children's advocacy groups when family violence is at issue, environmental advocacy groups when crimes against the environment by powerful corporations are at issue.

Empowerment: Non-domination does imply empowerment. In case readers misread non-domination to be a passive value, empowerment has been explicitly

---

[4] The next three pages of this paper draw upon Braithwaite (2002b) where a more detailed development of the argument is provided.

added to the list. Moreover, empowerment does the useful work discussed earlier; it trumps other values on our second and third list. For example, forgiveness is listed below. But if a victim rejects an apology, choosing to hate, the ideal is that the conference empowers them to do so. Empowerment takes precedence over forgiveness.

Honouring Limits: Enough said on this already. I simply add as someone who hypothesises that restorative justice processes have their positive effects through a dynamic of reintegrative shaming and work their most negative effects through stigmatisation, that it seems important to prohibit any degrading or humiliating form of treatment. We had a conference in Canberra where all the stakeholders agreed it was a good idea for a young offender to wear a T-shirt stating 'I am a thief'. This sort of outcome should be banned.

Respectful listening: Just as upper limits on sanctions constrain what citizens are empowered to decide in a restorative justice process, equally citizens are not empowered to howl others down. Respectful listening is a condition of participation; folk who persistently refuse to honour it should be asked to leave. It trumps empowerment of the one because it disables the empowerment of the many.

Equal concern for all stakeholders: Restorative justice programmes must be concerned with the needs and with the empowerment not only of offenders, but also of victims and affected communities. Programmes where victims are exploited as no more than props for the rehabilitation of offenders are morally unacceptable. Deals that are win-win for victims and offenders but where certain other members of the community are serious losers, worse losers whose perspective is not even heard, are morally unacceptable. Equal concern does not mean equal help. Help should vary according to need (Sullivan and Tifft, 2001).

Accountability, appealability: Principals to any restorative justice process about a legally significant matter, not just criminal matters, should have a right to appeal the restorative resolution to a court of law and a right to resolve the dispute in a court of law in preference to a conference/circle. This is my most radical prescription. In an era where legal aid is contracting it seems piously undeliverable. Elsewhere I have argued, relying heavily on Christine Parker's (1999) work, for the kind of radical transformation of the entire legal system along restorative justice lines that would make it affordable (Braithwaite, 2002: chapter 8). Not all of the accountability mechanisms of criminal trials, however, seem appropriate to the philosophy of restorative justice. For example, if we are concerned about averting stigmatisation and assuring undominated dialogue, we may not want conferences or circles to be normally open to the public. But if that is our policy, it seems especially important for researchers, critics, journalists, political leaders, judges, colleagues from restorative justice programmes in other places, to be able to sit in on conferences or circles (with the permission of the participants) so there can be informed public debate and exposure of inappropriate practices. Most importantly, it is critical that restorative justice processes can be observed by peer reviewers whose job it is to report on compliance with the kinds of standards under discussion here. It seems reasonable that offenders put into restorative justice programmes where any criminal sanctions are at risk be advised of their right to seek the advice of a lawyer on whether they should participate in the programme. Perhaps this would be an empty standard in poorer nations where lawyers are not in practical terms affordable or available for most criminal defendants. But wealthier nations can afford higher standards on this issue. Arresting police officers who refer cases to restorative justice processes should be required to provide a telephone number of a free legal advice line on whether agreeing to the restorative justice process is prudent.

Then in Braithwaite (2002b), I consider a second group of restorative justice values that participants are empowered to ignore. Their being ignored is not reason for abandoning a restorative justice process. It might, however, be reason for asking the participants to agree to an adjournment so that new participants might be brought in to give these values more chance of realisation. While the second group includes values that can be trumped by empowerment, they are values against which the success of restorative processes can be evaluated. Moreover they are values around which the restorativist is democratically active, seeking to persuade the community that these are decent values. They include very basic kinds of restoration like restoration of property loss and emotional restoration, and more abstract ones like restoration of dignity, compassion and social support. They are all essentially different forms of healing/restoration. Prevention of further injustice is also an obvious and central principle. There are as many modalities of evaluation of the performance of programmes against this principle as there are forms of injustice. The one being most adequately researched at this time is prevention of future crime, an evaluation criterion that has shown progressively more encouraging results over the past three years (Braithwaite, 2002a: chapter 3). I will not detail or defend any list of principles here, as what I want to emphasise is the method for clarifying the principles of restorative justice. That method, we will see, implies revisability of any such list and local adaptation.

My proposal for an initial formulation of the values was influenced by two sources. First, I attempted to craft them as consensus principles by choosing values which are used to justify the international human rights in the above-mentioned treaties that have been ratified by most nations (see Braithwaite, 2002b). Secondly, I selected values from these consensus documents that also come up repeatedly in the empirical experience of what victims and offenders say they want in restorative justice processes in the criminal justice system (see Strang, 2000). They represent what restoring justice means for participants. The privileging of empowerment on the constraining list of values above means that participating citizens are given the power to tell their own stories in their own way to reveal whatever sense of injustice they wish to see repaired. At times this can involve an utterly idiosyncratic conception of justice.[5] Again this is the pragmatic democracy of the restorative tradition. Elsewhere, with Pettit and Parker, I have elucidated my own, perhaps idiosyncratic, conception of what justice entails—republican justice (for an overview see Braithwaite, 2002: chapters 4, 5). The paradox of being a republican is that your commitment to non-domination means that when you yourself participate in a restorative justice process you are obliged not to try to force republicanism down anyone's throat. You try respectfully to make the republican case for justice; sometimes you persuade, sometimes you fail—then as the pragmatic democrat you live with the decision.

Providing social support to develop human capabilities to the full is one particularly indispensable principle because it marks the need for a consideration of transforming as well as restoring or healing values. Providing social support to develop human capabilities to the full is a corrective to the concern that restorative justice may be used to restore an unjust status quo. The key design idea here is that regulatory institutions must be designed so as to nurture developmental institutions. Too often regulatory institutions stultify human capabilities, the design of punitive criminal justice systems being a classic example. Regulatory institutions cannot do the main work of social justice; developmental institutions of families, civil society (eg charities), schools, workplaces, state welfare and global institutions of redistribution, such as the IMF and World Bank, must be reformed to deliver that. Yet, as I have attempted to argue in more detail elsewhere, punitive justice is a great disabler of social justice—causing unemployment, debt, disease, drug addiction, suicide and racial degradation—whereas restorative justice can be an important enabler of social justice (Braithwaite, 2002: chapters 5, 7). In evaluation research that tests such a developmental principle, the test is not whether human capabilities actually are developed to the full as a result of a restorative justice process, but whether a restorative process leads us closer to this ideal rather than leading us away from it, and closer than non-restorative alternatives.

Then in Braithwaite (2002b), I develop a third priority list of values that includes remorse over injustice, apology, censure of the act, forgiveness of the person and mercy. This list differs from the second list of values in a conceptually important way. It is not that the list three values are less important than list two. When Desmond Tutu (1999) says *No Future Without Forgiveness*, many restorative justice advocates are inclined to agree. Forgiveness differs from, say, respectful listening as a value of restorative justice in the following sense. We actively seek to persuade participants that they ought to listen respectfully, but we do not urge them to forgive. It is cruel and wrong to expect a victim of crime to forgive. Apology, forgiveness and mercy are gifts; they only have meaning if they well up from a genuine desire in the person who forgives, apologises or grants mercy. Apart from it being

---

[5] Barbara Hudson's paper in this volume gives the most profound reason why it is necessary not to rule such idiosyncrasy out of order as not manifesting restorative values: '[W]hat matters is whether restorative justice can provide a better opportunity for victims to tell the story they want to tell, and for their story-telling to be effective'.

morally wrong to impose such an expectation, we would destroy the moral power of forgiveness, apology or mercy to invite participants in a restorative justice process to consider proffering it during the process. People take time to discover the emotional resources to give up such emotional gifts. It cannot, must not, be expected. Similarly remorse that is forced out of offenders has no restorative power. This is not to say that we should not write beautiful books like Tutu's on the grace that can be found through forgiveness. Nor does it preclude us evaluating restorative justice processes according to how much remorse, apology, forgiveness and mercy they elicit. Some might be puzzled as to why reintegrative shaming does not rate on my list of restorative values. It is not a value, not a good in itself; it is an explanatory dynamic that seeks to explain the conditions in which remorse, apology, censure of the act, forgiveness, mercy and many of the other values above occur. There is redundancy in listing remorse, apology and censure of the act because my theoretical position is that remorse and apology are the most powerful forms of censure of the act since they are uttered by the person with the strongest reasons for refusing to vindicate the victim by censuring the injustice. However, when remorse and apology are not elicited it is imperative for other participants to vindicate the victim by censuring the act.

Let us clarify finally the distinctions among these three lists of restorative values. List one are values that must be honoured and enforced as constraints; list two are values restorative justice advocates should actively encourage in restorative processes; list three are values we should not urge participants to manifest—they are emergent properties of a successful restorative justice process. If we try to make them happen, they will be less likely to happen in a meaningful way. Constraining values, maximising values and emergent values.

Many will still find these values vague, lacking specificity of guidance on how decent restorative practices should be run. That specificity will come from shared sensibilities acquired by swapping stories about the implementation of the values (Shearing and Erickson, 1991). Standards of the good must be broad if we are to avert legalistic regulation of restorative justice that is at odds with the philosophy of restorative justice. What we need is deliberative regulation where we are clear about the values we expect restorative justice to realise. Whether a restorative justice programme is up to standard is best settled in a series of regulatory conversations (Black, 1998) with peers and stakeholders rather than by rote application of a rulebook. A value like restoration of the environment will be relevant to the inspection of factories, but not normally to the regulation of delinquency, unless perhaps what the delinquent has done is to light a forest fire. That said, certain highly specific principles from our first list are so fundamental to justice that they must always be guaranteed—such as a right to appeal.

Yet some conventional rights, such as the right to a speedy trial as specified in the Beijing Rules for Juvenile Justice, can be questioned from a restorative perspective. One thing we have learnt from the victims movement in recent years is that when victims have been badly traumatised by a criminal offence, they often need a lot of time before they are ready to countenance healing. They should be given the right to that time so long as it is not used as an excuse for the arbitrary detention of a defendant who has not been proven guilty.

This is an illustration of why, at this point in history, we need to aim for just a framework agreement on standards for restorative justice that is mainly a set of values for framing quality assurance processes and accountability in our pursuit of continuous improvement in attaining restorative justice values. There is some hope that the Committee of Experts established in pursuance of the Declaration of Vienna from the UN Congress on the Prevention of Crime and the Treatment of Offenders, 2000 will accomplish precisely that at the international level.

V. BOTTOM-UP VALUE CLARIFICATION

At the local level what we need to think about is how to make the quality assurance processes and accountability work well. We don't have to wait for the United Nations for this. For top-down value clarification the kind of UN process Dan Van Ness and his NGOs colleagues triggered is ideal (see Van Ness, this volume). While the worry now is that it will be dominated by 'experts' and states, a methodology of the kind I have advanced—informing the list of values (or principles or standards as the UN might prefer) by existing UN human rights accords and also by empirical research on what victims, offenders and their families say they want out of restorative justice processes—seems democratically defensible at the international level. The UN human rights accords have perhaps more than any other UN instruments been shaped by an inclusive, hotly contested dialogue (witness the 'Asian values' debate) over more than 50 years, thanks to the inspiring initial leadership of the regime by Eleanor Roosevelt. NGOs from many nations have participated in it; even the most oppressed political prisoners have had a voice through Amnesty and like organisations. And of course the rights enshrined in the world's many legal systems were put into contest in that dialogue. As comforting as that is, our objective now must be to connect this top-down process to a rich plurality of bottom-up value clarification processes.

A local restorative justice initiative can take a very broad list of values, such as the ones I have tentatively advanced, or preferably the ones that emerge from the UN dialogue, and use them as the starting point for a debate on what standards they want to see accomplished in their programme. A few discussion circles with all the stakeholders in the programme may be enough to reach a sufficient level of shared sensibility to make quality assurance and accountability work. Not every contested value or right has to be settled and written down. The unsettled ones can be earmarked for special observation in the hope that experiential learning will persuade one side of the debate to change their view (or all sides to discover a new synthesis of views).

The drafting of local charters for restorative justice programmes that have emerged from civil society in Northern Ireland (see Braithwaite, 2002b), is consistent with the approach commended here. There are a lot of similarities between these principles emerging from the Loyalist and Republican communities; it was a moving experience in Belfast in 2000 to see ordinary citizens and former combatants with diametrically opposed visions for the future of their country discover through dialogue that they shared a great number of restorative values. Statements such as the 'Standards and Values of Restorative Justice Practice' of Community Restorative Justice Ireland (from the Republican side) also has some distinctively interesting ways of framing standards, such as 'flexibility of approach' and 'evaluation.' There is also indigenous distinctiveness in the proposal that key elements of the charters 'are slated to appear as large murals at strategic locations, in spaces that have traditionally been reserved for the political iconography that is well known within and outside Northern Ireland.' (Mika and McEvoy, 2000). For all the local distinctiveness, both the Republican and Loyalist charters have values that sit comfortably beside the values I have derived from the UN human rights instruments and beside those that the Northern Ireland Office has derived from European human rights instruments (for example, in Restorative Justice and a Partnership Against Crime, 1998). Once there has been a preliminary discussion of the principles, standards and rights a local programme should honour, training is needed for all new restorative justice convenors to deepen the furrows of shared sensibility around them. Training carries a risk of professionalisation. This risk can be to some extent countered by making the training participatory, by giving trainees the power to reframe the curriculum. Elsewhere I have sought to develop in a little more detail how to resolve the contested values that emerge bottom-up through reflexive praxis—restorative justice practice that reflects back on its starting assumptions (Braithwaite, 2002b). Peer review—sitting in on one another's programmes and reflecting back constructive critique—is the key element of this reflexive praxis.

For republicans, bottom-up values clarification that actively involves disempowered people is superior to the imposition of a unicultural, univocal set of narrow legal values backed by a Diceyan conception of the sovereignty of parliament. As Christine Parker and I have argued elsewhere (Braithwaite and Parker, 1999), we need to restructure the rule of law by allowing the justice of the people to bubble up to reshape the justice of the law. That done, the justice of the law can then more legitimately constrain the justice of the people. This is particularly true in former colonies such as my own. Our criminal law, for example, was inherited almost entirely from England without any local debate, least of all from the prior Aboriginal owners of the continent. One reason that North Atlantic legal traditions should not be granted the legitimacy they are in a nation like Australia is that they were used to justify stealing the land from its owners, stealing children from their mothers, making Aboriginal elders trespassers on their own cultures and causing an epidemic of Aboriginal deaths in custody through infliction upon them of the Western institution of the prison.

The colonialism that concerns me about the retributive Anglo-American jurisprudence that was imposed on my land is not just a fact of our dim past. The most important recent change in our criminal law arose against a background of threat of coercive trade sanctions from the United States and the European Union. This criminalises a wide variety of intellectual property appropriations that were formerly torts, as well as extending the duration of patents and other intellectual property monopolies in knowledge. There is no way an undominated dialogue among Australian citizens would have led to the view that such criminalisation should occur or that substantial police resources should be diverted to enforcing these laws (as has occurred). As an intellectual property importing country— unlike net exporters such as the US, UK and Germany—we have no national economic interest in such laws. They are laws that have made us poorer and less free. Of course, the consequences for us have been minor compared to AIDS-ravaged nations in Africa that have been mercilessly threatened with litigation, trade sanctions and withdrawal of aid for importing generic AIDS drugs from India. The appropriation of seeds, medicines and other products of the indigenous cultures of the South by the multinational corporations of the North and then the imposition of new Northern laws to punish violators is making us all trespassers on our own cultures (Drahos with Braithwaite, 2002). China has been executing intellectual property 'pirates' as part of its campaign to gain admission to the World Trade Organisation. Republican justice, I submit, would quickly feed back the view that these kinds of laws enjoy no legitimacy with the people and would never be enforced by an undominated restorative justice process. Under a Diceyan view of parliamentary sovereignty, of course, the laws and enforcement practices enacted by colonised parliaments on behalf of the US-EU intellectual property order are legitimate.

VI. TRANSCENDING NORTH ATLANTIC JURISPRUDENCE

The greatest hope for forging productive new modalities of restorative jurisprudence lies beyond the North Atlantic core of the world system, all of which as part of Christendom fell victim to the 'theft' (Christie, 1977) of citizens' disputing first by the church under Canon Law and then by kings who turned what once were sins against god into felonies, failures of fealty to their king. Conceiving crime as an offence against the crown is a peculiarly obscure idea to have been taken seriously by the intellectuals of the North Atlantic for all these centuries. Of course it is wrong to see Northern jurisprudes as irredeemably fettered to being accomplices of this old project of their kings to dominate their peoples. On a wide front now, there is a problem-solving movement internal to North Atlantic traditions that Susan Daicoff (2002) has recently referred to as the comprehensive movement in law. It includes holistic lawyering, restorative justice, collaborative law, therapeutic jurisprudence, transformative mediation, procedural justice and preventive law, among other movements of the 1990s. Notwithstanding this North Atlantic legal ferment, my analysis is that the greatest hope for the radical transformation advocated here is in the South and East. At the time of writing, the South African parliament is debating a bill that would see *ubuntu,* a profoundly restorative and developmental ideal of human relationships, as the most fundamental guiding value of its juvenile justice system. Already South Africa has the most inspiring constitution in the world, one that incorporates many of the values discussed above, a Constitution used by the community peacemaking committees that Clifford Shearing has worked with in South Africa to guide and constrain their day to day peacemaking practices (Shearing, 2001; Roche, 2001).

There is much that all the world's peoples have learnt from European and North American liberal legalism. The ideas of legal rights, of having a criminal law that is distinguished from tort or delicts, have proved particularly important and useful for securing freedom as non-domination. But there are many features of it we should reject. One is the unicultural one-size-fits-all vision of law we have already discussed. Unlike some restorative justice advocates I suspect we should totally reject proportionality as a criminal law doctrine. We should abolish just deserts, retribution and stigma as doctrines. While I do not think we should totally abolish *mens rea* and intention as the fundamental doctrines that guide the allocation of criminal responsibility, such causal notions of fault should be relegated to a subsidiary role. Reactive fault (Fisse, 1983) is more useful for guiding a more restorative vision of responsibility, that empowers a more active kind of responsibility that citizens take, compared with the passive kind of Western criminal responsibility to which citizens are held (Braithwaite and Roche, 2000). Here Asian legal traditions are a more useful resource than Western ones.

As argued earlier, we can agree with the laudable objectives that motivate liberal desert theorists and at that level we can work together to realise them. More than that, I see no consequentialist dangers whatsoever in the formulation of retribution and proportionality advanced by Antony Duff when articulated in the following way in his essay for this volume:

> So whilst on this account we should not seek a strict proportionality between crime and reparation, or make proportionality our positive aim, we must respect the demands of a rough and negative proportionality: the reparation must not be *disproportionate* in its severity to the seriousness of the crime (p 57).

Retribution, just deserts and proportionality hold no dangers as doctrines so long as they explicitly rule out the legitimacy of the argument that a person should be put in prison for no better reason than that a failure to do so would be disproportionately lenient. Unfortunately, however, the Western legal tradition is for judges to give these concepts a meaning that does require them to imprison offenders when a failure to punish (or to punish severely) for a serious crime would be regarded as disproportionately lenient. We have seen appellate courts reason in just this way when they overturn decisions of restorative justice conferences as insufficiently punitive in cases like *Clotworthy.*[6] As Declan Roche (2001: 151) found in his study of accountability in 24 restorative justice programmes in six countries:

---

[6] *The Queen v Patrick Dale Clotworthy*, Auckland District Court T 971545, Court of Appeal of New Zealand, CA 114/98.

... internal review mechanisms generally intervene to prevent outcomes that are too harsh, while external mechanisms generally intervene to prevent outcomes that are too lenient. In other words, internal review mechanisms tend to enforce upper limits, while external mechanisms enforce lower ones.

Notwithstanding Antony Duff's careful limiting of proportionality to negative proportionality in his statement above, we should not be surprised if the average judge inferred from the following statement from the same paper an obligation of positive proportionality as well:

I will argue, however, that the retributivist slogan—that 'the guilty deserve to suffer'— does express an important moral truth; and that in the case of the criminally guilty it is the state's proper task to seek to ensure that they suffer as they deserve (p 48).

One whose central philosophical commitment is to freedom as non-domination must reject any such moral truth. More pragmatically, desert will have evil consequences if this conception of it is read as requiring imprisonment to honour it. In my country judges have interpreted their obligation to honour it as requiring sentencing of Aboriginal offenders to prison for very serious crimes when their people reject the justice of the prison as an institution, when imprisonment is viewed by them as something that removes them from spiritual contact with their traditional lands, sealing them off from any prospect of healing, thereby causing a high risk of suicide. Could an injustice be more profound? My plea to liberal retributivists would be that they be much more explicit in laying out how and why their position does not require putting a person in prison no matter how serious their crime. Indeed, why their position forbids any punishment being imposed for no better reason than to honour positive proportionality.

Until there is professional and popular clarity of understanding that retribution means upper limits while making the enforcement of lower limits on punishment an evil, the marriage of retribution and restorative justice is not a wedding we should want to attend.

VII. CONCLUSION

In this essay I have striven to conceive of restorative justice as a more ambitious project intellectually and politically than it is normally conceived. A republican case has been made for a set of limits upon restorative justice grounded in international human rights instruments. A beginning set of values we might seek to maximise through restorative justice has also been discussed based on an interplay between the values found in those human rights documents and the values revealed by empirical research on the aspirations of participants in restorative justice processes. A second reflexive methodology was then discussed for a more bottom-up generation of restorative justice values. Between these two methodologies the long-run hope is for a radical redesign of legal institutions whereby the justice of the people will more meaningfully bubble up into the justice of the law and the justice of the law will more legitimately filter down to place limits on the justice of the people.

Such a radical redesign project will be less democratically meaningful if it is restricted to a single area of law like criminal law. While the social movement for restorative justice of the 1990s has grown as a criminal justice reform coalition, restorative justice values have a longer history in the peace movement and in movements for democratising workplaces (industrial democracy) and democratising schools. Moreover, there is an obvious opportunity and challenge in linking the idea of regulating injustice restoratively to the aspirations of the women's movement to democratise family life and Indigenous rights movements for self-determination over their lives. Family, school, workplace, tribe, community and international relations all seem sites of restorative justice of comparable importance to law. Moreover the really interesting questions for both explanatory and normative theory seem to be about how the semi-autonomy (Moore, 1978) of say family and law, warfare and the International Criminal Court, are established (and should be established).

More broadly still, restorative justice can make a contribution to the institutional rethinking currently emerging under the rubrics of deliberative or discursive democracy. With a few exceptions, such as Fishkin's work on deliberative polling (Fishkin and Luskin, 1999), that tradition seems impoverished by an excess of political theory abstraction and a want of empirical research that dissects the speech conditions that nurture and discourage empowerment, procedural and substantive justice, equal concern for participants, accountability and competence in actually solving real problems like crime. The exciting combinations of micro-macro theory and rigorous empirical methods now being broached by restorative justice scholars should become a sophisticated resource for scholars of deliberative democracy. If the failure of the political theory of deliberative democracy is that it is too macro, the failure of theory and research on restorative justice has been that of being too micro. That deficiency is the one for which I have attempted to take some faltering steps toward remedy.

REFERENCES

Black, J (1998) 'Talking About Regulation' (Spring) *Public Law* 77–105.

Braithwaite, J (2002a) *Restorative Justice and Responsive Regulation* (Oxford University Press, New York).

—— (2002b) 'Setting Standards for Restorative Justice', 42 *British Journal of Criminology* 563–77.

Braithwaite, J and Parker, C (1999) 'Restorative Justice is Republican Justice' in L Walgrave and G Bazemore (eds), *Restoring Juvenile Justice: An Exploration of the Restorative Justice Paradigm for Reforming Juvenile Justice* (Criminal Justice Press, Monsey NY).

Braithwaite, J and Pettit, P (1990) *Not Just Deserts: A Republican Theory of Criminal Justice* (Oxford University Press, Oxford).

—— (2000) 'Republicanism and Restorative Justice: An Explanatory and Normative Connection' in H Strang and J Braithwaite (eds), *Restorative Justice: Philosophy to Practice* (Ashgate Dartmouth, Aldershot).

Braithwaite, J and Roche, D (2000) 'Responsibility and Restorative Justice' in L Walgrave and G Bazemore (eds), *Restoring Juvenile Justice: An Exploration of the Restorative Justice Paradigm for Reforming Juvenile Justice* (Criminal Justice Press, Monsey NY).

Braithwaite, J and Strang, H (2000) 'Introduction' in H Strang and J Braithwaite (eds), *Restorative Justice: Philosophy to Practice* (Ashgate Dartmouth, Aldershot).

Christie, N (1977) 'Conflicts as Property' 17 *British Journal of Criminology* 1–26.

Daicoff, S (2000) 'The Role of Therapeutic Jurisprudence Within The Comprehensive Law Movement' in DB Wexler, BJ Winick and D Stolle (eds), *Practicing Therapeutic Jurisprudence* (Carolina Academic Press, North Carolina).

Drahos, P with Braithwaite, J (2002) *Information Fendalism* (Earthscan, London).

Fishkin, J and Luskin, RC (1999) 'The Quest for Deliberative Democracy'. Paper presented to the European Consortium for Political Research, University of Mannheim, Bermand, 26–31 March 1999.

Fisse, B (1983) 'Reconstructing Corporate Criminal Law: Deterrence, Retribution, Fault, and Sanctions' 56 *Southern California Law Review* 1141–1246.

Haines, K (1998) 'Some Principled Objections to a Restorative Justice Approach to Working with Juvenile Offenders' in L Walgrave (ed), *Restorative Justice for Juveniles: Potentialities, Risks and Problems for Research*. A selection of papers presented at the International Conference, Leuven, 12–14 May 1997 (Leuven, Leuven University Press) 93–113.

Mika, H and McEvoy, K (2000) Unpublished paper to conference on International Perspectives on Restorative Justice, Belfast.

Moore, SF (1978) *Law as Process* (Routledge, London).

Morrison, B (2001) 'The School System: Developing its Capacity in the Regulation of Civil Society' in H Strang and J Braithwaite (eds), *Restorative Justice and Civil Society* (Cambridge University Press, Melbourne).

Parker, C (1999) *Just Lawyers* (Oxford University Press, Oxford).

Pettit, P (1997) *Republicanism* (Clarendon Press, Oxford).

Roche, D (2001) *First By Persuasion: Accountabilities of Restorative Justice*. PhD Dissertation, Australian National University.

Rokeach, M (1968) *Beliefs, Attitudes and Values: A Theory of Organization and Change* (Jossey-Bass, New York).

Shearing, C (2001) 'Transforming Security: A South African Experiment' in H Strang and J Braithwaite (eds), *Restorative Justice and Civil Society* (Cambridge University Press, Melbourne).

Shearing, C and Ericson, RV (1991) 'Towards a Figurative Conception of Action' 42 *British Journal of Sociology* 481–506.

Strang, H (2000) *Victim Participation in a Restorative Justice Process: The Canberra Reintegrative Shaming Experiments*. Unpublished PhD Dissertation, Australian National University.

Sullivan, D and Tifft, L (2001) *Restorative Justice: Healing the Foundations of Our Everyday Lives* (Willow Tree Press, Monsey NY).

Tutu, D (1999) *No Future Without Forgiveness* (Rider, London).

Van Ness, D and Heetderks Strong, K (1997) *Restoring Justice* (Anderson Publishing, Cinncinnati OH).

von Hirsch, A (1993) *Censure and Sanctions* (Clarendon Press, Oxford).

Zehr, H (1995) *Changing Lenses: A New Focus for Criminal Justice* (Herald Press, Scotsdale PA).

2

*Specifying Aims and Limits for Restorative Justice: A 'Making Amends' Model?**

Andrew von Hirsch, Andrew Ashworth and Clifford Shearing

I. INTRODUCTION

This paper explores the feasibility of clarifying aims and limits for Restorative Justice (hereafter, 'RJ'). It brings together three authors, two of whom (von Hirsch and Ashworth) have been associated with desert-oriented approaches to sentencing, and a third (Shearing) who has been exploring alternatives to traditional criminal-justice processes.

The essay proceeds by sketching a particular RJ model, which we shall term the 'making amends' model. We will describe the model, and then try to draw out some of its implications—regarding the scope of the model's application, modalities and techniques for achieving the model's ends, criteria for evaluating success or failure, and possible requirements regarding proportionality. We shall then examine two ways in which such a model might be implemented: first, ambitiously, as a comprehensive sanctioning approach designed largely to replace traditional criminal justice; and second, more modestly, as a scheme for a specified range of cases, within the broader framework of a proportionality-oriented sentencing system.

We make no ambitious claims for this 'making amends' model: at best, it will reflect some (albeit not all) of the aims discussed in the RJ literature. Moreover, we are not ourselves advocating this model here; rather, we wish to make heuristic use of it, to suggest how RJ's aims and limits might be specified more clearly.

Our approach will mainly be conceptual: we will be examining RJ as a set of ideas about dealing with offending. None of the authors deem themselves expert on RJ practice in various jurisdictions, and it is theory not practice that primarily concerns us. Our theoretical emphasis reflects our view that it is the aims and limits of RJ that are particularly in need of clarification. Because of this theoretical emphasis, we will be dealing with 'ideal' models—that is, models that are

* The authors are most grateful for the suggestions and comments of Anthony Bottoms, Kathleen Daly, Antony Duff, Nathan Harris, Shadd Maruna, Kevin Reitz, Julian Roberts, Declan Roche, Michael Tonry and Richard Young.

designed best to reflect the chosen aims. We do this both in sketching our 'making amends' model (s III), and also in considering a proportionalist sentencing scheme as a possible setting for the model (s VI).

We shall be dealing with RJ as it applies to criminal offending—that is, to conduct that has been found violative of a state's criminal statutes. Some writers (eg Braithwaite, this volume) suggest that restorative approaches might be extended beyond crime to address other social problems, but we shall not be discussing such matters.

II. THE CRITIQUE OF RESTORATIVE JUSTICE

We might begin the analysis by setting forth an 'internal' critique of Restorative Justice—namely, one that does not depend on strong ulterior (say, desert) assumptions. The aim of this critique is to scrutinise RJ in its own terms: to ask whether RJ conceptions, as usually represented, constitute a coherent theory capable of providing meaningful guidance.

1. The Critique

The 'internal' critique of which we are speaking points to a number of problematic features of RJ. These include the following:

(1) *Multiple and unclear goals:* The advocates of restorative justice put forward a variety of stated RJ goals: that, for example, the victim be 'restored'; the offender be made to recognise his wrong; the 'conflict' between victim and offender be healed; the breach in the community's sense of trust be repaired; the community be reassured against further offending; and fear of crime be diminished (see eg Zehr, 1990; Van Ness, 1993; Pettit and Braithwaite, 1993; Braithwaite, 1999; Bazemore, 1999; Braithwaite, this volume; Walgrave, this volume).[1] The goals may be ambitiously but vaguely formulated: for example, that the aim is to 'repair harm', but without considering whether this should address purely the consequential harms of the conduct, or should involve a normative response of some kind (see further, s V 3). Several goals may be proposed simultaneously, without priorities among them specified.[2] Some purported goals appear to have analogical rather than literal meaning. Restorative processes are supposed, for example, to resolve the 'conflict' between offender and victim (Christie, 1977); but crimes are different from disputes in that the offender seldom claims to be entitled to what he

---

[1] For a valuable analysis of the various RJ goals, see Zedner, 1994.
[2] See eg Pettit and Braithwaite, 1993, with the multiple proposed aims of giving recognition to the wrongdoing; recompensing the victim; and reducing crime and fear of crime; see also Braithwaite, this volume, with the multiple stated 'values' for RJ.

takes—so what 'dispute' is being resolved?[3] RJ processes are said to 'restore' the bonds of community frayed through the offence, but it is not explained what kind of bonds have been damaged or how this restoration is to take place. Such over-breadth of purpose dilutes the guidance that RJ conceptions can provide. An injunction to seek numerous imprecisely delineated good ends tells us little about what particular purposes should be pursued, and how those ends should be achieved.

(2) *Underspecified means and modalities*: Little has been done to specify the particular means for achieving the various RJ objectives—other than to assert that these may emerge through a deliberative process in which offender and victim participate. When, say, a 'group conference' meets to deal with a particular kind of case, what kind of interventions should it decide upon? When would monetary compensation to the victim be preferable, and when would something else be? If an apology by the offender is desired, when would this be desirable and when might it be counterproductive? With multiple and vaguely delineated goals, the means and modalities for achieving them are understandably difficult to identify.

(3) *Few or no dispositional criteria*: RJ proceedings tend to be largely discretionary: it is up to the group conference or other decision-making body in the individual case to decide what would be 'best'. Granted, there may be certain stated minimum requirements—such as that the participants must agree to a proposed outcome before it may take effect; and there may also be certain jurisdictional limits—for example, a ceiling on the amount of compensation. But within these wide bounds, an RJ conference may largely be free, in practice, to pursue any aim (including quite traditional ones such as deterrence); and to choose nearly any means it wishes to achieve such aims.

(4) *Dangling standards for evaluation*: RJ programmes are evaluated by a variety of criteria, including participant 'satisfaction' and impact on recidivism. Yet it is seldom explained how these criteria are related to the purposes to be achieved—again, not surprisingly, considering the multiplicity and imprecision of the stated goals.

In response to criticisms of this kind, it is sometimes asserted that RJ is only in its early stages; that it develops its aims inductively from actual practice; and that it emphasises procedural values rather than predefined substantive goals. None of these responses strike us as sufficient. First, RJ is no longer in its infancy; it has been influential for more than a decade and a half, and some of its texts go back a quarter-century (eg Christie, 1977). Secondly, while developing goals inductively is a possible way of proceeding, this approach succeeds only if well-defined and consistent goals eventually *do* emerge. Thirdly, procedural values cannot be

---

[3] The idea of 'conflict', moreover, also carries no necessary implication that either party has *wronged* the other (see s IV 3 below).

free-standing; the procedure must be *for* something. Having crimes dealt with through interaction between victim and offender has value only if it is possible to specify what goals such a procedure can accomplish.

2. Is RJ Primarily an Expression of Aspirations?

The characteristics just cited, a critic might argue, could suggest that RJ is primarily *aspirational* in character—serving to express wishes or aspirations rather than to adopt substantive goals that actually help to guide the choice of dispositions. True, RJ's stated aspirations are somewhat different than those of the traditional pre-1980s discretionary sentencing model (which also relied on multiple and possibly conflicting goals)[4] in that RJ's purported goals have more to do with 'healing', 'conflict-resolution' and the like. There is also a shift on who officiates: it would no longer be the judge, but rather the offender, victim and possibly other community representatives. But the point of RJ, on this interpretation, is to express what it is hoped might be accomplished, ranging from resolving the 'conflict' between offender and victim to reducing fear of crime in the community generally. There would be no need to choose among the ambitious and varying goals, because they are all worth desiring and the RJ process and its dispositions serve to express these desiderata.

What would be wrong with such an aspirational approach? Someone might wish to defend it along the following lines: *something* needs to be done about criminal offending, but what exactly should be done is difficult to decide and may not make much difference in its consequences for public safety. So why not have a discretionary response that expresses chiefly what we *wish* would occur? RJ advocates, however, do not view their efforts as merely expressing aspirations: they see themselves as serious reformers, wishing to implement better ways of dealing with criminal offenders. Something substantive needs to be accomplished through RJ, that goes beyond involving victims and members of the community in decisions, and expressing through the disposition the desire that various good things be achieved.

---

[4] The traditional sentencing model claimed to promote rehabilitation, deterrence, incapacitation and 'denunciation' of criminal conduct. However, no priority was set among these differing and potentially conflicting goals, few criteria were provided for deciding individual cases, and there were scant constraints on individual decision-makers' discretion. Such a system, I have argued elsewhere (von Hirsch, 2001: 410–12), might best be understood as expressing aspirations, rather than seeking to achieve substantive goals. Thus when judges responded to increasing rates of burglary by imposing tougher penalties on convicted burglars for the supposed sake of deterrence (without, however, showing any interest in what, if any, evidence there was to support such a deterrent strategy), the actual function of such sentences was to convey the public message 'Let there be deterrence!' Deciding priorities among the aims would not seem necessary because there are varying aspirations that might be publicly expressed through sentences. It would not be necessary to try to determine whether tougher burglary sentences actually help reduce the burglary rate, because even if this did not occur it would still be a good thing for an authoritative source to express on the public's behalf the sentiment that burglary ought better to be prevented.

3. The Importance of Specifying Aims and Limits

How might one respond to the foregoing critique? One way would be to try to specify aims and limits better. What needs to be done is to develop a more coherent and consistent formulation of these aims and related processes—that includes protections to help ensure that basic liberal democratic values are not compromised. Good reasons—ones suitable for the public sphere in a modern democratic society—need to be specified to justify RJ interventions. Such a specification calls at least for the following:

— Consistent and adequately prioritised goals for RJ;
— Adequate specification of means-ends relationships: why should a given kind of goal call for a given kind of response?
— Guidance for deciding individual cases that relate to goals and known means;
— Adequate fairness constraints on the severity of dispositions;
— Evaluation criteria, the use of which can be justified in terms of their relevance to the restated goals.

To see whether such a restatement of RJ is possible, we shall conduct a thought-experiment. It is to try to sketch a particular conceptual model for restorative justice, and examine whether it might satisfy these requirements of rationality better.

III. A POSSIBLE RJ MODEL: 'MAKING AMENDS'

The RJ model which we shall describe is one that involves the notion of 'making amends'. In the limited space available, our sketch will necessarily be incomplete but, we hope, sufficient to convey the concepts involved.

1. The 'Making Amends' Model

The 'making amends' model, which resembles in important respects that sketched by Antony Duff (this volume), involves a response negotiated between the offender and his victim, which involves (1) the implicit or explicit acknowledgement of fault and (2) an apologetic stance on the part of the offender, ordinarily conveyed through having him undertake a reparative task.

The model differs from the conception of punishment developed by desert theorists (see von Hirsch, 1993: ch 2). In a desert model, penal censure is *authoritatively* conveyed through the imposition of the punishment. Its aim, in part, is to convey blame which the offender, seen as a moral agent, may consider in evaluating his own conduct and deciding how to behave in future. That model involves a form of moral discourse but not a negotiated one: *A*, the punishing agent (usually the state), determines certain types of actions to be wrong, and adopts legal norms prohibiting such conduct and prescribing sanctions that convey disapproval for the conduct. If *B*, an actor, engages in the conduct, he will suffer the sanction and thereby be subjected to the disapproval. *B* and others may then take this into account in evaluating their own actions.

The 'making amends' model is also a form of moral discourse, but one which is closer in certain respects to informal moral discourse in everyday life. In this kind of response the victim's role is deemed central. The procedure is a *negotiated* process between offender and victim,[5] leading to a response that conveys acknowledgement of fault and the undertaking of a reparative task reflecting that acknowledgement. The reparative features of the sanction do not literally heal or 'take back' the wrong. Rather, they constitute a way of showing concern for the victim's interests, on the part of a person (the offender) whose lack of respect and concern was expressed, precisely, in his act of wrongdoing.

While the negotiated and discursive character of this response differs from the authoritative model of deserved punishment, the model is 'retributive' in the sense that it is primarily responsive to *past* wrongdoing: making amends is a way of conveying an apologetic stance for a misdeed that has occurred. Granted, if the process works as intended, there will also be some consequential effects: a regretful offender may (and it is hoped will) come to feel more empathy for his victims and others, and be less inclined to offend in future; and the victim may become less resentful and less alienated from the offender. But these consequences are not the sole point of the exercise, so that the making-amends response does not fail whenever they do not materialise—just as an apology is no less appropriate because the offended individual is unwilling to accept it (for further discussion of the normative mechanisms of apology, see Bottoms, this volume).

If 'making amends' were thus made the focus of RJ, would this have to be the exclusive aim? Not necessarily; other goals might also be pursued, so long as this were done consistently with the primary making-amends focus. (Providing support for the offender to help him avoid reoffending, for example, could be such a supplemental end—if this were done in a manner that comports with the appropriate making of amends for the offence.)[6] How such supplemental goals could be taken into account would call for further analysis, however and could complicate the model somewhat. Thus for the sake of simplicity, and because of limitations of space, we shall limit our discussion to the aim of making amends.

---

[5] In certain cases, where the victim wishes not to appear, it might be possible to designate a victim representative.

[6] For further discussion, see s III 6 below. A comparable issue arises in desert theory, concerning the extent to which ulterior (say, rehabilitative) goals may be pursued within a system of proportionate sanctions; see, von Hirsch, 1993: chs 6 and 7.

2. The RJ Intervention as an Imposition

In this volume, there is considerable divergence of view whether restorative responses are or are not 'punishments' (contrast Dignan with Walgrave, this volume). What should be clear, however, is that the making-amends model, even if it differs in significant respects from traditional punishment, is also one involving an *imposition*. It is so in two important respects. First, calling for acknowledgement of fault involves adverse judgements about the offender and his behaviour. Secondly, any disposition that results from the process may deprive the offender of important interests: of his property, if he pays compensation, of his freedom of action if he undertakes a reparative task, etc.

To say that an imposition is involved is no criticism: indeed, the adverse judgement and the burdens to be undertaken by the offender are central to the whole point of the process. Acknowledging that we are speaking of impositions means, however, that a burden of justification must be met: good reasons need to be supplied for why the offender must suffer these burdens, and fairness requirements need be observed to ensure that the burdens are justly imposed.

The character of making amends as an imposition cannot be avoided by pointing out that the offender's consent is required. The offender cannot choose simply to have nothing happen to him. If he refuses his consent, he will have to face whatever alternative sanctioning system awaits the non-consenting: a traditional criminal trial, or else possibly, Braithwaite's (1999) scheme of deterrent or incapacitative sanctions. He may have reason to fear that those latter responses would be (at best) no less unpleasant.

Where a negotiated procedure results in someone losing important interests, an imposition is involved—notwithstanding that the person agrees to participate in the negotiations. In simple contexts, this is obvious: being sentenced to prison as a result of a plea- and sentence-bargain obviously involves an imposition, and no less so because the person might have refused the bargain and faced the alternative legal consequences. The point holds also for restorative processes. So long as the offender engages in the process, it is that process—and not something else—which is responsible for any resulting deprivation of his interests. It does not matter that the offender could have withdrawn from the process, and faced an alternative sanctioning system.

3. Modalities and Guidance

The 'making amends' model represents a particular set of aims, which should influence the modalities of RJ intervention: only certain kinds of intervention are likely to be helpful in promoting the model's aims. Dispositions involving the making of restitution to the victim as a way of acknowledging fault appear to be legitimate ways of making amends. Purely unpleasant or humiliating sanctions might serve other (for example, deterrent) purposes, but not this purpose. There thus should be some explicit principles suggesting what kind of dispositions might be appropriate, and what kind might not be. Leaving this purely to the discretion of the particular group conference is likely to lead to dispositions which, if capable of being rationalised at all, would be so on grounds having little or nothing to do with the making of amends.

Even for those types of dispositions which appear generally to be appropriate to this model, it would be helpful to provide further guidance on specific means and techniques employed. What kind of apologetic ritual might help victim and offender understand that an expression of regret is involved? What kind is likely to bring the parties toward reconciliation and a better understanding? What kind of rituals and dispositions are likely to be counterproductive? As RJ programmes are tried and evaluated, there should develop some understanding on such matters, and individual decision-making groups should have available explicit guidance reflecting that knowledge. Calling for such guidance will mean that some rule-generating process needs to provide it, and will mean that the guidance will need to be set forth in some useful and readily available form.

4. Scope of Application of the Model

The making-amends model is addressed to a certain kind of case: one in which there is an identifiable person who is the offender, another identifiable person who is the victim, and a victimising act which infringes the latter's rights. A typical case which seems to suit this model is one where A unprovokedly vandalises B's flat. Here, there is an act of wrongdoing against someone, which would seem to warrant an apologetic response by the actor to the victim, conveyed in some act of making of amends.

There are, however, a variety of cases which seem less well suited to this kind of response. One 'unsuitable' category, in our judgement, would consist of crimes in which there are no individual victims. If A is charged with tax evasion, there is no person to whom he can convey an apologetic stance via some kind of restitutionary act. Saying the 'community' is here the victim is not illuminating.

There are also types of cases in which the appropriateness of an RJ approach should be a matter for further analysis. An example are crimes in which an individual 'victim' has been injured or threatened with injury, but in which this is a response to comparable previous behaviour on the victim's part directed against the present perpetrator. B has beaten A up last Saturday night, and now A beats up B this Saturday night and is apprehended for that act and placed before a group conference. In such cases it is less clear who should apologise to whom; or whether mutual apologies would be desirable. Having a more clearly stated goal—in our suggested model of making amends—might help resolve whether a restorative approach is appropriate here.

5. Evaluation Criteria

Evaluation criteria for assessing the success of RJ programmes at present tend to 'dangle': reasons are not provided why a given evaluation norm, rather than another, is being employed. Let us, however, examine some possible evaluation criteria, in the light of the 'making amends' model's aims.

(1) *Recidivism reduction.* Reduction in the rate of reoffending is a criterion often used in evaluating RJ programmes. The results have been mixed (see Kurki, this volume; Daly, 2002; Daly, this volume). But why should this be the basis of evaluation?

One possible claim is that reduced recidivism would show that RJ is an effective crime-prevention tool. Even if crime prevention were deemed the desideratum, however, that depends not on reducing recidivism per se, but on reducing citizen's net exposure to criminal victimisation. The debate over 'selective incapacitation' in the 1980s has made clear that reducing net victimisation rates depends on more than lowering the number of convicted offenders who return to crime. Critical other factors affecting crime rates include: (1) the number of new entrants into criminal activity and the number of those successfully avoiding conviction; (2) the estimated length of the residual criminal careers of convicted offenders, and the frequency with which they could have been expected to offend; (3) the extent to which the crimes involved are committed by co-offenders, some of whom remain unapprehended and continue active offending (see, National Academy of Science, 1986). Issues such as these are generally not addressed in the RJ evaluation literature.

Another (in our view more plausible) claim, would be that desisting from further crime is part of the making-amends process. An aspect of the offender's conveying a regretful stance for criminal behaviour is his making efforts to refrain from offending in future (see s III 1), and recidivism rates measure that. The difficulty remains, however, that lowered recidivism may be motivated not only by regret on the part of the offender elicited by the making-amends procedure, but possibly by a variety of ulterior factors. Even if many young offenders are unimpressed by the substance of the procedure, they might still desist from reoffending if they find it sufficiently disagreeable—so that special deterrence, rather than anything having to do with making amends, would be the major influence. Thus we would need evaluation techniques that help separate out these various possible effects.[7]

---

[7] In response, it might be asserted that the offenders' possible reasons for desisting from further crime would not matter, so long as they do desist. This, however, would be treating making-amends simply as a crime reduction technique. But then, lowered recidivism might be achievable by various strategies quite different from the making of amends—such as traditional incapacitative techniques. Were recidivism prevention the criterion for success, much would depend which approach—the making of amends or something quite different—were the most efficient.

(2) '*Satisfaction*'. Satisfaction on the part of those participating in the RJ processes has also been used as a test of success. But why should 'satisfaction' be the measure? A possible explanation is that the making-amends process, if it operates as it is supposed to, will lead to an accommodation between offender and victim from which both might derive some satisfaction. However, it would be necessary to consider what else might yield comparable satisfaction. Often, the research compares RJ with traditional court procedures, and finds that participants are more satisfied by RJ. But this may derive, in part, from the fact that RJ procedures are more friendly and informal, and give the participants more time and scope to discuss what has happened to them. Court procedures using traditional sentencing conceptions (say, of desert), might also evoke more satisfaction, if operated in a fashion that is less rushed, less peremptory, and gives more scope to the parties' explanations. If 'satisfaction' is to be a valid success measure, it would thus seem necessary to undertake comparisons of this kind.

(3) '*Meeting of minds*'. In her recent research, Kathleen Daly (this volume) uses as a measure of success whether, as a result of the procedure, the parties come to appreciate each other's perspectives better, and develop more empathy for one another. This does seem to be an appropriate evaluation norm for the making-amends model, one of whose express aims is to achieve a degree of reconciliation between offender and victim. But, as Daly notes (id), the occurrence rate of this phenomenon is relatively modest.

6. The Role of Proportionality

There exists considerable disagreement, among RJ proponents, about the need for proportionality constraints. Some RJ advocates have suggested that these should be jettisoned entirely (Pettit and Braithwaite, 1993), although Braithwaite (this volume) seems to have modified his position somewhat. Others, such as Dignan (this volume), suggest that there should be proportionality limits. However, the grounds for such limits have been little addressed in the RJ literature.

Outer proportionality requirements, that bar the use of very severe penalties for lesser crimes, are minimal requirements of fairness that any modern liberal state should observe. Indeed, a ban on grossly disproportionate penalties is constitutionally required in some jurisdictions.[8]

The interesting question is whether there should be proportionality requirements going beyond these minimal ones. For a punishment system, the argument for proportionality requirements is straightforward enough: such a system utilises sanctions that involve *censure*. In such a sanctioning system, the severity of the sanction signifies the degree of censure conveyed. Consequently, the severity of sanctions should fairly reflect the degree of comparative blameworthiness of the conduct (see more fully, von Hirsch, 1993: ch 2).

---

[8] The case-law jurisprudence of the German Constitutional Court includes such a ban, for example.

Could comparable themes be used to support proportionality requirements in a making-amends model? A possible argument might run as follows. An essential feature of the making-amends model is that the procedure and its sanction are designed to provide a moral evaluation of the conduct. The victim, it is assumed, has been *wronged* by the offender, and the procedure aims at giving adequate recognition to that wrongdoing. In tort law, there is no such aim: the point of tort is simply to decide who should bear the loss, the actor or the injured party; fault is deemed a ground—but not an exclusive one—for shifting the burden of loss to the actor. The making-amends model, however, is much more than a loss-shifting device: its point is to provide (through the imposition he undertakes to undergo) a method through which the actor can convey to his victim recognition of his wrongdoing. If such a moral evaluation of the conduct is thus centrally involved, the response should bear some reasonable relationship to how wrongful the conduct can fairly be characterised as being.

The foregoing point holds already for simple verbal apologies in everyday life. Suppose *A* negligently steps on *B*'s toes, and says that he is sorry to have hurt him. Suppose, however, that *B* insists that this is not enough; that *A* must admit that his conduct has not merely been clumsy but extraordinary reprehensible. *A* would rightly be entitled to resist such a suggestion: to say that while he was wrong thus to have hurt *B*, the injury was not great, and his fault was one of mere negligence; and hence, that the wrong was relatively minor. *A*'s apology should not be required to overstate his degree of fault.

This argument extends to the making-amends model, where what is to be negotiated is not just a verbal apology, but a burden undertaken by the offender that is designed to convey that apologetic stance. If the basis for the imposition lies in its recognition of wrongdoing, the degree of its onerousness necessarily conveys how reprehensible the conduct is treated as being. This implied valuation should, then, bear a reasonable relation to the actual degree of reprehensibleness of the conduct—that is, to its seriousness. The upshot is a requirement of proportionality. It should be noted, moreover, that this requirement has not been 'externally' derived from traditional criminal-justice principles; it derives from the logic of 'making-amends' itself.

In this kind of negotiated disposition, however, it would not seem feasible to impose the kind of rigorous ordinal-proportionality requirements that a desert model envisions for criminal punishments. (For a discussion of those requirements, see von Hirsch, 1993: ch 2.) This is because considerable leeway would be needed for the parties to choose a disposition that they feel conveys regret in a satisfactory manner. We will return below to the question of how large this leeway might need to be.

7. Is the 'Making Amends' Model Conceptually Coherent?

Our critique of RJ at the onset (s II) questioned whether, as usually formulated, it is a meaningful rationale at all. RJ's multiple and unclear goals, its underspecified conception of means and modalities, its lack of dispositional standards and fairness limits, its dangling measures of success—these all seem to point to a lack of a coherent conception. The question we posed was whether an RJ model could be formulated that avoids these deficiencies, and we sketched our 'making amends' models (s III 1) as a possible way of doing so.

The making-amends model, in our view, does seem to provide a modicum of conceptual coherence. It seeks to achieve, not all conceivable desiderata, but a particular, interrelated, and mutually consistent set of them: namely, the conducting of a dialogue between offender and victim about the former's wrongdoing; the expression by the wrongdoer to his victim of a regretful stance, carried out through reparative sanction; and the opportunity given to the victim to accept that expression of regret and thus possibly to achieve some measure of reconciliation. This model resembles in important respects a kind of moral dialogue that is carried out in everyday life, and that can be described directly and without reliance on metaphors such as 'healing' and the like.

The model also helps yield some norms of application. It points toward particular kinds of interventions, and standards of use (see s III 3); it provides some guidance regarding scope of application—that is, regarding the kind of cases for which this approach would or would not be suitable (see s III 4); it suggests what kind of evaluation criteria might be used to judge success or failure (see s III 5); and it tells us something about the standards of fairness—particularly, of proportionality—that should be utilised (see s III 6). A 'making-amends' model thus might be seen as seeking substantive ends, and not merely as constituting just the expression of aspirations.

Adopting a model such as this one involves, however, certain tradeoffs—for the model focuses on some possible RJ goals, and not others. The making-amends model is victim/offender-focused: it is conceived as a certain kind of discursive interchange between them. As a result, other possible goals are given less emphasis, if any; the model is not explicitly aimed at maximising crime-control effects, or reducing fear of crime, or the like. This kind of trade-off is inevitable: trying to accomplish all goals simultaneously is tantamount to having no meaningful goals at all.

IV. THE 'MAKING AMENDS' MODEL: SOME QUERIES

To say the making-amends model is conceptually coherent does not necessarily mean that it is right. A number of significant queries and apparent drawbacks exists, which we need to examine next.

1. Impartiality of Decision-Makers

For purposes of the present discussion, we shall assume that a fair procedure for determining the offender's guilt has been utilised. This would include having an impartial trier of the facts; giving adequate opportunity for defence; requiring that the evidence against the accused meets a high standard of proof; and giving full consideration of claims of exculpation. An RJ conference in which victim and accused are primarily decision-makers are not well suited for these purposes: the decision-makers are neither impartial nor are they trained to apply the relevant fairness standards. A fairer manner of determining guilt thus needs to be provided, preferably by a court with adequate procedural safeguards.

Impartiality of the decision-maker remains an issue, however, at the dispositional stages after guilt has been established. In an RJ group conference, two of the central participants—the victim and the offender—are clearly not impartial. (While there may also be an impartial facilitator at the proceeding, his or her role is likely to be primarily advisory). It would not be possible to remove the parties from having a central role in deciding the disposition of the case, as much of the point of the procedure lies in giving them this role.

It might be argued that impartiality need no longer be a concern where the sanction is not one imposed externally by an official, but rather negotiated in a process in which the offender is a participant. If the offender feels that he is not being treated fairly, he can withdraw. The feasibility of withdrawing, however, depends on what alternative processes and possible dispositions would then await him. He may have reasons for feeling that he must accept even a seemingly rather biased process, for fear of facing something worse. The lack of impartiality thus remains a drawback of the process.

2. The Problem of the Role of Attitude

An important safeguard of the human dignity of offenders is a ban on compulsory attitudinising: it is deeply demeaning to be compelled to express views or attitudes that are at variance with those one actually holds (see von Hirsch, 1993: ch 9). In the criminal process, this safeguard is not always observed; parole boards, for example, may insist on a showing of penitent attitudes, before granting parole release. But in punishment, the expressed attitudes of the offender are not of the essence; what matters is the authoritative expression of penal censure by the state through the sanction. Thus it would be possible to adopt principles against making the offender to show any particular set of attitudes (the defendant's entitlement to silence during the sentencing hearing being one such safeguard). On our suggested making-amends model, however, this issue becomes more difficult; here, the whole point is to negotiate a disposition that is meant to convey regret for the action. Attitude and its expression thus become more central.

It might be possible, on a making-amends model, to try to protect against the cruder kinds of compulsory attitudinising. If the offender is browbeaten into making an apology, that is no real apology at all. The problem lies, however, in the more subtle pressures to express the right attitudes—since those attitudes make so much difference for this kind of negotiated process.

Two kinds of constraints might be feasible to alleviate this problem. One would be a bar against requiring rituals of self-abasement (a well-known example being requiring the offender to wear an 'I am a thief' T-shirt). The other would be certain limits on attitudinal inquiries in the proceedings: the parties would negotiate on a disposition having an expressive form, but direct inquiries would not be permitted about what the offender actually believes or feels. Nevertheless, these are palliatives: the offender may still feel under pressure to express attitudes of repentance which he does not hold, in order to obtain a favourable disposition.

3. 'Privatisation'

A desert model treats punishment as a way of providing a *public* valuation of crime. The sanction is seen as an authoritative response by the state, that conveys censure to the offender—seen as a person capable of moral deliberation. The state's response serves also, through the implied public censure, to express a public evaluation—that certain kinds of conduct are injurious and reprehensible.

This public valuation has certain important normative functions. It conveys to the offender and potential offenders, and also to victims and potential victims, the message that the behaviour is deemed to be wrong in a certain degree. While the actual primary injury may be to a particular victim, the conduct is treated as infringing standards of conduct of the larger body politic. In providing that public acknowledgement of wrongdoing, the state gives public recognition to the value of the rights involved, and makes a moral (rather than purely prudential) appeal to citizens that they should desist from the conduct (see von Hirsch, 1993: ch 2).

Were RJ made the technique for dealing with victimising criminal behaviour, this would tend to *privatise* the response. The crime would be treated primarily as an affront to the particular victim, and the procedure and its sanctions would serve as a means by which the actor conveys regret for the affront to the victim. Additional actors—for example, the community representative at the hearing— would act primarily as facilitators for this process. Notwithstanding frequent references in the restorative-justice literature to communitarian themes, such a procedure would reflect chiefly the perspectives of the immediately interested parties.

A major drawback of this kind of privatisation is that it tends to blur the distinction between wronging and harming. On a wronging conception, the severity of the sanction should reflect how blameworthy the conduct is deemed to be. Harm is an important element in determining the conduct's degree of blameworthiness, but culpability is also vitally important—for example, the degree of foreseeability of the harm, the kind of intent involved, and the presence of any partially excusing conditions. Conventional depictions of RJ tend to blur this distinction, by describing RJ as largely focused on consequentialist goals such as 'repairing' the harm or resolving the 'conflict'. The making-amends model, as we have seen (see s III 1), more clearly treats the conduct as wrongdoing, and the response as a way of acknowledging the wrong. But if the procedure leaves decisions primarily to individual offenders and their victims, the process may too easily shift in practice from one of wronging to that of harming. What will come to matter is not so much how culpable the offender was in committing his wrong, but the particulars concerning how much the victim has been hurt. We shall return to this theme of privatisation and its implications below.

V. 'MAKING AMENDS' AS A REPLACEMENT FOR CRIMINAL JUSTICE?

Some of the RJ literature proposes the ambitious goal of having RJ largely or entirely replace traditional criminal justice. The institution of legal punishment is said to be fundamentally flawed, and should be replaced by a restorative approach (see eg Walgrave, this volume).

If RJ, with making-amends as its aim, were to replace criminal justice, how might such a system be constituted? An informal, negotiated process involving the victim and offender, aimed at the acknowledgement of fault and the undertaking of a reparative task, would become the *primary* response to victimising criminal behaviour. The procedure would apply not only to juvenile offenders, but after judicial adjudication of guilt,[9] to adult offenders as well. RJ's scope might thus extend to a wide variety of offenders, ranging from petty thieves and vandals to those convicted of serious violent offences. With this increase in scope would come wider dispositional powers (including possibly, the power to impose incarcerative dispositions for serious offences).[10] The formal criminal-justice system would be relegated to the status of a 'back-up' system, applying to cases deemed unsuitable to the making of amends (see s III 4), and to persons who fail to co-operate with RJ processes. What concerns would such a scheme raise?

1. Regulating Discretion

Earlier in this essay, we suggested the need for guidance concerning what kinds of procedures and dispositions would help implement a making-amends model (III 3). RJ proceedings tend, however, to be largely discretionary, with only limited controls (see Roche, 2002: chs 5 and 6). If the ambit of RJ is expanded so that it becomes the response of first resort for most victimising offences, this discretion would potentially be expanded still further; in order to deal with more serious cases, for example, the range of permissible sanctions would (as just noted) have to be widened substantially. This would make still more urgent the need for dispositional norms.

Yet for such an expanded system of 'free-standing' RJ, discretion would become much more difficult to regulate. The primary decision-maker would consist of lay

[9] For the need of judicial adjudication of guilt, see s IV 1.
[10] See Dignan, this volume.

persons not trained in applying and interpreting legal or other explicit norms. The legal system's usual way of policing the application of criteria—namely, having an appellate tribunal review the decision and possibly revise the disposition—would also be awkward to apply, because what matters is not just the disposition but the discursive process through which offender and victim reach it.[11] As a result, it would become harder to formulate and implement norms and review procedures that would help assure that the process serves to achieve making-amends goals, and does so in an equitable manner.

2. Uncooperative Offenders

Establishing a free-standing RJ system raises the question of what is to be done with uncooperative offenders. There are three types of persons potentially involved: those who refuse to participate in an RJ proceeding or who do not consent to any resulting disposition; those who do agree to undertake a reparative task, but then refuse to carry it out; and those who repeatedly reoffend, after previous RJ dispositions (see Dignan, this volume). The third category of recidivists is likely to be quite large—and would remain so, even if RJ were to have some success in reducing recidivism rates.

Some RJ theorists suggest strongly consequentialist responses, designed to strengthen incentives to participate, or to help combat recidivist crime. Braithwaite (1999), for example, recommends a system of deterrent and incapacitative back-up sanctions. Schemes of this kind would be open to two objections. One concerns fair treatment: purely incapacitative sanctions for recidivist offenders, for example, may lead to disproportionately severe responses (see, von Hirsch, 1985: ch 11; Dignan, this volume). The other objection concerns the adverse effect on the integrity of the making-amends process. The more the offender's failure to participate in the RJ process would involve risk of deterrent or incapacitative sanctions, the more offenders will feel compelled to participate in RJ on purely cautionary grounds and the less genuine any purported efforts at making amends are likely to be.

An alternative possible approach would be to retain a system of proportionate penal sanctions for those who do not co-operate. The difficulty is that such uncooperative offenders—multiple recidivists especially—tend to be especially resented. Even within sentencing systems that purport to follow a proportionalist sentencing rationale, the temptation to escalate sanctions for recidivists has not been easy to resist.[12] If the formal sentencing system becomes reduced to becom-

---

[11] If a court is given the power to reject a conference's disposals, for example, it will have to order a new proceeding, or alter the disposition agreed upon by the parties. Either approach would interfere with RJ's role as a discursive process through which the parties agree on an outcome. Alternatively, the facilitator could be given a larger role in explaining the range and limits of what the parties may agree upon; but then the question remains of enforcing such directives against unwilling parties.

[12] For example, Minnesota's sentencing commission, which employs a modified version of a desert model, has had particular difficulty maintaining moderate and proportionate sentences for recidivists; see more fully, von Hirsch, 1995.

ing mainly the repository of these most tiresome offenders, the prospects of a fair and parsimonious response to them becomes even less bright.

3. Routinisation

Making RJ the response of first resort would involve, given high rates of victim-ising crimes in most Western countries, shifting much of the large case-loads dealt with by the courts to RJ forums. It is these caseloads that have contributed so much to the routinisation of criminal justice, with its assembly-line procedures and truncated opportunities for meaningful discourse. This is problematic enough for the criminal justice system, as it makes for the remote, cut-and-dried character of criminal proceedings. But criminal sentencing is not essentially dia-logic in character, whereas RJ is. On a 'making amends' model, as we have seen, adequate communication and the reaching of understanding between the parties are central to the process. Here, routinisation undercuts the whole point of the procedure.

The Canberra RISE Project found that the average length of court hearings in the sample studied varied between seven and 27 minutes, depending on the type of case involved. Restorative conferences lasted much longer, averaging between 60 and 94 minutes (Strang, Barnes et al 1999). The longer duration doubtless gives a better opportunity to disclose the background to the case, and to permit offend-ers, victims and their supporters to put forward their perspectives on the event. But with large caseloads, will it be feasible to provide restorative hearings lasting between one to one-and-a-half hours? And if calendar pressures shrink the time available down to the ten to twenty minutes with which courts must make do, would that suffice for adequate restorative processes?

4. Aggravating the 'Privatisation' Problem?

If restorative proceedings are made the primary response to criminal behaviour, the problem of 'privatisation' spoken of earlier (see s IV 3) will be aggravated. After a finding of guilt by the courts, the focus shifts to a victim-centred negoti-ating process. In this process, what will tend to become central is the victim's degree of hurt. Even if the making-amends rationale relies on a 'wronging' stan-dard, such a victim perspective will be so difficult to limit—especially since exter-nal regulation of the process will be difficult to achieve, as just noted (see s V 1).

Consider the case of a relatively routine assault against a victim who unex-pectedly turns out to be more than usually vulnerable. A 'wronging' perspective, which the making-amends model purportedly would adopt, would focus on the offender's intent and how foreseeable the injuries were—thus ordinarily per-mitting the offence to be treated as a relatively minor one. Suppose, however, that such cases are dealt with restoratively. What would tend thus to matter is satisfying the victim's sense of grievance—which would be more strongly influenced by the actual injuries he or she has sustained. The focus will tend to shift from 'see the wrong that you have done' to 'see how I have been made to suffer'—which in this kind of case could point to a much more severe response.

A related drawback of this kind of privatisation concerns the watering down of horizontal equity requirements. When the response to crime is thus privatised, what will tend to matter is the *parties'* sense of the degree of wrongfulness of the behaviour, and of the disposition appropriate thereto; and if different negotiating pairs perceive these matters differently, so be it. Proportionality constraints—which we have said should be part of a making-amends model (see s IV 6)—may come mainly to constrain proposed dispositions which involve manifestly unreasonable views of the wrongfulness of the conduct.

VI. 'MAKING AMENDS' WITHIN A PROPORTIONALIST SENTENCING SYSTEM?

An alternative to the comprehensive RJ scheme just discussed would be to give restorative approaches, using a making-amends rationale, a more modest role within a larger structure provided by a proportionalist sentencing system.

How might such a scheme operate? We might begin by positing a hypothetical sentencing system, based on the principle of proportionate sentences. Penalties would be graded according to the seriousness of the offences, with limited adjustments for previous convictions (see von Hirsch and Ashworth, 1998: ch 4). Such a system would then be modified by introducing into it a 'making amends' scheme of more limited scope. This would apply to a specified range of victimising offences—say, property offences not involving significant violence. For such cases, guilt or innocence would continue to be determined by the courts, with traditional procedural safeguards. Upon a determination of guilt, the case would be referred to a victim-offender conference, with a facilitator presiding, which would seek a negotiated disposition—based on the making-amends rationale sketched above. The dispositions would be deemed to be punishments, and hence subject to proportionality requirements. These latter requirements, however, would be loosened somewhat (although not a great deal) to allow the participants additional leeway for agreeing upon a disposition. Would such a more limited scheme of making amends fare better?

1. Less Routinisation?

Routinisation could become somewhat less of a problem. With an RJ system of such limited scope, it will become possible to target this scheme to types of cases for which it seems most suitable. This targeting will also help limit the caseload, so that the system does not become overloaded and negotiations excessively routinised. Much will depend, however, on the breadth or narrowness of the eligibility requirements. Hence, this tension: keeping caseloads down points to narrower eligibility requirements—which, however, would reduce RJ's role. Expanding the eligibility requirements would make RJ become more important, but would increase caseloads and hence aggravate routinisation.

In such a scheme, non-co-operative offenders would be returned to the penal system, to receive the appropriate proportionate sanction. Any adjustment in the sanction for recidivists, for example, would be based on the system's general principles regarding recidivism (for discussion of such principles, see von Hirsch, 1998). As the penal system would itself be an intact sanctioning system, and not a mere repository for tiresome persons who refuse to participate in an alternate scheme considered preferable, it may deal with recidivists less inequitably.

2. 'Privatisation' and Horizontal Equity

This more limited scheme would also alleviate the 'privatisation' problem of which we have just spoken. While the making-amends process would aim at a meeting of the minds between the parties, the relevant standards—especially the proportionality limits—would ultimately be public standards, that represent not just the views of the parties but wider public understandings concerning the degree of blameworthiness of the conduct.

A potential objection to placing RJ within a proportionalist sentencing framework is that the two conceptions are too disparate. Here, the making-amends model should be helpful: while it is informal and discursive in ways that conventional criminal justice is not, the model utilises a *wronging* paradigm—and resembles penal censure in that it is retrospectively oriented, to give recognition to the degree of blameworthiness of the conduct (see s III 1).

Horizontal equity could be better safeguarded. True, the disposition would be based on the parties' views concerning how injurious and culpable the conduct was, and what a fair response should be; and ordinal-proportionality constraints would be relaxed to some extent to facilitate to parties' reaching accommodation. But these negotiations would still operate within firm proportionality limits, based on the system's assessment of seriousness and appropriate severity.

Imposing such limits on the degree of severity of the response might well facilitate, rather than retard, the negotiating process, by discouraging maximalist demands. In the case of a common assault, for example, the victim would be given to understand that—while he might point to the extra harm he has suffered—the negotiations will substantially be constrained by public understandings concerning the blameworthiness of this kind of conduct. The victim will not be able to get a severe response, merely by calling attention to his personal situation.

However, the degree to which these questions of privatisation and horizontal equity are resolved will depend on the specifics of the scheme. To what extent do the scheme's proportionality limits constrain dispositions? To what extent are the proceedings structured to favour a wrongdoing and not a purely harming perspective? Unless these questions are adequately addressed, the problem of privatisation and lack of horizontal equity will re-emerge.

VII. CONCLUSIONS

What conclusions might be drawn from this discussion? The following points seem to emerge:

— The conventional multi-purpose rationale for RJ has serious problems of coherence, and may serve a largely aspirational role.
— It is possible to sketch a 'making amends' model for RJ that is more coherent. Such a model could yield some standards of application, evaluation criteria, and proportionality limits. It does, however, raise concerns about impartiality of the decision-maker, the central role of attitude, and 'privatisation' of the response to criminal wrongdoing.
— An ambitious version of the making-amends model would be a 'freestanding' scheme, as the primary response to victimising crime generally. This, however, would present serious difficulties, concerning the regulation of discretion, the treatment of uncooperative offenders, routinisation, and the loss of horizontal equity.
— These difficulties of this ambitious version might be partially alleviated by giving RJ schemes more limited scope, within certain limits established by a larger sentencing framework emphasising proportionality.

Whether such a more limited scheme is worth implementing is something which we will not try to decide here. Our purpose in this essay has been to clarify some conceptual issues involved in RJ, not to try to settle the making-amends model's ultimate merits.

REFERENCES

Bazemore, G (1999) 'After Shaming, Whither Reintegration: Restorative Justice and Relational Rehabilitation' in G Bazemore and L Walgrave (eds), *Restorative Juvenile Justice: Repairing the Harm of Youth Crime* (Criminal Justice Press, Monsey NY) 155–194.

Braithwaite, J (1999) 'Restorative Justice: Assessing Optimistic and Pessimistic Accounts' in M Tonry (ed), *Crime and Justice: A Review of Research* (Chicago University Press, Chicago) vol 25, 1–127.

Christie, N (1977) 'Conflicts as Property' *17 British Journal of Criminology* 1–26.

Daly, K (2002) 'Restorative Justice: The Real Story' 4 *Punishment and Society* 55–79.

National Academy of Sciences, Panel on Research on Criminal Careers (1986) *Criminal Careers and 'Career Criminals'* (National Academy of Sciences, Washington DC) vol 1.

Pettit, P and Braithwaite, J (1993) 'Not Just Deserts, Not Even in Sentencing' 4 *Current Issues in Criminal Justice* 222–39. Reprinted as 'Republicanism in Sentencing: Recognition, Recompense and Reassurance' in A von Hirsch and A Ashworth (eds), *Principled Sentencing* 317–30, this bibliography.

Roche, D (2001) *Restorative Justice and Deliberative Accountability* (Australian National University, Canberra). PhD Dissertation.

Strang, H, Barnes, G et al (1999) *Experiments in Restorative Policing: A Progress Report on the Canberra Reintegrative Shaming Experiments (RISE)* (Australian National University, Canberra).

Van Ness, D (1993) 'New Wine and Old Wineskins: Four Challenges of Restorative Justice' 4 *Criminal Law Review* 251–76.

von Hirsch, A (1985) *Past of Future Crimes: Deservedness and Dangerousness in the Sentencing of Criminals* (Rutgers University Press, New Brunswick NJ).

——(1993) *Censure and Sanctions* (Oxford University Press, Oxford).

——(1995) 'Proportionality and Parsimony in American Sentencing Guidelines: The Minnesota and Oregon Standards' in C Clarkson and R Morgan (eds), *The Politics of Sentencing Reform* (Oxford University Press, Oxford).

——(1998) 'Desert and Previous Convictions' in A von Hirsch and A Ashworth (eds), *Principled Sentencing* 191–97, this bibliography.

——(2001) 'The Project of Sentencing Reform' in M Tonry and R Frase (eds), *Sentencing and Sanctions in Western Countries* (Oxford University Press, New York) 405–20.

von Hirsch, A and Ashworth, A (1998) *Principled Sentencing: Readings on Theory and Policy* (Hart Publishing, Oxford).

Zedner, L (1994) 'Reparation and Retribution: Are they Reconcilable?' 57 *Modern Law Review* 228–50.

Zehr, H (1990) *Changing Lenses: A New Focus for Criminal Justice* (Herald Press, Scottsdale PA).

3

Restoration and Retribution

Antony Duff

I. SEEKING RECONCILIATION

Though philosophers are as fond as other academics of confrontation, they some-times pursue a strategy of reconciliation, which seeks to resolve a controversy by dissolving the problem about which it rages. The reconciler argues that both sides are right in the important aspects of what they claim, but wrong to think that they must disagree if they are to maintain what matters to them: they are wrong, that is, on the very issue on which they agree—that their positions are incompatible.[1]

This paper seeks such a reconciliation in relation to the controversy over 'restorative' and 'retributive' justice. Advocates of 'restorative justice' argue that our responses to crime should seek restoration: we must therefore eschew retri-bution and punishment, since they preclude restoration. On the other side, advo-cates of punishment argue that the primary state response to crime should be to punish offenders in accordance with their deserts: 'restoration' should therefore not be the primary aim, since restoration precludes punishment, and is liable to be inconsistent with the values (justice, proportionality and fairness) which are central to punishment. Thus, it seems, we must choose between 'restorative' and 'retributive' justice,[2] or between the 'punishment paradigm' and the 'restorative paradigm' (Ashworth, 1993).

I will argue that restorative theorists are right to insist that our responses to crime should seek 'restoration', whilst retributive theorists are right to argue that we should seek to bring offenders to suffer the punishments they deserve; but that both sides to the controversy are wrong to suppose that these aims are incom-patible. Restoration is not only compatible with retribution: it *requires* retribu-tion, in that the kind of restoration that crime makes necessary can (given certain deep features of our social lives) be brought about only through retributive pun-ishment (see also Daly, 2000).

---

[1] A good example of this strategy is the compatabilist attempt to reconcile free will with deter-minism: see Watson, 1982.

[2] See eg Christie, 1981: 11; Marshall, 1988: 47–8; Zehr, 1990: 178–81; Walgrave, 1994: 57, and in this volume; Dignan, 1999: 54, 60; Braithwaite, 1999: 60, and in this volume. For further references and apt criticism, see Daly and Immarigeon, 1998: 32–34.

There are of course genuine contrasts that connect to the supposed contrast between 'restorative' and 'retributive' justice: most obviously, there are sharp contrasts between what goes on in the kinds of programmes that are formally labelled as 'restorative', and what goes on, under the name of punishment, in our criminal justice systems. Advocates of each species of justice also often hold *conceptions* of 'restoration', 'retribution' and 'punishment' given which the pursuit of one does preclude the pursuit of the other. I will argue, however, that those conceptions are inadequate, and that more plausible conceptions will enable us to see how retributive punishment is the appropriate way of achieving the kind of restoration that crime makes necessary.

This argument lays me open to attack from both sides. Advocates of 'restorative justice' might accuse me of a punitive obsession which blinds me to the non-punitive possibilities of restorative processes; and advocates of punishment might accuse me of abandoning the central principles of penal justice. I do not expect to persuade committed advocates of either position that they are wrong: but I hope at least to show that there is an alternative.

II. 'RESTORATION' AND 'RETRIBUTION'

To understand what 'restorative justice' could be, we must ask what is to be restored, to and by whom, when a crime has been committed. To see how it can require 'retributive justice', we must also ask what 'retribution' can amount to.

Restorative justice is 'a process whereby parties with a stake in a specific offence collectively resolve how to deal with the aftermath of the offence and its implications for the future' (Marshall, 1999: 5). Its purpose 'is the restoration into safe communities of victims and offenders who have resolved their conflicts' (Van Ness, 1993: 258). The vagueness of these definitions is inevitable, given the diversity of the 'restorative justice' movement (see Van Ness, this volume): but we must ask what it is about the 'aftermath' and 'implications' of an offence that the parties must 'deal with'—and what would constitute success or failure in dealing with it; what these 'conflicts' involve, and how they can be 'resolved'.

Crimes typically cause various kinds of 'harm' which we might then seek to 'repair'. The simplest case is that of material harm: someone's property is destroyed or damaged or stolen. Three features of this case should be noted. Firstly, such harm can usually be fully repaired: the property can be returned, or the damage made good, or a functionally equivalent replacement provided. Secondly, the harm can be understood as a harm independently of its causation by a criminal action: the same harm could be caused by an innocent action, or by natural causes (see Feinberg, 1984: 31). Thirdly, the harm could in principle be repaired by anyone—by the victim, by other people, by the state, or by the offender. It is just that the offender should pay for the repair if she has the resources to do so, since she culpably caused the harm[3]: but it could be adequately provided by anyone.

Of course, even in property crimes matters are not typically that simple: the 'harm' done is not limited to material damage to or loss of replaceable property. The property itself might not be reparable or replaceable: if the watch I inherited from my father is lost, a new watch cannot fully replace it. The victim might suffer psychological effects—anger, anxiety, loss of trust—which typically depend on how the harm occurred: the psychological effects of (what is perceived as) a crime typically differ from those of naturally caused harm. Such effects can spread beyond the immediate victim: his intimates might be distressed and angered on his behalf; those who know about the crime might be rendered anxious lest they become victims. We can also begin to talk here (as restorative theorists often talk) of damage to relationships: to the relationship between victim and offender, or between offender and wider community. We will need to look more carefully at the character of such 'damage', however, in particular at the question of whether it can be understood in empirical terms: is it just a matter of how the people concerned are now disposed to feel about and behave towards each other?

These points become even more obvious when we move from property crimes to other kinds of crime—especially those involving attacks on the person; the three features which characterised the case of simple material harm are no longer clearly present.

Firstly, it becomes less clear what, if anything, could count as 'fully repairing' the harm. This is true even when the crime causes a harm which can be identified as such independently of its criminal causation (a physical injury caused by an assault, for instance). Of course, many physical injuries can be repaired without long term physical effects: but some cannot; and even with those that can, it is not clear that their 'repair' can (as the repair or restoration of property can) make it as if they had never occurred. It is even more clearly true when we look at other kinds of harm—for instance the emotional distress caused to victims of criminal attacks. The victims of such harms might still be offered, and accept, financial compensation: but we need to explain the sense in which money could 'repair' these kinds of harm, since it cannot repair them in the straightforward way in which it can repair financial loss or loss of functional property.

Secondly, it becomes harder, if not impossible, to identify the harm independently of the crime that caused it. Such independent identification is doubtful even when it seems possible: it is at least arguable that one whose property is stolen, or who is physically attacked, suffers a *different* harm from that suffered by one who simply loses her property or suffers a natural injury—the harm of being stolen from, or of being wrongfully attacked (see Duff, 2002). But it becomes more clearly impossible in other cases. If we are to understand the harm suffered by a

---

[3] Which is how tort law would decide the matter, see Ripstein, 1999.

rape victim, for instance, or by someone who is burgled, we might see it as manifest in their psychological distress: but to understand that we must understand it as a response to the wrong that they suffered. The same is true of damage to relationships: even if we focus on the way in which the people concerned are now disposed to feel about and behave towards each other, we can understand those changed dispositions only as responses to a perceived wrong. I will return to this point shortly.

Thirdly, whatever kind of 'repair' is possible, it is not clear that it is something that anyone other than the offender could provide. Others can of course do much for the victims of crime: friends and fellow citizens can offer material help and sympathetic support, of a kind that is sensitive to the fact that the victim suffered criminal, not merely natural, harm; the state can provide more formalised versions of such help, as well as financial compensation—though this again raises the question of how money can help to repair such harm.[4] But once we move away from the straightforward repair or replacement of material property, the meaning and efficacy of reparative measures come to depend crucially on who offers them; and there may be kinds of repair that *only* the offender can provide. If, for instance, apology is an essential reparative measure, the offender must be involved: for whilst others might pay the financial compensation that I owe to the person I wronged, they cannot apologise for me.

These comments point towards something which should anyway be obvious enough: that any talk of 'restoration' in the context of crime must be sensitive to the fact that the victim of crime has been not just harmed, but *wronged*; he has suffered a wrongful, as distinct from a natural or merely unlucky, harm. Some restorative theorists reject the very concepts of crime and wrong: rather than talking of the 'wrong' the offender did or the 'crime' she committed, we should talk about the 'conflict' or 'trouble' that needs to be resolved.[5] Others, however, rightly insist that we must retain the concept of crime (and the criminal law as providing an authoritative specification of criminal wrongs), and recognise that crimes typically involve a victim who is wronged.

This does not yet distinguish criminal law from tort law, which enables those who suffer wrongful loss to gain redress or compensation, by making those who caused the loss pay for it. I cannot pursue this issue in detail here, but we can suggest two identifying features of the kinds of wrong that should be criminal rather than (merely) tortious.

First, in tort law the focus is on the loss or harm that was caused, which can typically be identified independently of its relation to any wrongful action. Fault becomes relevant only in deciding who should bear the cost of that loss: if it was caused by another's negligence, its cost can legitimately be transferred to her (see Ripstein, 1999: chs 2–4). By contrast, criminal law focuses primarily on the wrong

---

[4] On what the state owes to victims of crime, see especially Ashworth, 1986, 1993: the fact that the state offers victims of crime compensation that it does not offer victims of natural misfortune reflects the difference between criminal and natural harms.

[5] See eg Christie, 1977; Hulsman, 1986. In response see Duff, 2001: 60–64.

that was done. This is most obvious in the case of crimes—such as attempts or crimes of endangerment—that might cause no harm of a kind that could ground a tort claim, but that can still constitute serious criminal wrongs (see Ashworth, 1993: 285), but it is also true of crimes that cause such harm. The wrong done to the victim of rape, or wounding, or burglary, is in part constituted by, but also part constitutes, the harm that she suffers: to understand such harm, we must understand it as a *criminal* harm—as a harm that consists in being *wrongfully* injured.

Secondly, it is often said that crimes are 'public' wrongs: but it is hard to explain the sense in which they are 'public' wrongs, without denigrating the victim's standing by implying that they are wrongs against 'the public' *rather than* the victim. We could, however, say that they are 'public' in the sense that, while they are often wrongs against an individual, they properly concern 'the public'—the whole political community—as wrongs in which other members of the community share as fellow citizens of both victim and offender.[6] They infringe the values by which the political community defines itself as a law-governed polity: they are therefore wrongs for which the polity and its members are part-responsible in the sense that it is up to them, and not just up to victim and offender as private individuals, to make provision for an appropriate response.

This brings us back, however, to the question of what an 'appropriate response' would be when such a wrong has been committed, and what the notion of 'restoration' could amount to in this context; and we can now see more clearly why the three features that characterised the simple case of material harm do not carry across to criminal wrongs.

First, it is not clear what could count as 'repair' or 'restoration', or whether there could be a complete repair or restoration. Property can be repaired or replaced; physical injuries can be healed; psychological suffering and distress might be assuaged, traumas eventually healed: but what can 'repair' or 'restore' the wrong that has been done? It is here that talk of apology, of shaming, even of 'confession, repentance and absolution',[7] becomes appropriate: but I will argue that this brings us into the realm of punishment.

Secondly, we cannot separate the harm that needs repair from the wrong that was done: for the wrong partly constitutes the relevant harm. This is true even of crimes that involve some independently identifiable harm: the victim of wounding suffers not just the harm of physical injury, but the distinctive harm of being wrongfully attacked. It is also true when the harm is manifest in the victim's psychological suffering, or when we talk of damage to relationships. The victim's anger or fear expresses his understanding of what he suffered as a wrong, and it can be appraised as a reasonable or unreasonable response to that wrong—an appraisal which has implications for what we think is due to him by way of

---

[6] See Marshall and Duff, 1998; and on the relevant idea of political community, Duff, 2001: chs 2, 5.

[7] JO Hayley, as quoted by Van Ness, 1993: 255. See also Christie, 1977.

reparation. The damage done to the offender's relationships—with the victim, with others—might be described in apparently empirical terms: the victim, or others, no longer trust her, or feel at ease with her as a friend, or colleague, or fellow citizen. But it is crucial to a proper understanding of this kind of harm that these are reasonable responses to a wrong that was done—for instance that they cease to trust her because she showed herself, by committing that wrong, to be *untrustworthy*. There is also a significant kind of damage to the offender's relationships that does not consist in and need not involve (though it might be recognised in) any such actual responses: she has by her crime violated the values that define her *normative* relationships with her victim and with her fellow citizens. If I betray my friend, my action is destructive of the bonds of friendship even if she never finds out, and even if we can maintain what looks like an undamaged friendship: for such an action denies the values, the mutual concern, by which a friendship is defined. So too, when I wrong a fellow citizen, my action damages the normative bonds of citizenship,[8] which raises the question of how those bonds can be repaired.

Thirdly, we must ask who could provide the kind of 'reparation' or 'restoration' that crime, as involving wrongdoing, makes necessary—but also to whom such reparation must be made. Where there is an identifiable victim, she is the obviously appropriate recipient of reparation, since it is she who was harmfully wronged: but the political community as a whole is also owed something, since it shares in the victim's wrong as a violation of its public values. The community can of course do something towards repairing or restoring the victim, by offering help, and sympathetic recognition of what she has suffered: but in so far as the harm consists in a wrong done to the victim, or damage to the normative relationship between offender and victim (and between offender and wider political community), there is a kind of 'repair' that only the offender can provide.

In the next section I will flesh out this idea, which informs many restorative programmes, and will argue that it is a kind of 'repair' that involves the offender's punishment. However, since my claim is that we should seek restoration through retribution, I should say something about retribution, to ward off some likely misunderstandings.

Talk of retribution conjures up in many minds the image of a vindictive attempt to inflict hardship—to 'deliver pain' (see Christie, 1981)—'for its own sake'; and who could argue in favour of *that*? I will argue, however, that the retributivist slogan—that 'the guilty deserve to suffer'—does express an important moral truth; and that in the case of the criminally guilty it is the state's proper task to seek to ensure that they suffer as they deserve.

The retributivist slogan says nothing about *what* the guilty deserve to suffer; the crucial task in making retributivism morally plausible is to explain this. Once we recognise that the offender has done *wrong*, we can identify two kinds of 'suf-

---

[8] Thus even if victim and offender had no actual contact before the crime, they were related normatively as fellow citizens; and it is that relationship that the crime damages.

fering' that he deserves in virtue of that wrong. First, he deserves to suffer remorse: he should come to recognise and repent the wrong that he did—which is necessarily a painful process. Secondly, he deserves to suffer censure from others—which might be a formal censure, or the angry, ferocious censure of the victim or her friends; this too, if taken seriously, must be painful. There is also a third kind of 'suffering', a third kind of 'burden', that might be appropriate, that of making reparation to the victim. Some restorative theorists argue that the hardship involved in making reparation is a side-effect of the restorative process, not its aim, thus seeking to distance themselves from any species of 'punishment' (eg Walgrave, 1994: 66) but I will argue that reparation *must* be burdensome if it is to serve its restorative purpose.

I can best develop my argument that the kind of restoration that crime makes necessary should involve the offender's punishment by contrasting two models of mediation—a 'civil' and a 'criminal' model: this will occupy the next section.

III. MEDIATION: CIVIL VERSUS CRIMINAL

For restorative theorists, the process is as important as (or more important than) the product (see Dignan, this volume): restoration is achieved as much by the process of discussion and negotiation between victim, offender and others as by whatever reparative measures flow from that process. That process takes a variety of different forms in different programmes.[9] In particular, the range of people involved varies—as between, for instance, victim-offender mediation programmes in which individual victim and individual offender are the only lead players and group conferences that also involve their families, friends or 'supporters'. There is much to be said about who should participate (about who has responsibility, or standing, in the matter) but I will concentrate here on the simple case of victim-offender mediation, and on the contrast between two simple models of mediation.

Civil mediation is a matter of negotiation and compromise, aimed at resolving conflict. I am in conflict with my neighbour over her constant early morning Do-it-yourself work; my complaints have proved fruitless. Rather than going to law, we try mediation to resolve our conflict: we must find a way to live together as neighbours; going to law would probably be an expensive way of failing to achieve that. The mediation process consists initially in mutual explanation, and complaint. I complain about her DIY work; she argues that I am exaggerating things, and accuses me of keeping her awake with my late night parties. However, we recognise that we must move beyond trading complaints and harping on past misdeeds. Perhaps we should each admit that we have been variously in the wrong in the past, but now look to the future, to find a mutually acceptable *modus vivendi*. That will

---

[9] See generally Marshall and Merry, 1990; Daly and Immarigeon, 1998; Braithwaite, 1999; Kurki, 2000; also Roberts and Roach, Schiff, in this volume.

involve negotiating a compromise between our conflicting habits: we might agree that she will avoid noisy DIY work before 9.00 am, whilst I will hold no more than one late party a fortnight. We might also pay compensation for any past damage—damage to her hedge by my guests, to my walls by her building work; and we might exchange general apologies for any past wrongs. But the compensation will be focused purely on any material damage that was done; and the apologies might be formal (we do not aspire to the sort of friendship in which apologies are worthwhile only if sincere) and unfocused (we do not list every wrong).

Some such civil mediation process is often the appropriate way of dealing with conflicts, including many which involve criminal conduct. Perhaps my neighbour has committed what counts in law as criminal damage against me, as my guests have against her: but it would be stupid to call the police and demand that they press charges. This is partly because there have been similar, minor, wrongs on both sides, but also because our relationship is one of rough equality: neither has been oppressing the other. We have each failed to think carefully enough about our relationship, but we can remedy that through informal mediation.

Sometimes, however, such a process is inappropriate: if mediation is possible at all, what is required is *criminal* mediation, under the aegis of the criminal law.

Criminal mediation is focused on a wrong that has been done. A woman has been beaten by her husband, or her house has been burgled and vandalised; the parties agree to mediation. It matters, first, that the relevant facts be established, either before the mediation or as its first stage—that this was a serious criminal assault, or burglary and criminal damage. (Whereas in the civil case, it is less important or helpful thus to focus on the past.)

Secondly, the process will include discussion and mutual explanations of those facts: the victim can explain how the crime affected her; the offender might explain how he came to commit it. The offender's explanation might include mitigating factors: but he is not allowed to argue that his conduct was justified—that husbands have the right to 'chastise' their wives, for instance. For the criminal law, under whose aegis the process takes place, defines what counts as a crime and as a justification: whatever else is negotiable, the wrongfulness of the offender's conduct is not.[10] (Whereas in civil mediation each party might initially seek to justify their own conduct, before realising that this is futile.)

Part of the aim of the process is precisely this communication between victim and offender: the victim has a chance to bring the offender to grasp the wrong he did her, and to understand his action from her perspective; the offender has the chance to explain himself, and to grasp more clearly what he has done. Censure is integral to this exercise: to try to bring the offender to grasp the wrong that he did involves at least implicitly condemning his action as wrongful (not to condemn it would be implicitly to deny that it was a wrong, or that its wrongfulness mattered); and if he comes to grasp it as a wrong, he will censure himself for doing it.

---

[10] Compare Dobash and Dobash, 1992: ch 7, on the CHANGE project for violent men.

Thirdly, however, the process also aims to reconcile offender and victim: but what does this involve? Minimally, the aim is to reconcile them as fellow citizens (if they had no closer relationship that could be salvaged): to repair or restore the normative relationship of fellow-citizenship, so that they can treat each other with the acceptance and respect that fellowship in the polity requires. The offender's crime violated the values which define that normative relationship, and was thus injurious to it; that injury must be repaired.

Now in civil mediation, reconciliation is achieved partly by a compromise between the conflicting interests of the parties concerned: but since the wrongfulness of the crime is not negotiable, we cannot seek reconciliation in the criminal case through a similar compromise—for instance one that allows the husband to beat his wife occasionally. Nor can reconciliation be achieved merely by the kind of reparation that civil mediation can involve, for even if the independently identifiable harms suffered by the victim could be repaired, what is required is a response that addresses the *wrong* done to her. That must at least involve an apology, which expresses the wrongdoer's recognition of the wrong she has done, her implicit commitment to avoid such wrongdoing in future, and her concern to seek forgiveness from and reconciliation with the person she wronged. Apologies own the wrong as something that I culpably did, but disown it as something that I now repudiate; they also mark my renewed recognition of the person I wronged as one to whom I owe a respect that I failed to display, and with whom I must reconcile myself by making up for what I did to her.[11]

But a merely verbal apology might not be enough, for relatively serious wrongs. This is partly because verbal apologies can easily be insincere—mere words that lack depth or truth; but also because even a sincere verbal apology might not do enough to address the seriousness of the wrong. We often need to give more than merely verbal expression to things that matter to us. We express gratitude for services done to us by gifts or, in the public realm, by public rewards or honours; we express our grief at a death through the rituals of a funeral. Such more-than-merely-verbal modes of expression have two purposes: they make the expression more forceful, and they help to focus the expresser's attention on what needs to be expressed.

Similarly, an apology is strengthened if it is given a more than merely verbal form—if I make some kind of material reparation to the person I wronged. Thus the mediation process typically aims to end with an agreement on what reparation the offender should make. This might consist in something superficially identical to the reparation to which civil mediation can lead: if I damaged another's property, I might pay for its repair, or even repair it myself. But such direct repair is not always possible: the wrongdoer might need to find some other benefit he can provide for the victim (or for others; the offender might agree to undertake some charitable activity). Furthermore, even if such direct repair is possible, it has

---

[11] Compare Gaita, 1991: chs 1–4, on remorse as involving a recognition of the *reality* of the other person.

a different meaning in the criminal case, as a forceful expression of the offender's recognition of his wrongdoing—a forceful apology.

One striking difference between reparation in the civil and in the criminal case concerns its burdensome character. Civil reparation can be burdensome, depending on what is required and on the repairer's resources: but it is not designed to be burdensome, and repairs the harm no less efficaciously if it is entirely unburdensome. Criminal reparation, by contrast, must be burdensome if it is to serve its purpose: only then can it express a serious apology for a wrong done; if it cost the wrongdoer nothing, it would mean no more than empty verbal apology.[12]

I have spoken so far of how sincere apology can be adequately and forcefully expressed; and we could see the paradigm of moral reparation for a wrong as the voluntary undertaking of some designedly burdensome reparative task which will express the wrongdoer's sincerely remorseful apology. But life, especially of the kind that involves criminal mediation, is not always like that: what can I say about cases in which the offender is not sincerely apologetic, or in which the victim is not ready to accept such an apology? I will comment on the latter possibility in section V, but should make two initial points about the former possibility here.

Part of the purpose of criminal mediation is, as I have noted, to bring the offender (if she needs bringing) to recognise her crime as a wrong—and thus to recognise the need for some apologetic reparation. But that might not happen; and the question is whether, on my account, there can then be any appropriate point to requiring her to undertake a reparative task,[13] if it does not express a sincere apology. There is an appropriate point, in two ways.

First, the process of undertaking the reparation can help to induce what it is intended to express—the offender's repentant recognition of the wrong he has done. Just as the rituals of a funeral can serve both to express and to induce an understanding of the significance of the person's death by focusing the mourners' attention on it, so undertaking reparation can focus the wrongdoer's attention on the meaning of his wrongdoing, so inducing him to repent it as a wrong, and to see the reparation as an appropriate way of expressing that repentance.

Secondly, even if this does not happen, requiring the wrongdoer to undertake a reparative task serves a legitimate purpose. It makes it forcefully clear to him that he has done wrong, and that he owes this to his victim by way of apologetic reparation: we require him, in effect, to apologise to her in order to make clear to

---

[12] John Braithwaite asks why restoration must be burdensome: why can it not be achieved by a hug, or a gift from victim to offender (in discussion; see Braithwaite, 1999: 20 fn 6)? We need to know more about the context before we can understand whether a hug or a gift could have a suitably restoring meaning (in his example, the villagers' gift of rice to the thief expressed their shame that 'one from our village should be so poor as to steal', which implies their partial responsibility for the theft): but my concern is with what the offender owes the victim, rather than with what the victim or others can do for the wrongdoer.

[13] It might seem that I am here smuggling a 'requirement' into what was initially presented as, and what should surely be, a *voluntary* process of mediation resulting in an *agreed* mode of reparation: but I will argue that offenders could properly be required to enter mediation and to undertake reparation.

him why he ought to do so. It sends a message to the victim—that we recognise and take seriously the wrong she has suffered. There is also still a sense in which victim and offender are reconciled by the very ritual of reparation, even if it does not express a sincere apology. In more intimate relationships only sincere apologies have value: but in the more distant relationships in which we stand to each other simply as fellow citizens we can often make peace with each other by going through the ritual motions of making and accepting an apology without inquiring into its sincerity.[14]

We can, I suggest, see criminal mediation and reparation as a kind of secular penance: as a burden undertaken by the wrongdoer, which aims to induce and express her repentant and apologetic understanding of the wrong she has done, and thus to secure reconciliation with those she has wronged. Religious penances are addressed to God, against whom the sinner has offended. Secular penances are addressed initially to the direct victim of the wrongdoing (when there is one), as the person to whom apology is most obviously owed; but they are also addressed to the wider community, against one of whose members the wrong was committed and whose values were violated. Crimes as public wrongs require public apology: an apology addressed to the whole community as well as to the individual victim.

We should also, I claim, recognise criminal mediation and reparation as punitive, indeed as a paradigm of retributive punishment.

IV. CRIMINAL MEDIATION AND PUNISHMENT

Criminal mediation, as described here, certainly fits the standard definitions of punishment, as something intentionally painful or burdensome imposed on an offender, for her crime, by some person or body with the authority to do so—and, we can add, intended to communicate censure for that crime.[15]

It focuses on the offender and his crime: on what he must do to repair the moral damage wrought by his crime. It is intended to be painful or burdensome, and the pain or burden is to be suffered *for* the crime. The mediation process itself aims to confront the offender with the fact and implications of what he has done, and to bring him to repent it as a wrong: a process which must be painful. The reparation that he is then to undertake must be burdensome if it is to serve its proper purpose. The aim is not to 'make the offender suffer' just for its own sake: but it is to induce an appropriate kind of suffering—the suffering intrinsic to

---

[14] I do not pretend that the notion of apology, and the role I give it here, are unproblematic: some of the problems are highlighted by Bottoms, by Daly and by von Hirsch, Ashworth and Shearing in this volume. For preliminary attempts to deal with some of the problems, see Duff, 2001: ch 3.6 and ch 3.7.4.

[15] This is not the place for a detailed (and ultimately fruitless) exploration of the definitional complexities of the concept of punishment: see Scheid, 1980 on the definitional debate, and (on censure as a defining feature) Feinberg, 1970.

confronting and repenting one's own wrongdoing and to making reparation for it. Criminal mediation takes place under the aegis of the criminal law and the authority of a criminal court: a court must determine that the defendant committed the offence charged, supervise the mediation process, approve its outcome (the reparation the offender is to make), and deal with offenders who refuse to take part or to make the agreed reparation (see further section V below).

It might seem that criminal mediation and reparation still cannot constitute punishment, since punishment is imposed against or regardless of the offender's will, whilst mediation and reparation must be consensual: the offender must agree to enter mediation, and to undertake reparation. However, first, punishment can be *self*-imposed: an offender who willingly enters mediation and undertakes reparation can be said to be punishing herself.[16] Secondly, most of the punishments imposed by our courts are not strictly 'imposed' in the sense that the offender is simply their passive victim or recipient: more usually, they consist in *requirements*—to pay a fine, to undertake the specified community service, to visit the probation officer[17]—which it is up to the offender to carry out for herself; and offenders could likewise be required to take part in the mediation process and to undertake the specified reparation. There are, of course, sanctions against offenders who fail to do what is required of them, which will involve, in the end, something strictly imposed on the offender: but restorative processes must also be backed up by ultimately coercive sanctions against offenders who fail to do what is required of them.[18]

However, my claim that criminal mediation and reparation should be seen as punishment is not simply definitional: this process can serve the appropriate aims of criminal punishment.

First, mediation is a communicative process. The procedure consists in communication between victim and offender about the crime's implications, as a wrong against the victim; the reparation that the offender undertakes communicates to the victim and others an apology for that crime. But it is a process of *punitive* communication: it censures the offender for his crime, and requires some burdensome reparation for that crime. Criminal punishment must, I believe, be justified (if it can be justified at all) as a communicative enterprise between a state or political community and its members; criminal mediation is certainly such an enterprise.

Secondly, criminal mediation is retributive, in that it seeks to impose on (or induce in) the offender the suffering she deserves for her crime, and is justified in those terms. She deserves to suffer censure for what she has done: mediation aims to communicate that censure to her, in such a way that she will come to accept that she deserves it. She deserves to suffer remorse for what she has done:

---

[16] Compare Adler, 1992: ch 2, on the 'conscientious paradigm' of punishment.

[17] And even, in some countries, to present oneself on a specified date or at weekends to serve a prison term: see Walker and Padfield, 1996: 142–4.

[18] See Walgrave, 1994: 70–1, and this volume; Braithwaite, 1999: 56–7, 61–7.

mediation aims to induce remorse in her, by bringing her to recognise the wrong she has done. She ought to make apologetic, burdensome, reparation to her victim: mediation aims to provide for such reparation. By seeing criminal mediation as punishment, we can thus make plausible sense of the retributivist idea that the guilty deserve to suffer, by showing what they deserve to suffer, and why. What they deserve to suffer is not just 'pain' or a 'burden', but the particular kind of painful burden which is integral to the recognition of guilt: they deserve to suffer that because it is an appropriate response to their wrongdoing; and criminal mediation aims precisely to impose or induce that kind of suffering.

Thirdly, the reparation that the offender undertakes is a species of penal hard treatment: it is intentionally burdensome, making demands on his time, money or energies, independently of its communicative meaning. But we can now see how penal hard treatment can be justified as an essential aspect of a communicative penal process: the hard treatment that reparation involves is the means by which the offender makes apologetic reparation to the victim, and a vehicle through which he can strengthen his own repentant understanding of the wrong he has done.[19]

Fourthly, although criminal mediation is retributive, looking back to the past crime, it is also future-directed. It aims to reconcile victim and offender, through apologetic reparation by the offender. It aims to dissuade the offender from future crimes: to bring her to repent the wrong she has done is to bring her to see why she should not commit such wrongs in future. This is not, however, to posit a consequentialist 'general justifying aim' (see Hart, 1968) for criminal mediation or for punishment. On consequentialist accounts, the relationship between punishment and the good it aims to achieve is instrumental and contingent: punishment is, as a matter of fact, an efficient technique for achieving that good. But the relationship between criminal mediation and the goods it aims to achieve is not merely instrumental. For the ends themselves determine the means which are appropriate to them: the reconciliation which is to be achieved must involve a recognition of and apology for the wrong that was done, and must therefore be achieved by a process which includes such recognition and apology; the offender is to be dissuaded from future crime by her recognition of the wrong she has committed.[20]

Although I have argued that we should see criminal mediation of the kind described here as a paradigm of punishment, it might strike you that this process is still very different from the criminal punishments typically imposed under our existing penal systems; and so it is and should be. For although I believe that punishment is in principle a necessary and appropriate response to criminal wrongdoing, I am not seeking to justify our existing penal practices, or anything very like them. However, a criminal mediation process of the kind I have described will by no means always be possible or appropriate: I should therefore say something

---

[19] On 'hard treatment', and the problem of justifying it from a communicative perspective, see Feinberg, 1970; von Hirsch, 1993: 12–13.

[20] For a fuller account of the conception of punishment sketched here, see Duff, 2001.

about how criminal mediation should fit into a larger system of criminal justice—a system that will also impose more familiar kinds of punishment; this will also involve some comments on the proper role of the criminal courts, and will thus address some further concerns of critics of the 'restorative paradigm'.[21]

V.   RESTORATIVE PUNISHMENT AND THE COURTS

I have suggested that criminal mediation should be conducted under the aegis and authority of a criminal court. The court has an important role even when there is an identifiable victim, when both victim and offender are willing to engage in mediation, and when (with the help of a mediator) they agree on a suitable mode of reparation; but its role is more prominent when these conditions are not satisfied. In both cases, however, its central role is as guarantor of punitive justice.

The court's initial task is to establish whether the alleged offender did commit the crime charged, and to convict him if he is proved guilty. One of the protections that a liberal state should provide for its citizens is that they must not be subjected to the critical public attention that criminal mediation involves unless they are proved to have committed a public wrong—a task which cannot be safely left to informal procedures. It is also appropriate for the court to mark the public character of the wrong by convicting, and thus condemning, the defendant if his guilt is proved.

If victim and offender agree to mediation, the court has a role both as protector of each party's rights (protecting each against exploitation or bullying), and as guardian of the public interest: since the crime is a public wrong, the victim (and her supporters, if the mediation process includes them) must speak not just for herself, but for the community as a whole; and the offender must speak not just to her, but through her to the whole community. This role is best discharged by a court-appointed mediator, who can speak with the voice and authority of the law and of the polity whose law it is. Two other aspects of the court's role as guarantor of punitive justice are worth emphasising.

First, the court and the mediator must ensure that the offender is only required to discuss, and make reparation for, the crime proved against her. Restorative theorists sometimes take it to be a merit of 'informal justice' that it allows a wider, unconstrained discussion of whatever problems exist in the offender's relationships with others, or in her life as a whole: but this is not something in which offenders should be required to participate. What justifies mediation, and the demand that the offender take part in it, is her crime. A community that is to respect the privacy of its citizens must respect certain limits on how far it seeks to intrude into their lives or thoughts—which, in this context, means that it

---

[21] See also the 'making amends' model suggested by von Hirsch, Ashworth and Shearing in this volume: this section addresses some of the concerns that they raise.

should inquire only into the crime, her reasons for it, and its implications: that is their business, but other aspects of her life are not.

Secondly, the court must approve the reparation that is agreed between victim and offender to ensure that it is appropriate. What makes it appropriate depends in part on its character: is it, for instance, degrading? But it also depends on its proportionality to the crime: whilst the fact that a certain reparation has been agreed counts strongly in its favour as being just (as the outcome of a just, participatory process), it is not dispositive. The reparation must constitute an adequate apology to the victim, and to the wider community, and so must communicate an adequate conception of the crime to the offender, the victim and others: this must include a conception of its seriousness, which is marked by the onerousness of the reparation. So whilst on this account we should not seek a strict proportionality between crime and reparation, or make proportionality our positive aim, we must respect the demands of a rough and negative proportionality: the reparation must not be *disproportionate* in its severity to the seriousness of the crime.[22]

The court's role becomes more prominent when direct victim/offender mediation is not possible or appropriate. Mediation is clearly not possible if there is no identifiable individual victim; or if the offender or the victim refuses to take part, or cannot take part, in the process. In such cases, the offender will undergo a punishment of a more familiar kind: but I would argue, though I cannot develop the argument here, that the sentencing process should as far as possible be a formal analogue of the victim-offender mediation process (a mediation process, we might say, between the offender and the political community);[23] and that the offender's punishment should resemble, in its meaning and purpose, the reparation to which criminal mediation leads, as a kind of apologetic reparation that the offender is required to make to the wider community—the community which might be the only identifiable victim of the crime.

A trickier question is that of when direct victim-offender mediation followed by punitive reparation would be possible but inappropriate: are there kinds of crime for which mediation, even if it leads to onerous reparation, is not an appropriate response? I am not sure about this. Some might fear that even criminal mediation as I have described it makes crime too much of a private matter between victim and offender—and that for serious crimes we need a stronger public dimension to the response than mediation involves. But criminal mediation, as I have described it, presupposes a public condemnation of the crime

---

[22] The role of proportionality on my account thus has something in common with the role that Morris and Tonry give it, as a negative constraint on sentencing rather than a positive aim (eg Morris and Tonry, 1990: ch 4; Tonry, 1998): but see Duff, 2001: 137–9, 141–3. Note too that, since the focus is on the wrong done to the victim, the seriousness of the crime, and so the onerousness of the reparation, is to be measured by the seriousness of the wrong; the amount or cost of the harm caused will be relevant only insofar as it bears on the seriousness of the wrong. All this provides part of an answer to Ashworth's worries in Ashworth, 1993.

[23] Compare Cavadino and Dignan, 1998; for more detail, see Duff, 2001: chs 3–4.

through a criminal conviction; the wider community's voice is heard in the process through the mediator; and the reparation constitutes an apologetic communication to the victim and to the wider community.

Perhaps, however, one reason for insisting in some cases on a more public determination of sentence has to do with the nature and meaning of the sentence. For instance, the meaning of imprisonment is that the offender has, by his crime, made it morally impossible for his fellow citizens to live with him in ordinary community: the appropriate response to his crime is therefore temporary exclusion from such a community. Now such a punishment, with such a meaning, can be appropriate, for the most serious kinds of crime that deny the community's most basic values: but the judgement that it is appropriate should fall to be made not by victim and offender in a mediation process, but by a criminal court that speaks directly for the community from which the offender is to be excluded.

I cannot pursue this issue further here. What I have argued is that criminal mediation should be seen as a secular penance which, precisely as a kind of punishment for the wrong the offender has done, aims to secure repentance and apologetic reparation from the offender, and thus to achieve a reconciliation between the offender and those she has wronged. It aims, that is, to achieve restoration, but to achieve it precisely through an appropriate retribution. That is also, I would argue, the proper aim of criminal punishment more generally: but there is much more to be said about the relationship between criminal mediation and other modes of punishment than I can say here.

REFERENCES

Adler, J (1992) *The Urgings of Conscience* (Temple University Press, Philadelphia).

Ashworth, AJ (1986) 'Punishment and Compensation: Victims, Offenders and the State' 6 *Oxford Journal of Legal Studies* 86–122.

—— (1993) 'Some Doubts about Restorative Justice' 4 *Criminal Law Forum* 277–99.

Braithwaite, J (1999) 'Restorative Justice: Assessing Optimistic and Pessimistic Accounts' in M Tonry (ed), *Crime and Justice: A Review of Research* (University of Chicago Press, Chicago IL) vol 25, 1–27.

Cavadino, M and Dignan, J (1998) 'Reparation, Retribution and Rights' in A von Hirsch and AJ Ashworth (eds), *Principled Sentencing* 2nd edn (Hart Publishing, Oxford).

Christie, N (1977) 'Conflicts as Property' 17 *British Journal of Criminology* 1–15.

—— (1981) *Limits to Pain* (Martin Robertson, London).

Daly, K (2000) 'Revisiting the Relationship between Restorative and Retributive Justice' in H Strang and J Braithwaite (eds), *Restorative Justice: Philosophy to Practice* (Ashgate, Aldershot).

Daly, K and Immarigeon, R (1998) 'The Past, Present, and Future of Restorative Justice' 1 *Contemporary Justice Review* 21–45.

Dignan, J (1999) 'The Crime and Disorder Act and the Prospects for Restorative Justice' 1 *Criminal Law Review* 48–60.

Duff, RA (2001) *Punishment, Communication, and Community* (Oxford University Press, New York).

—— 'Harms and Wrongs' (2002) 5(1) *Buffalo Criminal Law Review* 13–45.

Feinberg, J (1970) 'The Expressive Function of Punishment' in J Feinberg, *Doing and Deserving* (Princeton University Press, Princeton NJ).

—— (1984) *Harm to Others* (Oxford University Press, New York).

Gaita, R (1991) *Good and Evil: An Absolute Conception* (Macmillan, London).

Hart, HLA (1968) 'Prolegomenon to the Principles of Punishment' in HLA Hart, *Punishment and Responsibility* (Oxford University Press, Oxford).

Hulsman, L (1986) 'Critical Criminology and the Concept of Crime' 10 *Contemporary Crises* 63–80.

Kurki, L (2000) 'Restorative and Community Justice in the United States' in M Tonry (ed), *Crime and Justice: A Review of Research* (University of Chicago Press, Chicago IL) vol 27, 235–304.

Marshall, SE and Duff, RA (1998) 'Criminalization and Sharing Wrongs' 11 *Canadian Journal of Law and Jurisprudence* 7–22.

Marshall, TF (1988) 'Out of Court: More or Less Justice?' in R Matthews (ed), *Informal Justice* (Sage, London).

—— (1999) *Restorative Justice: An Overview* (Home Office, London).

Marshall, TF and Merry, S (1990) *Crime and Accountability: Victim/Offender Mediation in Practice* (HMSO, London).

Morris, N and Tonry, M (1990) *Between Prison and Probation: Intermediate Punishments in a Rational Sentencing System* (Oxford University Press, New York).

Ripstein, A (1999) *Equality, Responsibility and the Law* (Cambridge University Press, Cambridge).

Scheid, DE (1980) 'Note on Defining "Punishment"' 10 *Canadian Journal of Philosophy* 453–62.

Tonry, M (1998) 'Interchangeability, Desert Limits and Equivalence of Function' in A von Hirsch and AJ Ashworth (eds), *Principled Sentencing* 2nd edn (Hart Publishing, Oxford).

Van Ness, DW (1993) 'New Wine and Old Wineskins: Four Challenges of Restorative Justice' 4 *Criminal Law Forum* 251–76.

von Hirsch, A (1993) *Censure and Sanctions* (Oxford University Press, Oxford).

Walgrave, L (1994) 'Beyond Rehabilitation: in Search of a Constructive Alternative in the Judicial Response to Juvenile Crime' 2 *European Journal of Criminal Policy and Research* 57–75.

Walker, N and Padfield, N (1996) *Sentencing Theory, Law and Practice* 2nd edn (Butterworths, London).

Watson, G (ed) (1982) *Free Will* (Oxford University Press, Oxford).

Zehr, H (1990) *Changing Lenses: A New Focus for Crime and Justice* (Herald Press, Scottsdale PA).

4

Imposing Restoration Instead of Inflicting Pain: Reflections on the Judicial Reaction to Crime

Lode Walgrave

I. INTRODUCTION: COERCION IN RESTORATIVE JUSTICE

In a previous publication, restorative justice has been defined as '*every action that is primarily oriented towards doing justice by restoring the harm that has been caused by a crime*' (Bazemore and Walgrave, 1999: 48). Restorative justice is thus characterised by its aim of doing justice by repairing the harm, which includes material damage, psychological and other forms of suffering inflicted on the victim and his proximate environment, but also social unrest and indignation in the community, uncertainty about legal order and the authorities' capacity for assuring public safety. It also encompasses social damage which the offender caused to himself[1] by his offence. Restorative justice is therefore not limited to resolving a tort according to civil law, but deals with crimes, which are also public events traditionally dealt with by criminal law.

(1) In contrast to both punitive or rehabilitative justice, restorative justice is not primarily characterised by the kind of action to which the offender must submit. Indeed, restoration can proceed a considerable distance without the involvement of the offender. If the offender is not caught, while the harm inflicted is assessed, (partial) justice should be done by trying to repair or compensate the victim, in order to restore the public's confidence that crime will be condemned.

The authorities' action in view of involving the offender in the aftermath of the offence is to be seen as a means of enhancing the restoration of the victim and addressing public confidence. It expresses disapproval of the norm transgression, and it contributes to the re-assurance of the norm and norm enforcement, among the public, victims and also offenders. The offender is implicated, not because something must be done to him, but because this will promote restoration. Any

---

[1] I shall use the male form as the general form. This may not be politically correct, but it is more practical to use one form coherently.

possible influence on the offender is a secondary objective, within the limits set by the primary goal of restoration. The nature and extent of obligation is determined by the needs of reasonable restoration, not by the needs of adequate treatment, nor of proportionate punishment.

(2) The quality of restoration will considerably improve if the offender cooperates freely. Many restorative justice proponents consider such cooperation to be the key element of restorative justice (Marshall, 1996; McCold, 2000). They rightly promote informal voluntary settlements as being crucial for achieving restoration. The offender's voluntary agreement to repair or compensate expresses his understanding of the wrongs committed and harms caused, as well as his willingness to make amends. This communicates compliance with social norms; the recognition of harm confirms the value and recognises the rights of the victim. The restorative value of such gestures is much greater than if the offender complies only to avoid further trouble. However, voluntary cooperation is not a value on its own, but rather a means of enhancing the quality of possible restoration.

In many cases, agreement cannot be reached or what is agreed may be insufficient. For a variety of reasons, coercion may then be needed. This can only be imposed by the judicial system. In the maximalist version of restorative justice,[2] judicial procedures and sanctions are also considered from a restorative perspective. Restorative sanctions include imposing formal restitution or compensation, paying a fine or doing work for the benefit of a victim's fund and/or community service. Other deprivations of liberty, like an enforced stay in a closed facility, are used to enforce compliance with the restorative sanctions, or to incapacitate offenders who are considered to represent a high risk with respect to public safety.[3] Because they are enforced and not a result of voluntary agreements, such sanctions do not completely fulfil the potential of the restorative paradigm. I shall develop my reasons why I consider them nevertheless to be preferable to other sanctions or punishments.

The remainder of this chapter will deal with the coercive imposition of obligations in view of restoration. It must, however, be clear by now that I strongly believe that face-to-face, informal and voluntary meetings will almost always provide the best prospects for restoration. I take their superiority for granted, but address what is in my view the most delicate but unavoidable issue in developing a maximalist restorative justice system, at the point where coercion finally appears to be the only possible way of doing justice.

This option provokes two questions: first, does accepting coerced restorative sanctions not undermine the essential elements of the restorative approach? This question is dealt with in sections one and two. Secondly, how can a systemic,

---

[2] The 'maximalist version of restorative justice' (Bazemore and Walgrave, 1999) aims at a fully-fledged justice system, consequentionally oriented towards doing justice through restoration. In the longer term, it would replace the existing punitive or rehabilitative justice systems.
[3] See Dignan, this volume.

restorative approach to crime be inserted into the principles of a constitutional, democratic state? This will be the subject of section three.

1. Coerced Restoration and Punishment

Accepting enforced restorative sanctions, imposed according to judicial procedures as a result of assessed accountability for the consequences of offending, seems to leave very few or no differences between such sanctions and traditional punishments.

McCold (2000), for example, rejects the possible inclusion of coercive sanctions within the restorative frame, because that would shift restorative justice back to being punitive. Others integrate the restorative models into the punishment philosophy (see Daly, 2000; Duff, 2001 and in this volume). They consider a punitive response to crime to be indispensable, but try to combine it with the social constructiveness of restorative responses. Restorative justice would then not offer 'alternatives to punishment', but 'alternative punishments' (Duff, 1992). This position overlooks critical differences between punishment and restoration.

1.1. Intentional Pain Infliction versus Awareness of Painfulness

'*Punishing someone consists of visiting a deprivation (hard treatment) on him, because he supposedly has committed a wrong, . . .*'[4] (von Hirsch, 1993: 9). Three elements are distinguished: hard treatment, the intention of inflicting it, and the link with the wrong committed. If one of these elements is lacking, there is no punishment. Intentionally inflicting pain which is not linked to a wrongful act is not punishment. Painful obligations which are not imposed with the intention to cause suffering are not punishments. That is the key difference between a fine and taxes. '*Pain in punishment is inflicted for the sake of pain . . .*' (Fatic, 1995: 197).

The crux lies in the intention. Equating every painful obligation after a wrong done with punishment is based on a mistaken 'psychological location' of the painfulness. The key lies in the mind of the punisher, not in that of the punished. It is the punisher who considers an action to be wrong and who wants the wrongdoer to suffer for it. Even if a juvenile sees the punishment as an event which will enhance his reputation among his peers, it will remain a punishment. Conversely, if he feels the obligation to repair as being hard and calls it 'a punishment', it actually is no punishment if the intention of the judge was not to make the juvenile suffer, but rather to request from him a reasonable contribution to reparation.

However, the relation between obliged restoration and pain is more complicated. Not taking the hardship of a restorative obligation into account could lead to draconian results. Obliging a deprived juvenile who stole and crashed a Jaguar

---

[4] Contrary to von Hirsch, I do not add disapprobation as another characteristic. Punishment is often administered routinely, and experienced as a 'price' to be paid, without any moral reflection at all.

to pay the full amount of the car would condemn him to a lifetime of working. This would be unacceptable. Even if there is no intention to inflict pain, there must be an awareness of the painful effects, which should be taken into account.[5] The boy will have to make an effort at reparation which will probably transcend the material repayment. The material part will be reduced to a small amount, in view of the boy's financial, mental and social capacities and his future. The remaining material damage to the victim should be repaid by insurance or by a victim's fund.

In deciding upon the restorative obligation, its possible painfulness is thus an element. It is, however, only a reason to eventually reduce the obligation, never to augment it. In retribution, in contrast, the painfulness is the principal yardstick, and its amount can be increased or decreased in order to achieve proportionality in punishment. In restoration, a relation may be sought between the nature and seriousness of the harm and the restorative effort, but painfulness can only lead to its decrease, never to its increase.

As we shall see, the importance of this difference lies in its ethical consequences. I shall argue that the intentional obligation to make up is ethically superior to the intentional infliction of pain, even if that is linked to a wrong committed.

1.2. Punishment as a Means, Restoration as a Goal

Punishment is a means which can be used to enforce any legal system. It is an act of power to express disapproval, possibly to enforce compliance, but it is neutral about the value system it enforces. Restoration, on the contrary, is not a means, but an outcome. Restorative justice is indisputably a consequentionalist approach to offending. It is characterised by the aim of doing justice through restoration. The broad scope of restoration inherently demonstrates its orientation to the quality of social life, as a normative beacon.

Traditional criminal justice conceives of punishment as the a priori means of the intervention with a view to achieving a variety of possible goals. In contrast, restorative justice advances restoration in the broader sense as the objective, and chooses among a diversity of social and legal means in view of this objective. Punishment is not the most appropriate means for achieving restoration. On the contrary, punishment generally represents a serious obstacle to possible restoration.[6] The priority for the procedure in view of determining the proportionate punishment is an often decisive interference with the attention for the harm and suffering done to victims; the penalty itself seriously hampers the offender's effort towards reparation and compensation.

---

[5] Richard Young suggested to me in Toronto the concept of 'oblique intention', which has put me on the track for nuancing the non-intentional infliction of pain in restorative obligations.

[6] The long tradition of criminological research on the effectiveness of criminal punishment leads to the conclusion that punishment is socially not really effective. The actuarial approach to criminal justice suggests that criminal punishment would even not function adequately as a moral agent, and thus not as an authoritative 'censurer' (Feeley and Simon, 1992).

1.3. Punishment, Communication and Restoration

Especially counterproductive for restoration is the communicative aridity of the punishment option. Probably the most important function of criminal justice is as a beacon of social disapproval, to show clear limits which are observable to all. After a crime has been committed, disapproval must be expressed in such a way that it is understood and accepted by all concerned. Society at large should see the social norm being re-confirmed and the authorities' determination to enforce the norm and to protect citizens from victimisation. The victim must feel supported in his victimisation and assured in his citizenship. The offender should be convinced to accept what is necessary to re-instate his position as an integrated citizen.[7]

The a priori option for punishment in criminal justice, however, interferes with effective and constructive communication. Disapproval expressed by the criminal sentence may communicate a clear message to the public at large, but it fails to communicate adequately to the other key actors in the crime, namely the victim and the offender. Good communication needs adequate settings. This is not the case in court, where confrontation prevails over communication, in front of the judge who will at the end decide upon the kind and degree of hard treatment. The offender does not listen to the moralising message, but tries to get away with as lenient a punishment as possible. He does not hear the invitation, but merely experiences the threat. It is the a priori option for inflicting hard treatment which is the major obstruction for good communication.

Hard treatment is not the only way to express blame. In daily life, in families and in schools, disapproval is routinely expressed without punishment. Morally authoritative persons without any power to punish are more effective in influencing moral thinking and behaviour than punishment. After a crime has been committed, the settings in view of restoration are more appropriate for communicating moral disapproval and provoking repentance, than are the traditional punitive procedures and sanctions. Victim-offender mediation or family group conferences, for example, intensely disapprove of the act through those who care for the offender and for whom the offender cares. Most offenders are open to communication if they themselves experience respect and elementary understanding. They can feel empathy for the suffering of their victims (Harris, 1999). Restorative settings position the harm and suffering centrally, presenting victimisation as the focal concern in the norm, and this provides huge communicative potential.

The writings of Duff (2001, also in this volume) take a special position here. Duff advances punishment as the necessary form of communication:

> 'the idea of a kind of censure that aims to bring offenders to face up to and recognise the wrongs they have done; . . . of burdensome reparation that expresses such an apologetic and repentant recognition; . . . of a reconciliation, mediated by such recognition and reparation, between victim and offender; . . .' (Duff, 2001: 99).

---

[7] Contrary to the retrospective retributivist view on disapproval, I have added a future oriented rationale to disapproval. We shall come back to this later.

Traditional punishments are rejected. There is a search to achieve 'constructive punishing', which favours communication with the offender. 'Criminal mediation'[8] and a combination of probation with community service are advanced as prototypes. The ideas seem to come close to restorative justice models, but three crucial differences remain.

First, Duff refers to wrongfulness, as opposed to harmfulness, in considering whether hard treatment after a crime is necessary. It is however not clear how wrongfulness can be understood separately from harmfulness (von Hirsch and Jareborg, 1991). Secondly, the approach focuses on what should be done to the offender, whereas restorative justice primarily focuses on how harm can be restored. Thirdly, criminal mediation and community service must in Duff's view necessarily include intentional infliction of a burden (more or less self accepted) on the offender. As argued here (see above), this a priori position does hamper possible communication in view of socially constructive solutions.

2. In Search of Ethics for Restoration

2.1. Ethical Problems with Punishment

Punishment

> '. . . involves actions that are generally considered to be morally wrong or evil were they not described and justified as punishments' (de Keijser, 2000: 7).

Punishment of offences by criminal justice is considered as evidence, while leaving unanswered why the general ethical rule not to inflict pain on others does not apply to responding to crime. Garland writes that:

> 'Punishing today is a deeply problematic and barely understood aspect of social life, the rationale for which is by no means clear' (1990: 3).

Penal theory provides a rich and complex variety of justifications for punishment (von Hirsch, 1998). These cannot thoroughly be described and discussed here. In my view, the a priori position that crime must be punished is both ethically questionable and instrumentally inefficient (Walgrave, 2001). Social rejection can be expressed in ways that do not involve punishment (see 1.3). Since the deliberate infliction of pain is in principle unethical, the alternative ways to express blame should be fully exploited. The blind acceptance of punishment as a means of condemning behaviour is therefore in itself morally questionable. This position might need revision if the punitive approach would appear to be the only or the most effective way of considerably reducing the amount of victimisation.

---

[8] The 'making amends' model, described by von Hirsch, Ashworth and Shearing in this volume, corresponds more or less to what Duff considers as 'criminal mediation'.

But it is not. The available research leads to the opposite conclusion (Lab, 1992; Sherman, 1993).

The a priori position that crime must be punished reflects a typical 'top-down' approach, based on an imposed rule of law, and does not adequately consider the social context of possible solutions. For society at large, penal criminal justice intervention offers a strong confirmation of legal order, but public safety is badly served. Pure punishment carries the seeds of more social discord, and thus of more crime and criminalisation (Braithwaite, 1999). Victims are principally used as witnesses, but then left alone to deal with their losses and grievances (Dignan and Cavadino, 1998). The priority given to the penal procedure and the penal sanction generally hinders the chances for victims to be compensated and/or repaired. For the offender, the sanction involves a senseless infliction of suffering. It does not contribute to public safety, nor to the victim's interests. It is a needless intrusion in the offender's freedom, causing an additional threat to his social future.

2.2. From Community to Communitarianism

Punishment is imposed after the transgression of any rule, even if that rule would be immoral itself. The intervention in view of restoration, on the contrary, not only expresses disapproval, but is also indicative of the moral system underlying the disapproval. The priority given to restoration focuses on social life rather than on an abstract moral or legal system of any kind. How can this ethical orientation be made more explicit?

Masters and Smith (1998) try to uncover the ethical foundations of restorative justice by referring to Gilligan's 'ethic of care', while traditional criminal justice would be based on Kohlberg's 'ethics of principles'. This would in fact reduce restorative justice to a variation of the rehabilitative approach, which cares for individual victims and offenders, whereas restorative justice also aims at preserving the quality of social life as a whole.

Boutellier (1999) proposes 'victimalisation'[9] as the *'normative minimum'*, a common moral basis for defining crime and for orienting crime policy. This is, however, not a sufficient ground for restorative justice, especially because victimisation is here limited to individuals and does not include social life as such.

Our search for the ethical foundations of restorative justice begins with the observation that community occupies a focal position in restorative rhetorics (Bazemore and Schiff, 2001).[10] This is understandable. Many of the critics of criminal justice were inspired by communitarian considerations, leading to a tendency to 'give back crime conflict to its owners' (Christie, 1977). The priority given to restoring the harm caused by crime inevitably draws attention to the social unrest

---

[9] The neologism 'victimalisation', is used by Boutellier to indicate the cultural trend to put the fact of being victimised in the focus of moral concern.

[10] See also Bottoms on Restorative Justice and Gemeinschaft thinking, this volume.

suffered by community. The living community is more directly victimised than is the state by the occurrence of an offence. Restorative interventions require a minimum of 'community': victim and offender must feel a minimal common interest in constructively settling together in the aftermath of the crime. Restorative justice also is presented to preserve the quality of community life.

However, the more restorative justice reflection goes beyond practice and aims at developing a coherent normative theory, the more problems with the community notion appear. These problems include the following:

— Community is hard to define. Even if it is not a territorial space (McCold and Wachtel, 1997: 3, or Marshall, 1994: 248), it must at least be an 'area', delineated mentally, structurally or territorially.

'Community is subjective in that the ascription to community membership or social identity is personal and does not necessarily carry any fixed or external attributes of membership' (Crawford and Clear, 2001: 135).

It is a psychological dimension, rather than a set of characteristics of given collectivities. Communitarianism may be useful to indicate a specific psychological attitude or to refer to a socio-ethical movement, but community is not a way to characterise part of social reality.

— Building on communities for developing restorative responses to crime presupposes that communities really exist, and this is far from evident (Braithwaite, 1993; Crawford, 1995 and 1996; Crawford and Clear, 2001). It is difficult to mobilise 'community' in the resolution of a street robbery in which victim and offender live many kilometres from each other and belong to totally different social networks. Most crimes occur in non community-like social settings, and the solution is to be found in the absence of such setting.

— Leaving 'community' the loose concept it is, is giving it away to possible misuses (Pavlich, 2001). Communities are not good per se. The supposed 'niche' of community may appear to be a hotbed of suffocating social control within the community, and to represent an exclusionary attitude towards the outside world. In the name of 'community', people are subjected to unreasonable control and local stigmatisation (Crawford, 1995). Local communities often support repressive police forces and judges, and vote for exclusionist politicians. To the outside world, communities may develop exclusionary tendencies. Defining community as an ontologic category fatally distinguishes between the inside-community and the outside. The outside is often considered to represent a threat, provoking possibly violent conflicts between communities based on territory, ethnicity or religion. 'Community' contains '*the seeds of parochialism which can lead. . . to atrocious totalitarian exclusions*' (Pavlich, 2001: 58).

Scepticism with respect to the community notion does not reject the ideals promoted by most communitarians: social unity, a form of harmonious living together, based on shared values and beliefs and mutual commitment. But do we need 'community' for promoting such ideals? We should instead promote socio-ethical attitudes and functions which are not limited to a given 'area' defined by 'community' (Pavlich, 2001: 67). Most communitarians in fact promote social ethics and values, not areas. 'Community' appears as a container for ethics and social values and the ethics and values must be unpacked from their container. Again, while rejecting community as the container, we consider communitarianism as a possibly useful label for a socio-ethical movement.

2.3. Towards Communitarian Socio-Ethics for Restorative Justice

Restorative justice is far more than a technical perspective on doing justice. It is an ideal of justice in a utopian ideal of society. Provisionally stated, the communitarian utopia makes the distinction between society and community meaningless, because collectivity is governed in view of individual and collective emancipation, in which autonomy and solidarity are not seen as opposed, but as mutually reinforcing principles. Collective life draws its strength not from threat, coercion and fear, but from motivation, based on trust, participation and support.

A collectivity aiming at this utopia promotes the socio-ethical attitudes which serve it. Respect, solidarity, and taking responsibility are advanced tentatively here as such attitudes (or 'behavioural guidelines' or 'virtues').

— In 'respect' the intrinsic value of the other is recognised. The recognition may be broad. It is ethical to respect not only humans, but also nature and objects. Respect for humans recognises the intrinsic value of a human being. This is why respect for 'human dignity' is a basic obligation for all social institutions.
— 'Solidarity' is more specific than respect. It is not evident to feel solidarity with objects or with nature. Solidarity presupposes more commitment than respect, because solidarity includes a form of companionship and reciprocity of support. Companionship goes with empathy and mutual trust, which is most visible in the attitudes towards those in trouble. Contrary to community rhetorics locating solidarity within the scope of a community, solidarity is no longer limited by a given 'area', but is a general ethical value. '... *this spirit of solidarity may be regarded as a forever-elusive promise of unpremeditated collective togetherness.*' (Pavlich, 2001: 67).
— 'Responsibility' links the person to his acts and its consequences. It confronts the self with its own actions. Passive responsibility means being confronted for one's actions by others; active responsibility is an awareness of the link between the self and the actions, and behaving accordingly (Bovens, 1998, in Braithwaite and Roche, 2001). Taking responsibility is an active form of responding autonomously to the obligations created by social life, which is in communitarian ethics oriented towards solidarity.

Other ethical guidelines might be superfluous if members of the collectivity behaved according to these three ethical guidelines. In my view, 'justice', for example, is currently advanced as a separate ethical rule only because respect, solidarity and responsibility are not achieved sufficiently.[11] Because people do not behave adequately according to these guidelines, it is necessary to stress specifically justice with its more restricting rules and balances.

At first glance, advancing respect, solidarity and responsibility as basics in a communitarian philosophy may seem to be mere rhetoric. Don't we all value these virtues? Do we really? Let us explore their presence in retributive justice.

— Is respect an ethical guideline in retributivism? Respect for the victim is absent, because he is not included in the retributivist reflections. Retributivism is focused on the offender. Considering the offender as a conscious moral agent, and treating him in a just (desert) way, recognises him as a human being, and as a citizen with guaranteed rights. But the respect is not complete. The offender is not respected as a whole person with personal interests and interpretations, including a possible willingness to make up for the misbehaviour. In the end, the offender has to be made to submit to a proportionate punishment. In fact, once the crime has been committed, respect for the person is withdrawn. He is seen as a moral agent to be considered guilty, but not to contribute to find a constructive response to the problems caused by his crime.[12]

— I do not see solidarity, the companionship including willingness for mutual support, in retributivism. Advancing the harm to 'the standard of living' as criterion for the degree of blameworthiness (von Hirsch and Jareborg, 1993), might suggest some solidarity with those victimised. However, the response does not support the victim, but merely punishes the offender, which often hampers possible reparation. In restorative justice, solidarity with the victim is evident, but solidarity with the offender is also present. The offender is not excluded, but encouraged to make up for the conduct, in order to preserve his position as an integrated member of the collectivity.

— Responsibility, the attitude of responding autonomously to the obligations created by social life, is central to retributivism. The offender is held responsible by having to respond autonomously to the obligation created by the misconduct, but again, the responsibility is incomplete. Responsibility only means accepting the negative consequences, but not searching for a constructive solution to the problems created. It is only a passive, retrospective form of responsibility (Braithwaite and Roche, 2001). The victim is not considered responsible for anything, except, perhaps to report the crime and serve as a witness during the trial. Retributivism burdens the criminal justice system with the crucial responsibility to censure criminal behaviour,

---

[11]   See also Duff: '*If people are bound together by strong bonds of mutual affection or concern, . . . there may be less need and less proper room for contractual definitions of their respective rights and obligations*' (Duff, 2001: 37).

[12]   Maybe this is less true in Duff's approach to punishment (2001, and this volume), but the problem remains that the offender must nevertheless undergo hard treatment.

and to impose proportionate punishments. Restorative justice extends the offender's responsibility to 'active responsibility' (Braithwaite and Roche, 2001), including the obligation to contribute to the reparation of the harm. The victim is encouraged, but not obliged, to assume the general citizens' responsibility for trying to find solutions, which promote peace. Restorative justice also stands for 'responsible collectivities, bound by obligations to search for socially constructive responses within the rules of law.

This superfluous exercise, of course, needs more exploration. It may, however, be sufficient to show that restorative justice promotes social ethical attitudes or virtues like respect, solidarity and taking responsibility more than retributive justice does, and that it is therefore more likely to contribute constructively to social life and relations. The priority for the quality of social life, as expressed in the communitarian utopia, grounds the 'bottom-up' approach in restorative justice, which appears through the preference for informal regulations, away from imposed procedures and outcomes. The point of departure for restorative justice, as in communitarianism, is that solutions primarily must be sought through the human and social resources in social life itself. This is opposed to the top-down approach in traditional criminal justice, where decisions are imposed according to strict rules, leaving restricted room, if any, for the views and interests of those directly concerned (see also Braithwaite, this volume).

3. Communitarian Ethics and The Rule of Law

The communitarian utopia is far from being realised. While 'justice' was considered as a derivative value only in the 'communitarian utopia', it must currently be seen as a value on its own in the non-ideal societies. This is especially true when agreed constructive solutions of the aftermath of a crime cannot be achieved, due to a lack of mutual respect, solidarity and/or taking responsibility. But also in free processes and agreements, respect and solidarity may be overruled by self-interest and abuse of power. It is therefore necessary to check these processes also according to a set of rights and duties.

We are seeking a combination in one system of a large margin for informal processes in line with the 'communitarian ethics', with rules of law and legal mechanisms of formal control. These rules and mechanisms should themselves express maximally the social-ethical guidelines described above.

3.1. Dominion

Braithwaite and Pettit's republican theory of criminal justice (Braithwaite and Pettit, 1990) claims to call for a '*rule of law*' that '*percolates down into restorative justice*' and '*restorative justice*' that '*percolates up into the rule of law*' (Braithwaite and Parker, 1999: 115–21).

The republican theory of criminal justice is built on the concept of 'dominion', which we can define as 'the set of assured rights and freedoms'. 'Freedom as non-domination' (or dominion)[13] is advanced as the ultimate criterion to evaluate restorative processes and values (Braithwaite, 2000). Dominion is the mental and social territory of which we freely dispose, as it is guaranteed by the state and the social environment. The assurance-aspect of rights and freedoms is crucial to the theory.[14] 'I know that I have rights, I know that the others know it, and I trust that they will respect it'. I am assured only if I trust my fellow citizens and the state, to take my rights and freedoms seriously. It is only then that I will fully enjoy my mental and social domain. Assurance provides the crucial distinction between the social concept of 'freedom as non-domination' and the liberal concept of 'freedom as non-interference'. In the liberal conception, the other potentially interferes with my freedom. In the republican view, the other is an ally in trying to extend and mutually assure dominion as a collective good.[15]

3.1.1. The Aim of Restorative Justice: Restoring Assurance in Dominion

A good state, according to Braithwaite and Pettit, must promote dominion for its citizens. Dominion is thus not delineated, but a value to be promoted. Dominion can be seen as a formalisation of the communitarian ideal into a political theory. The communitarian utopia can be achieved only in so far as the states' dominion is developed. Inversely, the assurance of rights and freedoms is achieved only in the degree to which citizens take their responsibilities in view of respect and solidarity.

The state seeks to extend and deepen dominion by promoting equality through more democracy, education, equitable socio-economic policy, welfare policy and the like. Criminal justice is the 'defensive' institution. Crime is seen as an intrusion upon dominion, and criminal justice must act to repair it (Walgrave, 2000).[16]

---

[13] In later publications, 'dominion' has been renamed as 'freedom as non-domination'. It may make it easier to oppose it to the liberal concept typified as 'freedom as non-interference', but I see no other advantage in complicating the wording. I will therefore stick to the 'old' name, 'dominion'.

[14] See also what Putnam (1993) called 'trust' in social capital. Social capital is defined as *'features of social organization such as trust, norms and networks, that can improve the efficiency of society by facilitating coordinated actions'* (1993: 167). Trust is crucial. Putnam does not limit trust to *'thick trust'* based on strong ties with family, friends and close neighbours. The strongest social capital lies in the generalised trust based on weak ties with the social organisations and with the generalised other. It is this trust which constitutes our assurance of rights and freedoms.

[15] von Hirsch and Ashworth (1993) raise serious critiques with respect to the republican theory. One of them is that it does not provide an appropriate basis for a decremental strategy with regard to punishment (despite Braithwaite and Pettit's claim). This criticism is in fact irrelevant here, because the theory is now not meant to ground the criminal justice system as a punishing machinery, but reconsidered as a theory of restorative justice. In view of the constructive claims of restorative justice, there is no need for a decremental strategy on restorative justice. Another critique is that censure cannot operate independently from severity of sanction, as suggested by the republican theory. There are two answers here: first, the sanctions in view here are not punitive, but restorative; secondly, the severity of censure is but one of the elements in 'restorative sentencing'. We shall come back to this in 3.2.2.

[16] The target of criminal justice must be repairing dominion, and not promoting it, as Braithwaite and Pettit advance, because promotion of dominion is an unsatiable target.

The intrusion most of all hurts the assurance in dominion. A burglary, for example, is a private and a public affair. Strictly speaking, the restitution or compensation of the concrete victim's losses could be private, to be arranged by civil law. But there is also a public side. The public matter is the loss of assurance: the burglary not only hurts the victim's trust that his privacy and possessions will be respected by his fellow citizens. The specific victim also stands as an example of what all citizens risk undergoing. If the authorities did nothing against the particular burglary, it would undermine citizens' trust in the right to privacy and possession.

Public intervention after a crime is therefore not primarily needed to put right the balance of benefits and burdens, nor to re-confirm the law. It is needed first of all to enhance assurance, by communicating the message that authorities do take dominion seriously. The intervention must reassure the victim and the public of their rights and freedoms, and to complete these rights and freedoms in a way that assures fully-fledged dominion. This happens by clearly censuring the intrusion and by involving, if possible, the offender in actions in view of restoring dominion. Voluntary co-operation of the offender is more effective to restore assurance, but only if it is backed by public institutions. The assurance indeed not only comes from the individual offender's repentance and apologies, but also from the authorities' determination to take the assured set of rights and freedoms seriously.

We began this chapter by considering all kinds of harm caused by a crime for possible restoration. We now make this statement more focused and precise: the aim of restorative justice as a public intervention model is to restore the assurance of rights and freedoms, which is essential for restoring dominion.

3.1.2. Limits to Restorative Justice: Rights and Freedoms in Dominion

Dominion is not only a value to be defended and promoted, in reality, it also has a hard core. The 'hard core' of dominion consists of actual rights and freedoms, which provide grounds for defining limits to (restorative) justice interventions. The intervention itself must be assuring for dominion by the respect it shows itself for rights and freedoms. Braithwaite and Pettit (1990) list four constraints: parsimony, checking of authorities' use of power, reprobation of crime, and reintegration of victims and offenders.

Here is not the place to elaborate on these constraints. Let me just mention that the second and the third constraints, 'checking of power' and 'reprobation', represent variations on principles which belong to the traditional deontological approach to criminal justice. The fourth constraint—reintegration of victims and offenders—is a typically consequentialist goal, reformulated in a restorative version.

The first constraint, parsimony, is crucial in the search for combining informal processes with the need for formal controls. In the republican theory, criminal justice must strive for satiable goals (repairing the intruded dominion), and is bound by the constraint of parsimony in using its coercive power. Parsimony is more restricting than satiability. We can eat until full satiation, but we can parsimoniously do with less in order to survive.

Satiability includes an obligation to set an upper limit, as required by the proportionality principle. Parsimony, however, excludes the setting of a lower limit. On the contrary, the parsimony constraint requires an active search for noncoercive ways to restore dominion. The more voluntary restorative processes can lead to satisfying and balanced outcomes, the less appeal to coercive judicial interventions is needed and thus, the more the parsimony principle is achieved. A fully-fledged restorative justice system should fulfil its parsimony obligation by leaving space for, and diverting to voluntary processes, wherein victim, offender and collectivity can seek together an agreed settlement in the aftermath of a crime that maximally restores the dominion.

Restriction on the length of this chapter precludes elaboration of these comments (see Walgrave, 2000), but this paragraph illustrates that the republican theory of criminal justice, built on the dominion concept, offers a base for principles and rules to limit and orient restorative justice.

3.2. Towards Legal Principles for Restorative Justice

A justice system which is primarily oriented towards doing justice through restoration would have some commonalities and crucial differences compared to the traditional criminal justice system.

Both the criminal justice and the restorative justice system express clear limits to social tolerance, and they hold the offender responsible for his behaviour, and use, if necessary, coercion according to legal standards.

The limits of social tolerance are clear, because the reason for the intervention outspokenly refers to the offender's behaviour. The interventions are retrospective, which is crucial to deduce legal safeguards. In penal justice, the seriousness of the crime committed is the yardstick upon which to determine the proportionate punishment. In restorative justice, the seriousness of the harm caused is the criterion to gauge the maximum amount of restorative effort that is reasonable (Walgrave and Geudens, 1997).

Holding the offender responsible is essential in both punitive and restorative approaches to crime. Both also can include personal and social circumstances in the sentencing decision. The amount of punishment or obligation to compensate will depend on personal capacities to understand, material resources, degree of premeditation, social and situational peculiarities. Such elements would evidently be considered more adequately and thoroughly in deliberative conditions like in the voluntary processes, but they are also crucial in judicial sentencing.

Both retrospectivity and (degree of) responsibility address the two crucial questions in traditional sentencing: have the facts been established and has the (degree of) guilt been established? (See Ashworth, 1986)

Sentencing in view of restoration, however, adds a third question: how can the sanction contribute maximally to restoration? This question is not asked in retributive justice, because of the a priori option for punishment, and because it is not prospective. Restorative justice, on the contrary, aims at restoring the harm, and is therefore prospective also. Again, voluntary deliberative processes are more adequate to assess the harm and to consider possible reasonable restoration, but the restoration question should also be central in judicial proceedings. Restorative justice thus is retrospective and prospective at the same time.[17]

This leads to a few principles in which judicial procedures in view of restoration would deviate from traditional criminal procedures.

— Because coercive intervention must be used parsimoniously, restorative justice procedures should at all stages allow easy access to voluntary, informal ways of responding to crime. Diversion is obligatory wherever possible. The decision to prosecute in court must be justified with positive arguments, and not simply because 'the law has been broken'. This is so because dominion must be intruded minimally, and because the restorative calibre of voluntary agreements is higher.

— Restorative justice procedures must allow large opportunities for input by victims and others affected by the crime. This input is crucial in defining the kind and amount of harm and in finding the best possible restorative outcome. However, because of legal rights, these actors may not be given any decisive power.

— Criminal investigation is not only focused on establishing the facts and guilt, but also on defining the harm, suffering and social unrest caused by the offence. It will also explore possible ways for negotiation, and thus for 'diversion', and for possible restorative sanctions if diversion would not be possible.

— As mentioned already, the sanction would not link the seriousness of crime to a proportionate punishment; but the seriousness and kind of harm to a maximum of reasonable restorative effort.

II. CONCLUSION

Restorative justice has evolved in the last twenty years to become a fundamental alternative to doing justice after a crime has been committed. It remains unclear how far its scope will reach. Some limit restorative justice to voluntary settlements, leaving the hard core reaction to crime to the traditional justice system. Others reformulate restorative practices as new forms of punishments. Neither of these views proposes an ethical and socially constructive alternative to the top down ideology nor to the ethically questionable a priorism that the response to crime must involve the infliction of pain.

This chapter adopts the maximalist version of restorative justice. It is believed that its empirical and social ethical benefits should be implemented maximally,

---

[17] See also Duff, 2001 and in this volume.

and should not be limited nor subordinated to the punitive. Taking the superiority of voluntary processes for granted, the maximalist option also reflects on how the coercive intervention, if needed, can be maximally oriented to restoration. This option is not an isolated view on how to respond to crime. Maximalism in restorative justice rests upon a comprehensive view on doing justice ideally in an ideal of society. Promoting restorative options as far as possible is believed to bring social life closer to a communitarian utopia.

The utopian view may however not be blind to reality. Retributivist scepticism, as described among others in this volume by von Hirsch, Ashworth and Shearing, must be taken seriously. The chapters by Dignan and by Van Ness, for example, make clear that restorative justice proponents are increasingly aware that due process and some kind of proportionality are important constraints to safeguard rights and justice in general. Contrary to the traditional deontologic version, however, these constraints must not be seen as top-down rules on how to do justice. They must be reformulated and integrated into the broader dominion concept which seems to integrate both safeguards for rights and freedoms, and the participatory bottom up approach in view of evolving social life in communitarian direction.

The communitarian ideal must be inserted into a model of the state. If there were no state, there would be no rights, and one would depend on the goodwill of others, or on one's own power to compete with the others and to oppress them. If there were only states, there would be no trust, and the other would be considered as a rival, a threat for one's own territory. Such a state would ultimately deteriorate into anarchy or tyranny.

REFERENCES

Ashworth, A (1993) 'Some Doubts about Restorative Justice' 4 *Criminal Law Forum* 277–299.

Bazemore, G and Schiff, M (eds) (2001) *Restorative Community Justice. Repairing Harm and Transforming Communities* (Anderson, Cincinnati).

Bazemore, G and Walgrave, L (1999) 'Restorative Juvenile Justice: in Search of Fundamentals and an Outline for Systemic Reform' in G Bazemore and L Walgrave (eds), *Restorative Juvenile Justice: Repairing the Harm of Youth Crime* (Criminal Justice Press, Monsey NY) 45–74.

Boutellier, H (1999) *Crime and Morality. The Significance of Criminal Justice in Post-Modern Culture* (Kluwer Academic Publishers, Dordrecht).

Braithwaite, J (1989) *Crime, Shame and Reintegration* (Cambridge University Press, Cambridge).

—— (1993) 'Shame and Modernity' 33 *British Journal of Criminology* 1–18.

—— (1999) 'A Future where Punishment is Marginalized: Realistic or Utopian?' 46 *UCLA Law Review* 1727–1750.

—— (2000) 'Decomposing a Holistic Vision of Restorative Justice' 3 *Contemporary Justice Review* 433–40.

Braithwaite, J and Pettit, P (1990) *Not Just Desert. A Republican Theory of Criminal Justice* (Clarendon Press, Oxford).

Braithwaite, J and Roche, D (2001) 'Responsibility and Restorative Justice' in G Bazemore and M Schiff (eds), *Restorative Community Justice. Repairing Harm and Transforming Communities* (Anderson, Cincinnati) 63–84.

Christie, N (1981) *Limits to Pain* (Norwegian University Press, Oslo/Oxford).

Crawford, A (1995) 'Appeals to Community and Crime Prevention' 22 *Crime, Law and Social Change* 97–126.

Crawford, A (1996) 'The Spirit of Community: Rights, Responsibilities and the Communitarian Agenda' 2 *Journal of Law and Society* 247–62.

Crawford, A and Clear, T (2001) 'Community Justice: Transforming Communities through Restorative Justice?' in G Bazemore and M Schiff (eds), *Restorative Community Justice. Repairing Harm and Transforming Communities* (Anderson, Cincinnati) 127–49.

Daly, K (2000) 'Revisiting the relationship between Retributive and Restorative Justice' in H Strang and J Braithwaite (eds), *Restorative Justice: from Philosophy to Practice* (Dartmouth, Ashgate) 33–54.

de Keijser, J (2000) *Punishment and Purpose. From Moral Theory to Punishment in Action*, Ph.D. thesis, University of Leyden.

Dignan, J and Cavadino, M (1998) 'Which Model of Criminal Justice Offers the Best Scope for Assisting Victims of Crime?' in E Fattah and T Peters (eds), *Support for Crime Victims in a Comparartive Perspective* (Leuven University Press, Leuven) 139–68.

Duff, A (1986) *Trials and Punishment* (Cambridge University Press, Cambridge).

——(1992) 'Alternatives to Punishment or Alternative Punishment?' in W Cragg (ed), *Retributivism and its Critics* (Steinder, Stuttgart) 44–68.

——(2001) *Punishment, Communication and Community* (Oxford University Press, Oxford).

Fatic, A (1995) *Punishment and Restorative Crime-Handling* (Avebury, Aldershot).

Feeley, M and Simon, J (1992) 'The New Penology: Notes on the Emerging Strategy of Corrections and its Implications' 30 *Criminology* 449–74.

Garland, D (1990) *Punishment and Modern Society* (Clarendon Press, Oxford).

Harris, N (1999) *Shaming and Shame. An Empirical Analysis*, PhD. Dissertation, RSSS, Australian National University, Canberra.

Lab, S (1993) *Crime Prevention. Approaches, Practices and Evaluations* (Anderson, Cincinnati).

Marshall, T (1994) *The Search for Restorative Justice: Reflections on the Leuven Mediation Project* (Koning Boudewijnstichting, Brussels).

——(1996) 'The Evolution of Restorative Justice in Britain' 4 *European Journal of Criminal Policy and Research* 21–43.

Masters, G and Smith, D (1998) 'Portia and Persephone revisited: Thinking about feeling in criminal justice' 2 *Theoretical Criminology* 5–27.

McCold, P (2000) 'Toward a Holistic Vision of Restorative Juvenile Justice. A Reply to the Maximalist Model' 3 *Contemporary Justice Review* 357–414.

McCold, P and Wachtel, B (1998) *Restorative Policing Experiment* (Community Service Foundation, Pipersville PA).

Pavlich, G (2001) 'The Force of Community' in H Strang and J Braithwaite (eds), *Restorative Justice and Civil Society* (Cambridge University Press, Cambridge) 56–68.

Sherman, L (1993) 'Defiance, Deterrence and Irrelevance: a Theory of the Criminal Sanction' 30 *Journal of Research in Crime and Delinquency* 445–73.

Van Ness, D (1999) 'Legal Issues of Restorative Justice' in G Bazemore and L Walgrave (eds), *Restorative Juvenile Justice: Repairing the Harm of Youth Crime* (Criminal Justice Press, Monsey NY) 263–84.

Van Ness, D and Heetderks Strong, K (1997) *Restoring Justice* (Anderson, Cincinnati).

Van Swaaningen, R (1997) *Critical Criminology. Visions from Europe* (Sage, London).

von Hirsch, A (1993) *Censure and Sanctions* (Clarendon Press, Oxford).

——(1998) 'Penal Theories' in M Tonry (ed), *The Handbook of Crime and Punishment* (Oxford University Press, New York/Oxford) 659–82.

von Hirsch, A and Ashworth, A (1993) 'Dominion and Censure. Chapter 3' in A von Hirsch, *Censure and Sanctions* (Clarendon Press, Oxford) 20–8.

von Hirsch, A and Jareborg, N (1991) 'Gauging Criminal Harm: A Living-Standard Analysis' 11 *Oxford Journal of Legal Studies* 1–38.

Walgrave, L (1999) 'Community Service as a Cornerstone of a Systemic Restorative Response to (Juvenile) Crime' in G Bazemore and L Walgrave (eds), *Restorative Juvenile Justice: Repairing the Harm of Youth Crime* (Criminal Justice Press, Monsey NY) 129–54.

——(2000) 'Restorative Justice and the Republican Theory of Criminal Justice. An Exercise in Normative Theorizing on Restorative Justice' in H Strang and J Braithwaite (eds), *Restorative Justice: from Philosophy to Practice* (Dartmouth, Ashgate) 165–83.

——(2001) 'On Restoration and Punishment: Favourable Similarities and Fortunate Differences' in A Morris and G Maxwell (eds), *Restorative Justice for Juveniles. Conferencing, Mediation and Circles* (Hart Publishing, Oxford) 17–37.

Weijers, I, (2000) *Trust, Shame and Guilt. An Educational Perspective on Juvenile Justice.* Paper Presented at the Symposium 'Punishing Children', Utrecht, 8–9 June.

5

Some Sociological Reflections on Restorative Justice

Anthony Bottoms

John Braithwaite is a master of the arresting aphorism. In his comprehensive 1999 review of the research literature on restorative justice, there are several examples of this; but here I want to focus on just two. First, Braithwaite tells us, 'restorative justice has been the dominant model of criminal justice throughout most of human history for all the world's peoples' (Braithwaite, 1999: 2). Secondly, in the abstract of his paper it is claimed that 'for informal justice to be restorative justice, it has to be about restoring victims, restoring offenders, and restoring communities' (Braithwaite, 1999: 1).

In dictionary definition, an aphorism is 'a concise pithy saying that expresses a truth' (Longman, 1984). In my view, both of the sayings I have quoted qualify as aphorisms under this definition, because they both—to some extent—'express a truth'. Those truths, however, require a good deal of contextualisation before they can be fully understood. Moreover, the fact that a saying expresses *a* truth does not mean that it necessarily expresses the whole truth, and I shall argue that neither of these sayings does so (although the second comes closer to doing so than does the first). The remainder of this chapter can be read, in one sense, as an elaboration of and commentary on Braithwaite's two aphorisms, and their relevance for our contemporary understanding of restorative justice.

Most of human history has been lived in what we now call pre-modern societies. Braithwaite's first aphorism is, therefore, another way of saying that restorative justice (RJ) is the dominant model of criminal justice in pre-modern societies. This reminds us of the fact that contemporary advocates of RJ have quite frequently used pre-modern societies as exemplars, arguing for example that such communities generally 'handled their own conflicts, and their primary aim was to make peace between the conflicting parties' (Johnstone, 2002: 12). Some consideration of traditional justice in pre-modern societies might therefore assist us in understanding more fully at least some features of RJ in contemporary societies.

But if RJ (or something like it) was an important form of justice in many pre-modern societies, it has certainly not been dominant in the criminal justice systems of modern Western states from the Renaissance onwards. Yet, as everyone knows, even in such states it has in the last quarter-century enjoyed a significant revival. Some careful sociological reflection on the reasons for this revival would therefore seem to be an important issue for those like myself who are interested in the sociology of contemporary criminal justice systems.

While Braithwaite's first aphorism focuses our attention on these historical and macro-sociological issues, his second aphorism raises a different, and more micro-oriented, set of considerations. 'For informal justice to be restorative justice, it has to be about restoring victims, restoring offenders, and restoring communities'. But, in this saying, what does 'restoring a community' or 'restoring a victim' actually mean? And, assuming that such phrases do mean something (as I shall argue that they do), then by what *social mechanisms* are these 'restorations' accomplished?

The topics raised in the preceding three paragraphs constitute the core subject matter of this chapter. To develop them, the remainder of the chapter is divided into four sections. In the first section, a classic early paper on the themes of RJ is reanalysed. Then, secondly, two of the intellectual roots of the RJ movement are examined: these are what might be described as the 'wisdom of pre-modern societies' argument, and the argument that civil methods of dispute resolution are preferable to criminal ones. In the third section, the social mechanisms of RJ are explored, in pursuit of the questions as to whether—and, if so, how—RJ can 'restore' victims, offenders and communities. These various discussions then pave the way for a final section on RJ in contemporary societies, in which a number of questions are raised, including the reasons for the revival of RJ in the last quarter century, the structural location of RJ in contemporary penal systems, and whether the social mechanisms of RJ can be expected to work effectively in contemporary advanced economies.

I. REVISITING A CLASSIC ARTICLE

I shall begin by discussing Nils Christie's (1977) celebrated paper 'Conflicts as Property', described by Braithwaite (1999: 5) as 'the most influential text of the [contemporary] restorative tradition'. This article was originally delivered as a public lecture on a formal occasion, and as one of those who was on the platform that day,[1] I have naturally retained a strong personal interest in the paper, and its subsequent influence.[2]

A key strategy in Christie's paper was to introduce, at an early stage, a description of a civil case from a small village in the Arusha province of Tanzania, about

---

[1] 'Conflicts as Property' was originally delivered on 31 March 1976 as the Foundation Lecture of the Centre for Criminological Studies at the University of Sheffield. As the first Director of the new Centre, I had the pleasure of proposing the vote of thanks at the conclusion of the lecture.
[2] The subsequent major influence of Christie's paper would have been predicted by very few of those who first heard it. It was initially regarded as an extremely interesting intellectual argument, but one that was unlikely to have much subsequent practical impact. How wrong first impressions can be!

the disposition of property after an engagement to be married had been broken. It rapidly becomes clear to the reader that this case is presented as a kind of normative ideal, an example of the kind of process that Christie wishes to advocate. In describing the case,[3] the following matters were especially emphasised:

(a) The two litigating parties were in the centre of the room, and at the centre of everyone's attention. Others, including relatives and friends but also a general audience, were present, but they did not take over (p 2). The case was thus, very obviously, focused upon the parties' own conflict; and that conflict had not in any sense been taken away ('stolen') from the parties by lawyers or by State professionals (p 4).

(b) The court hearing was very much a community occasion. No reporters attended; their presence was unnecessary because 'most grown-ups from the village and several from adjoining ones were there' (p 2). There was some oral participation from this wider audience, with 'short questions, information or jokes' (p 2). This participation 'crystallised norms and clarified what had happened', but without taking over the case from the main parties. The proceedings were described by Christie as a 'happy happening', with 'fast talking, . . . smiles, eager attention, not a sentence . . . to be lost' (p 2).

(c) The 'judges, three local party secretaries, were extremely inactive'.[4] They are described as 'obviously ignorant with regard to village matters', whereas all the other people in the room were 'experts' on such matters (p 2).

(d) It was 'not by chance that the Tanzanian case was a civil one', because 'full participation in your own conflict' (for Christie, a desirable attribute) 'presupposes elements of civil law' (p 3).

In sociological language, what is being described here is a *gemeinschaft* society settling a conflict. As Anthony Giddens (1990: 102) has pointed out, in such a society, typically, much emphasis and trust will be placed upon kinship relationships; upon the 'thick' social relations of people who live close together and know many aspects of one another's business; and upon tradition.

Later in his paper, Christie explicitly advocates for Western societies a 'model of neighbourhood courts' (p 10). Such courts would be strongly victim-oriented (p 10). They would also have an 'extreme degree of lay-orientation', so that both lawyers and behaviour experts would be viewed with suspicion, and 'if we find them unavoidable in certain cases or at certain stages [of the process]', it will still

---

[3] Christie gives no reference to indicate from what source he drew his description of this case.

[4] The unexplained reference to 'party secretaries' suggests that this is a post-independence case (independence from colonial rule was achieved in Tanganyika in 1963); hence Cain (1988: 53) refers to Christie's article as describing a 'post-colonial African community moot'. However, by being inactive the judges were, in a new context, remaining essentially faithful to the traditions of indigenous Arusha dispute-settlement, where there were 'no third parties recognised as having authority to resolve a dispute by decision, [so] settlement has to be by compromise reached through negotiation' (Roberts, 1979: 133). See further, n 7 below.

be necessary 'to get across to them the problems they create for broad social participation' (p 12).[5] The neighbourhood courts 'would represent a blend of elements from civil and criminal courts, but with a strong emphasis on the civil side' (p 11).

Christie is fully aware that his choice of an opening example from a Tanzanian village context is not accidental. The 'lack of neighbourhoods' in contemporary Western urban societies, he concedes, could be one of several significant 'blocks' against the establishment of the system of neighbourhood courts that he advocates. In response to this problem, Christie says he has only two weak arguments to offer (p 12). The first is that the death of real neighbourhood-based communities in modern societies 'is not complete'. The second is that his proposed neighbourhood courts are themselves intended as a 'vitaliser for neighbourhoods'; that is to say, neighbourhood courts would themselves, it is hoped, help to keep close-knit neighbourhoods alive.

In this key foundational text, then, RJ is explicitly linked to a particular kind of macro-social organisation deemed to be desirable, and that social organisation is fairly clearly of a *gemeinschaft* character. Christie, however, is under no illusions that *gemeinschaft* communities are plentiful in the neighbourhoods of modern cities. Since 1977, RJ has proliferated, but there is little or no evidence of it having been a 'vitaliser for neighbourhoods'. The reasons for its expanding influence must therefore lie elsewhere than in the sphere of neighbourhood *gemeinschaft*, a point to which I shall return in the final section.

But while Christie is explicit about the optimum macro-social context for his proposed neighbourhood courts, he is silent on meso-social structural contexts. Interestingly, however, a good illustration of the importance of such issues can be found in an earlier anthropological study by Gulliver (1963) of indigenous social control among the Arusha, the selfsame tribal group from whom Christie drew his Tanzanian example. According to Gulliver, in traditional Arusha society there were three distinct meso-structural sub-systems, respectively based on residence, lineage and age-set, and the existence of these separate sub-systems could significantly affect the procedures used in disputes.[6] Moreover, in a society where

---

[5] Christie (1977: 10–11) envisages a four-stage process for his proposed neighbourhood courts: (i) fact-finding about the incident; (ii) the victim's situation is considered in detail, including possible compensation and other assistance to her/him (first by the offender, and then by the wider community); (iii) possible punishment of the offender *in addition to* his/her restitutive actions to the victim; and (iv) possible social assistance to the offender. Christie is willing to consider the possible introduction of lawyers and behaviour experts into some of these stages (lawyers in stage (i); behaviour experts in stages (ii) and (iv)), but his underlying attitude is that 'experts are as cancer to any lay body' (p 11).

[6] As Roberts (1979: 129) summarises Gulliver's evidence: 'Arusha do not live in well-defined villages, but in homesteads located here and there across . . . arable lands . . . divided up into . . . geographical units which Gulliver describes as "parishes" '. But, unlike many pre-modern societies, residential groupings do not necessarily coincide with patrilineal descent groups; rather 'the homesteads of members of a given lineage are likely to be scattered all over Arusha country'. Since 'age-sets' (groups of persons of similar age who go through initiation rites together) are also important in traditional Arusha society, the social structures of that society have 'three distinct sub-groupings' [residence; lineage; age-sets], a feature that can have 'important consequences in the event of a dispute' (including giving the litigant 'a choice of forum before which disputes can be taken' (p 129), the principal options in the event of a public dispute being the 'parish assembly' and a lineage-based moot: Gulliver, 1963: 174).

disputes could not be settled by the decision of independent arbiters (see n14 above),[7] litigants with equivalently strong cases did not always achieve similar outcomes: rather, 'the degree of convergence between normative standards . . . and the details of actual settlements [could] vary considerably, according to the relative distribution of bargaining power between the two parties' (p 300). Bargaining power, not surprisingly, was intimately linked to the three sub-systems of Arusha society: '[t]he composition and strengths of the two conflicting parties in a dispute, [and] the identification of leaders and the scope of their influence . . . , are . . . direct functions of the sub-systems of Arusha society' (Gulliver, 1963: 301).

Gulliver's fieldwork was conducted in 1956–1958, and it is of course possible that some aspects of Arusha dispute settlement had altered by the time that Christie wrote, twenty years later (though radical change seems unlikely in a rural society, even in a pre/post-independence context: see n 4). However, the main point to be made is not specific to the empirical details of Arusha society, but rather the more general issue that in examining dispute-settlement processes in pre-modern societies, meso-structural questions (including issues of intra-societal power) need to be considered. This general point was well documented twenty years ago by Sally Merry (1982) in her literature review on mediation practices in non-industrial societies. Merry argued that some Western scholars had 'misunderstood the process of mediation' in such societies, 'focusing on its consensual and conciliatory qualities and ignoring the very important role of coercion and power' that was linked to the meso-structural context (Merry, 1982: 20). In the light of Merry's evidence, Maureen Cain (1988: 56) subsequently took the view that Christie, and writers like him, had fallen into the trap of constructing a 'romantic idealization of pre-capitalist (but non-feudal) forms' of legal or quasi-legal decision-making. These are harsh words; whether they are justified is an issue to be explored further as the argument of the chapter unfolds.

II. 'CIVILISATION' AND THE 'WISDOM OF PRE-MODERN SOCIETIES'

It can be plausibly argued that the intellectual roots of the modern RJ movement derive originally from two principal sources.[8] The first of these was a realisation

---

[7] See generally Gulliver (1963: ch 10). Neither in parish assemblies nor in moots (see note 6 above) were there any independent judges. Gulliver (1963: 228–9) notes however that there were several accepted 'general principles of proper behaviour' at these gatherings, including: (i) a degree of spatial separation of the disputants and their supporters; (ii) the right of each disputant to argue his/her case fully; and (iii) the presence of high-status 'spokesmen, counsellors [or] other notables' to support each party, these 'notables' being crucial to the maintenance of good order. ('Though avowedly on opposite sides in the dispute, they are generally ready to ally together against unruly behaviour, lengthy irrelevancies, and persistent contumely. It is only by their willingness together to maintain orderly discussion that an assembly can carry on its work adequately': p 229).

[8] I am grateful to Jim Dignan for this insight. It should be emphasised: (i) that the claim relates only to *principal* sources, and there were others (eg elements of Christian thought); and (ii) the claim relates only to the *origins* of the RJ movement, ie to the period preceding John Braithwaite's important book on reintegrative shaming (Braithwaite, 1989), which greatly influenced many later developments in RJ.

that, as Marjery Fry (1951: 124) put it in an early text (and using now outdated language) 'in primitive societies [the] idea of "making up" for a wrong done has wide currency', so that we should perhaps 'once more look into the ways of earlier men, which may still hold some wisdom for us'.[9] The second principal intellectual inspiration of the RJ movement derived from writers who argued that most crimes are an attack *on the individual victim*[10] (rather than the State or the community at large), and that the victim has been sidelined (if not completely displaced) in the modern Western criminal trial, where it is the State (and not the victim) that brings proceedings against the alleged offender. A key way of returning the victim to her/his rightful centre-stage position is therefore to reconceptualise the proceedings as primarily *civil* rather than *criminal* proceedings (sometimes described, in a deliberate *double entendre*, as a process of 'civilisation'). It is interesting that Christie's (1977) influential early article contains elements of both of these intellectual roots of the contemporary RJ tradition.

In this section, I shall briefly consider aspects of both these intellectual derivations, and I shall argue that neither is unproblematic for contemporary RJ advocates. I shall begin with the so-called 'civilisation thesis'.

1. The 'Civilisation' Thesis

The 'civilisation' thesis[11] can be dealt with fairly briefly, and I will discuss the thesis in what seems to me to be its most persuasive form, namely that propounded by Louk Hulsman (1981, 1982, 1986) in the 1980s.[12] Hulsman points out that, in contemporary societies, only a proportion of events which fit the official legal definitions of crimes such as 'theft' and 'assault' are dealt with by the criminal justice system, even where the identity of the offender is known. Instead, many of these events are dealt with informally in families, schools, workplaces, social clubs, among local neighbours, and so on. Not infrequently, the processes for handling such events have a restorative element within the group in question: as Johnstone (2002: 59) puts it, they are handled 'without the state's involvement and with an emphasis on recompense and contrition rather than punitive suffering'.

---

[9] Marjery Fry's claim here relates only to financial restitution, but a similar claim was later made in broader senses by RJ advocates.

[10] See for example the claim made in Zehr's very influential book *Changing Lenses* that even property crimes such as burglary, vandalism and car theft are essentially attacks on personal security, and are experienced as such: 'Crime is in essence a violation: a violation of the self, a desecration of who we are, of what we believe, of our private space. Crime is devastating because it upsets two fundamental assumptions on which we base our lives: our belief that the world is an orderly, meaningful place, and our belief in personal autonomy. Both assumptions are essential for wholeness' (Zehr, 1990: 24).

[11] Hulsman (1982: 46) defines the 'civilisation' thesis as 'an approach in which the compensatory model of civil law (by adaptation of civil procedure) is extended to areas in which it does not yet operate'.

[12] For other early contributions broadly within the 'civilisation' tradition, see Cantor (1976) and Barnett (1977).

Hulsman's argument is thus that restorative justice already exists informally (or indigenously) in many places in contemporary societies, and hence there is significant scope for developing it. All we have to do is to extend our horizons and realise that many more acts defined as 'crimes' could be dealt with in a similar informal fashion, or if necessary by the civil law. As he explicitly states in one of his articles, he has (like Christie) a strong preference for dispute resolution by those directly involved, ie the perpetrator and the victim, with settlements aimed at 'concrete restitution' (Hulsman, 1982: 45). He further complains that, from this perspective, the criminal justice system is seriously deficient:

> Conflicts which occur in society between persons or groups are defined in the penal system not in terms of the parties involved, but rather in terms of the regulations (criminal legislation) and the organisational requirements of the system itself. The parties directly involved in a conflict can exert little influence on the further course of events once a matter has been defined as criminal and as such has been taken up by the system . . . [Moreover] if we compare 'criminal events' with other events there is—on the level of those directly involved—nothing which distinguishes those 'criminal' events *intrinsically* from other difficult or unpleasant situations [such as] matrimonial difficulties . . . serious difficulties at work and housing problems . . . Nor are they singled out to be dealt with in a way differing radically from the way other events are dealt with
>
> (Hulsman 1981: 153–4, emphasis in original).

Hulsman's account is sociologically very useful in drawing attention to much 'hidden' informal justice even in countries with advanced economies. His normative thesis—that this approach should be extended, even to the point of abolition of the criminal justice system (Hulsman, 1991)—is of course much more controversial, and I shall not deal with it here.[13] Rather, I shall highlight two more general issues that arise from the 'civilisation' thesis.

The first issue is the extent to which RJ-type processes in contemporary societies should involve the wider community (however that concept is defined) as well as the direct participants. For Hulsman (1981: 157), one of the attractions of civil procedures is that the parties 'can to an important extent define the problem submitted to [the] system, and in the end they are not forced into a specific settlement of their conflict by the civil law judgement. They remain in a context of negotiation . . .'. Perhaps arising out of such thinking, many of the early practical experiments in RJ took the form of victim-offender mediation (see, eg Marshall and Merry 1990); but, as Johnstone (2002: 151) points out, this led to something of a backlash, where 'many who were sympathetic towards the ideas of restorative justice which arose from these experiments nevertheless criticised such . . . mediation for being too "private" and for failing to involve the community'. It

---

[13] Hulsman's core approach is illustrated in the quotation above by the phrase 'on the level of those directly involved, nothing . . . distinguishes these "criminal" events *intrinsically* from other difficult or unpleasant situations'. For desert theorists such as von Hirsch (1993), this is to ignore the crucial element of societal censure.

would seem that this 'private' versus 'community' debate is a continuing point of tension within the RJ movement, and it is worth exploring a little further.

In an important phrase, Braithwaite (2000a: 122) has described contemporary restorative justice as based on 'individual-centred communitarianism'. Both halves of this phrase are significant. Frequently occurring motifs in the RJ literature are the central role to be given to the parties directly involved ('participating in their own disputes' etc), and the weakness of traditional criminal justice in sidelining the victim. Hence, it is argued, the individual parties are crucial to RJ processes. Yet the importance of 'the community' is also frequently invoked, certainly in the literature on so-called 'family group conferencing', but also by 'civilisation thesis' writers such as Hulsman (see, eg Hulsman, 1981: 154–8).[14] So, what exactly should be the relative weight given to 'individuals' and 'communities' in the 'individual-centred communitarianism' of RJ; and what justifies these relative priorities? There is no clear or agreed answer. In a more formal sociological vein, one can also note, vis-à-vis the so-called 'civilisation thesis', that in contemporary societies civil proceedings are essentially *gesellschaft*-type law, while—from Christie onwards—RJ advocates have tended to emphasise many *gemeinschaft*-type elements within RJ processes.[15] There are significant conceptual tensions here.

The second general issue arising from the 'civilisation thesis' is related to the first. Nils Christie (1977: 8) makes clear that one of the things he is seeking, in his 'model of neighbourhood courts', is a set of *opportunities for norm-clarification*. This would constitute no less than 'what we might call a political debate in the court' about what facts are relevant to the decision, and ultimately about what should be done. For example, what if a petty thief steals from the owner of a big house? Or what if 'the other party is an insurance company, or if his wife has just left him, or if his factory will break down if he has to go to jail . . . or if he was drunk . . . ? There is no end to it. Any maybe there ought to be none' (p 8). Whether Christie is aware of it or not, there is a marked similarity between these comments and some aspects of traditional Arusha dispute-settlement practice.[16]

---

[14] It could be argued that victim-offender mediation projects are almost wholly individualistic, with little of a communitarian dimension. However, as Marshall and Merry (1990) make clear in their discussion of early projects of this kind in England, part of the philosophy of victim-offender mediation is that 'citizens generally ("the community") should be encouraged to play an active part in crime prevention and local social control' (p 6). Later, the same authors argue that, for example, 'as they become known as "experts" in mediation, the staff of such projects inevitably get asked to help train others in such techniques, even beyond the sphere of victim-offender mediation. In their work with corporate victims who suffer repeated crime, for instance, schemes could promote discussion of how to cope with the problem more constructively, and, through meetings with offenders, help to formulate ways of preventing it . . . All the schemes [studied] seem to be making some headway in these respects' (pp 209–10). Thus, while in these projects there was little direct community involvement in the formal mediation processes (pp 206–8), a communitarian dimension clearly remained, not least at an aspirational level.

[15] On *gemeinschaft*-type law and *gesellschaft*-type law, see the fuller discussion later in this chapter of the work of Kamenka and Tay (1975, 1980a, 1980b).

[16] As Gulliver (1963: 299–300) puts it: 'Arusha are inclined to view each new dispute as a unique phenomenon, to the solution of which the ideal norm and past precedent provide only the initial basis for negotiation'. Thus, Arusha dispute processes 'have a nature which can be characterised as mainly political rather than judicial'.

But if, in a modern context, matters of the kind that Christie describes are to be left to the parties involved to debate and decide in individual cases, then any hopes of consistency in decision-making vanish, and the principle of equal treatment before the law seems to be fatally compromised. As Johnstone (2002, p 146) shrewdly points out, Christie's agenda here has 'quite radical implications . . . which, when they become clear, are unlikely to appeal much to most mainstream advocates of restorative justice'. Christie seems to want endless normative/political debates; more mainstream advocates often see RJ as an effective instrument for consolidating and strengthening community normative standards.

In summary, then, detailed examination of the 'civilisation thesis' quickly exposes real uncertainties and disagreements within the RJ movement. What about the other strand in the original intellectual roots of RJ, the alleged 'wisdom of the pre-moderns'?

2. Wise Pre-Moderns?

The 'pre-modern' strand of contemporary RJ thinking has recently been usefully discussed in a textbook by Johnstone (2002: ch 3). Johnstone particularly focuses on Navajo peacemaking processes because of their prominence in the RJ literature, especially in North America.

Navajo peacemaking has some marked similarities to the Arusha civil case that Christie (1977) described, with the major difference that the 'peacemaker' or mediator (an apparently high-status individual) plays a significantly more proactive and interventionist role than the judges did in that case.[17] To quote Johnstone (2002: 45–6):

> The *naat'aanii*-peacemaker calls on the interested parties—the victim and the perpetrator and their families and clan relations—to participate in a meeting in which the aim is to resolve the dispute between them . . . [At the meeting, victims] have an opportunity to state what happened and to vent their feelings about it. The accused person then has an opportunity to speak. Frequently, they will put forward excuses or justifications. One of the purposes of the process appears to be to expose the weakness or unacceptability of the excuses which people habitually use to justify unacceptable behaviour such as drink-driving and spouse-abuse. . . . To achieve this, the plausibility of excuses are assessed, not by lawyers through Western methods of cross-examination, but by people who know the wrongdoer intimately and who will use their intimate knowledge of the wrongdoer to expose the frailty of their excuses . . . The group, *led by the peacemaker*, will then seek to construct a reparative plan of action. This search is guided by principles drawn, not just from legal precedents (in the Western sense), but from a rich range of traditional [teachings]. (Emphasis added).

[17] On mediators in small-scale societies, see Merry (1982). As she comments: 'mediators are respected, influential community members with experience and acknowledged expertise in settling disputes . . . they are experts in village social relationships and genealogy, bringing to the conflict a vast store of knowledge about how individuals are expected to behave toward one another as well as about the reputations and social identities of the particular disputants . . . To flout [a mediator's] settlement is to defy the moral order of the community' (Merry, 1982: 30).

According to Johnstone, some RJ advocates (and he cites examples) go on to claim that:

> Navajo peacemaking is a virtually universal process found among nearly all aboriginal groups and in all pre-modern societies. There is an implication that Navajo peacemaking represents a natural, authentic form of justice, a form abandoned by modern western societies in favour of a more 'artificial' system of state punitive justice. (Johnstone 2002: 44).

This claim, of course, is not dissimilar to (although more specific and more provocatively stated than) John Braithwaite's claim about restorative justice being 'the dominant model of criminal justice throughout most of human history' (see the introduction to this chapter).

So, what we have here is a kind of foundational myth about the 'naturalness' of RJ, based on the alleged universality or near-universality of RJ-type principles in pre-modern societies. To return to the dictionary definition of an aphorism, however (see the introduction to this chapter), while there is *some* truth in these claims, the claims are, without serious question, both overstated and decontextualised.

The alleged near-universality of RJ-style dispute settlement is quickly refuted by any serious look at the literature of legal anthropology. As Simon Roberts puts it in his classic textbook, in different stateless societies the 'approved means of handling disputes . . . are extremely varied' (Roberts 1979: 116). For example:

> In some societies it is recognized that quarrels *should* be resolved through talk rather than by fighting, ostracism or sorcery. In others no particular value is attached explicitly to talking but it may be used alongside other methods of handling disputes. Elsewhere different values prevail, demanding as a matter of honour some direct physical response to many types of wrong and resulting in the identification of conciliatory gestures with weakness. In the last case retaliatory violence may represent the likely reaction to a wrong, and where further injury is inflicted this may in turn lead to sustained fighting between kinsmen and co-residents of the principals. (Emphasis in original).

It is also clear from the relevant literature that, where conciliatory ('peacemaking') discussions are found in a given pre-modern society, they are sometimes set within a range of other procedures and sanctions that are much less obviously 'restorative'. Moreover, even within reconciliatory/restitutive processes, individuals may be 'coerced into settlements by the prestige of the mediator and the threat of sanctions, both secular and supernatural' (Merry, 1982: 28).

To illustrate these last points, I shall discuss in some detail Joan Ryan's (1995) recent anthropological study of the Dogrib hunter-gatherer tribal group (part of a larger community known as the 'Dene people') in the Canadian Northwest Territories. An important part of the purpose of Ryan's research was to recover (through oral accounts) how indigenous Dene traditional justice worked—

what the rules were, how children were socialised to obey rules, what happened when someone broke the rules, and so on (see especially Ryan, 1995: 33–4, 57–8).[18]

In traditional Dogrib society, there was no single mechanism of justice. The most serious offences were dealt with by banishment from the tribe, which 'was essentially a death sentence', because in the Dene territory (close to the Arctic Circle) no-one 'could survive out on the land on his own for long' (p 58). At the other end of the scale of seriousness, minor offences (such as a small theft) were dealt with by ridicule and shaming, which was intended to act as a deterrent (p 33).

Between these extremes came the intermediate offences. Some of these might be dealt with by the local camp *k'àowo* (each camp had a *k'àowo*, who was an assistant to the overall tribal leader or *yabahti*). An example might be theft of an animal from a trap; here the *k'àowo* would speak what are described as 'harsh words' to the thief, who would also 'be asked to acknowledge the theft and to return the fur (or another of equal value) to the person from whom it had been stolen' (p 34).

If the offender refused to comply with the *k'àowo*'s requirements, he would then be required to be 'put in the circle'. The same procedure would also be adopted for offences which the *k'àowo* considered too serious for him to deal with by himself. Here we reach the full RJ element within Dene traditional justice.

The 'circle' consisted of the whole local Dogrib community, presided over by the *yabahti* (tribal leader) and senior men and women of the tribal group. Joan Ryan (1995) describes the procedure as follows:

> The offender was kept [in the circle] until he or she admitted guilt,[19] at which point the senior people and leadership would give the person 'harsh words'. These words usually restated the rules and how the person should have behaved. They also made reference to the harm done to individuals and/or the group. Once the harsh words were spoken, the gathering shifted to discussing how the individual might make things better. People arrived at consensus about what the person might do to restore harmony [with the victim and within the community], compensate the victim, and end the matter.

> When the solution was proposed, the offender agreed to do what the elders had indicated would make things right. If the person did not agree, then the gathering [might decide] that he must leave the community since he would not follow the rules. [But] banishment was rare because few young people had the courage, or lack of respect, to 'break the words' of the elders.

[18] Ryan's concerns, in undertaking this research, were not only academic but also policy-oriented; that is, they were focussed on how the research team's findings about traditional justice 'might provide some directions and new ideas for the Dene to take back responsibility for their own ways of social control now' (Ryan, 1995: xxviii). These policy issues were addressed by Joan Ryan in her speech to a public meeting on restorative justice held at the University of Toronto in May 2001, linked to the discussions leading to this book.

[19] As Ryan several times emphasises, there is no concept of a 'not guilty' plea in Dogrib justice. However, 'no action is taken against an individual unless people are sure that something wrong has been done by the individual which affects the safety and well-being of the collective' (Ryan, 1995: 91).

Once [the offender had carried out what was considered appropriate to restore harmony], no further action was taken and no further mention of the offence was made.
(A composite of passages at pp 57–8 and p 34 of Ryan (1995)).

Ryan's perception of these processes is that 'the offender is not punished. Rather, the group demands that he or she face the victim, that restitution be made, that reconciliation start' (p 91). However, although in her view there is no punishment, Ryan is in no doubt that the processes described could be perceived as coercive, and indeed seemed to produce a deterrent effect:

In all our accounts, people said that they feared the discipline of their parents, they feared the power of the *yabahtis*, they feared 'harsh words' . . . As well, the reality of being shamed by all those gathered if one ended up in the circle, caused many people to think seriously before committing an offence (Ryan, 1995, p 58).

Additionally, Ryan (1995: 90–1) makes clear that there are a number of similarities—though not, of course, total similarity—between the traditional Dogrib procedure and the modern Canadian criminal trial. (The person accused of committing a wrong act is arraigned before a community tribunal, who may take harsh measures against him/her, and so on.)

Three points are of special interest about this account. First, restorative processes exist, but they are heavily buttressed by other processes (notably, the very real threat of banishment—hardly a 'restorative' sanction), in a way that must significantly affect the dynamics of the 'circle' process itself. Secondly, to use Emile Durkheim's (1893) celebrated distinction, traditional Dogrib society was apparently a society characterised more by *mechanical solidarity* than by *organic solidarity*.[20] In such societies, it is the group that is all-important, and any individual is secondary to the group. It is thus very noticeable that, in Ryan's account, although the end-results of the circle procedure are restitution and reconciliation, prior to that it is the elders who dominate the proceedings, acting essentially *on behalf of the victim(s)*, as well as on behalf of the community at large. The victim her/himself plays a somewhat passive role in the proceedings, so that this version of RJ, unlike those described by Christie and Hulsman, is apparently not in any serious sense akin to civil proceedings. This leads directly to the third key observation, which is that in Dogrib traditional justice the elders (or chairs of the circle)

---

[20] As Lukes (1973: 149) explains (quoting liberally from the original), Durkheim saw mechanical solidarity as ' "a solidarity *sui generis* which . . . directly links the individual with society"; it "arises from the fact that a number of states of consciousness (*conscience*) are common to all the members of the same society". It can be strong "only to the extent that the ideas and dispositions common to all the members of the society exceed in number and intensity those which pertain personally to each of them". Societies with organic solidarity are more internally differentiated, and have a more elaborate division of labour. In such societies ' "the individual depends upon society because he depends upon the parts which compose it", while society is "a system of different and special functions united by definite relations". It presupposes that individuals "differ from one another" . . . [and so, in such societies] "the yoke we submit to is infinitely less heavy than when the entire society weighs on us, and it leaves much more room for the free play of our initiative" ' (Lukes, 1973: 153).

are anything but inactive. All members of the circle are invited to participate, but it is the elders who dominate.

Two problems of sociological explanation arise directly from Ryan's account of Dogrib traditional justice. First, why are Dogrib penalties harsher, and their procedures less individualistic and more collective, than those often described for other societies? The answer to this question is almost certainly related to the fact that this was a hunter-gatherer society living in harsh physical circumstances. Under such conditions—according to other anthropological studies—'everything depends on the cohesion and co-operation of a group', so the group acts in a collective way to protect itself, because of 'the value that must be attached to relationships of mutual reliance' (Roberts, 1979: 98).

The second problem for explanation concerns the use of restitutive and reconciliatory techniques even for quite serious offences, and even in a society that is not afraid (where necessary) to use harsh sanctions such as banishment. At first sight, it seems surprising that offences falling just short of the seriousness threshold for banishment could nevertheless be dealt with by a restitutive procedure where, once the agreed restitution had been made, 'no further action was taken and no further mention of the offence was made' (Ryan 1995: 34). But, on further reflection, the reasons for this are not hard to discern. As Chris Hann (2000: 145) puts it:

> In a small-scale society where [direct enforcement options such as a prison system] are not available, the payment of compensation to the victim of a crime is likely to be more important than punishment. Reconciliation is especially important where the contesting parties have necessarily to continue sharing the same economic resources, to be part of a cooperative community in daily life.

This indeed seems to be the principal reason why settlement-directed talk, reconciliation and restitution is widespread (but by no means universal) in pre-modern societies. I shall return to the significance of this point when discussing the social mechanisms of RJ in the next section of this chapter.

Finally, what main conclusions can be drawn from this brief analysis of the 'wisdom of the pre-moderns' argument? I would suggest the following:

— Pre-modern societies are significantly more varied in their dispute-resolution procedures and sanctions than some RJ advocates have suggested.
— Reconciliatory/restitutive processes are nevertheless widespread in pre-modern societies, particularly because of the absence of direct enforcement mechanisms (which are much more readily available in contemporary societies), and also the imperative need for reconciliation in small-society contexts where people have to continue to live in close proximity to one another in a functioning economic and social community.
— Reconciliatory/restitutive processes always occur within the particular macro- and meso-structural contexts of the given society. These contexts can, however, vary quite widely as between different pre-modern societies,

with consequential differences for dispute settlement. (For an instructive contrast, compare Gulliver on the Arusha with Ryan on the Dogrib; the former has significantly more complex substructures).

— Despite the genuinely reconciliatory nature of dispute-settlement procedures in many pre-modern societies (see second point above), it remains the case that within such procedures there is frequently a strong degree of social pressure, so that 'individuals may be coerced into settlements by the prestige of the mediator and the threat of sanctions' (Merry, 1982: 28). The precise form of such social pressure is strongly linked to the social structural context of the particular society (see third point above), but coercive forces of various kinds can readily be identified in societies as different as the Dogrib and the Arusha.[21]

— As noted earlier in this chapter, contemporary RJ advocates tend to put forward a version of RJ based on 'individual-centred communitarianism' (see eg Braithwaite, 2000a; Christie, 1977), but some pre-modern societies were significantly more collectively-oriented than this model suggests (see the Dogrib example).

— In using examples from pre-modern societies in pursuit of contemporary RJ policy-formation, there is a particular need for care in generalising about the role of the president of the tribunal.[22] Even in this brief discussion, we have encountered very varied styles of chairperson activity, ranging from the inactive bystander (Christie on the post-colonial Arusha) to the respected and powerful mediator between individuals within a context of shared community norms (accounts of Navajo peacemakers) to dominant figures concerned above all with collective cohesion (Ryan on the Dogrib). In more comprehensive legal-anthropological accounts of dispute settlement in pre-modern societies, such as that of Roberts (1979), a similar range of roles can be found. This issue, of course, is linked to the tensions between 'individual' and 'community' emphases in RJ (already discussed in the context of the 'civilisation thesis'), since more collectively-oriented societies tend to assign stronger roles to those presiding over dispute-settlement procedures.

I noted earlier Maureen Cain's (1988: 56) claim that Nils Christie (1977) had constructed a 'romantic idealization of pre-capitalist (but non-feudal) forms' of legal or quasi-legal decision-making. After a more detailed examination of pre-

---

[21] For a full discussion of coercion in traditional Arusha dispute-settlement, see Gulliver (1963: ch 11).

[22] In contemporary RJ debates, disagreement sometimes arises about the appropriate role of the president(s) of a tribunal. For example, in the so-called Referral Orders established in the English youth justice system by an Act of 1999, some young offenders are mandatorily 'referred' from the Youth Court to a so-called 'Youth Offending Panel', a forum with intendedly restorative justice features. This panel consists of three community representatives, and some have argued that this constitutes an over-heavy community representation, for example by comparison with the New Zealand family group conferences (on which see Maxwell and Morris, 1993).

modern societies, it can be seen that there is some truth in such a characterisation, and that a similar tendency to idealisation of the pre-modern still exists among some RJ advocates (see some of the comments made by RJ advocates about the near-universality of processes akin to Navajo peacemaking). Despite this tendency, there remains some validity to claims—such as that by Braithwaite with which I began this chapter—about the widespread existence of processes of reconciliation and restitution in pre-modern societies. Those processes, however, vary widely in different pre-modern societies (see the third and sixth summary points above); and the widespread existence of reconciliatory/restitutive processes in such societies is itself connected to certain features of such societies which are either not present or not prominent in contemporary advanced urban societies (see the second and fourth point above). As Sally Merry (1982) argued twenty years ago, there is therefore no easy line of normative argument that can be drawn from reconciliatory/restitutive processes in pre-modern societies to the advocacy of RJ (or equivalent procedures) in contemporary societies. Contemporary societies will be considered more fully in the final section of this chapter, but first it is necessary to take a closer look at the social mechanisms of 'restoration'.

III. APOLOGY AND THE SOCIAL MECHANISMS OF 'RESTORATION'

I began this chapter with John Braithwaite's aphorism that 'for informal justice to be restorative justice, it has to be about restoring victims, restoring offenders, and restoring communities'. In looking more closely at this saying, we can begin by noting that if victims, offenders, or communities are to be 'restored', then it would seem that there must be some *social mechanism* that will restore them. Hedström and Swedborg (1996) have argued persuasively that sociologists need always to develop 'explanations that systematically seek to explicate the generative mechanisms that produce observed associations between events' (p 281), and if that is correct, then we need to ask ourselves what 'generative mechanisms' might produce an observed association between RJ procedures and/or sanctions, and the subsequent 'restoration' of the victim, the offender, or the community.

I shall begin this task by considering the community, bearing in mind that communities always consist of individuals in relationships, those relationships taking place within social structures and cultural contexts. Given this background, the most appropriate way for a social scientist to use the terminology of post-RJ 'community restoration' is, I would suggest, to speak of *a restoration of prior social relationships in a community, within an understood structural and normative framework*. Since many advocates of RJ claim that this is precisely what it can achieve, and since such a claim is not (see below) a meaningless statement,[23] then it can

---

[23] Indeed, it should be recalled that Ryan's evidence suggests this is what is actually achieved among the Dogrib: once an agreed restitution had been made, 'no further action was taken and no further mention of the offence was made' within the community (Ryan, 1995: 34).

be regarded as a testable hypothesis that the processes of RJ can in some way act as 'generative social mechanisms' to restore prior social relationships in communities. In saying this, it is explicitly assumed for present purposes that both the victim and the offender belong to the same social/moral community, although their direct personal linkage within that community might be tenuous (thus, while some offenders and victims might be linked through the 'thick' social relations of family members, or the 'thinner' relationships between, say, work colleagues or members of a social club, others might simply be residents of a town or village who barely know each other, but are both embedded in meaningful social networks which connect elsewhere within a functioning social/moral community).

So how might RJ 'restore prior social relationships' within such a context? It is at this point that we need to give special attention to one central feature of RJ processes, namely *the apology*. Almost all accounts of RJ emphasise the desirability of the apology as a prelude to meaningful reparation and reconciliation; and empirically, the evidence from the RISE randomised experiment in the Australian Capital Territory suggests that victims receive apologies far more often in RJ conferences than they do in courts (by a factor of six or seven to one: see Braithwaite, 1999: 24). Sociologically speaking, then, can the apology (followed usually by some restitution) be plausibly represented as a generative social mechanism that can potentially lead to the restoration of prior social relationships in a community (as defined above)?

In my view, the answer to this question is a straightforward affirmative. To understand why, we need to examine the pioneering monograph on the sociology of apology by Nicholas Tavuchis (1991)—a text that is sometimes cited in the RJ literature (see eg Braithwaite, 1999: 44; Johnstone, 2002: 135) but one that (to my knowledge) has rarely been carefully analysed in that literature.

Tavuchis examines the apology from two distinct but complementary perspectives. The first of these relates to the *social-structural context* of the apology, and here the key point is that the apology:

> speaks to an act that cannot be undone, but that cannot go unnoticed without compromising the current and future relationship of the parties, the legitimacy of the violated rule, and the wider social web in which the participants are enmeshed (p 13).

As we shall shortly see, every word of that formulation is important. Tavuchis's second perspective shifts our attention away from this 'social scaffolding of apology', and instead looks towards its 'experiential dynamics' (p 120). In the fully-accomplished apology, it is argued, we have first a *call* for an apology from the person(s) who regard themselves as wronged, or from someone speaking on their behalf; then the *apology* itself; and finally an expression of *forgiveness* from the wronged to the wrongdoer (p 20). Each of these moves can be emotionally fraught; thus, the whole apologetic discourse is (on both sides) 'a delicate and precarious transaction' (p vii). Yet it is important to emphasise that a successfully accomplished apology can have 'almost miraculous qualities' (p 6). This last point is explained as follows:

no matter how sincere or effective, [an apology] does not and cannot *undo* what has been done. And yet, in a mysterious way and according to its own logic, this is precisely what it manages to do (p 5, emphasis in original).

To understand more fully the 'social scaffolding' and the 'experiential dynamics' of the apology, let us take a closer look at three issues: the social background, the dyadic quality of apologetic discourse, and the allegedly 'miraculous qualities' of the successful apology. This approach can be regarded, in Max Weber's (1949) terminology, as the development of an ideal-typical analysis of a successful apology.[24]

(*i*) *The background*: In the ideal-typical apology, the parties already have some kind of relationship, even if that relationship is, at a personal level, tenuous and indirect (see above). But a social norm is violated, and so a 'moral imperative' (p vii) compels the wronged person to take note of that breach and to call for an apology. (The alternative is simply to forget the incident, but in any serious social/moral community, with pretensions to maintain an effective 'positive morality',[25] this is not a sustainable option.) The call for the apology therefore simultaneously:

— draws attention to the prior shared social relationships and understandings within the community;
— emphasises that the act complained of is a departure from the accepted positive morality of the group, and cannot be ignored if the legitimacy of the relevant moral rule is to be upheld; and
— potentially looks forward to a social situation where, after the apology has been offered, there will be a restoration of a prior state of relations between the parties, and within the community more generally (note the key word 'restoration' here).

In other words, both prior social relationships in community, and the accepted positive morality of the group, are deeply embedded as background characteristics (or part of the framework) of the ideal-typical apology.

(*ii*) *The structure of the apologetic discourse*: Tavuchis emphasises, rightly in my view, that the ideal-typical apology is essentially dyadic in its nature. That it to

[24] As Frank Parkin (1982: 28) explains: 'Ideal-types are conceptual abstractions that we employ in trying to get to grips with the complexities of the social world. Weber properly points out that we cannot grasp social phenomena in their totality. Patterns of behaviour and institutional forms like capitalism, or Protestantism, or bureaucracy, are each composed of a large number of interconnected elements, both normative and structural. In order to comprehend any such institution or social formation it is necessary to reduce it to its core components. We do this by singling out and accentuating the central or basic features of the institution in question and suppressing or downgrading those features that could be considered marginal to it'.

[25] The term 'positive morality', first used by nineteenth century utilitarians, was helpfully revived by HLA Hart forty years ago (see MacCormick, 1981: ch 4). Hart defined 'positive morality' as 'the morality actually accepted and shared by a given social group'; by contrast, he suggested that 'critical morality' refers to 'the general moral principles used in the criticism of actual social institutions including positive morality' (Hart 1963: 20).

say, while supporters of the two key parties may have much to offer by way of advice, support, censure, and so forth, at the end of the day it is those two parties who are the central players in the drama, and no-one can displace them in that role if the apologetic discourse is to be really meaningful: one must express genuine regret and remorse for an act that has breached a shared moral code, and the other must forgive.[26] Only in this way can prior social relationships be 'restored', although (see below) this process itself requires continual emotional work by the parties.

(iii) *The allegedly 'miraculous qualities' of successful apologies:* Why does a successfully accomplished and accepted apology seem 'miraculous'? It seems so because, in one sense, nothing at all has happened (except that some words have been exchanged); and yet in another sense, everything has changed. The apology, as Tavuchis repeatedly emphasises, does not (and indeed cannot) annul the wrong that has occurred; but the *pain* and the *regret* of the sincere apology (often a difficult matter for the offender to express), followed by the equally difficult act of forgiveness offered (perhaps uncertainly) by the wronged person, have the power to effect a social transformation. The complex experiential dynamics of apology can therefore be 'a prelude to reunion and reconciliation' (p 22), even though that process of reconciliation might encounter further emotional difficulties on both sides before it is fully accomplished. We are not far here from Braithwaite's (1999: 2) aspirational words about RJ at its best: 'Crime is an opportunity to prevent greater evils, to confront crime with a grace that transforms human lives to paths of love and giving'.

To bring these points down to earth, consider a hypothetical case, that of a seriously wrong act committed by one party to a 'thick' social relationship, directly against another party (say, an adult son, with a close relationship with loving parents, committing an act that seriously wrongs his mother). Reflecting on such a scenario, we quickly realise that a true apology has much to offer. The reason for this resides in the dual facts of (i) the shared commitment to a particular social group (in this case, the family unit) *and* (ii) a genuine shared belief in the importance of the moral rule that has been broken. Given a real social/moral community of this kind, often an apology offers by far the best hope of repairing the social/moral breach, and paving the way for the resumption of something like the previous set of relationships. Those few words of apology may seem to the hypothetical Martian observer to be nothing; but to the participants they can be everything, especially if backed up by practical action to put right—so far as possible—the wrong caused by the original action. This, in a nutshell, is the sociological explanation of the 'miracle' of the successful apology: it is a social mecha-

---

[26] Even in collective societies such as the Dogrib, note the language used by Joan Ryan (1995: 91): 'the group demands that [the offender] face the victim, that restitution be made, that reconciliation start'. There is very strong collective pressure here, but also a recognition that meaningful apology and reconciliation is ultimately dyadic: the offender must 'face the victim', and only in this way can reconciliation 'start'.

nism that can help to transcend breaches of the normative order within a given group or community, and to begin to restore prior relationships within that community. The key to its success lies squarely in the normative and relational realms.

I have focussed so far on 'community restoration', deliberately leaving aside Braithwaite's apparently wider agenda when he spoke of 'restoring victims, restoring offenders and restoring communities' (see above). At first blush, talk of 'restoring victims' or 'restoring offenders' might seem to have a somewhat mystical ring to it, and it is not at all clear how one could identify the generative social mechanisms that might lead to such 'restorations'. However, I would suggest that these ideas are again best considered in relational terms. How can victims, having suffered a perhaps traumatic shock, be brought again into something like their prior set of social relationships and activities, regaining their self-esteem and the confidence to live their lives without undue anxiety? How can offenders, having been rightly censured (perhaps severely) for their offence, nevertheless be reintroduced into society so that they—and the society—may 'move on' after the offence? So understood, these apparently more individualistic kinds of 'restoration' may also be understood within the framework I have previously suggested, namely the 'restoration of prior social relationships in a community, within an understood structural and normative framework'.[27]

The preceding discussion has deliberately been conducted on the basis of two explicit assumptions: first, that we are speaking of the ideal-typical apology; and second, that the victim and the offender are part of the same social/moral community (although perhaps with only a tenuous or indirect relationship within that community). It is time to address the question of what difference it makes if either or both of these assumptions is not instantiated in a given case.

We have seen that, for Tavuchis (1991), the ideal-typical apology is essentially dyadic in its nature. It follows that, where third parties become involved, there are potential complications; and these can include, according to Tavuchis, 'eliciting and exacerbating latent anger, self-righteousness, moral indignation, and, most perniciously, the development of a punitive atmosphere' (p 52). Hence, an apology forced out of someone by a group of others encircling him and threatening to beat him up is a long way from the ideal-typical apology.[28] The presence of third parties, however, does not necessarily have such pernicious effects, and the best kind of third party is a true mediator, who is 'a kind of moral stand-in or surrogate, a necessarily temporary social actor', (p 66), who can assist the parties towards genuine apology and reconciliation. These issues highlight the delicate balancing act that is required of chairpersons of RJ-style tribunals in

---

[27] It should be noted that, once again, these formulations do not necessarily presuppose that the offender and the victim have any direct relationship. As before, however, it is assumed for present purposes that both the offender and the victim belong to the same identifiable moral/social community.

[28] For a worst-case scenario of this kind in a criminal justice context, see the description by Karp (1998) of the coerced apologies ordered by courts in some American jurisdictions, in some cases combined with debasement gestures such as requiring the defendant to make the apology while on his hands and knees.

contemporary societies, where the offender has broken the criminal law. As the experience of pre-modern societies attests, the involvement of third parties (such as mediators), and a degree of social pressure or coercion, do not in themselves preclude a sincere and eventually socially effective apology. Nevertheless, the presence of such factors certainly might not assist the emergence of really genuine apologetic discourse, perhaps especially in contemporary societies where the parties are not necessarily members of the same social/moral community.

Which brings us to our second explicit assumption in the discussion to this point; namely, the assumption that the victim and the offender are part of the same moral/social community. On this issue, Gulliver's (1963: 263) study of indigenous Arusha dispute settlement contains a finding with significant admonitory resonance for the contemporary RJ movement:

> Most serious disputes occur between people who are directly and fairly closely related to one another in one or more ways—members of a single lineage, or of a single parish, . . . etc . . . Arusha indigenous procedures are on the whole able to deal with these relationships because the procedures themselves arise out of the social sub-systems in which these relationships operate. 'Unrelated' people[29] are less likely to come into serious dispute; but when they do, indigenous procedures are cumbersome and not altogether efficient. Injuries may have to be tolerated under the circumstances because of the difficulty, perhaps impossibility, of taking useful action.

The reasons for this finding are interesting. One reason relates to the previously-quoted comment by Chris Hann (2000: 145) about reconciliation being 'especially important where the contesting parties have necessarily to continue . . . to be part of a continuing community in everyday life'; by definition, this consideration is much less relevant for 'unrelated' than for 'related' parties. Secondly, in 'unrelated' cases the linkage to the moral/social attachments and structures in the society is necessarily weaker; in a society like the Arusha, this may make a formal dispute settlement procedure harder to convene,[30] and any settlements reached harder to enforce. The general implication is that, where the offender and the victim are not part of the same moral/social community, the genuine apology—and the social mechanisms of reconciliatory justice more generally—may be significantly harder to orchestrate. This obviously raises questions about RJ mechanisms in the anonymous urban societies of the contemporary world, and this is an issue to which we must return in the final section of this chapter.

Finally, we should return again foursquare to Braithwaite's aphorism, with which this discussion began ('for informal justice to be restorative justice, it has

---

[29] Gulliver deliberately places inverted commas around the word 'unrelated'. As he explains elsewhere, among the Arusha everyone is structurally related to all other people through the patrilineal descent system; nevertheless 'those who live more than a few miles apart and whose patrilineal link is relatively remote, may be said for practical purposes to be "unrelated"' (Gulliver, 1963: 258).

[30] Among the Arusha in the 1950s this led to 'unrelated' people not infrequently taking their case to the courts of the colonial power (Gulliver, 1963: 266, 204ff), notwithstanding that the Arusha in general regarded these courts as 'alien-imposed institutions' which were over-formal, and in which they lacked faith (pp 273–4).

to be about restoring victims . . . (etc)'). In the light of the analysis in this section, we can now see that Braithwaite has formulated a very demanding test. What he is saying is that informal justice (say, a family group conference) is one thing, but true *restorative* justice (in my preferred formulation, justice that will restore social relationships in community) is quite another matter. In other words, just because a given part of a particular criminal justice system claims that it is running a 'restorative cautioning system' (or whatever), it does not follow, for Braithwaite, that this system truly is 'restorative'—that is, restoring relationships through the kinds of generative social mechanisms explored in this section. Given the complexity and the often fraught emotional character of the process of ideal-typical apology, it would in fact not be at all surprising if officially-sponsored 'restorative justice schemes' in contemporary societies sometimes succeeded, but sometimes failed to deliver the kind of 'restoration' to which Braithwaite aspires; and, to his credit, John Braithwaite (1999) clearly recognises this. We shall explore these issues further as we move to an analysis of RJ in contemporary societies.

IV. RESTORATIVE JUSTICE IN CONTEMPORARY SOCIETIES

In this final section, I shall first discuss the view that RJ is an apparent anomaly in contemporary penality, and then go on to consider sociological reasons for the rapid growth of RJ in recent decades, an analysis which includes some discussion of the structural location of RJ in contemporary societies. Finally—and building on the analysis in the preceding sections—I shall assess the extent to which we can expect the truly 'restorative' elements of the mechanisms of RJ to be routinely delivered in contemporary societies.

1. The Anomaly of RJ in Contemporary Penality

Contemporary sociologists have developed, as one of their main preoccupations, an extensive discourse and set of theorisations about, for example, 'globalisation', 'late modernity' or 'post-modernity', 'the risk society' and so forth (see for example Harvey, 1989; Giddens, 1990 and 1991; Beck, 1992; Beck et al 1994; Lash and Urry, 1994; Bauman, 1997; Lupton, 1999). Criminologists, also, have become interested in applying such theoretical ideas to a wide variety of topics. To take just one example, Ericson and Haggerty's (1997) *Policing the Risk Society* sees contemporary public police services as primarily information-brokers in a knowledge-based society, where they co-ordinate activities with, for example, the insurance and private security services. Even so-called 'community policing' is, these authors argue, really 'risk communication policing', providing a basis for risk management, that is, the pre-identification of, and subsequent containment of, risks seen as undesirable.

In the specifically penal sphere, rather similar arguments have been developed about the so-called 'new penology' (Feeley and Simon, 1992, 1994), and anyone interested in the correctional services must now actively engage with the impact of managerialism upon those services (see for example James and Raine, 1998). Quite sophisticated tools of risk assessment are now routinely deployed in the penal sphere (Robinson, 2002). Additionally, one of the most astonishing features of the penal scene in many countries at the end of the twentieth and the beginning of the twenty-first century is the apparently inexorable rise of prison populations. All this has led David Garland, one of the leading writers on the sociology of punishment, to entitle his recent book *The Culture of Control* (Garland, 2001). Nor finally, in this brief inventory of contemporary penality, must one forget the growing importance of human rights protections enforced by the law, well exemplified by the very significant impact of the European Convention on Human Rights on various aspects of criminal justice in the United Kingdom.

Every one of these various issues seems rather remote from the main preoccupations of RJ. Unquestionably, RJ is now an international movement, and in a number of countries it has come to have a significant influence on mainstream criminal justice policies. This has been achieved from a position of almost complete marginality of quarter of a century ago. Yet, in achieving its phenomenal growth, RJ has remained predominantly small-scale and communitarian in its preferred operating style, with—for example—usually only at best a very marginal role for lawyers[31] and other professionals, and certainly very little use of such late modern devices as risk assessment profiles. Neither RJ practitioners, nor most academics sympathetic to RJ, show any sustained interest in the issues of 'managerialism' and 'risk' in relation to criminal justice,[32] and even the legal protections arising from human rights conventions are on occasion downplayed. In all these respects, the RJ movement has remained faithful to the wariness of 'experts' (both legal and behavioural), and to the preference for ordinary people to have a direct say in their own conflicts, expressed by Nils Christie (1977) a quarter of a century ago. But, equally, all this makes RJ distinctly *anomalous* in contemporary penality, in the sense that RJ has genuinely grown in influence in the last quarter-century, yet this has occurred within a penal policy context that in many ways seems to operate on a set of assumptions very different from its own. If this analysis is correct, then the apparently 'anomalous' growth of RJ in contemporary societies requires serious sociological attention.

2. The Appeal and Growth of RJ in Contemporary Societies

Why, then, has RJ's influence spread so rapidly, especially given the apparently inauspicious context (see above)? Any answer to this question must be,

---

[31] For example, the recent English legislation concerning 'Referral Orders' (see n 22 above) expressly excludes state-assisted legal aid from being available in the Youth Offender Panel proceedings.

[32] An important exception here is John Braithwaite, whose work on restorative justice in relation to 'the new regulatory state' (Braithwaite, 2000b) is considered later in this chapter.

in part, speculative, but a number of possibilities can, I think, be reasonably suggested.

(i) *The appeal of the gemeinschaft in late modern societies:* Kamenka and Tay (1980a), influential writers on the sociology of law, have identified three major types of law in Western societies. These types, they emphasise, are not necessarily evolutionary, and indeed all three types are often co-present in a given legal system. Their analysis, although perhaps over-schematic, can I think help us in our task of explanation.

The first of the three types is *gemeinschaft*-type law, which 'takes for its fundamental presupposition and concern the organic community' (p 19). By contrast, *gesellschaft*-type law takes for its fundamental presupposition and concern the individual, who is 'theoretically—for the purposes of law—free and self-determined, limited only by the rights of other *individuals*' (p 19, emphasis in original). In the third type of law, so-called 'bureaucratic-administrative law', the presupposition and concern is 'neither an organic human community nor an atomic individual, it is a non-human ruling interest, public policy, or ongoing activity, of which human beings are subordinates, functionaries or carriers' (p 19).[33]

In the contemporary world, it is often not at all difficult to discern each of these three kinds of law in operation on a co-present basis in a given legal jurisdiction. For example, in the sphere of criminal justice one might find, in a particular jurisdiction, a Human Rights Act (or equivalent) enshrining basic legal rights and freedoms for individuals (*gesellschaft*-type law); together with risk-based legislation on parole release, or on the community-based monitoring of sex offenders (bureaucratic-administrative law); together with provisions for restorative justice conferences for certain categories of persons who have admitted offences (*gemeinschaft*-type law).

Of the three legal types, individualised *gesellschaft*-type law is in an important sense the foundation-stone of legal rules in any modern liberal-democratic state. But a central problem for such states is that *gesellschaft*-type law 'is not attuned, in its underlying individualism, to the fact of social interconnection and interdependence, or to the supra-individual requirements of social activities and

---

[33] Kamenka and Tay (1980a: 19–20) explain this more fully by reference to laws and regulations relating to railways. 'The (*Gesellschaft-*) law concerning railways is oriented toward the rights of people whose interests may be infringed by the operation of railways or people whose activities may infringe the rights of the owners or operators seen as individuals exercising individual rights. (*Bureaucratic-administrative*) regulations concerning railways take for their primary object the efficient running of railways or the efficient execution of tasks and attainment of goals and norms set by the authorities and taken as given. Individuals as individuals are the object of some of these regulations but not their subject; they are relevant not as individuals having rights and duties as individuals, but as part of the railway-running process and its organization, as people having duties and responsibilities. Such people are seen as carrying out roles, as not standing in a "horizontal" relation of equivalence to the railway organization or to all their fellow-workers, but as standing in defined "vertical" relations of subordination and sub-subordination. The relation of the bureaucratic to people as subjects and not objects is never direct but mediated through the policy, plan or regulations that purport to have human needs as well as technical requirements for their foundation.'

social living' (Kamenka and Tay, 1975: 140). These supra-individual requirements, insofar as they are properly within the province of law at all, must therefore be provided either by *gemeinschaft*-type or by bureaucratic-administrative law, or by some mixture of the two. In practice, however, in contemporary societies there is a tendency for bureaucratic-administrative values and arrangements to be favoured for such purposes, since 'the necessary structure, the resources and control in a world of atomic individuals not shaped in and by coherent [social] institutions, can only be provided by the State', or by other organisations acting ostensibly in the public interest (Kamenka and Tay, 1980b: 108).[34] Hence, in criminal justice systems, the rapid development of 'managerialism' and of 'risk' paradigms, which are undoubtedly predominantly bureaucratic-administrative in their approach, and are designed to meet the 'supra-individual requirements of social activities and social living' in late modern societies (see further, Bottoms, 1995; Bottoms and Wiles, 1996).

This analysis, however, whilst prioritising the bureaucratic-administrative approach to 'supra-individual requirements', nevertheless allows us to see why there might be, in modern legal arrangements, something of a hunger for *gemeinschaft*-type approaches, as policies that could help to provide, at a minimum, 'a certain humanising cosmetic for bureaucratic practice' (Kamenka and Tay, 1975: 142), and perhaps substantially more than that. Such a hunger for the *gemeinschaft* could of course be purely nostalgic (the hankering after a lost world of 'thick' social relationships and neighbourhood-based communities), but it could also be, in part, completely genuine (the search for an organic rather than a bureaucratic approach to at least some supra-individual requirements within modern legal systems).

Such considerations would be consistent with the rise of RJ arrangements in a globalised, risk-oriented, bureaucratic-administrative world. But if this approach to explanation has any validity, then two things follow. First, on this view RJ conferences (or their equivalents) are not—contrary to Christie's (1977) original vision—in any serious sense organisations that will be a 'vitaliser for neighbourhoods', but rather organisations that are allowed to exist in certain spaces of late modern societies where it is thought that a *gemeinschaft* approach might have some value (as an addition to the bureaucratic-administrative and *gesellschaft* approaches that are elsewhere dominant in criminal justice). And secondly, if the first proposition is correct, then it will be worth paying some serious attention to those 'structural spaces' where, in practice, RJ seems to be most often allowed to flourish in contemporary societies. The most obvious such 'structural space', empirically speaking, clearly lies in the field of youth justice:[35] it follows, therefore, that our search for explanation needs to consider why youth justice is seen as a particularly appropriate site for RJ approaches.

---

[34] Writing in the early 1980s, Kamenka and Tay did not appreciate the extent to which the State would in the near future withdraw from the direct provision of the 'structure, resources and control' of which they speak, in favour of a more regulatory role. On this, see further subsection (v) below.

[35] Almost all contemporary jurisdictions that have developed RJ-style approaches have developed them more quickly and extensively for juveniles than they have for adults.

(ii) *Victims and moral clarification:* Sociologically speaking, the RJ movement can unquestionably be read as part of the 'victimological turn' in criminal justice policies in many jurisdictions since about 1960—a movement that has seen a host of innovations such as increases in victim compensation, victim impact statements, 'Victim Charters' and the like. Such movements can be, and have been, analysed in detail on a country-by-country basis, notably in the distinguished work of Paul Rock (1986, 1990). But for present purposes, perhaps a more macro-level, broad-brush explanation is of greater relevance to an understanding of the international growth of RJ.

Possibly the most interesting contribution in this regard has come from the Dutch criminologist Hans Boutellier (1996, 2000). In contemporary societies, sources of social trust typically shift from traditional, localised social groups and communities to a more individualised and technologically-based set of social arrangements. These developments tend to produce moral individualism and some moral relativism, which in turn mean that the criminal law 'cannot be legitimised any more by the self-evident moral cohesion of the community' (Boutellier, 1996: 15). Moreover, and as Durkheim (1901) long ago indicated, such moral shifts result in changes in the way in which we see crimes in contemporary societies—the crime is less often seen as an offence against the State (or collectivity), and more often as against the individual victim. In such a social context, the victim and his or her suffering can and does tend to become the organising focus for a new moral code that is simultaneously more individualistic and more concrete than its predecessors. Members of contemporary societies (especially younger members) can see the point of a moral code based on preventing the sufferings of a flesh-and-blood victim more easily then they can relate to the abstract violation of a traditional collective norm. Giving the victim a prominent role in the courtroom (or its equivalent) may therefore be a way of helping to 'find a criterion that draws a line on moral relativism and pluralism' (Boutellier, 1996: 15). RJ, on this reading, is therefore attractive as a social policy because it helps to provide an element of *normative clarification* in a morally changing society, struggling to develop a new 'positive morality' (Hart, 1963) for our times. (On morality, crime and criminal justice, see further Bottoms, 2002.)

In short, RJ, on this view, can be seen as helping to provide an attractive form of *moral clarification* and *moral pedagogy* (based on the suffering of the victim) to contemporary penal policymakers. And if that view is correct, then it becomes much easier to see why RJ has become structurally focussed especially on juveniles, the traditional subjects of moral pedagogy. The focus on juveniles also links back to the first possible explanation (based on the work of Kamenka and Tay), because juveniles are one group of offenders who many people would wish to see treated within a *gemeinschaft*, rather than a bureaucratic-administrative, policy approach.

A final comment may be made on Boutellier's thesis. His proposal is that there is a contemporary shift in perception of the nature of crimes, now seen less often as the violation of an abstract moral principle, and more often as a harm to a specific victim. Such a shift in perception, of course, would not only produce a 'victimological turn' in criminal justice, it would also encourage a shift away from perceiving incidents necessarily as 'crimes' at all. In other words, the previously-discussed 'civilisation thesis' might itself in part be the product of the kind of social changes to which Boutellier has drawn attention.

(iii) *The questionable legitimacy of courts*: In its origins, the RJ movement had links not only with the 'victim movement' but also with the 'informal justice' movement (on which see eg Abel, 1982; Matthews, 1988). Important reasons for the growth of the informal justice movement are well captured by Merry (1982: 17), in a passage that reminds one of Hulsman's emphasis on 'naturally occurring' restorative justice processes:

> The increasing urbanism, transiency, and heterogenity of American society in the twentieth century has undermined informal dispute settlement mechanisms rooted in home, church, and community and increased the demand for other means of dealing with family, neighbor, and community disputes. However, many legal experts argue that the formality of the courts, their adherence to an adversary model, their strict rules of procedure, and their reliance on adjudication render them inappropriate for handling many kinds of interpersonal quarrels arising in ongoing social relationships.

Since the early 1980s, the informal justice movement has lost some of its impetus,[36] though RJ has not. But the RJ movement, like the informal justice movement, has gained part of its strength from the perceived deficiencies of the courts. These deficiencies have also been more fully exposed owing to some macro-social developments to which we must now turn.

Those who have lived through the second half of the twentieth century in Western societies have witnessed a sustained period of economic growth, yet also the decline of manufacturing industry in most countries, as such goods can now be produced more cheaply in the low wage economies of developing societies. The apparent paradox of manufacturing decline despite sustained growth is explained, of course, by a massive switch into service industries in most Western economies, and by the stimulation of demand (through advertising and the like) for luxury goods, and for leisure and personal services. This rapid development of a *consumer* rather than a *producer* economy (to adopt the usual shorthand phrase) has cultural as well as economic consequences (see generally Lash and Urry 1994). In a service-led, consumer-oriented society, consumers have realised that they can make their demands assertively where they consider that the product is not up to standard. As is well known, they have learned to make such demands not only in their private purchasing, but also in relation

---

[36] Part of the reason for this loss of impetus probably lies in the decline in the influence of socialism since about 1990, and the linkage of socialist analyses with some aspects of the informal justice movement (see eg Cain, 1988). For an account of optimism and pessimism in the informal justice movement of the 1980s, see Matthews, (1988).

to public sector organisations such as schools, the police and (in Britain) the health service.

Two key issues that public organisations have had to address in response to these developments are demands for the enhanced *accountability* of professionals (who are no longer afforded the automatic deference that they once were); and, on occasion, demands for *lay participation* in decision-making. The growth of RJ appears to fit well with these sociological trends, since RJ typically uses a primarily lay and participatory forum, and tends to have a suspicion of professionals. Hence, it is not surprising that on the question of *procedural justice*—as developed in the work of Tom Tyler (1990) and others—both the RISE and the SAJJ research evaluations in Australia have produced very high ratings of satisfaction, among both offender and victim participants in RJ conferences, on questions such as having a proper chance to have one's say, and being treated with respect within the forum. In the RISE study, ratings for the conference samples on these variables were consistently higher than those for the court sample (for further details see Kathleen Daly's chapter in this volume).

These matters undoubtedly help to explain the worldwide growth of RJ, yet they perhaps do not explain it fully. For the advocates of RJ, it is ultimately what Kathleen Daly (2002; see also her chapter in this volume) has called the *restorative justice* elements of RJ (that is, the possibility of really engaging with and influencing the other party) that is substantially more important than the *procedural justice* elements of participation and so forth, important though these also are. Moreover, the 'participation/accountability' approach seems to offer little by way of explanation as to why RJ has become structurally concentrated in the youth justice sector. On balance, therefore, it seems likely that the doubtful legitimacy of courts in the contemporary era has been a contributory factor, rather than a major force, in the rapid development of RJ in the last quarter-century.

(iv) *Political contexts of contested legitimacy.* As is well known, the first jurisdiction to incorporate restorative justice processes into its justice system in a really major way was New Zealand with its 'family group conferences' (see Maxwell and Morris, 1993). It is sometimes asserted that family group conferences are a replication of Maori indigenous (pre-colonial) practice, but this is not the case (Maxwell and Morris, 1993: 4). Kathleen Daly (2002: 63) tells the story briefly:

> conferencing emerged in the 1980s, in the context of Maori political challenges to white New Zealanders and to their welfare and criminal justice systems. Investing decision-making practices with Maori cultural values meant that family groups (whanau) should have a greater say in what happens, that venues should be culturally appropriate, and that processes should accommodate a mix of culturally appropriate practices. New Zealand's minority group population includes not only the Maori but also Pacific Island Polynesians. Therefore, with the introduction of conferencing, came awareness of the need to incorporate different elements of 'cultural appropriateness' into the conference process. But the devising of a (white, bureaucratic) justice practice that is *flexible and accommodating* towards cultural differences does not mean that conferencing *is* an indigenous justice practice. (Emphasis in original).

Rather similar stories can be told for other jurisdictions. The Canadian 'sentencing circles', for example, are an attempt to provide a sentencing context that will be more culturally appropriate for the Canadian indigenous peoples.[37] In the rather different political context of Northern Ireland, following the so-called 'peace process' and the Good Friday Agreement of 1998, a formal Review of the Criminal Justice System was set up, designed to be acceptable to both principal communities (Unionist/Loyalist and Nationalist/Republican) in the jurisdiction. That review recommended the general development of RJ approaches for juvenile offenders, and the formal integration of RJ principles into the official juvenile justice system (Northern Ireland Office, 2000: chs 9 and 10), and subsequently these recommendations were accepted by the U.K. government (Northern Ireland Office, 2001).

What all the above jurisdictions share is the presence of a minority group of a significant size that has, over time, become significantly alienated from the official criminal justice system in the light of a colonialist or quasi-colonialist history. In each case, RJ processes now seem attractive to policymakers as a way of trying to heal past conflicts and wrongs, and to incorporate greater awareness of differing cultural traditions into the criminal (and especially juvenile) justice systems. It is not hard to see that such developments draw on at least two important features of RJ: these are, first, the reconciliatory elements in RJ philosophy; and secondly, the element of 'normative clarification' sometimes present in RJ-style fora, to which Christie (1977) drew attention long ago (see earlier section). This 'normative clarification' dimension, however, has its own dangers in a situation of seriously contested legitimacy, because the official policymakers' gesture of setting up RJ processes—within a State formation still dominated by the previous majority group—can easily be attacked as being insufficiently aware of cultural differences, insufficiently aware of the depth of the 'legitimacy deficit' (Beetham 1991) that the majority community's past actions have engendered, and so forth. Exactly such responses have sometimes been encountered in all of the jurisdictions mentioned above. Despite these continuing tensions, there seems little doubt that a political context of seriously contested legitimacy is, in the contemporary world, a powerful motivating factor (along with the other factors already discussed) that makes more likely—although, of course, not inevitable—the establishment of RJ-type processes.

(v) *The new regulatory state*: John Braithwaite (2000b) has proposed a very interesting additional explanatory suggestion concerning the rise of RJ. This suggestion arises out of the political science literature, and can be regarded as

---

[37] Restorative justice has also expanded rapidly in the various Australian jurisdictions, mostly but not exclusively in a juvenile justice context (see Daly and Hayes, 2001). However, while there are of course serious anxieties in Australia about the social exclusion of the aboriginal communities, and the over-representation of aboriginals in the criminal justice system, the rise of RJ in Australia—unlike the parallel process in New Zealand—mostly seems not to have occurred in direct response to aboriginal 'political challenges to white [settlers] and to their welfare and criminal justice systems' (Daly, 2002: 63).

potentially complementary to some of the earlier explanations discussed, notably explanations (i) and (ii) above.

Braithwaite follows Osborne and Gaebler (1992) in distinguishing between two possible approaches to the exercise of State power in society, namely 'rowing' (where, as in a rowing boat, the State does the principal work) and 'steering' (where, like a coxswain, the State provides direction, but the 'rowing' is done by others, notably private firms, voluntary agencies and local communities). In a somewhat overschematic, but nevertheless very heuristically useful discussion, Braithwaite suggests that in the last two hundred years we have witnessed three different types of State formation: *first*, the 'nightwatchman state', where 'most of the steering and rowing was done in civil society'; *secondly*, the Keynesian state, where the State did 'a lot of rowing, but was weak on steering civil society'; and *third* the new 'regulatory state', 'which holds up state steering and civil society rowing as the ideal' (Braithwaite, 2000b: 233). The shift from Keynesian to regulatory politics has involved massive privatisation of former State functions (from nationalised industries to policing and prisons), but also a pattern of insisting that individuals and groups should make provisions for their own welfare (a process sometimes described as 'responsibilisation'). Yet, in thus withdrawing from previous 'rowing' functions, the State has frequently set up 'regulators' whose task is to ensure that the public interest is protected: hence, the State offers a strong 'steering' guideline to markets and to civil society in the 'new regulatory state'.

From this perspective, contemporary RJ procedures—where, typically, people are asked to settle their own conflicts under the guidance of a State-appointed mediator or chairperson—can be viewed as an 'important manifestation of the new regulatory state in criminal justice' (Braithwaite, 2000b: 227). However, Braithwaite is uneasy about a policy of total State withdrawal in this area (save for the provision of the mediator), since he argues that in contemporary societies 'restorative justice founders when the welfare state is not there to support it' with appropriate services to victims and offenders (Braithwaite, 2000b: 233). He therefore concludes that what we should aspire to is a new regulatory state that is strong on steering, *combined with* a strong market economy and with 'communities in civil society that are . . . strong on both steering and rowing' (including indigenous dispute settlement), *combined with* State retention of certain 'Keynesian' rowing functions as a support to markets and to civil society.

Braithwaite's interesting analysis does, I believe, further help to explain the revival of some RJ-style practices in contemporary societies. As presented by Braithwaite, however, the analysis is somewhat less successful in explaining what I called (earlier in this section) the anomaly of the rise of RJ in the predominantly managerialist and control-oriented penal systems of contemporary Western societies (since many of these developments look distinctly like State 'rowing'). A possible development of Braithwaite's argument would, however, be to see the criminal justice in the era of the regulatory state as having a dual focus: a coercive, 'rowing-based', risk-focussed State criminal justice system for more serious and persistent criminality, and a delegation to local communities of the process of dealing with non-persistent, low level criminality.[38]

(vi) *Overview:* As I indicated at the beginning of this subsection, any answer to the question 'why has the influence of RJ spread so rapidly?' must be, in part, speculative, and I do not claim that the preceding analysis is in any sense definitive. Nevertheless, I think it is reasonable to claim that, at least on a preliminary basis, many of the explanations suggested here have some potential validity. RJ sceptics, in particular, need to come to terms with these matters, for their implication is that there are in contemporary advanced-urban societies some apparently plausible reasons for the revivication of RJ-related ideas. Policymakers, too, could perhaps benefit from considering some of the specific reasons that I have outlined, and reflecting upon how they relate to the development (and potential development) of RJ processes in their particular jurisdiction.

3. The Mechanisms of RJ in Contemporary Societies

Sally Merry (1982: 34), in her literature overview of mediation processes in pre-industrial societies, offered a warning about the simple transplantation of mediation practices from one social context to another:

> The efficacy of mediation depends on the existence of a cohesive, stable, morally integrated community whose powers of informal social control can be harnessed to informally achieved settlements . . . [But in contemporary America] disputants are rarely embedded in a close, cohesive social system where they need to maintain cooperative relationships. Evan when disputants come from the same neighborhood, unless they are integrated into a unitary social structure their conflicts in one relationship do not have repercussions for others.

The potential importance of this issue had, of course, already been raised by Christie (1977) in his landmark early paper (though with little precision about the social mechanisms involved). As we have seen, Christie's proposed solution was to try to revivify 'thick' social relationships in the neighbourhoods of contemporary cities; but there is little evidence that this has occurred. Not surprisingly, therefore, scepticism about the viability of RJ processes within contemporary urban contexts is a topic that has resurfaced fairly regularly in the RJ literature (see eg the recent textbook discussion in Johnstone, 2002: ch 3). RJ advocates tend to deal with this issue by offering three counter-arguments:

> *First*, while 'thick' social ties have diminished in contemporary societies, the nature of a globalised economy means that we are all now more socially interdependent with a larger number of other people than was the case in traditional societies;

---

[38] More than any other writer, Braithwaite (1999) has additionally drawn attention to the importance of RJ mechanisms in dealing with white-collar and corporate crime in contemporary societies. These developments, of course, fit extremely well with the 'regulatory state' thesis that Braithwaite (2000b) has also advanced; but they are not the principal concern of the present chapter.

Secondly, and relatedly, that while communitarian relationships *in neighbourhoods* have diminished, non-geographic relationships (fostered by the easy communication afforded by developments such as email) and 'communities of fate' (Braithwaite, 2000b) have flourished. Accordingly, for example, 'one cannot withdraw from the disapproval of one's international professional community by moving house' (Braithwaite, 1993: 14); *Thirdly*, that the communitarianism of RJ is an 'individual centred communitarianism that can work in a world of weak geographical communities', because it 'looks for community on many and any bases that can be built around a single person' (Braithwaite, 2000a: 122); and everyone has at least some community ties that can be used in support of RJ processes.

There is, of course, some prima facie merit in all of these arguments. However, the real issue is whether the *social mechanisms* of RJ (exemplified *par excellence* in the apology) can work in contemporary urban societies. Certainly they can work in international professional relationships and the like (see the second point above), but this is of very limited relevance to street crime, most perpetrators of which are anything but globalised in their social relationships (see Wiles and Costello, 2000). 'Interdependence' (see the first point) is in itself of very little significance; the issue is whether, in contemporary societies, adequate meso-social structures exist to support RJ-type approaches, and the social mechanisms on which successful reconciliation depends, and it is not obvious that globalised interdependence helps at all in these respects. Hence, at least for dealing with street crime, it is the third of the above arguments that is crucial. Here, the central point seems to be that while indeed *some* (perhaps vestigial) element of 'community' can be built around almost every single person, that 'community' might or might not be a strong enough social-structural base to make the social mechanisms of RJ work effectively.

If all this is correct, a corollary would seem to be that one would expect detailed empirical examinations of RJ in contemporary societies to show a very mixed picture, with (for example) apologies sometimes being received as sincere and sometimes not; sometimes a real meeting of hearts and minds among the participants, sometimes not; and so on. And that is, indeed, exactly what the current empirical evidence seems to show. Fortunately, however, there is no need for me to offer details of this evidence here, since the task has been very well accomplished elsewhere in this volume by Kathleen Daly (see also Daly, 2002).

V. CONCLUSION

Finally, I shall offer seven brief conclusions that can, I believe, reasonably be derived from the analysis in this chapter.

First, there seem to be some good sociological reasons for the growth of RJ in contemporary societies. Policymakers (and RJ sceptics) should take these matters seriously.

Secondly, for a number of reasons (including mainstream developments in contemporary penal systems, and the kinds of generative social mechanisms on which successful RJ depends) it is extremely unlikely that, in contemporary societies, RJ will ever completely replace existing criminal justice systems.

Thirdly, there remains among RJ advocates a significant lack of agreement as to whether the 'individual-centred communitarianism' of RJ should primarily offer a 'civil justice' or a more 'communitarian' vision of RJ.

Fourthly, the social mechanisms on which RJ depends work less well in contemporary than they do in traditional societies, because of the different social-structural context; hence, a 'blanket' delivery of RJ (to all cases in a given category) is always likely to achieve modest and/or patchy results in contemporary societies.

Fifthly, a version of informal RJ will always exist alongside the official criminal justice system, in families, schools, and so on (see the analysis by Hulsman).

Sixthly, and taking into account the previous five conclusions, a key policy debate (which has as yet barely begun) is that contemporary societies should start to consider seriously the kinds of case for which we might wish to develop formal RJ-type responses (and why), and the kinds of case in which we would prefer to retain standard criminal justice processes. For the kinds of case that we might wish to develop RJ approaches, we will need to specify the relative degree of emphasis on the 'private' and the 'communitarian' elements (a matter that might of course vary between different kinds of case).

Seventhly, in all these policy debates, we should always hold at the forefront of our minds the social mechanisms that apparently underpin successful social reconciliations, and the social structures that best support these social mechanisms.[39]

REFERENCES

Abel, RL (ed) (1982) *The Politics of Informal Justice*, 2 vols (Academic Press, New York).
Barnett, R (1977) 'Restitution: A New Paradigm of Criminal Justice' 87 *Ethics* 279–301.
Bauman, Z (1997) *Postmodernity and its Discontents* (Polity Press, Cambridge).
Beck, U (1992) *Risk Society: Towards a New Modernity* (Sage, London).
Beck, U, Giddens, A and Lash, S (1994) *Reflexive Modernization* (Polity Press, Cambridge).
Beetham, D (1991) *The Legitimation of Power* (Macmillan, London).
Bottoms, AE (1995) 'The Philosophy and Politics of Punishment and Sentencing' in C Clarkson and R Morgan (eds), *The Politics of Sentencing Reform* (Clarendon Press, Oxford).
—— (2002) 'Morality, Crime, Compliance and Public Policy' in AE Bottoms and M Tonry (eds), *Ideology, Crime and Criminal Justice* (Willan Publishing, Cullompton, Devon).
Bottoms, AE and Wiles, P (1996) 'Crime and Insecurity in the City' in C Fijnaut, J Goethals, T Peters and L Walgrave (eds), *Changes in Society, Crime and Criminal Justice in Europe: vol. 1: Crime and Insecurity in the City* (Kluwer Law International, Antwerp).

[39] I am most grateful to Jim Dignan for several clarificatory discussions, and for his comments on an earlier draft of this chapter. The chapter has also benefited from my conversations with Kathleen Daly, John Braithwaite and Paul Crosland. Of course, none of these colleagues should be held responsible for the final product.

Boutellier, H 'Beyond the Criminal Justice Paradox' (1996) 4(4) *European Journal on Criminal Policy and Research* 7–20.
—— (2000) *Crime and Morality: The Significance of Criminal Justice in Post-Modern Culture* (Kluwer Academic, Dordrecht).
Braithwaite, J (1989) *Crime, Shame and Reintegration* (Cambridge University Press, Cambridge).
—— (1993) 'Shame and Modernity' 33 *British Journal of Criminology* 1–18.
—— (1999) 'Restorative Justice: Assessing Optimistic and Pessimistic Accounts' 25 *Crime and Justice: A Review of Research* 1–127.
—— (2000a) 'Survey Article: Repentance Rituals and Restorative Justice' 8 *Journal of Political Philosophy* 115–31.
—— (2000b) 'The New Regulatory State and the Transformation of Criminology' 40 *British Journal of Criminology* 222–38.
Cain, M (1988) 'Beyond Informal Justice' in R Matthews (ed), *Informal Justice?* (Sage Publications, London).
Cantor, G (1976) 'An End to Crime and Punishment' 39 *The Shingle* (Philadelphia Bar Association) 99–114.
Christie, N (1977) 'Conflicts as Property' 17 *British Journal of Criminology* 1–15.
Daly, K (2002) 'Restorative Justice: The Real Story' 4 *Punishment and Society* 55–79.
Daly, K and Hayes, H (2001) *Restorative Justice and Conferencing in Australia* (Trends and Issues in Crime and Criminal Justice No 186) (Australian Institute of Criminology, Canberra).
Durkheim, E (1893) *De la Division du Travail Social* (Alcan, Paris) English translation: *The Division of Labour in Society* (Macmillan, Basingstoke 1984).
—— (1901) 'Deux Lois de l'Evolution Penale' 4 *L'Année Sociologique* 65–95. English translation: 'The Evolution of Punishment' in S Lukes and A Scull (eds), *Durkheim and the Law* (Martin Robertson, Oxford 1983).
Ericson, RV and Haggerty, KD (1997) *Policing the Risk Society* (Clarendon Press, Oxford).
Feeley, M and Simon, J (1992) 'The New Penology: Notes on the Emerging Strategy of Corrections and its Implications' 30 *Criminology* 449–74.
—— (1994) 'Actuarial Justice: The Emerging New Criminal Law' in D Nelken (ed), *The Futures of Criminology* (Sage, London).
Fry, M (1951) *Arms of the Law* (Victor Gollancz, London).
Garland, D (2001) *The Culture of Control* (Oxford University Press, Oxford).
Giddens, A (1990) *The Consequences of Modernity* (Polity Press, Cambridge).
—— (1991) *Modernity and Self-Identity* (Polity Press, Cambridge).
Gulliver, PH (1963) *Social Control in an African Society: A Study of the Arusha* (Routledge & Kegan Paul, London).
Hann, C (2000) *Social Anthropology* (Hodder & Stoughton, London).
Hart, HLA (1963) *Law, Liberty and Morality* (Oxford University Press, London).
Harvey, D (1989) *The Condition of Postmodernity: An Enquiry into the Origins of Cultural Change* (Basil Blackwell, Oxford).
Hedström, P and Swedborg, R (1996) 'Social Mechanisms' 39 *Acta Sociologica* 281–308.
Hulsman, LHC (1981) 'Penal Reform in the Netherlands: Part I—Bringing the Criminal Justice System under Control' 20 *Howard Journal of Penology and Crime Prevention* 150–59.
—— (1982) 'Penal Reform in the Netherlands: Part II—Reflections on a White Paper Proposal' 21 *Howard Journal of Penology and Crime Prevention* 35–47.

Hulsman, LHC (1986) 'Critical Criminology and the Concept of Crime' 10 *Contemporary Crises* 63–80.

—— (1991) 'The Abolitionist Case: Alternative Crime Policies' 25 *Israel Law Review*.

James, A and Raine, J (1998) *The New Politics of Criminal Justice* (Longman, London).

Johnstone, G (2002) *Restorative Justice: Ideas, Values, Debates* (Willan Publishing, Cullompton, Devon).

Kamenka, E and Tay, AES (1975) 'Beyond Bourgeois Individualism: The Contemporary Crisis in Law and Legal Ideology' in E Kamenka and RS Neale (eds), *Feudalism, Capitalism and Beyond* (Edward Arnold, London).

—— (1980a) 'Social Traditions, Legal Traditions' in E Kamenka and AES Tay (eds), *Law and Social Control* (Edward Arnold, London).

—— (1980b) ' "Transforming" the Law, "Steering" Society' in E Kamenka and AES Tay (eds), *Law and Social Control* (Edward Arnold, London).

Karp, DR (1998) 'The Judical and Judicious Use of Shame Penalties' 44 *Crime and Delinquency* 277–94.

Lash, S and Urry, J (1994) *Economies of Signs and Space* (Sage Publications, London).

Longman, (1984) *Longman Dictionary of the English Language* (Longman, Harlow, Essex).

Lukes, S (1973) *Emile Durkheim: His Life and Work* (Allen Lane The Penguin Press, London).

Lupton, D (1999) *Risk* (Routledge, London).

MacCormick, N (1981) *H. L. A. Hart* (Edward Arnold, London).

Marshall, T and Merry, S (1990) *Crime and Accountability: Victim/Offender Mediation in Practice* (HMSO, London).

Matthews, R (1988) 'Reassessing Informal Justice' in R Matthews (ed), *Informal Justice?* (Sage Publications, London).

Maxwell, G and Morris, AM (1993) *Family, Victims and Culture: Youth Justice in New Zealand* (Social Policy Agency and Victoria University of Wellington, Wellington, NZ).

Merry, SE (1982) 'The Social Organization of Mediation in Nonindustrial Societies: Implications for Informal Community Justice in America' in RL Abel (ed), *The Politics of Informal Justice: vol 2, Comparative Studies* (Academic Press, New York).

Northern Ireland Office, (2000) *Review of the Criminal Justice System in Northern Ireland* (The Stationery Office, Belfast).

—— (2001) *Criminal Justice Review: Implementation Plan* (The Stationery Office, Belfast).

Osborne, D and Gaebler, T (1992) *Reinventing Government* (Addison-Wesley, New York).

Parkin, F (1982) *Max Weber* (Ellis Horwood, Chichester and Tavistock Publications, London).

Roberts, S (1979) *Order and Dispute: An Introduction to Legal Anthropology* (Penguin Books, Harmondsworth, Middlesex).

Robinson, G (2002) 'Exploring Risk Management in Probation Practice: Contemporary Developments in England and Wales' 4 *Punishment and Society* 5–25.

Rock, P (1986) *A View from the Shadows: The Ministry of the Solicitor General of Canada and the Making of the Justice for Victims of Crime Initiative* (Clarendon Press, Oxford).

—— (1990) *Helping Victims of Crime: The Home Office and the Rise of Victim Support in England and Wales* (Clarendon Press, Oxford).

Ryan, J (1995) *Doing Things the Right Way: Dene Traditional Justice in Lac La Martre, NWT* (University of Calgary Press and Arctic Institute of North America, Calgary).

Tavuchis, N (1991) *Mea Culpa: A Sociology of Apology and Reconciliation* (Stanford University Press, Stanford, California).

Tyler, TR (1990) *Why People Obey the Law* (Yale University Press, New Haven, Connecticut).

von Hirsch, A (1993) *Censure and Sanctions* (Clarendon Press, Oxford).

Weber, M (1949) *The Methodology of the Social Sciences* (Free Press, New York).

Wiles, P and Costello, A (2000) *The 'Road to Nowhere': The Evidence for Travelling Criminals* (Home Office Research Study No. 207) (Home Office, London).

Zehr, H (1990) *Changing Lenses: A New Focus for Crime and Justice* (Herald Press, Scottdale, Pennsylvania).

6

Restoration and Retribution in International Criminal Justice: An Exploratory Analysis

Paul Roberts*

I. RESTORATIVE JUSTICE INTERNATIONAL

Restorative Justice (RJ) is an international phenomenon. Cultural borrowing, cross-fertilisation of ideas and practices between jurisdictions, and—more recently—explicitly supra-national initiatives (Van Ness and Nolan, 1998; Van Ness, this volume) are prominent characteristics of the RJ movement. RJ has attracted an international fellowship of exceptionally committed, able and hard-working practitioners and advocates across three continents. The motives of politicians who embrace RJ-inspired reforms are, inevitably, always open to question. But amongst others whose motivation is not in doubt, RJ is invested with the most extravagant hopes for penal (and broader social) transformations (eg Fatić, 1995: chapter 8; cf Daly and Immarigeon, 1998) and commands practitioners' deep loyalty and affection.

Any reasonable explanation of the rise and rise of RJ must surely give serious consideration to the possibility that RJ is both valuable and timely. Part of RJ's immediate appeal lies in its association with intuitively attractive ideas of empowerment, democracy, community, autonomy, healing, reconciliation, and crime reduction. These positive virtues draw further, negative reinforcement from all we now know about the harmfulness and failure, of existing criminal justice systems in general, and of prisons in particular. The timeliness of RJ, in other words, is a function of enduring moral principles of human flourishing and social organisation, and recent crises in penal administration. New recruits are likely to be plentiful wherever the depressingly predictable pattern of penal failure, common to many western democracies, is found: rising crime *and* rising expenditure on policing and criminal process; prevalent fear of crime; high rates of recidivism; an increasingly punitive penal climate fuelled by populist media and reactionary policy-making; prejudice and discrimination, on grounds of race, class and

* I am indebted to all the organisers and participants of the Cambridge and Toronto colloquia for enlightenment in the ways of RJ. Particular thanks are due to Andrew Ashworth and Rob Cryer for comments on previous drafts, and to Kathy Daly for being a supportive discussant.

gender; police brutality and corruption; shameful conditions of penal confinement. When things are so bad, it might reasonably be felt, there is little to be lost, and yet much that might be gained, from radical innovation (cf Zedner, 1994). It is a sure sign that something of great significance is occurring, at all events, when the Chief Constable of Thames Valley Police starts promoting Canadian sentencing circles as a model for re-orientating English penal process towards a victim-centred approach (Pollard, 2000).

If RJ's current appeal is readily explicable, however, deeper issues of justification, priority and implementation remain unresolved. Are the philosophy and practice of RJ compatible with traditional penal thinking, or is radical revision in the basic objectives and structure of criminal process and punishment required? Is RJ a supplement to traditional criminal process, or its (partial) substitution? Does RJ operate at the margins of a penal system, or aspire to be its centre of gravity? What are the normative and practical constraints on RJ-inspired policy and practice? Fundamental objectives, moral values and juridical limits are now receiving closer attention, both from advocates and from critics of RJ. But the discussion to date, like most debates on penal affairs, has largely been restricted to RJ's status and impact in particular national jurisdictions. Domestic preoccupations have engendered (some) reflection on issues of multiculturalism within states, but have rarely incorporated explicitly international or comparative (cf Miers, 2001) dimensions.

Their omission is regrettable. An exclusively municipal focus is estranged from experiences and developments in the international arena, almost in defiance of RJ's patently international pedigree. The traditional state-centred (or state-obsessed?) approach, which characterises the greater part of criminology as well as legal studies, fails to register significant trends towards internationalisation in modern domestic legal orders, with the countervailing vice that the supra-national potential of penological innovations like RJ remains largely unrealised. In a tentative and impressionist effort to glimpse beyond conventional disciplinary horizons, this chapter refracts some of RJ's foundational claims and presuppositions through the prism of an emerging new penological and jurisprudential sub-specialism, for which 'International Criminal Justice' is the most appropriate rubric, and ICrimJ the best abbreviation.[1] ICrimJ is too raw and recently-minted to have agreed conceptual boundaries, settled subject-matter or conventional taxonomy. A key task for the following two sections is to provide some basic pointers—a *definition* would be strained and redundant here—to the essential content and contours of the discipline, as a basis for further reflections on RJ developed through case studies in the second half of the chapter.

ICrimJ retains that vitality and innocence that older disciplines tend to forfeit through torpor and ossification. The sense that 'everything is up for grabs' invigorates ICrimJ as an intellectual pursuit, and often seems to propel much of its policy

---

[1] ICJ already being the accepted abbreviation for the International Court of Justice.

and practice (albeit with uneven implications: the novelty and contingency which fire classroom debate are less welcome in the courtroom, or on the battlefield). When the familiar props, crutches, and well-rehearsed scripts and catchphrases of penal argument are stripped away, scholars and policymakers alike are forced to confront afresh the most basic existential questions of objective and motivation. In short order ICrimJ demands renewed meditation on the fundamentals of criminal process and retributive punishment. And beyond these perennial—but frequently ill-attended—questions, prominent recent developments, including the work of the UN's *ad hoc* criminal tribunals for the Former Yugoslavia (ICTY) and Rwanda (ICTR) and the Rome Statute for an International Criminal Court (ICC), bear strong RJ resonances, and some modest influences and inputs.

II. INTERNATIONAL CRIMINAL JURISPRUDENCE

When in due course ICrimJ spawns treatise and canon, the dynamic tension between peace, security, truth, justice and reconciliation will be their organising principle. A less ambitious initial approach to ICrimJ is to stake out its *juridical* constitution. The jurisprudence of ICrimJ is a worthy point of departure, since it immediately confronts us with the agitated morphology of modern legality (generally, see Twining, 2000: chapters 6 and 7; Harding, 2000).

For its positive legal content, ICrimJ draws most directly and most heavily on public international law (PIL), and in particular on the laws of war, generally known today as international humanitarian law (IHL). This comprises the treaty and customary law, significantly developed in the Nuremberg and Tokyo war crimes trials, as well as the Geneva Conventions 1949 and their associated Protocols (Sassòli and Bouvier, 1999). IHL finds limited application in peacetime, and has traditionally been restricted to 'international' armed conflicts (thus excluding civil wars and other 'internal' conflict situations from its aegis). Nonetheless, even in dualist countries where PIL is at best a secondary source of law, the impact of globalisation is being felt in the increasing penetration of supra-national norms and institutions into domestic legal practice. Most western powers, including the United Kingdom, are signatories to major multilateral treaties, including the Genocide Convention and the various suppression conventions relating, inter alia, to torture, drug-trafficking and international terrorism (see Sunga, 1997: chapters 2 and 3). The old concepts and theories, of state sovereignty and mutually exclusive legal orders, are being shunted into anachronism by the juridical realities of the modern world. Especially in the guise of EC/EU criminal law (see Baker, 1998; Peers, 2000), ICrimJ is beginning to exert a direct and potentially extensive influence on the legal jurisdictions of the United Kingdom (and of course on the other 14 Member States of the EU).

After IHL and EC/EU law (and in various ways overlapping with them), a third significant strand of ICrimJ is contributed by international human rights law (IHRL: generally, see Steiner and Alston, 2000). Rule-of-law restrictions on the deprivation of individual liberty and familiar bundles of fair trial rights are main-stays of IHRL treaties (including the UN's flagship International Covenant on Civil and Political Rights), widely replicated in modern national constitutions and codes of criminal procedure (Bassiouni, 1993). IHRL imposes limitations on municipal criminal justice practice and reform, limitations which, moreover, cannot easily be renegotiated or disavowed at the behest of national authorities. This realisation has a particular local charge for English lawyers after October 2000, when the European Convention on Human Rights (ECHR) became a (sup-plementary) source of domestic English law under the Human Rights Act 1998 (HRA). The HRA should in some respects provide a boost to RJ-inspired policies and practices, inasmuch as it may guarantee certain process rights to victims of crime and their families (Emmerson and Ashworth, 2001: chapter 18; Wadham and Arkinstall, 2000). At the same time, however, the HRA will also place new, and perhaps progressively stringent, constraints on deviations from traditional criminal process. Whilst firm predictions would be premature, existing Strasbourg (ECtHR) jurisprudence contains enough clues to infer a battery of Convention-based arguments utilising Articles 3, 5, 6 and 7 that, were they to find favour with the judges, could fetter RJ initiatives. Employing the common law precedential method, and unrestrained by any European 'margin of appreciation', English judges might well give (some) Convention rights greater definition and bite under the 1998 Act than the ECtHR would ever be empowered, or inclined, to achieve through direct application of the Convention. This potential has already been realised in one notable case concerning Article 6(2)'s presumption of innocence (see Roberts, 2002).

National criminal, criminal procedure (including evidence), sentencing, and penal laws constitute a fourth bundle of ICrimJ norms. National laws replicate, transpose, replenish, overlap with, reinforce, and execute PIL norms, or yet may contradict, undermine, or otherwise frustrate them, with simultaneous (not nec-essarily co-ordinated, sometimes wholly unanticipated) legal consequences in multiple legal systems, and with diffuse and often unpredictable effects. Modern legality breeds horizontal complexity—different strands of PIL intersect and overlap, for example—compounding the unmistakable, albeit uneven and differ-entiated, globalising processes of vertical integration in legal and political systems. National legal systems' contributions to ICrimJ are too extensive, various and sub-stantial to recount in brief survey (for examples, see Wexler, 1994; Marschik, 1997; Wenig, 1997; Triggs, 1997; Williams, 1997; Hirsch, 2001). A fifth generic source of ICrimJ norms is more illustrative for present purposes.

In addition to the better-known ICrimJ-related sources of PIL and IHRL norms, there is now an accumulating corpus of 'soft law' international instru-ments relating to penal affairs, emanating in particular from the UN,[2] the EU[3] and

---

[2] See *Compendium of United Nations Standards and Norms in Crime Prevention and Criminal Justice*, excerpted in Bassiouni (1994), and on-line at http://www.uncjin.org/Standards/compendium.pdf.
[3] Eg 2001/220/JHA, EU Council Framework Decision on the Standing of Victims in Criminal Proceedings, OJ 2001 L 82/1, Eur-Lex doc 301F0220.

the Council of Europe, to which sponsoring governments should have regard in the development of related domestic policies. Most of these international commitments and obligations are not directly enforceable in English criminal proceedings, and in some cases do not even give rise to enforceable obligations in international law. Cynically, one might dismiss such measures as empty rhetoric with no bearing on RJ's municipal aspirations. Yet if we grant our political leaders and their vaunted ethical foreign policy an ounce of integrity, we should also insist that integrated, joined-up government must strive to co-ordinate the foreign policy right hand and the home affairs left into coherent, concerted penal action. A conscientious administration would bring domestic arrangements into conformity with international agreements, or else explicitly renounce inconsistent international policies and suffer consequent loss of standing amongst the community of nations.

Pertinent international treaties and other instruments repeatedly endorse restitution, compensation, mediation and victims' process rights. Indeed, the UN's *Basic Principles of Justice for Victims* states that '[i]nformal mechanisms for the resolution of disputes, including mediation, arbitration and customary justice or indigenous practises, should be utilised where appropriate to facilitate conciliation and redress for victims' (para 7: see above, n 2). Yet in other respects even soft law international legal commitments should temper RJ-inspired policies and practices in domestic criminal proceedings. The Council of Europe Recommendation on *Mediation in Penal Matters*,[4] for example, promotes victim-offender mediation within a robust framework of procedural safeguards. More generally, there would be a troubling lack of consistency in, say, diverting juvenile rapists to domestic sentencing circles yet insisting that young soldiers who commit rape during armed conflict, perhaps under extreme duress, should be tried and punished as war criminals. Such inconsistency would expose government policy to charges of incoherence and hypocrisy, which can only be answered by identifying defensible distinctions between the objectives, modalities or pragmatics of international as opposed to municipal criminal justice (assuming that the levels and fora of justice are genuinely discontinuous: cf the Kantian position reviewed by Waltz, 1962).

III. INTERNATIONAL CRIMINAL JUSTICE

Any discussion of the juridical constitution of ICrimJ should be balanced by a health warning against *positivitis*, the peculiarly juristic tunnel vision induced by exclusive preoccupation with doctrinal technicalities. For all its stubbornly (and gloriously) irreducible depth and sophistication, international criminal *law* is only part of the picture: serious engagement with international criminal *justice*,

---

[4] Committee of Ministers Recommendation No R(99) 19 Concerning Mediation in Penal Matters (15 Sept 1999), on-line at http://cm.coe.int/ta/rec/1999/99r19.htm.

whether in its predominantly theoretical or practical registers, requires sympathetic appreciation of the political, social and cultural contexts of legality, and therefore also of its historical and philosophical foundations.

The international legal order, personified in the United Nations Organisation (UN) and its Charter, does not embrace criminal justice as its primary concern or objective. International peace and security rank highest on the UN's explicit list of priorities. More fundamentally, the UN and the international community at large are committed to promoting human flourishing by safeguarding the vital interests of individual human beings. IHRL is the principal juridical instrument adapted to this end, but the preferential status of individual rights is balanced— or we might better say *enriched*—by international legal agreements devoted to the promotion and protection of the social groups, cultural practices and natural environments that afford context, form and sustenance to material human existence. This is entirely as it should be in any community, whether local, municipal, international, or global. A community formed solely or primarily to enforce the criminal law would provide a thin basis for sociability and human flourishing. Indeed, we would probably have gone past the point where anything was worth saving if human societies ever became so preoccupied with criminal justice that they devoted themselves exclusively to penal objectives.

Yet it is a fact of life that state members of the international community sometimes shirk their responsibilities and inflict unjustified harm on neighbouring states,[5] or on their own peoples, just as individuals and groups trespass against their municipal neighbours. At a minimum, everyone agrees that miscreants must be brought into line, lest they ruin things for everybody by destroying the planet. But opinions divide sharply as to what should be done, and for what reasons. On these questions there have been recent, and rapid, developments which shed interesting light on the topics of this volume.

For most of the modern period (which international lawyers conventionally date to the rise of the nation state after the Peace of Westphalia in 1648) international criminal justice has been eclipsed by international diplomacy (McCormack, 1997 provides a useful potted history). Powerful nation states claimed exclusive territorial authority over the prescription and enforcement of criminal law within their own national borders, refused to submit to external authority in such matters (except unwillingly, through war or annexation), and paid the mutual compliment of staying off each other's national turf, unless a state's own nationals happened to be involved as offenders or, later and more controversially, as victims of crime. Throughout this period there is evidence of occasional, uncoordinated and unsystematic attempts to secure a kind of international criminal justice, but without permanent and powerful supra-national institutions or, crucially, the political will to demand that justice be done, little of lasting significance could be achieved. Fast-forwarding to the more recent past, the failure of the Treaty of

---

[5] In a globalising world of the internet and smart bombs, 'neighbouring states' are any other states in the world.

Versailles 1919 as a penal instrument marks the twentieth century's darkest days for international criminal justice, representing, as it did, the almost complete subordination of the pursuit of justice to the machinations of international diplomacy. By mid-century, and despite the jurisprudential landmark of Nuremberg, commentators were saying that the whole notion of international criminal law was utopian nonsense, a 'contradiction in terms' (Schwarzenberger, 1950: 295), a dead duck beyond resuscitation.

But the idea did not die; far from it. Nurtured through the unpropitious years of the Cold War by a handful of enthusiasts in the law schools and the International Law Commission, the cause of international criminal justice spectacularly re-emerged in the 1990s with a potency that must have surpassed the expectations of even its most optimistic advocate. UN-sponsored *ad-hoc* tribunals to try war criminals in the Balkans and *genocidaires* in Rwanda, still fully operational today, were followed by the adoption of a Statute for a permanent International Criminal Court (ICC) at a conference of plenipotentiaries in Rome in 1998 (McGoldrick, 1999). When ten states simultaneously ratified the Rome Statute in April 2002, the required total of 60 ratifications were exceeded, and the Statute duly entered into force on 1 July 2002. In the meantime, initiatives such as the trial of the *Lockerbie* suspects in the Netherlands and the furore surrounding the extradition of the former Chilean dictator Pinochet (Webber, 1999) have kept the topic of international criminal justice in the media eye, which in turn has raised public awareness and made references to 'international (criminal) law' a staple of informed political commentary and debate. The terrible events of 'September 11' and the ensuing hunt for Osama bin Laden have intensified these developments, and put paid to any prospect of US isolationism (though not necessarily unilateralism).

The longevity and remarkable tenacity of the aspiration to international criminal justice, as well as ICrimJ's rapid progress once favourable political conditions allowed, may hold some important lessons for domestic criminal process in general, and for RJ-inspired initiatives in particular. This story of ultimate triumph over centuries of false starts and setbacks attests, I suggest, to the deep-seated conviction that particular types of harm, marked out as crimes, should call forth particular forms of organised social response: public trials of guilt followed by sanctions calibrated to communicate an offender's blameworthiness. It is increasingly clear, moreover, that part of the rationale for such responses is the intrinsic value and importance of censuring wrongful conduct, in the correct way and to the right degree, whatever additional collateral benefits might also be in view (for philosophical underpinnings, see especially, Duff, this volume; Moore, 1997: chapters 2–4; Murphy and Hampton, 1988; von Hirsch, 1993). This clarity is admittedly clouded by the fact that Chapter VII of the UN Charter, from which the ICTY and ICTR derive their legal authority, is couched in terms of peace and security, not doing justice; and it is fair comment that President Bush's talk of bringing back bin Laden 'dead or alive' evokes more of the Wild Western posse than the formal solemnities of justice. Nonetheless, it is evident from official statements of the Tribunals' objectives,[6] as well as from the Tribunals' legal framework and practice, that their mission is to restore peace and security *by* doing justice (see eg Akhavan, 1997). UN Secretary General Kofi Annan (1997: 365) has encapsulated this policy in memorable idiom:

> Peace and justice are indivisible. They are indivisible in the former Yugoslavia, in Rwanda, and in all post-conflict situations where the dawn of peace must begin with the light of justice.

Nor can rapid recent developments be dismissed as the latest, more cunningly camouflaged, manifestation of *realpolitik*. Even if the new 'war on terrorism' is primarily an artefact of American self-interest (a proposition lacking neither evidence nor adherents, but too cut-and-dried for my tastes), there is scarcely any better explanation for the international community's involvement in otherwise uninteresting, economically insignificant regions, than the ethical foreign policy desire to promote regional security by bringing international criminals and perpetrators of crimes against humanity to justice. Let it not be forgotten that the latest wave of activity leading to the Rome Statute was initiated by Caribbean states, minnows of international diplomacy and geopolitics, aided and abetted by NGOs endowed with no greater political leverage than the moral argument to persuade, or shame, nation states into living up to their own rhetoric of justice and rights. And though the ICTR, as constituted, disappointed Rwanda's post-genocide political administration (partly for the dubious reasons recounted below), that should not eclipse the significant fact that Rwanda initially begged the international community to intervene, and that equal treatment for (black) Africans was part of the clinching argument. Meanwhile, the ICC bandwagon rolls on, over the objections of the world's last superpower (Wedgwood, 1999 and 2001)—though one should add, with the wise poultry farmer's caution, that it remains to be seen whether anything concrete will ever materialise if the USA cannot be persuaded to climb on board or at least allow itself, sullen and grumbling, to be dragged along behind.

The form, as well as the fact, of international penal developments merits emphasis in the present discussion. For the Statutes constituting the *ad hoc* Tribunals and the ICC faithfully reproduce, with the endorsement of the entire international community,[7] an ideal-typical model of criminal process incorporating the foundational elements on which modern domestic criminal justice systems converge. This mutually reinforcing, overlapping consensus[8] of national and supra-national norms represents the best practically conceivable foundation

---

[6] Full documentation is available on-line: http://www.un.org/icty/; and http://www.ictr.org/.

[7] This is part of the response to objections that ideal models of criminal process are a peculiarly 'western' or 'Christian' or 'bourgeois' etc construction. History and cultural tradition, certainly, demand proper respect. But history and cultural tradition are contested and changing, and must today be read against the homogenising influences of globalisation.

[8] Terminology and associated ideas transparently lifted from Rawls (1987), with the caveat that I remain unclear in my own mind how much of a Rawlsian (which Rawls?) I want to be.

for both the legitimacy and the political stability of international criminal justice. Subjective culpability, rule of law values, the presumption of innocence, adversarial defence rights, independent and impartial adjudication, and humane and proportionate punishment—what might be described as the *normative core* of criminal process—are all explicitly guaranteed (cf Bhattacharyya, 1996).

The long and recently eventful story of international criminal justice can thus be seen to underscore both the indispensability of retributive (blaming) sanctions for criminal wrongs, and the precipitation of a maturing international consensus on the proper form of criminal process. If these developments should exert a generalised downward pressure on RJ enthusiasts' aspirations, however, other aspects of contemporary ICrimJ practice bear a more positive message for RJ. The traditional (international) law paradigm of retributive justice has not gone unchallenged by informed ICrimJ observers and participants. A minority has even expressly invoked RJ principles as a model for international penal policy and practice.

Turning now to more specific case studies, the next section re-evaluates rival conceptions of justice in the crucible of the Rwandan genocide of 1994, before focusing in Section V on *reconciliation*, a bundle of associated ideals, objectives and practices which, I will suggest, are RJ's first cousins in ICrimJ. This section features South Africa's Truth and Reconciliation Commission (SA TRC) as a paradigmatic alternative to criminal prosecution for serious and systematic human rights violations. Although first and foremost a domestic affair, the TRC was also of intense concern to the international community, since—and this is a familiar pattern in post-conflict situations—*regional* peace and security were riding on its outcome. As Kadar Asmal (2000: 3) observes, 'it is in fact impossible to separate large international questions of war and peace from seemingly local matters of civil disorder.'

IV. JUSTICE AFTER GENOCIDE

In 1994 some 800,000 Rwandans—about 10 per cent of the total population—were systematically slaughtered in a carefully orchestrated, mercilessly executed genocide. The dead were mostly of the minority Tutsi population who, through western colonial occupation, had became Rwanda's political and social elite. Their killers were Hutus, the formerly disenfranchised majority. The international community's—belated—response to this atrocity was the creation of a second *ad hoc* criminal tribunal, the ICTR, on the model pioneered in the previous year to deal with Balkan war crimes (including the genocidal policy of 'ethnic cleansing'). The ICTR's distinctive mandate is to support the efforts of Rwanda's domestic criminal process in convicting and punishing the perpetrators of genocide. A foundational assumption, notably prominent in the recitals of UN Security Council Resolution 955/94 establishing the ICTR, is that lasting peace and security imply (retributive) justice:

Expressing once again its grave concern at the reports indicating that genocide and other systematic, widespread and flagrant violations of international humanitarian law have been committed in Rwanda,
Determining that this situation continues to constitute a threat to international peace and security,
Determined to put an end to such crimes and to take effective measures to bring to justice the persons who are responsible for them,
Convinced that in the particular circumstances of Rwanda, the prosecution of persons responsible for serious violations of international humanitarian law would enable this aim to be achieved and would contribute to the process of national reconciliation and to the restoration and maintenance of peace,
Believing that the establishment of an international tribunal for the prosecution of persons responsible for genocide and the other above-mentioned violations of international humanitarian law will contribute to ensuring that such violations are halted and effectively redressed . . .

The Security Council's belief that penal justice must pave the way for 'national reconciliation and . . . the restoration and maintenance of peace,' and deter future atrocities, is echoed in the reported statements of Rwandan victims and officials. Chief prosecutor Gerald Gahima told a *Guardian* reporter:

'Of course, we cannot kill all those who deserve to die, it would not stabilise our society. But in the aftermath of genocide there was an overwhelming feeling that there must be accountability, people must be punished so it will not happen again' (quoted in Brittain, 2001).

Several hundred *genocidaires* have been tried in Rwanda's domestic criminal courts, where the death penalty is mandated for those found to have planned and orchestrated the genocide. Executions have been performed in football stadia, before packed houses and in a carnival atmosphere. A Spanish journalist was present when the first four convicts were executed in April 1998 (eighteen further executions took place elsewhere on the same day):

From early morning thousands of ordinary people began converging on the football ground where the Kigali executions would take place. They were driven by that atavistic fury that goes back to the times when human beings moved in packs and ate raw meat. There were women dressed in their Sunday best, men in suits, beggars, businessmen and children, above all, children. There were probably more than 100,000 people. Some had clambered into trees, others on to traffic lights. Most were squashed together pushing, protesting, dodging the blows of the police in a desperate attempt to get a better view. . . . The crowd was growing impatient when two white four-wheel drive vehicles arrived at one side of the field. At first no-one paid any attention. Then, suddenly, the doors opened and five young men wearing the blue uniform of the municipal police tore out of them with black masks over their faces and Kalashnikovs in their hands. They headed quickly for the stakes and, when they were a meter away, opened fire. . . . The spectators, who up to then had been silent, anxious and expectant, went wild. Many of them ran to the stakes to see the blood close up, others shouted and screamed and the whole affair began to take on the air of a festival. 'Justice has been done. But it is not enough,' a man with a long scar on his face said. 'It would have been better to cut off their fingers one by one and kill them slowly the way they killed our children.' . . . The Rwandan president, Pasteur Bizimungu . . . has emphasised that the executions are intended only as a 'lesson' to those that kill the innocent. 'We are not sadists,' he said. 'But it is necessary for justice to be done' (Rojo, 1998).

Parallels between President Bizimungu's statement and stock justifications of retributive justice are easily drawn, and may be seized on by RJ enthusiasts as confirmation of the moral bankruptcy of retributivism. However, the sickening spectacle of Rwandan executions, which, I agree, represents the betrayal of justice, fundamental rights and respect for human dignity, does not refute the retributive ideal, but rather offers a graphic illustration of its susceptibility to corruption, indeed thoroughgoing perversion, from a measured, institutionalised reckoning with criminal wrongdoing, into manic, depraved revenge. It confronts us with the stark realisation—too little credited by penal philosophers, in my estimation— that proportionate censure is difficult to communicate effectively, even for a wise and well-motivated polity. (Demagogues fond of stoking the fires of populist punitiveness need not even apply.)

The ICTR has encountered related difficulties, though it boasts the acme of international criminal due process and impressive liberal credentials—the death penalty was withheld from the Tribunal over the vociferous objections of the Rwandese authorities and to the approbation of international penal reformers (eg Schabas, 1996). Obstacles to effective communication, which in western democracies may be subtly camouflaged or partially sublimated, in the Rwandan context are easily identifiable. The ICTR has its seat in Arusha, Tanzania. To the Rwandan populace, who are mostly poor, illiterate, lack basic amenities, and are struggling to rebuild some kind of life for themselves in the aftermath of the most horrific slaughter imaginable, the ICTR must seem an impossibly abstract entity, operating in a foreign country, according to unfamiliar rules and procedures, generating precious few and long-awaited verdicts, which anyway appear anomalous by national penal standards. Few ordinary Rwandans will have seen or even know about the work of the ICTR, and fewer still must care. In these political, socio-economic and cultural circumstances it is questionable whether the ICTR is capable of communicating *any* message to the Rwandan people. It defies credulity to suggest that the subtleties of retributive justice are being conveyed effectively.

Communicating penal messages to suspects, defendants, and convicts is no less fraught, or crucial. Responsibility for the genocide is routinely denied by its undoubted perpetrators; indeed many accused dispute that genocide even occurred. Denials are maintained in the teeth of ample evidence that perhaps a million Hutus directly participated in brutal slaughter at close quarters, hacking at prone and defenceless human prey with knives, clubs, and machetes. Many more besides assisted or looked on. In a sense, the killing has been normalised— everybody did it, and if nobody is innocent, none can be singled out as guilty. Moreover, circumstances conspire to nurture and reinforce these brazen inversions of moral scruple. The Rwandan criminal justice system is hopelessly ill-equipped to detain, prosecute and try the 120,000 suspects held on remand these past seven years. Characterising the situation as 'sclerotic,' Drumbl (2000a) estimates that at the present rate of progress it would take hundreds of years to clear the backlog of cases. Meanwhile, imprisoned together in appalling conditions and with no real prospect of release, the detainees nurse their ethnic hatreds and confirm each other in the conviction that, once again, it is they who are the real victims, of Tutsi political oppression. Set against this penal and political backdrop, it is easier to comprehend the chilling words of Jean-Paul Akayesu on becoming the ICTR's first convict: 'Although the decision of my guilt has already been taken, I am sure in my heart that I am not guilty.'

Retributive messages can only be conveyed successfully to those whose ears, and hearts, are open to receive them. It does not follow, however, that attempts to reach Akayesu, and others like him, should not be made. For it is sometimes necessary and worthwhile to say things that one knows in advance will probably fall on deaf ears, because one owes it to the intended recipient, or to a third party, or to oneself, to try to convey that message. Even if the ICTR is failing to communicate with Rwandan perpetrators and victims, it has a duty to express proportionate penal censure to, and on behalf of, the international community.

In the desperate political and social circumstances of post-genocide Rwanda it is appropriate, nonetheless, that retributive penal responses have come to be questioned, even with regard to the most heinous offences. Mark Drumbl recounts arriving in Rwanda as a rookie volunteer public defender flushed with the ideals of constitutional due process, to be brought up short by the realities of a society rent by ethnic division and a crumbling penal process in gridlock (Drumbl, 2000a: 292). Explicitly invoking the RJ paradigm and John Braithwaite's theory of reintegrative shaming, Drumbl (2000b: 1323) now argues that

> accountability for genocide, and the deterrence of future interethnic violence, can be pursued more effectively though restorative justice initiatives (motivated by the cultivation of shame) as opposed to the retributive justice of the criminal trial (motivated by the imposition of guilt). Restorative justice initiatives, which emphasize the need for atonement, shaming, and reintegration, may be well-suited for societies moving past mass atrocity where both victims and aggressors need to be accommodated within the same polity, society, and government.

Drumbl is not alone in challenging the normative priority accorded by international lawyers and the international community to trials and retributive justice (also see Alvarez, 1999), or in promoting RJ ideals to facilitate national reconciliation and reconstruction in the wake of mass atrocity (Howland and Calathes, 1998: 154). In Rwanda, an indigenous system of local *gacaca* tribunals has supplied the raw material for institutional adaptation in furtherance of a more holistic response to the genocide. *Gacaca* proceedings compass multiple objectives: holding perpetrators to account, piecing together an accurate and authentic historical record of the genocide, providing compensation for victims, reintegrating offenders into civil society, and promoting a new Rwandan national identity based on principles of equality, democracy and respect for human rights. But nobody is under the illusion that success is assured. Adapting an informal system for resolving minor village disputes into a credible programme of accountability for genocidal murder would present a stiff challenge under any circumstances, the more so for Rwanda with its history of ethnic strife and daily confrontation with looming political, financial, and administrative collapse.

Gacaca tribunals might be an effective way of easing the remand population and freeing up court-time in the short term (though, there again, previous efforts to divert cases from formal process through confession and expedited guilty pleas have not been conspicuously successful: Schabas, 1996; Drumbl, 2000b). But grander long-term objectives—national reconstruction and reconciliation at the pinnacle of their ambition—will require *gacaca* tribunals to generate a sense of legitimacy in their proceedings and outcomes. This is asking a lot of offenders, and still more of their victims. As one survivor tried to explain: 'Foreigners can never understand the void we widows live in. We have lost the whole of our large families, our husbands' families, everyone is gone. . . . We see these people, we are forced to forgive them, but they don't recognise what they've done. . . . It will not be easy to live with them again, it will be very, very hard to welcome them' (Margaritte Salome Uwamliya, quoted by Brittain, 2001).

A review of Rwanda's post-genocide condition converges on the conclusion that accountability through retributive censure and punishment is an essential part of the process by which individuals and communities try to come to terms with mass criminal atrocity. Categorical, non-negotiable rejection of impunity is not confined to those directly involved as victims, or their families and fellow citizens, but also extends to the attitudes of third party States and peoples, and ultimately to the international community as a whole. Notwithstanding his chastening experiences of Rwandan criminal proceedings, Drumbl still maintains that criminal trial and punishment are the appropriate responses to 'paradigmatic violations of human rights' (2000a: 296). Yet it remains undeniable that retributive justice is vulnerable to forms of corruption that betray the foundational premises of liberal criminal justice and imperil a society's best efforts to promote personal healing, social reconciliation and national reconstruction after criminal catastrophe. Retributive justice and the normative core of criminal process are too important to be dispensed with, we seem to be saying, and yet the policies holding out the best hopes for political stability, peace, security, social harmony and individual well-being may be jeopardised by retributive censure and punishment.

This conclusion is only disappointingly bland, or infuriatingly evasive, when confined in abstraction. It is trite to observe that no two episodes of genocide or systematic human rights violations are exact carbon copies. Drumbl, Asmal (2000) and others are surely right to insist that boiler-plate, 'one-size-fits none' approaches must give way to contextualised, targeted, pluralistic (Drumbl prefers 'blended') responses, attuned to the unique conditions and possibilities of each particular time and place. The prominence of retributively-orientated international criminal proceedings has not dispensed with the need to make principled trade-offs between a range of potentially conflicting values and objectives in international penal affairs. Nor should it be expected or vaunted to do so. Any mature system of criminal justice, whether international or municipal, must confront the need for such trade-offs, which flow ineluctably from any conception of political morality incorporating plural and incommensurable values (Raz, 1986: Parts IV and V; Stocker, 1990). Value pluralism opens up the conceptual and normative possibility of a harmonious integration of ends. But it also implies the risk of irreconcilable conflict between incommensurable values and objectives, which must be confronted and managed when flashpoints ignite. A clear articulation of the relevant values and objectives, and some kind of context-sensitive normative hierarchy for choosing between them, are essential first steps towards effective policy formation and implementation.

Whether RJ-enthusiast or international criminal jurist, the message remains the same: sweeping generalisations and inflexible dogma must give way to particularistic analyses and reasonable compromise. Superficial impressions to the contrary, this is neither a deplorable cop-out nor a recipe for justice compromised, but merely the candid recognition of a banal moral reality. It is something we should all be mature enough to acknowledge and to live with, in order to get past it, in order to live together.

V. RESTORATION AND RETRIBUTION IN RECONCILIATION

Reconciliation is not synonymous with restoration, but they are closely related. Both could be achieved, or at least aimed at, by the same process. Victim-offender mediation, for example, might aspire to restore the personal security of the victim and also to reconcile her to the experience of victimisation, or even, more ambitiously, to reconcile victim and offender in full and equal citizenship. Reconciliation might be achieved *through* restoration, or vice versa. Compensation or restitution might reconcile through the restoration of property or its value. Conversely, a reconciliation effected by the offender's sincere and remorseful apology to his victim might be the means by which the victim's personal security, confidence and psychological well-being are restored (as where the victim learns that the youth who burgled her house is a pathetic junkie who was only looking for money for another fix, neutralising the experience of victimisation as 'nothing personal').

The close affinity between restoration and reconciliation suggests further parallels between international criminal justice and RJ-inspired developments in municipal criminal proceedings. Judicial punishment, even when meticulously administered and fully deserved, risks precipitating factionalised tit-for-tat reprisals and an escalating cycle of violence. In Drumbl's contention that retributive justice must defer to reconciliation in the service of lasting peace and security, there are clear echoes of RJ ideals: criminal/international justice as peacemaking, as triage for personal and social perturbations, as conflict resolution through collective healing. Blame and punishment, RJ advocates and reconciliation's international sponsors might urge in unison, must not be allowed to derail the pursuit of more valuable social ends.

But in highlighting with unusual clarity inescapable normative choices and tradeoffs, ICrimJ also testifies to the formidable practical obstacles ranged against grand social designs. Genuine reconciliation is difficult to foster. People who are hurt, frightened and (rightly) affronted will not easily be led to reconcile with their tormentors, even if genuine remorse is forthcoming—which is no mere formality, as former president Botha's refusal to appear before the SA TRC graphically demonstrated and as Rwandan experiences daily reconfirm. It must be conceded that the pursuit of truth and reconciliation in South Africa or Rwanda, in Chile or Guatemala, seems a long way removed from the crime problems confronting the average British council estate tenant or metropolitan magistrates' court. Yet people forced into extreme situations are, for all the singularity of their circumstances, still people with predictably human responses and preoccupations. On further reflection, the objectives and working practices of truth and reconciliation commissions are not so very distant from the aspirations and operations of RJ in municipal settings.

It strikes me as too complacent, at any rate, to assume that restoration is necessarily more easily accomplished amongst the victims of muggings and residential burglary. Virtually by definition, political crimes at least have appreciable motivations, which is one essential precondition for a synaptic spark of (self)recognition to cross sectarian divides.[9] Mindlessly violent or gratuitously greedy municipal crime, though in objective terms trivial by comparison, may be no more comprehensible to its victims, and no better candidate for forgiveness, restoration or reconciliation. Meditation on these intuitions underscores the difficulty of achieving victim restoration in any context, international or domestic. Human psychology, personal character and the structure of the moral emotions—including, especially, retributive emotions of resentment and righteous indignation—place real, if imprecise and subjective, limits on the prospects for achieving reconciliation or securing restoration in practice. Still, for all their daunting ambition, reconciliation and restoration may be the best, and possibly only, options for responding to international or domestic crimes without making matters worse. But sober and informed assessment of any policy's practical prospects remains vital. The longer the odds against success, the more a conscientious policy-maker should focus her efforts—and the community's resources—in another direction.

When reconciliation is combined with more traditional penal objectives, as it often has been in both national and international contexts, a further set of challenges arises. Bias or discrimination in the formulation or application of selection criteria are elementary pitfalls requiring careful monitoring and speedy correction, or the legitimacy of the entire enterprise may suffer irreparable harm. Even with meticulous planning and preparation, some individuals will foreseeably

---

[9] This much can be said even for bin Laden's outrages. (But does this just prove that so much amounts to not very much at all?)

complain about the allocation of cases involving them. Victims may prefer ret-ributive justice to 'truth and reconciliation.' Suspects and defendants, for their part, might insist on the full panoply of defence rights and protections, uncon-cerned that elaborate procedural guarantees could distort the relative informality of reconciliation processes. Judges are, in general, culturally well-disposed to appeals for due process, and may insist on the rigours of formal legality, even if this diminishes the prospects for reconciliation. Whilst legislative policies may ultimately prevail, the judges are the guardians of constitutional propriety, and the executive must respect judicial authority. The South African TRC was assailed by the full range of these challenges and objections, and was forced by the courts to make procedural concessions (see Dugard, 1998).

A third problem area for ICrimJ is the corruption of genuine objectives like peace, truth and reconciliation into a cloak for offending with impunity, a kind of dictators' 'get-out-of gaol-free' card. For some commentators, the popularity of truth and reconciliation commissions, amnesties, special or military court pro-ceedings and the like, smacks of the old corrupt deal between nation states to leave each other free to terrorise and oppress their own citizens without fear of being held accountable to international law. Committed advocates of criminal prosecu-tion argue that diversionary devices should attract searching critical scrutiny (eg Bassiouni, 1996 and 2000). The cult of impunity must be exposed and resisted whenever it is to be found lurking behind weasel-worded, hand-wringing excuses for declining to bring perpetrators of past crimes to book.

Non-prosecution strategies have undoubtedly been abused in this way: witness, for example, the truth commissions and related amnesties absolving Pinochet and other Latin American dictators (Webber, 1999; Roht-Arriaza and Gibson, 1998). In other cases, the motivation is not so much impunity as (genuine) practical necessity. Thus, without promises of amnesty the South African security forces would have boycotted the new dispensation, destabilising its fledgling democracy with foreseeably catastrophic consequences (Sachs, 2000). More positively, in its tri-cameral composition, institutional innovation, democratic pedigree, and broad social and political agenda; in its sensitivity to victims' needs and narra-tives *and* to offender rehabilitation; in the dramatic public spectacle of anguished confessions and collective expiation, the SA TRC can be viewed as a model—human, and therefore necessarily flawed[10]—institutional reconciliation of peace, truth and justice (Asmal, 2000). Egregious crimes of the apartheid state would have remained forever hidden, denying closure to both victims and offenders, without the carrot of immunity from criminal prosecution. However, amnesty was restricted to proportional political crimes and had to be *earned* by full public disclosure to the TRC; and *refusniks* have been vigorously prosecuted (Dugard, 1998). Particular compromises can be justifiable in terms of practical necessity,

---

[10]   Cf Sachs (2000: 202): 'Nobody is fully happy with the Truth Commission. But to me that is almost a proof that it is a real human experience. If everybody was happy it would be too neat, it would mean someone was paying an undue price. Instead everybody is a bit uncomfortable.'

without implying any *general* priority of reconciliation over retributive justice. Opting for a truth commission in preference to criminal prosecutions *would* be abusive, at all events, if appeals to practical necessity turned out in reality to mask executive convenience or cronyism, allegations from which the SA TRC has not been immune (Johnson, 1999).

RJ-inspired policies and practices are similarly vulnerable to hijack by alternative agendas. In the domestic setting this threat comes from political expediency in penal policy, and from institutional practices and imperatives, rather than from evil dictators. The political attractions of a superficial commitment to RJ, and the threat this poses to the long-run success of RJ programmes, are by now notorious (see eg Morris and Gelsthorpe, 2000). A second source of vulnerability is perhaps less obvious. In the modern actuarial state the work of the police, prosecutors and courts is assessed by reference to a battery of performance indicators (cf Lord Chancellor's Department et al 2001; Home Office, 2001). Each agency operates under constant pressure to improve its 'efficiency,' 'productivity' and 'outputs'. This regulatory environment reinforces the natural tendency of all organisations towards conservative inertia. Externally-imposed objectives and other pressures are reinterpreted, so far as possible, in conformity with pre-existing objectives and values, keeping life as pleasant and uncomplicated as possible for an organisation's personnel. The tendency for police officers, for example, to redirect RJ-initiatives towards traditional crime-fighting objectives has been noted in the evaluation literature, and more general concerns have been expressed about the co-option of RJ policies and practices to different, and possibly competing, penal objectives. Vigilance and zealous advocacy to keep RJ initiatives 'pure' are qualities that RJ's proponents might require in equal measure to sponsors of reconciliation in international penal affairs.

VI. FOR INTERNATIONAL CRIMINAL JUSTICE

This short chapter has engaged with large and enduring themes, and I am well aware that the analysis is superficial, speculative and very incomplete. But consciousness-raising exercises are often inevitably question-begging, if not so by design.

My principal aim was to demonstrate that ICrimJ's historical development and contemporary policies and practices present an ideal testing-ground, and a fruitful source of examples and illustrations, for reconsidering RJ's conceptual coherence, ethical purchase, normative (including juridical) limitations, and practical possibilities. Political settlements that some hail as reconciliation in furtherance of community peace and prosperity, others condemn as impunity for the powerful and injustice for the weak. These counter-posed moralities, competing conceptual frameworks and practical dilemmas—vividly illustrated by the African case studies presented in Sections IV and V—are close analogues, if they are not direct continuations, of the municipal RJ debate.

A further, subsidiary programmatic objective runs through the chapter: to raise the general profile of ICrimJ materials, and exemplify the argument for their inclusion across the broad sweep of criminal justice curricula (also see Frase, 1998).

REFERENCES

Akhavan, P (1997) 'Justice and Reconciliation in the Great Lakes Region of Africa: The Contribution of the International Criminal Tribunal For Rwanda' 7 *Duke Journal of Comparative and International Law* 325.

Alvarez, JE (1999) 'Crimes of States/Crimes of Hate: Lessons from Rwanda' 24 *Yale Journal of International Law* 365.

Annan, K (1997) 'Advocating for an International Criminal Court' 21 *Fordham International Law Journal* 363.

Asmal, K (2000) 'Truth, Reconciliation and Justice: The South African Experience in Perspective' 63 *Modern Law Review* 1.

Baker, E (1998) 'Taking European Criminal Law Seriously' *Criminal Law Review* 361.

Bassiouni, MC (1993) 'Human Rights in the Context of Criminal Justice: Identifying International Procedural Protections and Equivalent Protections in National Constitutions' 3 *Duke Journal of Comparative and International Law* 235.

——(1994) *The Protection of Human Rights in the Administration of Criminal Justice* (Transnational Publishers, NY).

——(1996) 'Searching for Peace and Achieving Justice: The Need for Accountability' 59 *Law and Contemporary Problems* 9.

——(2000) 'Combating Impunity for International Crimes' 71 *University of Colorado Law Review* 409.

Bhattacharyya, R (1996) 'Establishing a Rule-of-Law International Criminal Justice System' 31 *Texas International Law Journal* 57.

Brittain, V (2001) 'Time for Truth as Rwanda Strives for Reconciliation' *The Guardian*, 6 April.

Daly, K and Immarigeon, R (1998) 'The Past, Present, and Future of Restorative Justice: Some Critical Reflections' 1 *Contemporary Justice Review* 21.

Drumbl, MA (2000a) 'Sclerosis: Retributive Justice and the Rwandan Genocide' 2 *Punishment and Society* 287.

——(2000b) 'Punishment, Postgenocide: From Guilt to Shame to *Civis* in Rwanda' 75 *New York University Law Review* 1221.

Dugard, J (1998) 'Reconciliation and Justice: The South African Experience' 8 *Transnational Law and Contemporary Problems* 277.

Emmerson, B and Ashworth, A (2001) *Human Rights and Criminal Justice* (Sweet & Maxwell, London).

Fatić, A (1995) *Punishment and Restorative Crime-Handling: A Social Theory of Trust* (Avebury, Aldershot).

Frase, RS (1998) 'Main-Streaming Comparative Criminal Justice: How to Incorporate Comparative and International Concepts and Materials into Basic Criminal Law and Procedure Courses' 100 *West Virginia Law Review* 774.

Harding, C (2000) 'The Identity of European Law: Mapping Out the European Legal Space' 6 *European Law Journal* 128.

Hirsch, D (2001) 'The Trial of Andrei Sawoniuk: Holocaust Testimony Under Cross-Examination' 10 *Social & Legal Studies* 529.

Home Office, (2001) *Criminal Justice: The Way Ahead*, Cm 5074 (TSO, London).

Howland, T and Calathes, W (1998) 'The UN's International Criminal Tribunal, Is It Justice or Jingoism for Rwanda? A Call for Transformation' 39 *Virginia Journal of International Law* 135.

Johnson, RW (1999) 'Why There is No Easy Way to Dispose of Painful History' *London Review of Books*, 14 Oct.

Lord Chancellor's Department, Home Office and Attorney-General's Office, (2001) *Criminal Justice System Business Plan 2001–2002*, http//www.criminal-justice-system. gov.uk.

McCormack, TLH (1997) 'From Sun Tzu to the Sixth Committee: The Evolution of an International Criminal Law Regime' in TLH McCormack and GJ Simpson (eds), *The Law of War Crimes: National and International Approaches* (Kluwer: The Hague).

McGoldrick, D (1999) 'The Permanent International Criminal Court: An End to the Culture of Impunity?' *Criminal Law Review* 627.

Marschik, A (1997) 'The Politics of Prosecution: European National Approaches to War Crimes' in TLH McCormack and GJ Simpson (eds), *The Law of War Crimes: National and International Approaches* (Kluwer: The Hague).

Miers, D (2001) *An International Review of Restorative Justice*, Crime Reduction Research Series Paper 10 (Home Office RDS, London).

Moore, MS (1997) *Placing Blame: A General Theory of the Criminal Law* (Clarendon Press, Oxford).

Morris, A and Gelsthorpe, L (2000) 'Something Old, Something Borrowed, Something Blue, but Something New? A Comment on the Prospects for Restorative Justice Under the Crime and Disorder Act 1998' *Criminal Law Review* 18.

Murphy, JG and Hampton, J (1988) *Forgiveness and Mercy* (Cambridge University Press, Cambridge).

Peers, S (2000) *EU Justice and Home Affairs Law* (Longman, Harlow).

Pollard, C (2000) 'Victims and the Criminal Justice System: A New Vision' *Criminal Law Review* 5.

Rawls, J (1987) 'The Idea of an Overlapping Consensus' 7 *Oxford Journal of Legal Studies* 1.

Raz, J (1986) *The Morality of Freedom* (Clarendon Press, Oxford).

Roberts, P (2002) 'Drug-Dealing and the Presumption of Innocence: The Human Rights Act (Almost) Bites' 6 *Evidence and Proof* 17.

Roht-Arriaza, N and Gibson, L (1998) 'The Developing Jurisprudence on Amnesty' 20 *Human Rights Quarterly* 843.

Rojo, A (1998) 'Justice is Revenge in Kigali's Bloody Arena' *The Guardian*, 25 April.

Sachs, A (2000) 'The Truth and Reconciliation Commission in South Africa' in S Doran and JD Jackson (eds), *The Judicial Role in Criminal Proceedings* (Hart Publishing, Oxford).

Sassòli, M and Bouvier, AA (1999) *How Does Law Protect in War?* (International Committee of the Red Cross, Geneva).

Schabas, WA (1996) 'Justice, Democracy, and Impunity in Post-Genocide Rwanda: Searching for Solutions to Impossible Problems' 7 *Criminal Law Forum* 523.

Schwarzenberger, G (1950) 'The Problem of an International Criminal Law' *Current Legal Problems* 263.

Steiner, HJ and Alston, P (2000) *International Human Rights in Context: Law, Politics, Morals* 2nd edn (Oxford University Press, Oxford).

Stocker, M (1990) *Plural and Conflicting Values* (Clarendon Press, Oxford).

Sunga, LS (1997) *The Emerging System of International Criminal Law: Developments in Codification and Implementation* (Kluwer, The Hague).

Triggs, G (1997) 'Australia's War Crimes Trials: All Pity Choked' in TLH McCormack and GJ Simpson (eds), *The Law of War Crimes: National and International Approaches* (Kluwer: The Hague).

Twining, W (2000) *Globalisation & Legal Theory* (Butterworths, London).

Van Ness, DW and Nolan, P (1998) 'Legislating for Restorative Justice' 10 *Regent University Law Review* 53.

von Hirsch, A (1993) *Censure and Sanctions* (Clarendon Press, Oxford).

Wadham, J and Arkinstall, J (2000) 'Rights of Victims of Crime—I & II' 150 *New Law Journal* 1023 and 1083 (7 and 14 July).

Waltz, KN (1962) 'Kant, Liberalism, and War' 56 *American Political Science Review* 331.

Webber, F (1999) 'The Pinochet Case: The Struggle for the Realization of Human Rights' 26 *Journal of Law and Society* 523.

Wedgwood, R (1999) 'The International Criminal Court: An American View' 10 *European Journal of International Law* 93.

——(2001) 'The Irresolution of Rome' 64 *Law and Contemporary Problems* 193.

Wenig, JM (1997) 'Enforcing the Lessons of History: Israel Judges the Holocaust' in TLH McCormack and GJ Simpson (eds), *The Law of War Crimes: National and International Approaches* (Kluwer, The Hague).

Wexler, LS (1994) 'The Interpretation of the Nuremberg Principles by the French Court of Cassation: From Touvier to Barbie and Back Again' 32 *Columbia Journal of Transnational Law* 289.

Williams, SA (1997) 'Laudable Principles Lacking Application: The Prosecution of War Criminals in Canada' in TLH McCormack and GJ Simpson (eds), *The Law of War Crimes: National and International Approaches* (Kluwer, The Hague).

Zedner, L (1994) 'Reparation and Retribution: Are They Reconcilable?' 57 *Modern Law Review* 228.

7

Towards a Systemic Model of Restorative Justice: Reflections on the Concept, its Context and the Need for Clear Constraints[1]

Jim Dignan

I. INTRODUCTION

The road to penal reform, like the road to hell, is paved with good intentions: just deserts, the 'treatment model' and, before that, the reformatory. Yet all too often in the past, well-intentioned penal reform programmes have raised expectations that turned out to be unrealistic, failed to achieve their intended objectives and brought about terrible injustices of their own. One of the main challenges facing any penal reform movement is therefore to learn from the mistakes of the past by acknowledging the limitations to which it may be subject, accepting the need for appropriate safeguards and adapting both theory and practice in the light of experience. This is particularly important in the case of restorative justice initiatives because of the often evangelical and uncritical way in which their virtues have been promoted by some of their early proponents. At a time when the relationship between restorative justice initiatives and the regular criminal justice system is being more intensively debated than ever there is now a need to engage in fresh thinking about the way restorative justice is conceptualised, the part it might play in reforming current penal policies and also the normative constraints that will need to be adopted if this reformative potential is to be realised.

The aim of the paper is to explore the scope for a principled alliance between restorative justice advocates and just deserts proponents in pursuit of a radical reform of the existing criminal justice and penal systems in the interests of victims, offenders and the wider community. I will argue that restorative justice has the potential to contribute to such a programme of reform by furnishing the kind of 'replacement discourse' concerning the purpose and practice of

[1] This chapter has benefited from comments made by Michael Cavadino, David Miersard Gwen Robinson, though none of there colleagues should be held responsible for the final product.

punishment that Andrew Ashworth (1997) has called for. This will only be possible, however, if restorative justice advocates are prepared to accept firstly that restorative justice has to be concerned just as much with *outcomes* as with *processes*; secondly that, however well-intentioned and benevolent they might be, restorative justice interventions do constitute a form of punishment; and thirdly that they therefore stand in need of moral justification and should be subject to principled normative constraints relating to the nature and intensity of any restorative justice intervention.

II. CONCEPTUAL CONSTRAINTS: PROCESS VS. OUTCOME DEFINITIONS

Although it would be wrong to overstate the degree of consensus on the issue, one of the most influential definitions of restorative justice (Marshall, 1999: 5) portrays it as a distinctive type of decision-making *process*: one that enables those who have a stake in a specific offence to 'do justice', by collectively resolving how to deal with its aftermath and also its implications for the future. Not all restorative justice advocates are convinced, however, and some critics (eg Bazemore and Walgrave, 1999: 48) have correctly pointed out that the definition is at best a partial one since it has nothing to say on the subject of '*restorative outcomes*' or how these might be defined.[2]

Those restorative justice advocates (eg Bazemore and Umbreit, 1995: Brown and Polk, 1996) who do refer to restorative outcomes tend to do so rather obliquely, by speaking generally about the need to 'restore victims', 'restore offenders' and 'restore communities'. Reparation is often referred to in this context, as is the aim of reintegrating offenders into the community. More specifically, John Braithwaite (1996; 1999: 6) has suggested that, from a republican perspective, restorative outcomes would include the restoration of property loss, injury, a sense of security, dignity, a sense of empowerment, deliberative democracy, harmony— based on a feeling that justice has been done—and social support. However, he has also made clear that what restoration means in a specific context is determined by the deliberation of the relevant stakeholders: victims, offenders and communities affected by the crime. In other words, restorative outcomes are once again defined exclusively with reference to the restorative justice *processes* from which they are expected to emanate.

Most restorative justice advocates and practitioners also accept that restorative justice processes should be regulated by procedural constraints founded on certain core ethical values. They include the need for consensual participation by the

---

[2] It is, of course, true that restorative processes, involving as they do, some form of dialogue between the principal stakeholders, may often elicit a variety of 'outcomes'. One such outcome is a subjective sense of 'having been restored', as a result of the process. But other, more tangible outcomes in the form of material reparation are also possible. However, for many restorative justice advocates it is the dialogue process itself that constitutes the essential meaning of restorative justice, rather than any consequential outcomes to which it may give rise.

principal stakeholders, dialogue based on mutual respect, non-coercive practice and agreements, and the need to address the interests that are in play in a balanced way. Where such values are respected and enforced they may provide welcome safeguards against some obvious forms of abuse to which informal restorative justice processes might otherwise be subject. However, they would also appear to restrict the scope of restorative justice processes to those cases in which both parties are willing to participate and abide by the ground-rules, the implication being that all other cases will need to be dealt with by the 'regular' criminal justice system.[3] However, this raises two important questions: first regarding the extent to which parties, particularly victims, may be willing to participate in informal restorative justice processes; and second about what should happen in cases where they are unwilling to do so.

Although very high victim participation rates have been reported for some Australian police-led conferencing initiatives,[4] these seem exceptional, and most other studies have reported much lower levels of victim participation. They include the early New Zealand evaluations of family group conferencing, where victims attended only half the conferences (Maxwell and Morris, 1996), and also the Bethlehem police-led conferencing project, where the victim participation rate was 42 per cent (McCold and Wachtel, 1998: 95). However, in England and Wales the rates of victim participation that have been reported from a variety of restorative justice-style processes in England and Wales have been far lower still. Umbreit and Roberts (1996: 27), for example, reported that only seven per cent of all referrals to two English Victim Offender Mediation Projects (Coventry and Leeds) during 1993, participated in direct (face to face) mediation.[5] Similarly, following the introduction of reparation orders in the Crime and Disorder Act 1998, only nine per cent of these involved mediation between victims and offenders during the pilot evaluation (Holdaway et al 2001: 89). Reports on the evaluation of the referral order pilots also indicate a low rate of victim participation in the new youth offender panels (Newburn et al 2001a and b, 2002). Finally, the Thames Valley restorative cautioning project has also reported levels of victim participation that are much closer to those encountered in other restorative justice processes in England and Wales than to its Australian or North American counterparts.[6]

The significance of these more pessimistic findings is that they raise serious doubts about the proportion of criminal cases in which a fully participatory

---

[3] In practice this may not be the case, since victims do not always participate in restorative justice processes such as conferencing. But this makes it all the more important to reflect on the *outcomes* that might emanate from such processes as well as the manner in which these outcomes are decided. It also raises doubts concerning the extent to which such processes can be considered to be fully restorative, at least in terms of Marshall's definition.

[4] Notably the Canberra RISE experiment, and also the Wagga Wagga conferencing evaluation, for which the reported rates of victim participation are 85% (Braithwaite, 1999: 22) and over 90% (Moore and O'Connell, 1994) respectively.

[5] See also Miers et al (2001: 25).

[6] The overall rate of victim participation was 16%, averaged over the three years of the project and showed a slight tendency to diminish over time (Hoyle et al 2000).

restorative justice process would present a viable alternative to the regular criminal justice system,[7] at least in an English context. So if the definition of restorative justice is indeed tied to a particular kind of informal dispute-resolution processing the effect will be to drastically restrict the scope of restorative justice theory and practice. And restorative justice initiatives themselves are likely to remain confined for the most part to diversionary processes that will, at best, have a marginal status at the periphery of the regular criminal justice system. Moreover, restorative justice advocates will continue to find it difficult to respond when asked how cases that do not lend themselves to this kind of process should be dealt with.

This tendency to adopt a restrictive process-linked definition of restorative justice is unfortunate, since it represents a missed opportunity to consider how restorative justice thinking might contribute to a broader and more far-reaching programme of penal reform. Before developing this line of argument, however, we need to consider an additional shortcoming that stems from the tendency to equate restorative justice with a particular kind of *process* while failing to consider the need for safeguards with regard to the kind of *outcomes* with which it might be associated. This has to do with the type of normative constraints to which restorative justice initiatives might be subject.

III. NORMATIVE CONSTRAINTS: PRINCIPLES OF PENALITY

Debates about punishment tend to concentrate on two types of moral questions. The first asks *what justifies* the infliction of pain or suffering on a person, which raises a further question about *whom* we are entitled to punish. The second is concerned with the severity of punishment and asks *how much* punishment we are entitled to inflict? There is a third question, which is usually overlooked, or at any rate the answer to which is normally taken for granted: viz. *what kind* of punishment we are entitled to impose?

Restorative justice advocates need to be able to provide convincing answers[8] to the first two sets of questions if they are to allay the well-founded concerns of those who fear that, well-intentioned though it might be, restorative justice could all too easily result in unintended and unjust consequences for some. The response to these questions from most restorative justice advocates so far has not been entirely convincing, however. Some have appeared to question the need for such normative constraints, while others have failed to particularise the limits that they would be prepared to countenance, or even the principles by which such limits might be determined. In the sections that follow I will argue that there is ample

---

[7] Much less a new paradigm that might displace the existing system altogether, as some early advocates portrayed it.

[8] Quite apart from the issue of principle that is raised, there is also a sound pragmatic reason for taking the question seriously since the group of sceptics includes many penal reformers who might otherwise be sympathetic towards a restorative justice approach if they thought it might advance the case for penal parsimony (see especially Ashworth, 2000).

scope for an accommodation to be reached which would meet the main concerns raised by just desert theorists without compromising the integrity of a restorative justice approach.

When it comes to the third question, relating to the *kind* of punishment we are entitled to impose, a restorative justice approach would in principle seem to be capable of generating a much more convincing set of answers than desert theory (or any other theory of punishment) has so far been able to come up with. Indeed, it may even have the potential to furnish the kind of 'replacement discourse' that Andrew Ashworth (1997) has called for, which could potentially change the terms of reference with which the debate about punishment is conducted. Or so I shall be arguing. But it will only do so if it stops assuming that the concept of restorative justice refers exclusively to a particular kind of process, and overcomes its reluctance to talk about what might count as just and unjust outcomes.

1. The Need to Justify Restorative Justice Interventions

In response to the first question, relating to the justification for punishment, some restorative justice advocates (eg Wright, 1991: 15 and 1996: 27; Walgrave, 1999: 146) seem to deny that measures of a restorative nature stand in need of moral justification in the way that conventional forms of punishment do. Their argument is based on a purported distinction between 'punitive' measures that are intended to inflict pain or unpleasantness for its own sake, and 'restorative' interventions which 'cannot be defined as punishments' because their intended purpose is said to be constructive. However, this line of reasoning relies for its effect on the confusion of two distinct elements in the concept of intention. One relates to the motive for doing something, but the other refers to the fact that the act in question is being performed deliberately or wilfully. In the case of punishment (and all analogous practices), it is the fact that pain or unpleasantness is *deliberately* imposed on a person that calls for a moral justification, regardless of the motive for doing so. Restorative justice advocates would do well to recall that similar 'motivational' arguments were used by past generations of penal reformers in support of ostensibly more benevolent rehabilitative measures, and were also justifiably challenged[9] on the grounds that they failed to provide adequate safeguards to protect offenders from being treated unjustly.

2. Limiting the Severity of Restorative Justice Interventions: The Inadequacy of 'Republican' Constraints?

Other restorative justice advocates (notably Braithwaite and Pettit, 1990; see also Braithwaite and Parker, 1999) have acknowledged that restorative justice

---

[9] See for example the American Friends Service Committee (1971); and also the Canadian Ouimet Report (Canada, 1969) as cited by Roach (2000: 265).

interventions do stand in need of moral justification. And they have articulated a coherent and elaborate normative theory (based on the concept of 'dominion', or freedom as non-domination) that they claim is more likely to generate just outcomes than the rival 'just deserts' theory.

However, Braithwaite's republican theory of restorative justice has failed to convince just deserts' theorists that he has an adequate answer to the second question, relating to the *amount* of punishment we are entitled to impose. This is largely because of his insistence (1999: 73) that restorative justice amounts to no more than a procedural requirement that 'the parties talk until they feel that harmony has been restored on the basis of discussion of all the injustices they see as relevant to the case'. Consequently, there can be no guarantee that even restorative justice conferences will be able to avoid unjust outcomes in which authoritarian figures like 'Uncle Harry' call the shots (Ashworth, 2000: 8, commenting on Braithwaite, 1999: 66–7).

Braithwaite's response takes two forms, though neither has assuaged the concerns raised by his critics. One line of defence (Braithwaite and Parker, 1999: 109) is to rely on the moderating influence that a vigorous 'republican' political discourse is expected to exert on the deliberations that take place within restorative conferences, the effect of which should be to defend powerless minorities against the tyrannies of the majority. The problem with this argument is that it assumes the existence of a particular kind of polity within which restorative justice processes are most likely to produce acceptable outcomes. Where this is not the case, however (as will often be the case in practice), there are genuine concerns that even a partial switch to informal dispute-settlement processes could result in unjust outcomes being perpetrated at the hands of 'authoritarian' communities (Lacey and Zedner, 1995; Cavadino et al 1999; and Dignan and Lowey, 2000).

Braithwaite's second line of defence (1999: 89) is to preserve an absolute right for the accused (and victims) 'to walk out of the restorative justice process and try their chances in a court of law'. The problem with this argument is that it leaves the parties exposed to the vagaries of a legal lottery.[10] By equating restorative justice with a particular kind of informal dispute resolution process, and refusing to specify what might count as a just or unjust outcome, it is impossible for Braithwaite to assuage the concerns of those who fear that the kinds of punishments that are inflicted by the courts are themselves all too often excessive and unjust. Indeed, those concerns are heightened by Braithwaite's professed willingness to resort to more conventionally punitive strategies based on the principles of 'active deterrence' and incapacitation, both in cases where restorative justice has been tried repeatedly and failed, and also as an implicit threat, lurking in the background, to encourage a responsible restorative approach on the part of offenders.

---

[10] What, for example, if the offender has already made admissions as part of the process, or has even undertaken some form of reparation by the time the process is abandoned?

3. Limiting the Severity of Restorative Justice Interventions: A 'Rights-Based' Approach

So how *might* restorative justice advocates respond to the legitimate question that has been posed by just deserts theorists regarding the amount of punishment we are entitled to impose, whether in the context of an informal restorative justice process (such as a restorative or community conference or victim offender mediation) or by a regular criminal court? Mick Cavadino and I have argued elsewhere (1997) in favour of a 'compromise' theory of punishment, which sets out a principled accommodation between a form of retributivism, as espoused by the 'justice model' that is associated with Andrew von Hirsch and Andrew Ashworth, and restorative justice. Our argument is based on a form of human rights theory (of the kind propounded by Ronald Dworkin (1978) and Alan Gewirth[11] (1978)) and may be summarised as follows.

One of the most important human rights is the equal right of individuals to maximum 'positive freedom',[12] by which we mean the right to make effective choices about their lives.[13] Rights' theory insists that any kind of punishment (whatever form it takes, and whatever the motivation for imposing it might be) requires special moral justification, since it reduces the freedom of the person being punished. It is difficult to see how a purely retributive justification for punishment could be reconciled with the positive freedom principle. For if retribution was all that punishment achieved, the offender's freedom would be gratuitously diminished without doing anything to improve anyone's prospects for exercising choice. However, the theory allows for one person's right (including even the right to positive freedom) to be restricted in certain circumstances, *provided* this is justified on the basis of another person's 'competing rights' (Dworkin, 1978).

This provides a prima facie moral justification for two different types of response to a given offence. First, if the offence has resulted in harm to a victim, that person is likely to have experienced some reduction in positive freedom: to function free from physical or psychological pain or disability, or to choose how to use or dispose of their resources. And it is this 'special harm' that entitles victims to reparation at the hands of their offenders, even though *their* positive freedom

---

[11] While Dworkin justifies rights on the relativistic ground that people in our society happen to accept that such rights exist, Gewirth maintains that human reason can establish certain definable fundamental rights which human beings in any society possess. We are more attracted by the latter, non-relativistic approach.

[12] This has some affinity with Braithwaite's concept of freedom as 'non-domination', but is arguably more 'content-specific', and therefore more capable of generating limiting principles by which it is possible to evaluate outcomes as either just or unjust.

[13] As such, it entails much more than the absence of coercion or constraint imposed by others, which is the classical Liberal concept of 'negative freedom'. The latter is a *necessary* component of positive freedom, but is not sufficient by itself in the absence of the requisite physical and psychological capabilities and also the material resources that might be needed in order to perform a given action.

may be diminished thereby. Rights' theory thus provides a principled justification for restorative justice processes that provide a forum in which victims and offenders may deliberate about the offence and its consequences, including the kind and amount of any reparation to which the victim may be entitled. Moreover, if victims are to be treated with *equal* concern and respect, which is also in line with a rights-based approach (Dworkin, 1978), then their entitlement to seek reparation should apply *irrespective* of the nature or seriousness of the offence in question. Indeed, the victim's entitlement to reparation should prevail even if the offender is unwilling to participate in an informal restorative justice process such as conferencing or victim offender mediation. However, the *kind* of reparation that an offender might be obliged to make in such a case would almost certainly be quite different from the kind of reparation that might be expected to emanate from such a process (see below).

Secondly, where it may plausibly be argued that punishing an offender does something to reduce the incidence of crime, and thereby prevents the diminution of some other people's positive freedom, this *may* also provide an independent prima facie justification for restricting the positive rights of an offender. However, the pursuit of *both* these punitive aims—the provision of appropriate reparation for victims and the reduction of offending—must be pursued in a manner that is consistent with the human rights of the offender.

Consequently, there would be no justification for punishing someone unless they had deliberately and wrongfully broken a just law, thereby exercising a freedom to which they are not entitled (because to do so has diminished or threatened to diminish other people's positive freedom). It also follows that the *amount of* punishment (of whatever kind) that we are entitled to impose is itself subject to limits. Although offenders are liable to forfeit certain of their rights (including, to some extent, their right of positive freedom) because of their infringement of the rights of others, the response to this infringement should not be excessively severe, taking into account the moral gravity of their offence (see below).

The human rights based precept of positive freedom is thus consistent with a general principle of proportionality in the maximum amount of punishment that is imposed on an offender. This is sometimes referred to as the principle of 'limiting retributivism' (as advocated by Morris, 1974: 75; and Morris and Tonry, 1990), which prescribes an upper limit for the response to an offence, whatever form this may take. At the other end of the scale, the principle of limiting retributivism *may* also (particularly in the case of more serious offences) be consistent with a lower limit for the response to an offence, whatever the parties may feel and agree is appropriate by way of reparation. However, it would be difficult to reconcile the principle of positive freedom for both offenders and victims with an insistence on the kind of strict proportionality that is favoured by just deserts' advocates.[14] I will return in a later section to the kind of proportionality con-

---

[14] See Cavadino and Dignan (1997) for a more detailed rejection of the principle of strict proportionality that is favoured by some desert theorists.

straints that might be appropriate in respect of restorative justice interventions. But in the meantime, it is necessary to turn to the remaining and frequently neglected question concerning the *kind* of punishment that we may be entitled to impose for a given offence.

4. What Kind of Punishment? The Limits of Just Deserts

Just deserts' theorists deserve credit for focusing the minds of restorative justice advocates on such issues as the need for a defensible moral justification for restorative justice interventions, and the importance of determining acceptable limits on the degree of punitiveness that is warranted. However, the recent emergence of restorative justice as a distinctive philosophy and practice in its own right has focused attention on a third aspect of penality that has hitherto been sadly neglected, concerning the *kind of* punitive response that is appropriate and morally justifiable. And on this issue desert theory looks much more vulnerable in the face of the credible challenge that is posed by the theory and practice of restorative justice, particularly one that is founded on a rights-based approach of the kind sketched out above.

Hitherto, most debates about punishment have focused on the moral principles that either justify its imposition or regulate its distribution and severity without specifically addressing the equally important moral and practical question *how* we punish. Desert theorists (eg von Hirsch, 1993; Duff, 1996; 2000) have tended to simply assume the answer by taking for granted that punishment comprises two key elements: first 'censure' and second some form of 'hard treatment'. Both elements are highly problematic, however.

The 'censure' component suffers from three principal shortcomings, which relate to the form it takes, the forum in which it is administered, and its possible consequences. Although desert theorists contend that the institution of punishment is a valuable mechanism for conveying blame or censure,[15] this seems highly dubious for two main reasons. First, the rather crude form of instrumentalist reasoning that it relies on is unlikely to be the most effective method of communicating normative standards to offenders, or of eliciting compliance with those standards (see Cavadino and Dignan, 2002: 198ff). And secondly, the moral attitudes of non-offending members of the public towards particular offences are equally unlikely to be affected by the severity of the punishment that is (or which they believe to be) inflicted (Walker and Marsh, 1984; cf. Tyler, 1990).

A second and related shortcoming relates to the court-based forum within which the censure is conveyed since this affords extremely limited opportunities for any meaningful censure-based communication to take place, and virtually no

---

[15] In part because it enables differences in the degree of censure that is merited to be reflected in the level of hard treatment (or deprivation) that is imposed, and thereby communicated to both the offender and the outside world.

possibility of any constructive engagement on the part of either victim or offender (see also Walgrave, 2001). The third shortcoming is linked to Braithwaite's well-known critique of the potentially criminogenic consequences that may follow when the process of censuring an offender results in indelible, open-ended, stigmatic shaming.

In marked contrast, restorative justice processes that involve some form of dialogue between victims, offenders and other interested parties provide an opportunity for censure to be expressed in a normative way. They are based on a moralistic form of reasoning that offenders may find it harder to reject, and to which they may consequently be less likely to object. The forum in which this dialogue takes place is more likely to afford an opportunity in which both victims and offenders are able to participate constructively in the communicative enterprise. And, if handled sensitively, it may be possible for censure to be communicated in a non-stigmatising way that offers a better prospect for the offender's successful reintegration back into the community. In short, the challenge for desert theory that is presented by restorative justice processes is that they provide an alternative, and arguably far more effective form of normative discourse through which to convey censure without stigma.

The 'hard treatment' component within desert theory is also problematic on a number of counts. One major shortcoming is that it ties the expression of censure and denunciation to a relatively limited range of retributive-style punishments, the primary purpose of which is to inflict some form of deprivation on offenders. This has undesirable consequences from the victim's point of view because few such punishments do anything to redress the personal loss or injury that they may have experienced. Even those that do (such as compensation orders) are only capable of addressing part of the harm that is caused by an offence: comprising the physical injury or loss or damage to property. However, they are likely to do little to repair any emotional or psychological upset that is caused by an offence, or to restore the moral equilibrium that has been disturbed by undermining the victim's presumption of personal security (Watson et al 1989). Once again, the attraction of restorative justice processes is that they facilitate the negotiation of much more flexible forms of reparation that should, in principle, be capable of responding more appropriately to more of the particular harms that victims may have experienced.

Desert theory's insistence on the retention of 'hard treatment' as the only possible medium through which to express censure and denunciation also poses serious problems for penal reformers who support an overall lowering of penalty levels. One reason for this is that, as Ashworth (2000: 6) has pointed out, the 'parsimony principle' is not deducible from the bare bones of desert theory. This renders the theory especially vulnerable to political hi-jacking in pursuit of higher levels of punishment, even though its supporters may be right to maintain that this is by no means an inevitable process. A second problem relates to the fact that desert theory's unshakeable attachment to the principle of 'hard treatment' renders it manifestly incapable of furnishing the kind of 'replacement discourse' that Ashworth himself (1997) has called for. The latter calls for a new set of assumptions about the purposes of punishment and the confidence to articulate

ASSUMPTION

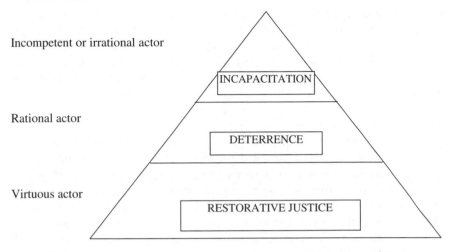

Incompetent or irrational actor

Rational actor

Virtuous actor

Fig 1: Toward an integration of restorative, deterrent and incapacitative justice

more constructive and less harmful ways of responding to and preventing crime than by imposing more imprisonment or by making community punishments ever more restrictive simply to enhance their 'credibility' in the eyes of the courts or public at large.

IV. RESTORATIVE JUSTICE AS A FORM OF REPLACEMENT DISCOURSE?

The question I now wish to address is whether restorative justice might be capable of providing such a replacement discourse relating to the kind of punishment practices we should be pursuing. It is difficult to see how this might be achieved while restorative justice continues to be conceptualised solely in terms of a particular kind of informal dispute-settlement process that functions entirely separately from the 'regular' criminal justice process. John Braithwaite's (1999: 61) recently proposed model for integrating restorative justice processes within the regular criminal justice system, which is reproduced in Figure 1, above, demonstrates the inadequacy of this position and the need to adopt a more systemic approach.

1. Braithwaite's 'Integrated' but Non-Systemic Model of Restorative Justice

Although Braithwaite refers to the model as an *integration* of restorative, deterrent and incapacitative strategies, it may be more apposite to think of it as incorporating a *twin-track* approach, in which restorative justice processes operate alongside deterrent and incapacitative measures rather than one that is systemically reorganised according to restorative justice principles. Thus, at the base of the enforcement pyramid, a restorative justice approach to criminal law enforcement is reserved exclusively for virtuous or well-intended actors (including repeat offenders up to a point) who are willing to enter into informal restorative justice negotiations in good faith. To guard against the risk of rational actors who might be tempted to pursue a 'free-loading' strategy by making a deceitful pretence at participating in a restorative justice negotiation, however, Braithwaite envisages an enforcement strategy based on the principle of 'active deterrence'. The latter involves the strategic use of *escalating* threats in response to recalcitrance on the part of the offender, and could result in custodial incapacitation. This aspect of Braithwaite's approach has provoked understandable concerns on the part of deserts-based theorists who are alarmed at the absence of proportionality constraints. Indeed, far from serving as a 'replacement discourse', there is a danger that this kind of twin-track approach could readily lend itself to an escalation in the level of punitive responses towards repeat and recalcitrant offenders.[16]

If restorative justice is to furnish a comprehensive 'replacement discourse' it will need to be founded on a very different type of enforcement strategy. This in turn will necessitate a reconceptualisation of restorative justice itself so that it is no longer tied to an informal consensual decision-making *process* requiring active participation by all the relevant stakeholders. For provision will also need to be made—if necessary in the form of court-ordered restorative *outcomes*—for all those cases that are deemed ineligible or inappropriate for referral to a diversionary informal restorative justice process (the 'recusants, the rejected and the recalcitrant', to use Ashworth's (2000: 9) alliterative terminology).[17] In the next section I will outline and develop an alternative enforcement model that I have previously proposed in a slightly different context (Dignan, 1994).

2. Towards a Systemic Model of Restorative Justice

Figure 2 is based on an alternative enforcement pyramid in which restorative justice is intended to provide a 'replacement discourse' as part of a systemic and fully integrated reform of the regular criminal justice system.[18] As in Figure 1, the standard response for the vast majority of criminal offences[19] would be for the

---

[16] Such concerns are by no means fanciful. In England and Wales the Halliday report (2001: 15) recommends the introduction of an explicit presumption that the severity of a sentence should no longer be determined primarily by the seriousness of a given offence, but also by the degree of persistence shown by an offender.

[17] Similar considerations may also apply even in those jurisdictions (for example New Zealand), where restorative justice processes such as conferencing have been mainstreamed, in cases where victims decline to participate or offenders prove recalcitrant.

[18] This model was itself adapted from an original version proposed by Braithwaite (1991) in the context of business or agency regulation.

[19] Including most minor property offences, minor assaults and also the great majority of regulatory offences.

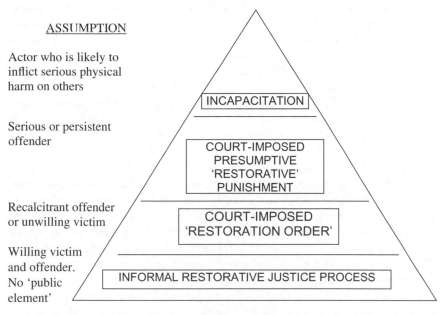

ASSUMPTION

Actor who is likely to
inflict serious physical
harm on others

INCAPACITATION

Serious or persistent
offender

COURT-IMPOSED
PRESUMPTIVE
'RESTORATIVE'
PUNISHMENT

Recalcitrant offender
or unwilling victim

COURT-IMPOSED
'RESTORATION ORDER'

Willing victim
and offender.
No 'public
element'

INFORMAL RESTORATIVE JUSTICE PROCESS

Fig 2: Toward a form of replacement discourse based on a 'systemic' model of
restorative justice

matter to be dealt with where possible by means of the most appropriate restorative justice process (victim offender mediation, restorative conference etc). Provided that reparation is agreed and performed to the satisfaction of both parties, and at least where there is no evidence of a lengthy history of similar offences, the fact that the offender has been willing to make suitable amends should normally be taken as evidence of a renewed respect for the rights of others. In the absence of any other 'public element', the case for any additional punishment in such cases would appear very weak. However, in order to safeguard the public interest (ie the human rights of people other than the individual victim and offender) it would be desirable to incorporate some form of 'judicial oversight',[20] if only to ensure that whatever is agreed by the parties does not exceed a reasonable level of reparation.

Recourse to the courts would not normally be allowed unless either the accused denied guilt, the victim was unwilling to participate, the parties were unable to reach agreement on the subject of reparation or the offender refused to make reparation as agreed. In cases such as these (which include not only Braithwaite's rational free-loading actor but the many other cases in which informal restorative justice processes would not be considered suitable) the sentencing powers of the courts would be restricted to the imposition of a 'restoration order', comprising

[20] As in the New Zealand family group conferencing model.

either compensation, reparation for the victim or some form of restorative justice-based community service. There would thus be no need for a strategy of 'active deterrence' since the court would in principle be able to enforce compliance on the part of offenders making a deceitful pretence at co-operation.

In more serious cases, (including cases in which the offender has unreasonably refused to make adequate amends, or there is a prolonged history of repeat offending followed by a refusal to make adequate reparation), greater weight would need to be placed on the 'public' aspect of the offence. Such cases could be said to represent a potential threat to the rights of other law-abiding citizens, whose interests need to be taken into account in determining the final outcome. However, the adoption of a rights-based approach also requires the 'private element' to be addressed. Consequently, an opportunity should still be afforded for suitable reparation to be informally negotiated in such cases. And due weight would need to be given by the court to the outcome of such negotiations when determining the kind and amount of additional punishment that might be appropriate, since a willingness to undertake reparation represents an acknowledgement that an offender has done wrong. It could also indicate a commitment to respect other people's rights in future. Where no adequate reparation is forthcoming, however, or reparation alone is not an adequate response to the 'public' element that needs to be addressed, what principles should apply regarding the type and amount of punishment to which an offender should be liable?

3. Reconceptualising Punishment within a Systemic Model of Restorative Justice: Rethinking the Role of Non-Custodial Penalties

If restorative justice *is* to furnish a more constructive form of 'replacement discourse' to counter the current repressive approach, it will be necessary to reformulate the existing range of punishments so that, as far as possible, every kind of penalty applies restorative justice principles in the pursuit of restorative outcomes. Some existing forms of punishment are already geared (in principle at least) towards the pursuit of broadly restorative outcomes—notably compensation orders and reparation orders. At present, however, the way in which compensation works is far from ideal from a restorative perspective (Cavadino et al 1999: 175). Compensation orders are not always considered despite a statutory duty on courts to do so. And even when compensation is imposed, the duty to take the offender's financial circumstances into account means that it may not represent the full amount that the victim has lost as a result of the crime, particularly where the offender has committed a number of offences with multiple victims. Moreover, the victim often has to wait a considerable time for any compensation to be paid, frequently in small sums according to the means of the offender; and often having to go back to the court when instalments are missed.

Furthermore, the *kind* of reparation that such penalties are capable of providing is inferior in many respects to the kind of reparation that might be expected to emanate from an appropriate restorative justice process. For example, it is far less flexible, is less likely to address the particular needs and sensitivities of the parties, and lacks the empowering potential that may ensue when victims and offenders are given the opportunity to participate actively in the offence resolution process. But in cases that do not lend themselves to restorative justice processes for one reason or another, the use of a compensation (or reparation) order is likely to result in a more constructive and restorative outcome than is likely to emanate from most other conventional forms of punishment, particularly if it is modified to take account of some of the operational shortcomings identified above.

Another conventional form of punishment that could in principle be modified in pursuit of restorative outcomes is the fine. This is not the case at present, since the revenue that is generated by fines is paid to the Treasury. But in principle it would be possible to strengthen the reparative potential of the fine. One way of achieving this would be to develop closer links between the fine and the compensation order, which might also attend to some of the deficiencies that have already been noted. For example, the income from fines (and also from proceeds that are confiscated from convicted offenders) could be used to create a 'Reparation Fund' that would enable victims to be compensated immediately.[21] The fund could then be reimbursed by the offender at whatever rate the court feels is appropriate after taking account of the offender's financial circumstances. There is still an important distinction between the fine, a financial compensation order that is imposed on an offender by the court, and a voluntary agreement on the part of an offender to make reparation (whether financial or non-financial) to a victim. Although the latter is preferable, it is not always achievable and, in such cases, it would be consistent with the idea of restorative justice as a form of replacement discourse to develop a much more explicit and transparent link between crimes which infringe the right and well-being of others, including the community at large, and the principle of reparation for such wrongs.

It may also be possible to adapt other penalties, such as the community service order, to ensure that they are capable of producing more reparative outcomes (Walgrave, 1999; Cavadino et al 1999: ch 4), though it will almost certainly be necessary to divest them of their more overtly repressive and denunciatory elements in order to do so. Thus, as Tony Bottoms (2000) has recently pointed out, the community service order can be, and often is, conceptualised in an unambiguously punitive manner as a 'fine on the offender's time', as where an offender is required to undertake meaningless and sometimes demeaning tasks that are

---

[21] Similar forms of hypothecation already operate within the criminal justice system; for example the channelling of the confiscated financial gains of drug offenders into programmes working to combat drug abuse and proposals to channel income from speeding fines to cover the cost of installing and operating road-side cameras. Moreover, the government has recently indicated (Home Office, 2001: para 3.118), that it is contemplating the creation of a Victims Fund to ensure that every victim receives immediate payment of any compensation that is ordered.

unrelated to the crime.[22] However, it can also be conceptualised either in a straightforwardly reparative manner as a more constructive and meaningful undertaking that is more closely related to the original offence; or as a potentially restorative or reintegrative intervention, for example where the task is related to the offender's skills or interests, or is intended to reinforce the offender's sense of self-esteem by providing a meaningful and worthwhile service to others.

With regard to other forms of non-custodial punishment, the restorative potential may not be so clearly discernible, but is rarely completely absent. In the case of probation, for example, attempts to promote compliance with the law by engaging in normative dialogue with an offender have some affinity with the kind of discourse that is encouraged during restorative justice processes such as conferencing. In principle it would be possible to move probation practice much closer to a model involving the 'dialogic regulation of social life' of the kind that is posited by Braithwaite (1999: 60) as part of the conferencing process. This might be done, for example, by encouraging probation officers to involve other people—including those that the offender cares about and also victims where appropriate—during discussions about the offence and the offending behaviour that gave rise to it.

Even the imposition of more restrictive measures such as curfew orders (with or without electronic monitoring) could in principle help to promote restorative outcomes; for example if they are adopted to enable an offender to maintain a job and so undertake financial reparation for a victim instead of being given a custodial sentence.[23] However, there is also a danger of 'up-tariffing' where such measures are used as substitutes for other forms of non-custodial punishment, or the conditions that are imposed are so restrictive that the offender faces an increased likelihood of imprisonment in the event of a breach (see also Roberts and Roach, this volume). The risk of up-tariffing is likely to be lower where such measures are introduced within the context of a 'systemic' model that prioritises restorative outcomes, but it would be naïve to imagine that it could be eliminated altogether; hence the need for effective constraints on the amount of punishment that can be imposed, and for effective procedural safeguards to ensure that those constraints are observed.

It is also worth noting that even within a punishment system in which the primary aim is to repair the harm caused by an offence and promote the restoration of victims, offenders and communities, this does not necessarily preclude the pursuit of other sentencing aims such as rehabilitation or even public protection in appropriate cases (see below). Indeed, irrespective of their views on the subject of personal reparation for themselves, many victims would like to feel that any

[22] For example one of the areas piloting reparation orders under the Crime and Disorder Act 1998 routinely required offenders to redecorate 'derelict' houses that no one lived in (Holdaway et al 2001: 91).

[23] The use of conditional sentences of imprisonment in Canada provides an interesting example of an attempt to pursue restorative outcomes in sentencing as an explicit alternative to imprisonment (see Roberts and Roach, this volume) even though the sentencing system as a whole falls a long way short of the 'systemic' approach that is advocated here.

response to their offence would reduce the likelihood of others being victimised in the way they have been.

4. Reconceptualising Punishment within a Systemic Model of Restorative Justice: Rethinking the Role of Imprisonment

So far I have been arguing that, even in cases for which informal restorative justices processes may be inappropriate, inapplicable or inadequate by themselves, it is possible to envisage a range of non-custodial court-imposed punishments that could be adapted to promote restorative outcomes. To this extent, at least, restorative justice could form the basis of a replacement discourse in which the emphasis would be on more constructive and less repressive forms of intervention. The use of custody would not normally be permitted within this kind of approach because it is rarely consistent with the pursuit of restorative outcomes. For that reason, it would not be routinely available as either a purely punitive or a deterrent measure, whether in an active or passive sense.

The use of custody would not be prohibited altogether, however, since some offenders do threaten the positive freedom of others to such an extent that protective measures are called for. But it would need to be strictly reserved instead for offenders who pose a serious and continuing threat to the personal safety of others.[24] Even where custodial sentences are warranted, however, much more could and should be done to promote restorative outcomes, for example by enabling offenders to undertake adequately paid work in prison in order to provide financial compensation for or on behalf of victims. Moreover, experience in a wide range of penal jurisdictions has shown that there is also scope for facilitating victim offender mediation in appropriate cases within a prison context. In England and Wales, for example, some victim offender mediation services (notably those serving the West Yorkshire and West Midland areas) have regularly mediated in serious cases where the offender is either still serving, or has recently been released from, a custodial sentence. In Belgium each of the 30 prisons now has its own restorative justice counsellor, whose responsibilities include the facilitation of a wide range of restorative activities (including but not restricted to mediation between victim and offender where requested) during the detention period (Verstraete et al 2000).

Equally important, however, is the need to apply wherever possible relevant insights that are derived from experience with informal restorative justice processes to the regulation of social life *within* the prison setting. Thus, much more could and should be done to foster constructive and mutually respectful relationships between staff and prison inmates, since such interactions normally

---

[24] There may also be a case for using imprisonment as a default sanction in order to secure compliance with a non-custodial order, but this would only be justifiable in fairly limited circumstances where the offence itself was serious and all other non-custodial options had been tried and failed.

afford the only context within which any kind of constructive dialogue, emotional engagement and behavioural or attitudinal change is likely to be possible (Cavadino and Dignan, 2002: 214ff). Within this setting, there is also a strong argument for adopting normative or 'moralistic' forms of reasoning with offenders. This kind of 'relational' approach is not only more humane and respectful of the rights of offenders, but offers a potentially much more constructive and effective approach than the cruder forms of instrumental reasoning based on sanctions and incentives that have typically been favoured—all too often with predictably damaging consequences—in the past (Liebling, 2001).

5. Revisiting the Need for Proportionality Constraints within a Systemic Model of Restorative Justice

I believe that the adoption of a restorative justice approach as outlined above could provide the basis of a more constructive 'replacement discourse'. If our existing range of punishments were to be reconceptualised in order to promote the pursuit of restorative outcomes as the primary sentencing aim it seems probable that this could in itself have a beneficial decremental effect on the overall level of punishment that is imposed. First, it would invalidate the use of purely retributive or deterrent sentencing strategies; and secondly, it should restrict the incapacitative use of imprisonment to cases in which an offender poses a serious and continuing threat to the personal safety of others that cannot be dealt with in any other way.

These optimistic predictions cannot be taken for granted, however, since the history of penal reform initiatives provides a constant reminder that benevolent intentions provide no guarantees against unintended and frequently malevolent consequences. For that reason, restorative justice advocates need to be able to at least specify the principles that might help to determine the overall amount of reparation or additional punishment to which an offender might be liable in the absence of the kind of 'strict proportionality' constraints that are favoured by just deserts' supporters.

One possible approach that might find favour with some restorative justice advocates would be to relate the severity and intensity of the response to the amount of harm that is caused. A slightly more sophisticated variant on the same theme might be to adapt the kind of 'living-standard analysis' that has been proposed by von Hirsch and Jareborg (1991) within a just deserts context, and relate the onerousness of any response to the extent to which the victim has been deprived of his or her positive freedom. Both approaches are problematic, however (Ashworth, 1993), and do not appear to lend themselves to the kind of decremental approach that has been advocated in this paper.

A better approach might be to link the proportionality constraint to the seriousness of the *wrong* that has been done to the victim—by violating the standards of behaviour that s/he is entitled to expect from fellow citizens—and possibly the wider community, rather than the *harm* that may actually have been caused (see also Duff, this volume). One advantage of this approach is that it detaches the scale of the overall response from the particular harm (or loss of positive freedom) that the victim may have experienced, while still acknowledging the latter's entitlement to appropriate reparation. Unless this is done, it may be much more difficult to resist calls for the response to 'equate' in some way with the harm that has actually been caused.

A second advantage is that it acknowledges that the 'wrongfulness' of a criminal act may be determined in part by the way the offender responds to it, and the extent to which s/he is prepared to undertake appropriate reparation for it. This reinforces the need to give due weight to the reparative response that the offender is prepared to undertake (for example, by participating in a restorative process that affirms the wrong to the victim, apologising and, possibly, undertaking other forms of reparation). Finally, a third advantage is that by focusing attention firmly on the reparative or restorative action that may be required in order to redress the wrong that has been done, the 'seriousness' of this wrong should place an upper limit on the severity of any response that may be deemed appropriate; for example by limiting the scope for deterrent, rehabilitative and preventive measures.

V. CONCLUSIONS

This paper is based on the premise that restorative justice advocates and desert theorists share a common strategic agenda that seeks a radical reform of our existing penal and criminal justice systems. It assumes that they would broadly agree that these systems are not only excessively repressive in the way they deal with offenders but also fail to adequately address the needs of victims. The paper suggests that while restorative justice advocates need to address the well-founded normative concerns that have been raised by critical desert theorists, a reformulated concept of restorative justice may be capable of providing the kind of decremental 'replacement discourse' that has so far eluded desert-based penal reformers. This will only be possible, however, if both sides are prepared to accept that restorative justice should be just as much concerned with the promotion of restorative outcomes (for *all* victims and offenders) as it has been with the pursuit of restorative processes. This in turn will require a radical reappraisal of the aims and scope of restorative justice approaches, and a willingness to engage in fresh thinking about the part that restorative justice values and practices might play within the wider penal system.

REFERENCES

American Friends Service Committee (1971) *Struggle for Justice* (Hill and Wang, New York).
Ashworth, A (1993) 'Some doubts about restorative justice' 4 *Criminal Law Forum* 277–99.
—— (1997) 'Sentenced by the Media' 29 *Criminal Justice Matters* 14–15.

Ashworth, A (2000) 'Assessing the R.J. Paradigm'. Paper presented to the Restorative Justice Colloquium, 12 Sep 2000, Cambridge UK.

Bazemore, G and Umbreit, M (1995) *Balanced and Restorative Justice: Program Summary.* Balanced and Restorative Justice Project (US Office of Juvenile Justice and Delinquency Prevention, Washington DC).

Bazemore, G and Walgrave, L (eds) (1999) *Restorative Juvenile Justice: Repairing the Harm of Youth Crime* (Criminal Justice Press, Monsey NY).

Bottoms, AE (2000) Oral contribution in the course of a conference on Restorative Justice: Exploring the Aims and Determining the Limits, held 6–8 Oct 2000, Cambridge UK.

Braithwaite, J (1991) 'The political agenda of republican criminology'. Paper presented at the British Criminological Society Conference, 27 July 1991, York UK.

——'Restorative Justice and a Better Future' (1996) 76(1) *Dalhousie Review* 9–32.

——(1999) 'Restorative justice: Assessing Optimistic and Pessimistic Accounts' in M Tonry (ed), *Crime and Justice: A Review of Research* (Chicago University Press, Chicago IL) vol 25, 1–127.

Braithwaite, J and Parker, C (1999) Restorative Justice is Republican Justice' in L Walgrave and G Bazemore (eds), *Restoring Juvenile Justice: An Exploration of the Restorative Justice Paradigm for Reforming Juvenile Justice* (Criminal Justice Press, Monsey NY).

Braithwaite, J and Pettit, P (1990) *Not Just Deserts: A Republican Theory of Criminal Justice* (Oxford University Press, Oxford).

Brown, M and Polk, K (1996) 'Taking the Fear of Crime Seriously: The Tasmanian Approach to Community Crime Prevention' 42 *Crime and Delinquency* 398–420.

Canadian Committee on Corrections (1969) *Report of the Canadian Committee on Corrections, Toward Unit: Criminal Justice and Corrections (The Ouimet Report)* (Queen's Printer, Ottawa).

Cavadino, M and Dignan, J (1997) 'Reparation, Retribution and Rights' 4 *International Review of Victimology* 233–53.

——(2002) *The Penal System: An Introduction,* 3rd edn (Sage, London).

Cavadino, M, Crow, I and Dignan, J (1999) *Criminal Justice 2000* (Waterside Press, Winchester).

Dignan, J (1994) 'Reintegration through reparation: a way forward for restorative justice?' in Duff et al (eds), *Penal Theory and Penal Practice: Tradition and Innovation in Criminal Justice* (Manchester University Press, Manchester).

Dignan, J with Lowey, K (2000) *Restorative Justice Options for Northern Ireland* (Criminal Justice Review Commission/Northern Ireland Office, Belfast).

Duff, A (1996) 'Penal Communications' in M Tonry (ed), *Crime and Justice: A Review of Research* (Chicago University Press, Chicago IL) vol 20, 1–97.

——(2000) *Punishment, Communication and Community* (Oxford University Press, New York).

Duff, A, Marshall, S, Dobash, RE and Dobash, RP (1994) *Penal Theory and Practice: Tradition and Innovation in Criminal Justice* (Manchester University Press, Manchester).

Dworkin, R (1978) *Taking Rights Seriously* (new impression) (Gerald Duckworth, London).

Gewirth, A (1978) *Reason and Mortality* (University of Chicago Press, Chicago IL).

Halliday, J (2001) *Making Punishments Work: Report of a Review of the Sentencing Framework for England and Wales* (Home Office Communications Directorate, London).

Holdaway, S, Davidson, N, Dignan, J, Hammersley, R, Hine, J and Marsh, P (2001) *New Strategies to Address Youth Offending: The National Evaluation of the Pilot Youth Offending Teams*. RDS Occasional Paper no 69. (Home Office Research, Development and Statistics Directorate, London). Also available on-line at http://www.homeoffice.gov.uk/rds/pdfs/occ69-newstrat.pdf.

Home Office (2001) *Criminal Justice: The Way Ahead* Cm5074 (The Stationery Office, London).

Hoyle, C, Young, R and Hill, R (2002) Proceed with Caution: an evaluation of police-led restorative justice (Joseph Rowntree, York).

Lacey, N and Zedner, L 'Discourses of Community' (1995) 22(3) *Journal of Law and Society* 301–25.

Liebling, A (2001) 'Policy and Practice in the Management of Disruptive Prisoners: Incentives and Earned Privileges, the Spurr Report and Close Supervision Centres' in E Clare and K Bottomley (eds), *Evaluation of Close Supervision Centres*. Home Office Research Study no 136. (Home Office Research, Development and Statistics Directorate, London).

Marshall, TF (1999) *Restorative Justice: An Overview* (Home Office Research, Development and Statistics Directorate, London).

McCold, P and Wachtel, B (1998) *Restorative Policing Experiments: The Bethlehem Pennsylvania Police Family Group Conferencing Project* (Community Service Foundation, Pipersville PA).

Maxwell, G and Morris, A (1996) 'Research on Family Group Conferences with Young Offenders in New Zealand' in J Hudson, A Morris, G Maxwell and B Galaway (eds), *Family Group Conferences: Perspectives on Policy and Practice* (Federation Press and Criminal Justice Press, Sydney).

Miers, D, Maguire, M, Goldie, S, Sharpe, K, Hale, C, Netten, A, Doolin, K, Uglow, S, Newburn, T and Enterkin, J (2001) An Exploratory Evaluation of Restorative Justice Schemes. Home Office Crime Reduction Series, paper 9.

Moore, DB and O'Connell, T (1994) 'Family Group Conferencing in Wagga Wagga: A Communitarian Model of Justice' in C Alder and J Wundersitz, *Family Conferencing and Juvenile Justice* (Australian Studies in Law, Crime and Justice, Australian Institute of Criminology, Canberra).

Morris, N (1974) *The Future of Imprisonment* (University of Chicago Press, London).

Morris, N and Tonry, M (1990) *Between Prison and Probation: Intermediate Punishments in a Rational Sentencing System* (Oxford University Press, New York).

Newburn, T, Masters, G, Earle, R, Goldie, S, Crawford, A, Sharpe, K, Netton A, Hale, C, Uglow, S and Saunders, R (2001a and b) *The Introduction of Referral Orders into the Youth Justice System*. RDS Occasional Paper no 70 and 73. (Home Office Research, Development and Statistics Directorate, London). Also available on-line at http://www.homeoffice.gov.uk/rds/index.html.

Newburn, T, Crawford, A, Earle, R, Goldie, S, Hale, C, Hallam, A, Masters, G, Netten A, Saunders, R, Sharpe, K and Uglow, S (2002) The Introduction of Referral Orders into the Youth Justice System. Final Report (Home Office Research, Development and Statistics Directorate, London). Home Office http://www.homeoffice.gov.uk/index.html.

Roach, K 'Changing Punishment at the Turn of the Century: Restorative Justice on the Rise' (2000) 42(2) *Canadian Journal of Criminology* 249–80.

Tyler, TR (1990) *Why People Obey the Law* (Yale University Press, New Haven).

Umbreit, M and Roberts, A (1996) *Mediation of Criminal Conflict in England: An Assessment of Services in Coventry and Leeds* (Centre for Restorative Justice and Mediation, University of Minnesota, St Paul MN).

Verstraete, A, Verhoeven, H and Vandeurzen, I (2000) 'Introducing Restorative Justice in Belgian Prisons'. Paper presented at X International Symposium on Victimology, August 2000, Montreal.

von Hirsch, A (1993) *Censure and Sanctions* (Clarendon Press, Oxford).

von Hirsch, A and Jareborg, N (1991) 'Gauging Criminal Harm: A Living Standard Analysis' 11 *Oxford Journal of Legal Studies* 1–38.

Walgrave, L (1999) 'Community Service as a Cornerstone of a Systemic Restorative Response to (Juvenile) Crime' in G Bazemore and L Walgrave (eds), *Restorative Juvenile Justice: Repairing the Harm of Youth Crime* (Criminal Justice Press, Monsey NY).

—— (2001) 'Restoration and Punishment: Duet or Duel? In Search of Social Ethics for Restorative Justice'. Paper presented to the Restorative Justice Symposium, 12–13 May, 2001, Toronto.

Walker, N and March, C (1984) 'Do Sentences Affect Public Disapproval?' 24 *British Journal of Criminology* 27–48.

Watson, D, Boucherat, J and David, G (1989) 'Reparation for Retributivists' in M Wright and B Galaway (eds), *Mediation and Criminal Justice: Victims, Offenders and Community* (Sage, London).

Wright, M (1991) *Justice for Victims and Offenders* (Open University Press, Milton Keynes).

—— (1996) *Justice for Victims and Offenders: A Restorative Response to Crime* 2nd edn (Waterside Press, Winchester).

8

Proposed Basic Principles on the Use of Restorative Justice: Recognising the Aims and Limits of Restorative Justice

Daniel W Van Ness

What are the aims of restorative justice? What are its limits? Critics complain that restorative justice advocates are prone to offering visionary and expansive answers to the first question, and reluctant to concede anything in answering the second. Part of the reason for the apparent lack of clarity is that the term 'restorative justice' is used in multiple ways. Sometimes it describes a visionary look at a whole new understanding of crime and justice—a new paradigm. Other times it refers to a public policy for responding to crime, one that emphasises the need to 'make things right'. In the past few years, some have used the term to apply to a possible future system of justice capable of responding to all crimes, solved or unsolved, all defendants, guilty or innocent, and all victims, whether or not their offenders have been convicted. The label 'restorative' is applied to particular kinds of programmes—mediation, conferencing or circles—whose purpose is to allow victims, offenders and those close to them to meet, to talk about their specific crimes and to consider ways to address the harm that resulted. Finally, the term is applied to particular kinds of arguably reparative but judicially imposed sentences, such as restitution or community service.

This chapter will not address the first three usages (vision, public policy or system). Instead, it will focus on the narrower and more tangible expressions of restorative justice found in the programmes frequently identified with the movement. Some of these programmes establish alternative procedures to conventional criminal justice; we could call them restorative processes. Others implement restitution or community service sentences that have been negotiated or imposed; we could call those restorative outcomes.

The aims of restorative justice as a vision or policy are much broader than the aims of restorative processes or outcomes. Because restorative processes and outcomes are more tangible, their aims and limitations are more readily apparent. This can be seen in a set of Basic Principles on the Use of Restorative Justice Programmes in Criminal Matters developed by NGOs and subsequently used as the basis for UN debate and action on restorative justice guidelines. This chapter will offer a brief history of the development of the basic principles followed by an annotated review of their provisions.

I. BACKGROUND TO THE PROPOSED BASIC PRINCIPLES

Every five years, the United Nations convenes a Congress on Crime Prevention and the Treatment of Offenders for discussion and debate on topics related to crime, criminal justice, treatment of offenders and more recently, treatment of victims. The Congresses offer an opportunity for countries to discuss national experiences with programmes and problems in criminal justice. They also are used to discuss joint strategies and mutual co-operation in matters that transcend national boundaries.

Non-governmental organisations in consultative status with the United Nations are actively involved in the Congresses as well. One of the most visible ways in which this happens is through ancillary meetings open to delegates at the Congresses that explore issues of concern to the NGOs. At the Congresses in 1990 and 1995, NGOs sponsored ancillary meetings on the topic of restorative justice. During this period of time, as countries witnessed the growing spread of restorative programmes, interest and participation in these sessions expanded.

The Ninth Congress, conducted in Cairo in 1995, included several sessions on the theme of restorative justice. While interest in the topic seemed to be strong, it was apparent that neither the presentations during ancillary meetings nor the growing domestic experience of Member States with restorative programmes had any effect on debate during the Committee and Plenary Sessions of the Congress itself. As a result, a group of NGOs participating in the Alliance on Crime Prevention and Criminal Justice (NY) decided to form a Working Party on Restorative Justice.

The Alliance had a long history of convening working parties around issues of common concern. These groups followed a fairly consistent pattern. They began with a literature review and a survey of criminal justice officials and NGO representatives in different countries on the issue of interest to the working party. Based on this research, the working party would issue a report and recommendations. Often these became the basis for an ancillary meeting at a Crime Congress.

The Working Party on Restorative Justice had a different agenda. Its objective was to stimulate sufficient international awareness of and interest in restorative justice to make it an item of discussion at the Tenth Crime Congress to be held in 2000. Members of the Alliance believed that this topic was of enough import and interest that it deserved discussion in the Committee and Plenary Sessions of the Congress itself, not simply in the ancillary meetings.

The Working Party was made up of representatives of NGOs in consultative status with the UN as well as other NGOs and individuals who had practical, research or academic expertise in the subject. During the early research stages of the Working Party, its members included many who were active in restorative justice work but did not represent NGOs in consultative status. Over time, and as the work of the Working Party focused increasingly on the expected Tenth Congress, participation narrowed to representatives of member organisations of the Alliance.

The Working Party's initial efforts focused on collecting and organising existing research and experience concerning restorative justice. Out of those efforts came several resources:

1. A Restorative Justice Handbook which proposed a working definition and key principles of restorative justice, descriptions of typical restorative programmes, a lexicon of terminology commonly used in discussions about restorative justice, and so on.
2. An annotated bibliography of articles and research concerning the use of restorative justice worldwide compiled by Dr Paul McCold and subsequently published by Criminal Justice Press in 1997.[1]

This phase of the Working Party's activities came to a close at about the time the UN began planning for the Tenth Crime Congress. In 1997, the Commission on Crime Prevention and Criminal Justice adopted a provisional agenda for that Congress. Item four on the agenda was 'Offenders and victims: accountability and fairness in the justice process'. It was understood that this topic opened the door to discussion of restorative justice as well as issues related to the rights and roles of victims in criminal justice.

A year later, the Commission approved a discussion guide for the regional preparatory meetings that traditionally precede a Congress. Included in the discussion guide for item four was a lengthy description of restorative justice (concept and programme) and a request for comment by the preparatory meetings on whether standards and norms were needed to guide member states in implementation of restorative programmes.

At its meeting in 1999, the Commission debated and approved a draft declaration for consideration by the Crime Congress. Paragraph 25 of this draft referred to restorative justice and established the year 2002 as a date for States to review their practices in support of crime victims, 'including mechanisms for mediation and restorative justice'.

In addition, the government of Italy proposed a resolution on mediation and restorative justice. Among other things, this resolution requested that the Commission 'consider the desirability of formulating United Nations standards in the field of mediation and restorative justice'. This resolution was approved by the Commission and referred to United Nations Economic and Social Council (ECOSOC), which adopted it later that year.

Just before the Tenth Congress convened, the International Scientific and Professional Advisory Council (ISPAC) released a study entitled 'An Overview of

---

[1] P McCold (1997), *Restorative Justice: Annotated Bibliography* (Criminal Justice Press, Monsey NY). The entries in the bibliography have since been put online and are regularly updated as a searchable database on restorative justice. See Research Centre at www.restorativejustice.org.

Restorative Justice Programmes' drafted by Professor Paul Friday. This study concluded as follows:

> **Guidelines and standards are desperately needed.** There is a danger that programs that are initially restorative in outlook recreate the courtroom process and, in turn, undermine rather than cultivate restoration. There is also the danger that the legal basis for initiating the process can get lost. And there is a third danger that the etiological factors producing crime—poverty, racism, cultural/social values, individualism will not be addressed as they are uncovered in the process.[2]

II. THE WORKING PARTY PREPARES BASIC PRINCIPLES

Meanwhile, the Working Party had begun drafting basic principles on restorative justice. That project had grown naturally out of the initial research phase, during which it had discovered a growing interest in the development of guidelines and standards for countries intending to use restorative programmes. This concern was reflected in the activities of the Council of Europe and in several independent efforts by researchers and policymakers to create such standards.

1. Council of Europe Recommendation R(99)19

In 1995, the Council of Europe appointed an Expert Committee to evaluate and assess the use of mediation in criminal proceedings within Europe. Between 1996 and 1999 the Committee met to review reports from countries with experience in mediation of criminal matters, and to consider what if any recommendations to make. The reports contained descriptions of the use of mediation, outcome evaluation, legal and policy issues raised by mediation, and so on. Based on the reports and substantial discussion, the Committee prepared a draft recommendation and Explanatory Memorandum and submitted it in June 1999. The Committee of Ministers adopted the recommendation later that year.[3]

---

[2] Pl C Friday (1999) 'An Overview of Restorative Justice Programmes and Issues', paper presented for the International Scientific and Professional Advisory Council, 35 (emphasis in original).

[3] Council of Europe Committee of Ministers (1999) 'Mediation in Penal Matters' Recommendation No R(99)19, adopted 15 Sept 1999. For a brief history of the Committee's work, see the accompanying Explanatory Memorandum at pp 11–12. Mediation is defined as 'any process whereby the victim and the offender are enabled, if they freely consent, to participate actively in the resolution of matters arising from the crime through the help of an impartial third party (mediator)'. The principles are divided among five sections:
1. general principles: addressing consent, confidentiality, the general availability of mediation geographically and within all phases of the criminal justice system, and the autonomy of mediation within the criminal justice system
2. legal basis: the need for legislation, guidelines and protection of fundamental procedural safeguards
3. the operation of criminal justice in relation to mediation: referring cases to mediation, informing parties about mediation, avoiding unfair inducement, protecting minors and persons not

The Appendix to the recommendation defines 'mediation' and offers 34 principles for Member States of the Council of Europe to consider when using mediation in penal matters.

2. Declaration of Leuven

In 1997, the International Network for Research on Restorative Justice for Juveniles convened the first of what have become annual conferences on 'Restorative Justice for Juveniles'. At the conclusion of that conference, the Network adopted a declaration 'on the advisability of promoting the restorative approach to juvenile crime'. This came to be known by the name of the location of that conference, Leuven, Belgium.

The Declaration begins with a preliminary section entitled 'The Potential', containing five optimistic observations based on experience with restorative justice for juveniles to that date (its scope is worldwide, initial results are positive, no decisive limits have been observed, it offers potential for increased peacemaking, and wider applications appear promising). It follows with ten propositions, many broken into multiple parts, based on then-current research and experience.[4]

3. Standards for Restorative Justice

The Restorative Justice Consortium is a group of individuals and organisations in the UK interested in promoting restorative justice practice in their country. The

---

capable of understanding the process, requiring acknowledgement of the facts of the case, dealing with disparities between the parties, setting reasonable time-frames, and responding to both successful and unsuccessful outcomes

4. the operation of mediation services: standards, qualification and training of mediators, handling cases, and outcomes, and

5. continuing development of mediation: ongoing consultation and research.

[4] Declaration of Leuven. In summary, the ten propositions are:

1. crime should be responded to as harm to victims

2. the purpose of the social response to crime should be to restore the range of harms resulting from crime

3. public authorities should make restorative responses available to victims and juvenile offenders

4. participation of the victim and juvenile offender should be voluntary

5. competency-building and rehabilitative programs should be made available to juvenile offenders

6. incarceration should be used only for purposes of public safety, and when it is used the juvenile offender should have opportunities to participate in restorative activities

7. any coercion should be imposed only by a judicial body, and the outcomes of restorative programs should not exceed the maximum in a range of sanctions proportionate to the seriousness of the harm and the responsibility and capabilities of the juvenile offender

8. juvenile justice should be reformed to incorporate restorative responses by both public authorities and community-based agencies

9. process, outcome and theoretical research should continue

10. lessons learned in juvenile justice may be applicable to adult criminal justice as well.

Consortium's purposes are to educate the public and criminal justice officials about the benefits of restorative justice, to encourage policy makers to use restorative approaches, to share information among themselves, and to recommend standards for restorative justice projects. In 1999, the Consortium issued their Standards for Restorative Justice.[5]

The standards are presented in six sections, organised around the rights, needs, obligations, and responsibilities of different parties. Noting that use of restorative justice programmes leads to greater flexibility in the criminal justice system, it cautions that this could undermine existing protections of individual rights. The standards are proposed as a means of preserving human rights and ensuring ethical practice as victims, offenders, communities, criminal justice officials and programme practitioners participate in restorative justice.[6]

---

[5] In March 2002, the Consortium adopted a new document, Statement of Restorative Justice Principles, to replace the Standards. This Statement may be found at www.restorativejustice.org.uk/standard.html. Because it was not available to the Working Party as it drafted the basic principles, this paper does not summarise its contents or describe the process leading to its adoption.

[6] The Consortium works through committees. The standards committee was known as SINRJ (Standards in Restorative Justice) and included not only members of the Consortium but also an international advisory panel. TF Marshall, (1999) *Restorative Justice: An Overview* (Home Office Research Development and Statistics Directorate, London), 9.

The six sections address the following groups:

1. The rights and needs of victims, offenders and others involved in restorative justice processes
    a. In relation to the criminal justice system: standards, equal access, swiftness, contextualisation, judicial oversight, voluntariness, integrity of program purpose, renegotiation when necessary
    b. In relation to criminal justice agencies: offered to all, screening of criminal justice agents, impartiality and training of criminal justice agents, complaints systems
    c. In relation to restorative justice programs: fair procedures, confidentiality, safety, adding participants, legal advice, preparation of parties, minors and parents/guardians, power imbalances, duress, withdrawal, facilitator's role, interpreters, insurance, assessment of programs
2. The rights and needs of victims: voluntariness, ensure victim's needs are addressed, time and place convenient to victim, priority where there is a personal victim, priority of meeting victim's needs, agreements should be kept, offenders should respond to victims, no obligation to accept offers from offender, victim involvement in design and oversight
3. The rights, needs and obligations of the accused: right to refuse participation without penalty, admission of act (but not necessarily legal culpability) required, presumption of innocence may be reasserted, criminal justice decisions should consider inability/willingness to make reparation, criminal justice decisions should consider rehabilitation programs needed, right to voluntarily offer reparation, companies are not victims because they insured the victim, protection against cruel, demeaning or degrading experience, proportionality of reparation to harm caused
4. The needs of the local community: need for restoration, healing and safety, minimise public expenditure, consultation, resources and education, official support of community initiatives, involvement in agency and program operations
5. Society's responsibility to effect rehabilitation of offenders: crime reduction through rehabilitation, reintegration is primary objective, punishment only when justifiable, priority to cases of likely recidivism, apply restorative justice in all types of cases, at all ages, in all stages of criminal careers, alleviation of criminogenic factors, repeated use even after initial failure
6. Need to ensure program integrity: clear aims, partnerships, values and principles, application to whole criminal justice process, clear and reasonable agreements, training of referral agencies, training of staff and volunteers, accreditation, monitoring, codes of practice and standards

4. VOMA Recommended Ethical Guidelines

The Victim-Offender Mediation Association consists of 350 individual members and 30 agency members in 40 states and seven countries. It grew out of an informal network of restorative justice practitioners, researchers and advocates in the early 1980s. Its purpose is to promote and provide best practices, guidelines, and peer support for its members and others in the field. One way in which it has done so is through its 'Recommended Ethical Guidelines.'[7]

The guidelines are directed to practitioners, and cover the process and procedures to be used in handling cases, impartiality and neutrality of the mediator, confidentiality and the exchange of information, the rights of the parties to self determination and professional advice, the training of mediators, their advertising and fees, and how mediators should relate to their peers and to the media.

5. ABA Victim-Offender Mediation/Dialogue Programme Requirements

In 1994, the American Bar Association adopted a resolution urging incorporation of victim-offender mediation/dialogue programmes into the criminal justice system provided that these programmes are run consistently with 13 'program requirements'. These concern the programme's goals, monitoring, funding and evaluation; screening of victims and offenders; voluntary participation with no

---

[7] For more information on VOMA, see its website at www.voma.org. The guidelines are divided into fourteen sections. The first defines mediation (which includes victim-offender mediation, victim-offender dialogue and conferencing) as 'the process of bringing together the victim of a crime and his or her offender in a safe, controlled setting that is assisted by a trained mediator.' It also provides a list of purposes and principles or values that underlie mediation. The second section describes the process, beginning wit training for mediators, screening of cases, use of a model of mediation it describes as 'humanistic/transformative', preparation of victims and offenders, disclosure by the mediator, and follow-up after sessions. The third provides for negotiated understanding among the parties on matters such as confidentiality, legal consultation, additional parties, and the responsibilities of the mediator and participants. The fourth obliges the mediator to maintain impartiality and neutrality toward the parties, including disclosure of prior relationships and conflicts of interest. The fifth addresses a number of issues related to confidentiality and disclosure or exchange of information by the mediator. The sixth indicates that primary responsibility for the outcome and rests with the parties. While the mediator is not to coerce either party to accept or reject participation or outcomes, the mediator is also expected to help participants understand the views of others. The seventh encourages mediators to refer participants to expert information and advice and to seek legal assistance when relevant matters arise. The eighth give suggestions for protecting weak parties from being dominated by strong parties during mediation. The ninth discusses reasons for termination of mediation because of agreement, restitution, termination by the parties or the mediator, and impasse of the participants. The tenth requires training in mediation and urges continuing education. The eleventh addresses situations in which the mediator wishes to charge fees; the fees must be reasonable and explained to the participants. Contingent fees and referral fees are prohibited. The twelfth permits advertising only concerning the mediation process, its costs and benefits, and the qualifications of the mediator. The thirteenth relates to relationships between mediators. The last section deals with media relations, supporting general education on the topic of mediation, but urging caution when the media wishes to follow particular cases.

adverse effects upon the offender for refusal to participate; face-to-face meetings; the inadmissibility of statements made in mediation/dialogue; selection and training of mediators; and involvement of prosecutors and defence attorneys.[8]

Each of these documents was informative and useful, but they had several limitations. First, three of the five addressed only one dimension of restorative justice: mediation. Secondly, four of the five were the product of researchers and experts in the field, not the result of a process that included the political support of governments. Thirdly, for the most part they made no attempt to be global, but instead involved geographical, subject matter or age limitations.

The Working Party began exploring development of standards or guidelines for countries on the use of restorative justice programmes that could be offered for debate and discussion in the political processes of the United Nations. Its initial idea was that this could take place during the Tenth Crime Congress.[9] Beginning with the standards mentioned above, and in particular the Council of Europe Recommendation on the Use of Mediation in Penal Matters, the Working Party sought to draft a document that would reflect the range of restorative justice programmes (its subject matter would be broader than simply mediation, for example) as well as the experience of countries around the world, not just those of Europe or North America. The results of various studies by Law Reform Commissions and Justice Ministries in New Zealand, Australia and South Africa were informative in this process. The Working Party was also guided by existing standards and norms of the UN, such as the Declaration of Basic Principles of Justice for Victims of Crime and Abuse of Power.

The Working Party circulated successive drafts to restorative justice researchers, practitioners and policy-makers around the world and incorporated their suggestions in subsequent drafts. It also circulated drafts to governments, requesting advice on whether such an instrument might be useful to consider during the course of the Tenth Congress or the following Crime Commission meetings. As a result of this consultation, the governments of Canada and Italy introduced a resolution to the Crime Commission proposing development of UN basic principles on the use of restorative justice programmes, with the Working Party's draft annexed as 'Preliminary draft elements' of such a declaration. This resolution was adopted by the Crime Commission in April 2000, and subsequently approved by ECOSOC in July.

Pursuant to that resolution, the Secretary General circulated the resolution and preliminary draft elements to Member States requesting comment on the advisability of adopting guidelines on the use of restorative justice, as well as on the substance of the preliminary draft elements. The UN subsequently created a Group of Experts to review those comments and recommend further UN action

---

[8] American Bar Association, 'Criminal Justice Policy on Victim-Offender Mediation/Dialogue', approved Aug 1994.

[9] As it turned out, rules governing the Congress did not permit that. Instead, Canada and Italy introduced it for debate in the meeting of the Commission on Crime Prevention and Criminal Justice that followed the Crime Congress.

if necessary. This body met in Ottawa, Ontario in late 2001 and in the course of its four-day meeting reviewed and revised the preliminary draft elements into a set of UN basic principles on the use of restorative justice programmes in criminal matters.

III. COMMENT ON THE WORKING PARTY'S BASIC PRINCIPLES ON THE USE OF RESTORATIVE JUSTICE PROGRAMMES IN CRIMINAL MATTERS

The 23 basic principles proposed by the Working Party are grouped into five sections dealing with definitions, use of restorative justice programmes, operation of restorative justice programmes, facilitators, and continuing development of restorative justice programmes. The remained of this paper will provide background comment on the document as a whole, on each section, and on the proposed basic principles themselves.

1. Basic Principles on the Use of Restorative Justice Programmes in Criminal Matters

The UN has issued standards and norms related to many aspects of criminal justice. Sometimes these take the form of basic principles, sometimes of standard minimum rules, and sometimes of conventions or treaties. *Basic principles* provide governments with general guidance related to a particular topic, but they do not address in detail how the principles should be implemented. Examples include the Basic Principles of Justice for Victims of Crime and Abuse of Power, the Basic Principles for the Treatment of Prisoners, and the Basic Principles on the Use of Force and Firearms by Law Enforcement Officials. *Standard minimum rules* are more comprehensive directives to Member States that provide detailed guidance. They are much longer and more specific than basic principles, and consequently offer less flexibility once promulgated (both to Member States, and to the UN if subsequent practice prompts change). Examples include the Standard Minimum Rules for the Treatment of Prisoners and the Standard Minimum Rules for the Administration of Juvenile Justice (the Beijing Rules). *Treaties or conventions* are agreements between Member States concerning how they will co-operate in certain tasks or ways in which they agree to restrain their own internal conduct. Examples include the Model Agreement on the Transfer of Foreign Prisoners and the Convention against Torture and Other Cruel, Inhuman or Degrading Treatment or Punishment.

The Working Party concluded that basic principles rather than standard minimum rules were appropriate at this time for several reasons. First, what countries had requested during regional preparatory meetings prior to the Tenth Congress was guidance about use of restorative justice programmes in criminal matters, not clear-cut rules. Secondly, in the opinion of restorative justice experts the movement had not yet developed common and global agreement on the particular rules that should apply to restorative programmes, and that as a result standard minimum rules would be premature. Thirdly, one of the administrative and practical concerns for the UN in adopting standards is that they can lead to requests for UN technical support to implement them. This is another reason why the basic principles were written as *principles* and not as *standard minimum rules*. They are designed to give guidance, not to impose rules or standards on countries.

Unlike other topics the UN has addressed, no country is required to use restorative justice programmes. Consequently, in adopting basic principles on the use of restorative justice, the UN would not be imposing burdens on countries, since there is no obligation to use restorative justice programmes. Every country has prisoners, victims, law enforcement officials, juveniles, courts and so forth, and the UN standards adopted on those topics apply to every country. But not every country will choose to use restorative processes, so the development of guidelines for those countries that do will not impose a burden on those who don't. What the Basic Principles do is make it possible for countries considering restorative justice programmes to draw upon the experience of other countries.

I. Definitions

The proposed basic principles do not attempt to define 'restorative justice'. This was an intentional omission based on several considerations. First, the basic principles themselves do not address restorative justice at the level of vision, public policy or a comprehensive system. Rather they address particular programmatic expressions of restorative justice. Therefore, it was necessary only to define those expressions. Secondly, there is no general agreement on a definition of restorative justice, and it seemed unwise to embed a particular definition into a United Nations document not likely to change significantly in future years.

1. *'Restorative Justice Programme' means any programme that uses restorative processes or aims to achieve restorative outcomes.*
The limited scope of the basic principles is reflected in the title, which refers to 'restorative justice programmes'. This term is given particular meaning by reference to the two following definitions. Together the three definitions indicate that these principles apply to the various forms of victim-offender mediation, conferencing and circles, and to restitution and community service obligations arising out of those restorative processes. They also include any other restorative process that may emerge, and to the agreements that come out of those processes in addition to restitution and community service.

2. *'Restorative Outcome' means an agreement reached as the result of a restorative process. Examples of restorative outcomes include restitution, community service and any other programme or response designed to accomplish reparation of the victim and community, and reintegration of the victim and/or the offender.*

Restitution and community service are commonly linked to restorative justice (and to other sentencing philosophies). This definition is an expansive one: it incorporates all elements of the agreement, including those that are done because the victim or community has requested it as well as those that have a rehabilitative or reintegrative purpose. All aspects of the agreements reached in the course of restorative processes are subject to the basic principles.

3. *'Restorative Process' means any process in which the victim, the offender and/or any other individuals or community members affected by a crime actively participate together in the resolution of matters arising from the crime, often with the help of a fair and impartial third party. Examples of restorative process include mediation, conferencing and sentencing circles.*

This definition adapts an increasingly used definition offered by Tony Marshall: 'Restorative Justice is a process whereby parties with a stake in a specific offence collectively resolve how to deal with the aftermath of the offence and its implications for the future'.[10] It substitutes 'the victim, the offender and/or any other individuals or community members affected by a crime' for Marshall's more general 'parties with a stake in a specific offence'. It also notes that this collaborative resolution often requires the assistance of a skilled third party, the facilitator. The Declaration of Leuven applies the term 'restorative process' to the approach described by Marshall.[11]

4. *'Parties' means the victim, the offender and any other individuals or community members affected by a crime who may be involved in a restorative justice programme.*

Throughout the basic principles, the term 'parties' is used more broadly than simply the victim and the offender. It also incorporates individuals and community members who are touched by crime.

5. *'Facilitator' means a fair and impartial third party whose role is to facilitate the participation of victims and offenders in an encounter programme.*

The term 'facilitator' was chosen rather than 'mediator' because the latter term is not used in conferencing or circles. The term 'encounter programme' should read instead 'restorative process'. A comment about impartiality is found after paragraph 18.

II. Use of Restorative Justice Programmes

6. *Restorative justice programmes should be generally available at all stages of the criminal justice process.*

---

[10] Marshall, at p 5.
[11] See paras 1 and 3.

A similar principle appears in the CE Recommendation (see Guidelines 3 and 4). This does not mean that programmes will operate the same at all stages of the criminal justice process, nor that they will have a similar effect. An agreement reached prior to the sentencing of an offender may shape the sentence. An agreement reached after the sentence may have no effect on the sentence at all. One example of this are the victim-offender dialogue programmes that exist in several US states, which provide victims with an opportunity to meet with their offenders while they are serving their sentences in prison (or in some instances even, awaiting execution). It is understood that the programmes will not influence the prisoners' sentence; the programmes serve other purposes related to the victim's recovery.

7. *Restorative processes should be used only with free and voluntary consent of the parties. The parties should be able to withdraw such consent at any time during the process. Agreements should be arrived at voluntarily by the parties and contain only reasonable and proportionate obligations.*

This paragraph incorporates two guidelines appearing in the CE Recommendation (Guidelines 1 and 31). The first two sentences speak of voluntary participation by the parties in restorative justice processes. Since those processes are dependent on the full participation of the parties, they must choose to enter the process and be given the option of leaving the process at any time. It will be important that referring agencies and restorative justice practitioners inform the parties of this right at the outset.

The third sentence relates to restorative outcomes. The principle of voluntariness continues here: the agreement reached during a restorative process is not to be imposed in the same way as a judge imposes a sentence. Furthermore, the agreement must be reasonable and proportionate. The Explanation provided with the CE Recommendation notes that 'reasonable' means that the agreement must have some relationship to the offence, and that 'proportionality' means that 'within rather wide limits, there should be correspondence between the burden on the offender and the seriousness of the offence; for instance, compensation should not be excessive'.[12]

8. *All parties should normally acknowledge the basic facts of a case as a basis for participation in a restorative process. Participation should not be used as evidence of admission of guilt in subsequent legal proceedings.*

This is a slightly reworded version of the fourteenth Guideline in the CE Recommendation. This separates an acknowledgement of what took place from the question of legal guilt. Restorative justice processes typically require a general agreement on the facts, which implicitly includes recognition of some sort of culpability on the part of the offender.[13] Related to this is the 'flipside': that agreeing

---

[12] Explanation, p 24.

[13] In some jurisdictions, 'declining to deny guilt' is treated as a sufficient recognition of wrongdoing by the offender (J Braithwaite and S Mugford, 'Conditions of Successful Reintegration Ceremonies: Dealing with Juvenile Offenders,' (1994) 34(2) *British Journal of Criminology* 139–71.)

to participate in a restorative process cannot be treated as an admission of legal guilt. The presumption of innocence in criminal proceedings must continue, even if the accused has at one time agreed to participate in a restorative process.

9. *Obvious disparities with respect to factors such as power imbalances and the parties' age, maturity or intellectual capacity should be taken into consideration in referring a case to and in conducting a restorative process. Similarly, obvious threats to any of the parties' safety should also be considered in referring a case to and in conducting a restorative process. The views of the parties themselves about the suitability of restorative processes or outcomes should be given great deference in this consideration.*

The first sentence of the paragraph is drawn from the fifteenth Guideline in the CE Recommendation. What are addressed here are several factors to be considered in screening cases and in conducting restorative processes. When there is sufficient disparity between parties in power, age, maturity or intellectual capacity that the parties cannot discuss the crime as equals, it will be difficult to conduct meaningful conversation during the process. Furthermore, when one party finds their safety threatened because of their participation in the process, the party cannot negotiate meaningfully. The paragraph urges great deference to the parties' view on whether a restorative process is suitable, although it does not leave the decision on that with the parties.

10. *Where restorative processes and/or outcomes are not possible, criminal justice officials should do all they can to encourage the offender to take responsibility vis-à-vis the victim and affected communities, and reintegration of the victim and/or offender into the community.*

There are a number of ways in which a restorative process or outcome can fail. One or more of the parties may be unknown or unwilling to participate. They may be unable to reach agreement in the course of a restorative process. One of the parties may fail to carry out the terms of the agreement once it has been reached. Perhaps the power imbalances referred to in paragraph 9 make a restorative process inadvisable. Under such circumstances the matter will be returned to the referring agency (see paragraphs 15 and 16). This paragraph recognises that the failure of the restorative process or outcome does not remove the need for redress for those who were harmed, or for reintegration of the parties into their communities. It urges that criminal justice officials do what they can to encourage such restorative aims even when the restorative process and outcomes cannot be used.

III. *Operation of Restorative Justice Programmes*

11. *Guidelines and standards should be established, with legislative authority when necessary, that govern the use of restorative justice programmes. Such guidelines and standards should address:*

(a) *The conditions for the referral of cases to restorative justice programmes;*
(b) *The handling of cases following a restorative process;*
(c) *The qualifications, training and assessment of facilitators;*
(d) *The administration of restorative justice programmes;*
(e) *Standards of competence and ethical rules governing operation of restorative justice programmes.*

There is a need for oversight and standards for restorative justice programmes. The informality and flexibility that characterise restorative processes and outcomes increase the ability of the parties to tailor a response to the crime that fits the offence, the offender, the victim and others who are affected. This flexibility, however, 'may make current protections of individuals rights and interests less secure'.[14] Furthermore, it may mask incompetent or unethical practices by programme administration or facilitators, and/or by the criminal justice personnel who refer cases to restorative justice programmes. While self-regulation and training can do much to address these problems, the protection of certain right and interests of the parties may require involvement of the legislative and administrative breaches of government.

12. *Fundamental procedural safeguards should be applied to restorative justice programmes and in particular to restorative processes:*
    (a) *parties should have the right to legal advice before and after the restorative process and, where necessary, to translation and/or interpretation. Minors should, in addition, have the right to parental assistance;*
    (b) *Before agreeing to participate in restorative processes, the parties should be fully informed of their rights, the nature of the process and the possible consequences of their decision;*
    (c) *Neither the victim nor the offender should be induced by unfair means to participate in restorative processes or outcomes.*

This paragraph is drawn from Guidelines 8, 10 and 11 of the CE Recommendation. It provides that procedural safeguards of the parties must be protected by informing them of their rights, giving them access to legal advice before and after the restorative process, and ensuring that they have the assistance of translators/interpreters when necessary, and of parents in the case of minors. It further requires disclosure to the parties about the nature of the restorative process and the consequences of deciding to participate in such a process. Finally, it acknowledges that some inducements given to parties to encourage them to participate in restorative justice programmes can be unfair. Examples include pressure by criminal justice officials on a defendant to participate when the defendant claims innocence, or a threat or bribe by the offender to the victim in order to coerce the victim's involvement. Such unfair inducements are prohibited.

Some countries have raised the concern that the right to legal advice referred to in subparagraph (a) would bestow rights that do not exist in their current laws.

---

[14] Standards for Restorative Justice, Preface, 3.

In particular, this section could be read to require free legal assistance to victims of crime. It may be that this concern can be dealt with by providing for 'the right to obtain legal advice'.

13. *Discussion in restorative processes should be confidential and should not be disclosed subsequently, except with the agreement of the parties.*

This paragraph is drawn from Guideline 2 of the CE Recommendation. The reason for confidentiality is to encourage the exchange of information among the parties. A major emphasis and benefit of restorative processes is that they allow the parties an opportunity to ask and answer questions that the other may have. In some instances those are questions that are not legally relevant, but are important to the party. In other instances they might be highly relevant—and incriminating—if revealed in a court setting. In an adversarial setting, there are no incentives for disclosing damaging information, and there are many incentives for hiding it. Restorative processes permit parties to disclose to the other party things they would be unwilling to disclose in court.

But confidentiality is not limited here to use in subsequent legal proceedings. It also concerns disclosure to other individuals or to the community. Criminal justice is conducted in a public setting; restorative processes are more private. Even in the case of circles, which any interested person may attend, that openness is typically limited to those who are willing to participate in the circle to seek resolution of the crime. Those who would sit outside the circle and observe are not permitted to attend.

14. *Judicial discharges based on agreements arising out of restorative justice programmes should have the same status as judicial decisions or judgements and should preclude prosecution in respect of the same facts (non bis in idem).*

This paragraph is Guideline 17 of the CE Recommendation. It applies to the situation in which a restorative process has led to an agreement and the court has therefore dismissed the case. As long as the agreement is met, criminal justice officials are forbidden from initiating a new prosecution based on the facts of that case. Paragraph 16, below, provides for situations in which the agreement is not kept.

15. *Where no agreement can be made between the parties, the case should be referred back to the criminal justice authorities and a decision as to how to proceed should be taken without delay. Lack of agreement may not be used as justification for a more severe sentence in subsequent criminal justice proceedings.*

The first sentence is drawn from Guideline 18 of the CE Recommendation. This paragraph refers to the situation where a restorative process has, for some reason, failed to result in an agreement. In those instances, the case should be returned to the referring criminal justice authorities who should decide without delay how to proceed. These determinations should be based on the normal considerations for such cases, but given the time it has taken to attempt to reach an agreement through restorative processes, that determination should be made without delay.

The second sentence is a logical extension of the provisions protecting against unfair inducements (12) and involuntary participation (7), as well as of provisions on confidentiality (13) and presumption of innocence (8). If lack of agreement could be used later to justify a more severe sentence, the offender could be unfairly induced to accept an onerous or disproportionate agreement by a victim or community member. Furthermore, it would erode the right of the offender to withdraw from a restorative process at any time. An attempt by the offender to explain the failure to agree could breach the provisions on confidentiality and threaten the presumption of innocence.

Furthermore, judicial oversight of restorative justice programmes is one thing. The kind of scrutiny that would be required if courts were to attempt to reconstruct what took place during the restorative process in order to determine whether the fault for failure lay with the defendant could 'legalise' restorative processes in such a way as to reduce or eliminate flexibility. The way to avoid all these problems is to treat the attempt to reach a restorative resolution as an interlude in the criminal justice process and simply resume that process when the case is returned.

16. *Failure to implement an agreement made in the course of a restorative process should be referred back to the restorative programme or to the criminal justice authorities and a decision as to how to proceed should be taken without delay. Failure to implement the agreement may not be used as justification for a more severe sentence in subsequent criminal justice proceedings.*

This paragraph follows from the last, and addresses the situation in which an agreement was reached, but was not implemented. The fault for such a failure could lie with the offender or with individuals, groups or agencies outside the control of the offender. For example, an offender who loses his job may not be able to keep his restitution agreement, or an offender who has agreed to perform community service at an agency selected by the victim may discover that this agency does not need (or want) his services. Furthermore, the offender could refuse to complete the agreement because as he began he experienced aspects of it as degrading or humiliating.

The reason to impose a more severe sentence would be because the court found fault on the part of the offender in relation to how he approached the restorative process and outcome. To find fault, the court would need to examine what took place, and this would raise the issues mentioned in the comment on paragraph 15. Once again, the way to avoid undue interference by courts in the powerful and informal dynamics of restorative processes (including the agreements that come out of them), is to treat the failure of the restorative justice programmes as only an occasion to resume criminal justice proceedings.

IV. Facilitators

17. *Facilitators should be recruited from all sections of society and should generally possess good understanding of local cultures and communities. They should be able to demonstrate sound judgement and interpersonal skills necessary to conducting restorative process.*

This paragraph is drawn from Guidelines 22 and 23 of the CE Recommendation. It means that facilitators should come from ethnic and racial minority groups and not just the dominant groups within a community or local culture. Both sexes will be represented. The Comment to the CE Recommendation on Guideline 22 notes that no age limitations are included, although the 'sound judgement' called for in the second sentence suggests a level of maturity on the part of the facilitator.

The other qualities of the facilitator mentioned in this paragraph are a 'good understanding of local cultures and communities' and 'interpersonal skills necessary to conducting restorative processes'. Both are important in facilitating restorative processes, particularly when the participants are from different cultures, races, religions and so on. The abilities of the facilitator to listen, to help the parties communicate with one another, to maintain impartiality while making sure that no one is unfairly disadvantaged by how the restorative process unfolds, are critical to a successful process.

18. *Facilitators should perform their duties in an impartial manner, based on the facts of the case and on the needs and wishes of the parties. They should always respect the dignity of the parties and ensure that the parties act with respect towards each other.*

This paragraph is drawn from Guideline 26 of the CE Recommendation. Facilitators must be impartial in relation to the parties, meaning that they are not to choose sides but instead should make it possible for both parties to find a solution that meets their needs and wishes. The facilitator is not neutral, however, if that word implies inactivity or an emphasis on procedural fairness. The work of the facilitator is based on the facts of the case, which means that the wrongdoer is usually understood to be in a morally different place than the victim and to have incurred obligations as a result. Furthermore, the differing needs of the parties may require the facilitator to take steps to help the parties overcome imbalances in age, power, intelligence, and so forth (see paragraph 9). The touchstones for the facilitator are the dignity and respect due to each party, the facts of the case, and the needs and wishes of the parties. The discussion and any resulting agreements should be the result of the parties' efforts, not the facilitator's proposals.

19. *Facilitators should be responsible for providing a safe and appropriate environment for the restorative process. They should be sensitive to any vulnerability of the parties.*

This paragraph is drawn from Guideline 27 of the CE Recommendation. Just as the facilitator is to be impartial between the parties, so the place chosen for the restorative process should be one that is conducive to an effective exchange between the parties. At a minimum the environment should be safe, private and comfortable for the parties. The facilitator needs to consider how to conduct the restorative process in such a way that both parties are able to participate effectively.

20. *Facilitators should receive initial training before taking up facilitation duties and should also receive in-service training. The training should aim at providing skills in conflict resolution, taking into account the particular needs of victims and offenders, at providing basic knowledge of the criminal justice system and at providing a thorough knowledge of the operation of the restorative programme in which they will do their work.*

Portions of this paragraph are drawn from Guideline 24 of the CE Recommendation. While the selection of people with interpersonal skills is important (see paragraph 17), they also need initial and ongoing training. The training needs to provide skills and basic knowledge. The skills relate to conflict resolution and to the roles they are expected to play in the particular restorative justice programme that they are involved in. The knowledge has to do with the needs of victims and offenders, the operation of the criminal justice system as well as of the restorative justice programme in which they will work.

Groups that work closely with victims and with offenders are the best sources of information about the needs of those parties. The purpose of understanding victims and offenders generally, as well as the criminal justice and restorative justice apparatus, is so that the facilitator is oriented to the needs and issues facing the participants.

V. Continuing Development of Restorative Justice Programmes

21. *There should be regular consultation between criminal justice authorities and administrators of restorative justice programmes to develop a common understanding of restorative processes and outcomes, to increase the extent to which restorative programmes are used and to explore ways in which restorative approaches might be incorporated into criminal justice practices.*

The first part of this paragraph comes from Guideline 33 of the CE Recommendation. If restorative justice programmes are to become available at every stage of the criminal justice process (see paragraph 6), criminal justice authorities and restorative justice administrators will need to understand what restorative processes and outcomes can do, how they can be made available to parties, and the ways in which cases can be effectively handed back and forth between the criminal justice system and restorative justice programmes.

The latter part of this paragraph suggests that consultation can do more than simply build a common understanding. It can and should lead to increased use of restorative programmes and to the incorporation of restorative approaches into the criminal justice system. The tendency of institutions is to focus on self-preservation, and to resist steps that might reduce their influence. Consequently the temptation of criminal justice officials may be to refer only marginal cases to restorative justice programmes, and the tendency of restorative justice administrators may be to discourage innovation by criminal justice officials who want to use restorative approaches in their own systems. The importance of this principle is that it requires both groups to overcome those inherent tendencies.

22. *Member States should promote research on and evaluation of restorative justice programmes to assess the extent to which they result in restorative outcomes, serve as an alternative to the criminal justice process and provide positive outcomes for all parties.*

Restorative justice programmes have demonstrated that they can play an important role for many victims and offenders. Research and evaluation into why this happens and what the implications of that may be on criminal justice is critically important. This research should be directed toward the outcomes of those processes, toward the effect that these programmes are having on criminal justice caseloads, and toward documenting the ways in which they are positively affecting the participants.

23. *Restorative justice processes may need to undergo change in concrete form over time. Member states should therefore encourage regular, rigorous evaluation and modification of such programmes in the light of the above definitions.*

The definitions of restorative processes and restorative outcomes are expansive. Examples of specific programmes are provided in each, but implied is the expectation that new forms will emerge over time. This principle acknowledges that restorative justice programmes will continue to develop, and provides that new programmes claiming to be restorative be subjected to evaluation and modification as needed in order to increase the likelihood that the purposes of restorative processes and outcomes will be accomplished.

The need for evaluation will be particularly important as criminal justice officials become involved in restorative justice programmes, and as those programmes are incorporated into criminal justice systems. Without regular and rigorous evaluation those programmes may lose their restorative distinctiveness and become just one more fad in the history of criminal justice reform.

IV. CONCLUSION

At the Ninth Session of the Commission on Crime Prevention and Criminal Justice, held in April 2000, the governments of Canada and Italy introduced their resolution proposing development of basic principles on the use of restorative justice, noting that the year before the Commission had adopted a resolution calling for consideration of the creation of standards or guidelines on the use of restorative justice and mediation. Annexed to the resolution were the basic principles reviewed above, labelled 'preliminary draft elements' of possible basic principles. Thirty-eight other countries joined as co-sponsors during the three-day meeting of the Commission, and the resolution was approved unanimously and referred to the Economic and Social Council. It was adopted by ECOSOC in July 2000.

The resolution called on the Secretary-General to circulate the resolution and its annex to the Member States, requesting comment on whether an international instrument on restorative justice would be useful, on the substance of the provisions found in the annex, and on whether an Expert Meeting to consider country responses would be useful. Under UN procedures, unless 30 or more countries respond to such requests, it is assumed that the topic is of insufficient interest to warrant further consideration.

The Secretary-General sent a *note verbale* to Member States in early December 2000, requesting comment on the matters raised in the resolution. By early April over 30 countries had responded with comments. The government of Canada hosted the Expert Meeting in the Fall of 2001, at which time the country comments were reviewed, discussed, and a revised version of the Basic Principles was approved. This version was endorsed by the Eleventh Session of the Commission in April 2002, and by ECOSOC in July of that year.

REFERENCES

American Bar Association (1994) *Criminal Justice Policy on Victim-Offender Mediation/Dialogue*, approved Aug 1994.

Braithwaite, J and Mugford, S, 'Conditions of Successful Reintegration Ceremonies: Dealing with Juvenile Offenders' (1994) 34(2) *British Journal of Criminology* 139–71.

Council of Europe Committee of Ministers (1999) *Mediation in Penal Matters*, Recommendation No R(99)19, adopted 15 Sept 1999.

Friday, PC (1999) 'An Overview of Restorative Justice Programmes and Issues'. Paper prepared for the International Scientific and Professional Advisory Council, 1999.

Marshall, TF (1999) *Restorative Justice: An Overview* (Home Office Research Development and Statistics Directorate, London).

McCold, P (1997) *Restorative Justice: Annotated Bibliography* (Criminal Justice Press, Monsey NY).

9

Victims and Offenders

Barbara Hudson

I. INTRODUCTION

Restorative justice has at its core the bringing together of victims and offenders. In this chapter I want to consider some aspects of this bringing together of victims and offenders, raising questions about the extent to which victims' and offenders' rights, interests and perspectives may be shared, separate, or conflicting. The main point of the chapter, is to consider whether or not it is reasonable to expect one process to be able to 'do justice' to both victims and offenders.[1]

Established criminal justice has been concerned predominantly with offenders: punishing actual offenders and deterring potential offenders. Restorative justice has been promoted at a time when offenders are being punished increasingly harshly, whilst victims' complaints that they are neglected in established criminal justice proceedings have received more attention then previously. Restorative justice has appealed to those who have long advocated abolition or reduction of punishment whilst recognising the legitimacy of claims for greater concern with victims, and from those whose starting point has been neglect of victims but who have not wished to add to the penal burdens on offenders. Christie's classic article 'Conflicts as Property' is the paradigmatic case here: well-known as an abolitionist, in this article he extends his concern for the dehumanisation of offenders to victims, arguing that established criminal justice 'steals' the conflict event (the crime) from those to whom it properly belongs, ie victims and offenders (Christie, 1977).

Another example of this movement between concerns for victims and offenders is, of course, exemplified by Braithwaite, who started by looking at the *lack* of punishment in white-collar crime, and was particularly concerned with lack of redress for victims of malpractice in the pharmaceutical industry. Contrasting this with the over-penalisation of offenders in criminal justice, especially marginalised young offenders, he did not, like some in the field of corporate crime, call for

---

[1] Restorative justice is, of course, concerned with 'restoration' to and of communities, as well as victims and offenders. In this chapter, however, communities will only enter the discussion in relation to victims and offenders.

greater penalisation of white-collar offenders, but for mainstream criminal justice to become more like the restorative, compliance-inducing processes by which corporate crime is dealt with. As Kurki rightly points out, therefore, restorative justice is concerned with providing constructive outcomes for both victims and offenders, and is not simply part of the victim movement (Kurki, 2000). Essentially, it is a way of moving away from the 'zero-sum' approach to victims and offenders, which sees rights for one being at the expense of rights of the other, concern for one being at the expense of concern for the other. Restorative justice is envisaged as a way of dealing constructively with both victims and offenders, jumping off rather than on the populist bandwagon, which believes that what *helps* the victim must necessarily *hurt* the offender (Zimring, 2001).

Braithwaite's (1999) review of the demonstrable or predictable successes and potential deficiencies of restorative justice is so comprehensive that the issues I raise will echo his to a large extent, but as well as looking at restorative justice's response (or possible response) to challenges from desert theorists, I will focus on the potential of restorative justice for providing remedies for some of the defects I see in putting desert theory into practice. My argument has been that desert in practice tends to reduce to an over-simplified proportionality to offence gravity, which is not the same as proportionality to offender culpability. The parallel argument is that the notion of harm in proportionality systems is a correlative over-simplification, since it does not take adequate account of the difference in harm suffered by differently situated victims.

The essence of this chapter, then, is to join my own reflections on 'doing justice' to offenders, with restorative justice's promise and achievements in 'doing justice' to victims, and exploring the potential for satisfying both parties' claims so that 'justice' is more closely approached than with established systems. This of course begs the question of what I mean by 'justice'. My own understanding of the idea is close to, or at the very least compatible with Braithwaite's republican idea of 'justice as dominion'. Like Young and other feminist theorists who want to pre-serve the baby of liberal rights whilst throwing out the bath water of the white male worldview embodied in law and other institutions, my preferred definition of justice is 'freedom from oppression' (Young, 1990).

Justice in practice has two elements: a formal, or distributive element which consists in dealing equitably between people (justice as fairness), and a qualitative or substantive element, which consists in dealing with individuals appropriately to their own needs (justice as alterity). The argument of 'difference theorists' in relation to liberalism generally, and which I share as regards deserts theories of criminal justice in practice if not in principle, is that the distributive element, formal justice, has been promoted at the expense of the qualitative element, substantive justice. My questions about restorative justice are whether it offers a better prospect of substantive justice, by allowing for fuller consideration of victims and offenders in the individual case, rather than reducing cases to general categories; but does it thereby raise a new—or at best fail to solve an existing—distributive injustice, ie inequity between victims and offenders.

In my analysis I will draw freely on examples of restorative justice programmes whether they are for young offenders; adult offenders; minor crimes; more serious crimes; whether they are court ordered or diversions from court; whether they are police-led or whether they use non-police facilitators etc. I will use a distinction which seems to me to be important for the purposes of this chapter. This is a distinction between offences which are not targeted at a certain victim, and those which are so targeted. The latter type of crime I call 'relational' crimes: the relationship may be an existing one between the offender and an individual victim, as in domestic violence, or it may be a contemplated or sought-out relationship between an offender and a category of victim, as in racial violence; the point is that the victim is not targeted randomly or on the basis of something other than personal characteristics, such as their dwelling or car appearing insecure.

Additionally, I will raise questions about whether or not restorative justice is putting too much responsibility for crime reduction on victims and offenders. Is restorative justice a welcome returning of conflicts to those to whom they rightfully belong, or is it another example of the state divesting itself of onerous and expensive burdens, washing its hands of things for which it ought to continue to take responsibility?

II. ELEMENTS OF JUSTICE: (1) SEEING 'THE OTHER' AS A REAL PERSON

All versions of restorative justice have at their centre the opportunity provided for the victim to recount what the offence meant to her. Instead of giving evidence in answer to questions, having to follow rules and maintain relevance to the questions at issue, she is able to say whatever is important to her. In established criminal justice proceedings, if an offence is admitted she may not be called upon to speak at all. The victim may be questioned about her memory of events; her eyesight and ability to recognise the offender; her whereabouts, lifestyle, carefulness or carelessness in locking her car, her home, guarding her possessions and her person. The victim will be known to the court ground-hog-day style, going over and over the events of the day of the crime, a day extracted from a life in which the court has no other interest.

Like the victim, the offender must present those aspects of his life and character which are judged by others to be relevant to the offence. Where the victim may well feel excluded *from* the proceedings, the offender is excluded *by* the proceedings. He will be talked about through the reports of probation officers or other professionals; he may be placed at the scene of the crime by police and other witnesses; he may be described as a nuisance, a menace, a danger to society by judges and magistrates. The invitation 'have you anything to say' at the end usually results in silence, or something mumbled, or it may even be a last-ditch declaration of innocence, appearing perverse in the light of a finding of guilt. Most offenders, and especially first-time offenders, are rendered mute or incoherent by the time they get the opportunity to have their say. Courtrooms are, in many countries, designed so that there is maximum distance between the judge and the defendant, with the result that offenders quite often cannot hear what is being said. If they do manage to hear the question, they may well not know what they are allowed, or expected, to say.[2]

Having a say, telling one's story, is then, a part of restorative justice that is of great value to victims and offenders, but it is of course nowhere near enough of itself. Telling one's story must have an impact if it is to be satisfying. This is demonstrated by evaluations of victim impact statements in England and Wales, which show that as proceedings progress, initial satisfaction can turn to dissatisfaction if it appears that the statement has no effect on outcomes (Sanders et al 2000). The dilemma of victim impact statements is that if they have no impact on sentencing then they are merely tokenistic, but if they are allowed to influence sentence then this introduces distributive unfairness. If a burglar unwittingly selects the home of a specially vengeful or unusually traumatised victim, does he deserve more punishment than someone who happens upon the premises of a laid-back, tolerant victim with generous and prompt-paying insurers? A similar dilemma attaches to offenders' statements—if they do say something on their own behalf and it has no effect then they will feel the judge was merely going through the motions; but should an articulate criminal, alert to the importance of appearing remorseful and wise to the sorts of motivational stories that are likely to 'play well', achieve a more lenient outcome than a tongue-tied miscreant whose body-language may come from embarrassment but is interpreted as defiance or heartlessness?

For restorative justice to contribute to substantive justice, victims' and offenders' telling of their stories needs to be effective communication: the hearing is at least as important as the saying. The telling of the harm suffered and of the reasons for the offence must make the victim and offender real to each other, if the harm and its causes and circumstances are to be acknowledged as real.

For the offender to acknowledge responsibility and feel remorse, he must first acknowledge the victim as a real individual. Restorative justice builds on the insight that crime comes easily if the victim is denied. Perpetrators of run-of-the-mill crimes often deny there is any victim at all—the shoplifter who thinks there is no real victim, only a faceless retail chain; the burglar or car thief who tells himself the insurance will make good any damage or loss; the tax-fiddler who thinks that everybody does it, and it's 'our own' money anyway. Perpetrators of the greatest harms deny the humanity of their victims—the war criminal; the torturer; the genocide; the exploitative low-payer; the routine enforcer of discriminatory rules, do not feel they are harming an 'Other' who is like themselves. The racist attacker, the woman beater, the sexual predator, all deny the commonality

---

[2] Many of us will have experienced something similar when asked if we have any questions to put, as a job interview draws to a close. It is only with increasing experience and confidence that we learn to combine information gathering and imparting, with impression management. For a classic study of courtroom rituals, see Carlen (1976).

with themselves of those they victimise. For restoration to be effected, the first step is that the victim becomes as real to the offender as those who encourage him, those who give him status because of his offending.

A parallel communication needs to be achieved for substantive justice to be obtained for the offender as well as for restorative effects to be experienced by the victim: the offender must be revealed as a real person to the victim. Fear of crime research finds that 'fear' is a complex amalgam of anger at crime and fear of troublesome people, (stereo)typically fear of young males (Farrell, Bannister and Ditton, 1997). If a large part of 'fear of crime' is in fact a more generalised 'fear of strangers' (Merry, 1981), then making the offender real and known to the victim is an important step in reducing fear. Sensationalist media reporting of crime adds to commonplace feeling, building images of criminals larger, more aggressive, more confident, more focused, than flesh-and-blood offenders often turn out to be.[3] For victims, the general public imagery of fear can be heightened by the feeling that they have been personally invaded and violated by crimes such as burglary, as well as by offences against the person. The offender's denial of the crime having a real victim has as its counterpart many victims' feelings of having been personally targeted. Consider the following incident report:

Thief Raids Dead Man's Home
Young mum Lisa Smith thought life could not get any worse when her partner died in a horrific motorbike accident.

But she had not counted on the cruelty of a thief who heard about Glyn Browett's death and thought his home would make an easy target.

Lisa surveyed her ransacked home today and condemned the thief as evil. The heartbroken 20-year-old said the burglar struck just as she was starting to pick up the pieces of her life following Glyn's death a month ago.

She and their two-year old son Zach were visiting her parents when the burglary happened. She returned home . . . to find . . . a TV, video and hi-fi stolen.

. . . Speaking publicly for the first time, his girlfriend of four years said today . . . "I can't believe someone could be so heartless.

"They are evil. They will have known Glyn and known he was dead.

Glyn's things were all I had left."

(Lancashire Evening Post, 10 April 2001.)

No-one has been arrested for this crime, so there is no way of knowing whether the burglar did in fact know of the death of the victim's partner, but there is no doubting that this victim feels herself to have been personally rather than randomly targeted, and that her circumstances made her specially vulnerable to any further form of loss. Most research on, and work with, burglars would suggest that the key factor in selection of the home to burgle would be the fact that it was

[3] People in the north east of England were amazed at how small the so-called 'rat boy' was when he appeared in court. Although the reason for the name he was given by the local press indicates his smallness—he avoided arrest on many occasions by fleeing through the pipework in the blocks of flats he burgled—the diminutive 12-year old was nonetheless a surprise to observers who had expected a larger, older, intimidating 'thug'.

unoccupied, so the circumstance of visiting her parents, or being out for whatever reason, was more likely to be the main opportunistic factor rather than that she was recently bereaved. Only a procedure allowing for full and direct communication between victim and offender could reassure this victim that she is not being selectively targeted by the local villains, and could allow the burglar to reveal him(her)self as not the heartless monster he is portrayed as being.

In my work on criminal justice and poverty, I have argued that established procedures do not allow for adequate assessment of culpability because they necessarily operate with a restricted notion of choice (Hudson, 1995, 1998, 2000). I have argued that established legal reasoning constructs 'responsibility' in a way that over-emphasises *agency*—the physical and mental capacity wittingly to carry out an action—and both under-conceptualises and under-emphasises *choice*. Whereas agency has an either/or quality, choice is a matter of degree, a continuum from none, to few, to some, to many options. Choice is made among a range of alternative actions; a range which is structured by opportunity; a range which in our societies is structured by race, gender, economic status and age. Without appreciation of this differential opportunity structuring and consequent differential range of choice, desert cannot properly be assessed.

In my previous work I have suggested that in the case of property crime, what has to be considered is the range of opportunity available to obtain necessary and/or generally valued goods—food, shelter, excitement, esteem—legitimately. One can then envisage a spectrum of choice ranging from someone who has no access to legitimate income, through people with limited incomes, to people with perfectly adequate incomes. Whether or not their available means are the result of their own choices is, of course, also relevant.

So far I have had in mind offences where the victim is chosen more or less randomly, offences where there is no prior relationship between victim and offender. If we think about offences where there is a prior relationship—where the crime stems in some way from the relationship—then the issue of 'seeing the other as a real person' becomes even more crucial. In these kinds of cases, what needs to happen for the victim is that she become real to the offender as a person in her own right, upheld in her own evaluation of what happened, and that she can move outside the relationship in the offender's perception. 'Denial of the victim' in these relational crimes may not be in the form of denying that there was a victim, but certainly takes the form of denying his separate personhood. The offender may project the sparking of the incident onto the victim—'he dissed me'; 'she was asking for it'—or may see the crime as some form of expression of self or of the relationship, turning the victim into an object rather than respecting her as an active subject.

There are too many accounts of victims of sexual assaults feeling re-victimised in established criminal justice proceedings, of being inhibited by the court setting, being restricted by evidentiary rules and relevance considerations, to need repetition here; what matters is whether restorative justice can provide a better opportunity for victims to tell the story they want to tell, and for their story-telling to be effective.

The restorative justice claim in the case of offences such as domestic violence is that the conference or meeting offers the victim the opportunity to choose how to present herself; to abstract herself from the relationship; to select her own supporters and representatives. The abuser cannot ignore her, as he could in a conventional court while she is giving her evidence; her story will not be refracted through legal language, it will be told in her words, the words with which she always communicates with him, so he cannot claim not to have understood any more than he can claim not to have heard. Her story will be about her: she will not be confined to dwelling on those elements that relate to him, elements relevant to establishing his guilt and his culpability. He cannot claim, then, not to have been told about *her* feelings, her understanding of events, her wishes and demands for the future. The tessellation of the relationship with other parts of her life will be relevant if she wishes it to be, she does not need to confine her narrative within the relationship. With racial as well as with gendered crime, conferencing or similar procedures can force the offender to see the victim as a 'real' person, with qualities, commitments and emotions other than those attributed to him by the offender through stereotype or fantasy.

Relationships between abusers and abused are relationships of dominance and submission, and so the principle of restorative justice that empowerment of the victim is the prime element of 'justice' in these cases is absolutely right. The victim needs the offender not just to hear her story, but for it to be validated by others, and for him to hear that validation (Morris and Gelsthorpe, 2000). As all those who see a potential for restorative justice in these kinds of cases say, there must be strong procedural safeguards to ensure that the power relationship of the crime is not recreated in the conference. This is important for all crimes, but is a *sine qua non* for relational crimes. Different restorative justice programmes may do this well or badly, but at least they aim to do it at all, and this is one of their strongest claims to superiority over established criminal justice.

Addressing offender choice is also important for culpability in relational crimes. Male violence against women, sexual offences against children, are often rationalised by offenders to themselves in terms of having no choice. He was provoked, he was defending his honour, he was aroused; she nagged, she mocked his sexual prowess, she slept with his friend, she brought shame on her relatives, he couldn't stop himself—the common element in the litany of familiar excuses is that the point of choice was passed. 'Getting real' about choices may sometimes reduce culpability, but at other times it can reinforce it.

Much of the most effective work with offenders over recent decades has been based on inducing them to acknowledge not only that the behaviour has caused harm, but that they could have chosen to have acted differently. Often, facing up to choice is part of a rehabilitative package, unavailable to offenders unless they are sentenced to probation, or to custody in an institution which includes such a programme: but making it central to decision-making procedures seems to me essential to offender accountability. Quite apart from restorative value, it is surely important for criminal justice legitimacy. People respect the law if they feel it treats them fairly (Tyler, 1990); offenders will not feel they have been treated fairly if they continue to believe that they have been punished for something they had no choice but to do.

III. ELEMENTS OF JUSTICE: (2) CONFLICTING PERSPECTIVES AND AGREED OUTCOMES

When offenders and victims have told their stories, there is no guarantee that they will agree on a version or meaning of events. This seems most obvious in offences of heterosexual violence where there may well be two seemingly irreconcilable perspectives: his and hers (Finstad, 1990). Other offences, however, may also present hermeneutic difficulties. The burglar may view 'home' as only a collection of material possessions and not realise the sense of violation and insecurity consequent upon one's home having been entered; the shop thief may not realise that the Asian shopkeeper feels his premises to have been targeted because of his ethnicity; the woman whose bag is snatched may be able to stop her credit cards but may no longer be able to enjoy walking around the town. For example:

> A woman who betrayed the trust of her friend and stole her credit card is today start-
> ing a seven-month prison sentence . . .
> The court heard that [X] sought solace in her friend when she began to worry that
> she was pregnant and did not know who the father was.
> Defence counsel . . . told the court that in distress [X], who was homeless at the time,
> called her friend on the evening of January 11 and was invited round to talk.
> [X] stayed the night but became agitated in the morning when her friend left her to
> sleep, causing her to miss a housing appointment.
> The pair argued and [X] alleges she became angry when she asked her friend to
> repay a loan and was refused.
> [X] then stole her friend's credit card, left the premises in a taxi and bought groceries.
> . . .
>
> (Lancashire Evening Post, 10 April 2001.)

To the victim, this is a betrayal by someone she had befriended, even extending hospitality to the extent of inviting her to stay in her home; to the offender, this is taking what was rightly hers, the victim having refused to repay a loan even though she was aware of *X*'s straitened circumstances.

Established criminal justice could not effect a reconciliation of these perspectives, nor would it attempt to. Although it does not necessarily afford the actual victim a hearing, it assumes the perspective of the victim, it becomes the surrogate victim. Established criminal justice does not need to make special arrangements to *hear* the victim, because it *is* the victim. Restorative justice is not, therefore, innovative in privileging as it does the victim's account; what is innovative is its aspiration to change the offender's perspective. (Although communicative retributivism emphasises the message of censure that is conveyed to the offender, what is essential is that it is conveyed, not that it is accepted by the offender, though this is desirable (Duff, 1986, 1996).)

Proponents of restorative justice readily accept that a single conference could not shift entrenched misogynist or racist views,[4] but there is a regrettable lack of clarity about what follows from this. Does it mean that restorative justice is inappropriate, or that a series of meetings is needed, or what? For some, acceptance by the offender of the victim's perspective is a precondition of proceedings:

> There may be two quite separate views on "what happened", but in restorative processes the victim's perspective is central and the meeting can only proceed on the basis of the offender's acceptance of responsibility. (Morris and Gelsthorpe, 2000: 419.)

What is unclear here is firstly, what is meant by 'acceptance of responsibility', and secondly, what is it to 'proceed'? Most restorative justice projects (but not all) require an admission of guilt, as does cautioning. If the offender contests the fact of having committed the crime at all, then clearly they are not going to accept responsibility or 'make amends'. So presumably what is at issue is something more than acceptance of the fact of having carried out the act. But if this is the case, then surely the offender's 'acceptance of responsibility' must be an outcome of the process rather than a precondition? Daly's idea that 'Ideally, the conference setting is a dialogic encounter' and that the dialogue is 'ongoing', seems better to encapsulate the spirit of restorative justice (Daly, 2000).

Braithwaite's vision of an 'undominated speech situation', echoing Habermas's discursive rules for 'ideal speech', also seems to capture the essence of a form of justice that could be genuinely new in its treatment of victim and offender perspectives. His review takes account of various different possibilities of speech domination: victim; offender; representative of one or the other; community representative; facilitator, especially if the facilitator is a police officer. As he says, rules of procedure need to be carefully established to ensure that conferences or meetings are not allowed to be dominated by any powerful individual, and I would add, by any one perspective, at least *at the outset.*

But however carefully rules of procedure are designed, and however free from domination proceedings may be in fact, there is no guarantee that a fusion of horizons can be accomplished. Restorative justice proposals are usually vague on how long proceedings might continue, and just how much of a change of heart is required of offenders.

A change of heart at least sufficient to bring forth an apology, is perhaps the most general view on that last question. An apology is widely suggested as an essential first step in reparation, and it is an explicit prime objective of some restorative justice schemes, including Thames Valley's 'restorative cautioning' in England (Young and Goold, 1999). Again, there is nothing new in this stress on apologising: reports of trials under established procedures often mention whether or not the offender assumed a remorseful demeanour; probation reports and

---

[4] See Stubbs (1997) for this objection to the use of restorative justice in domestic violence cases.

defence solicitors comment on offenders' expressions of remorse, and parole/early release is often dependent on assessments of 'genuine remorse'. What is new, is that in restorative justice apology is to be made directly to the victim; that it is to be backed up by reparative actions, and that it is to be witnessed by other participants in the meeting who are significant to the offender.

Whether or not the offender adopts the victim's perspective, a set of measures is to be agreed that is supposed to satisfy the needs/interests of both parties. For the victim, the measures are to be adequate reparation, and in relational crimes they usually include a safety agenda to assure her future protection. For the offender, they are to be adequate to express her regret for the harm done, and to restore to the victim that which has been lost or damaged by the offence. They may also include rehabilitative elements such as education, employment or addiction programmes to help his reintegration as a crime-free citizen.

Here restorative justice encounters its own distributive problem: that of equating the victim's interests in adequate reparation to the offender's interests in impositions proportionate to her culpability and remorse. One argument made by retributivists against a more elaborated and emphasised assessment of choice in attributing culpability is that it may lead to penalties which are inadequate reflections of harm. For desert theorists, the best (or at least, most viable) solution to this conundrum is the assumption of the standard victim and the standard offender in grading offence seriousness. Allowances can be made, as in the range of defences and mitigations recognised by criminal law, and, for example, in regarding offences with certain kinds of victims or relationships targeted as aggravated forms of the crime category (elderly householders, children, ethnic minorities, relationships of trust), but more thoroughgoing examination of victim harm and offender choice is thought to risk injustice either through inadequacy as a measure of harm, or through inconsistency between different offenders (von Hirsch and Jareborg, 1992). Established criminal justice prioritises the victim perspective in the sense that it makes the penalty relate to the harm done to victims, allowing for offender interests by the contrivance of a standard victim.

Although restorative justice individualises cases more than established justice does and so allows for greater variation between cases, it solves the problem of equilibrium in the single case in the same way that established criminal justice does, by coming down clearly on one side—that of the victim. Offenders have the option of reverting to established justice procedures if they don't agree the measures decided upon by the conference or meeting, but as with cautioning or plea-bargaining, this is an option that is hardly free from coercion. Proponents increasingly take account of the need to protect offenders' rights and interests, but what these are is not clearly enough specified. As Braithwaite concludes, 'Restorative justice practices can trample rights because of impoverished articulation of procedural safeguards' (Braithwaite, 1999: 101ff). If the conference privileges the victim's perspective then articulation of what are to count as 'just outcomes' for offenders is urgently needed. If the victim is granted procedural rights such as vetoing agreements, halting procedures, then it seems that a corresponding articulation of offenders' rights is required, and that if they remain—as seems likely—less well specified and accorded less priority, then offenders ought to have legal representation throughout (although how legal representatives would uphold rights which have not been recognised is unclear).

While I can of course see the force of the argument for prioritising victim rights over offender interests, I am disturbed by the absoluteness with which this priority is sometimes stated. Though it may seem obvious that a victim's right to safety must have priority over an offender's right to privacy or to freedom of movement, the scales should not be weighted so that the one is everything and the other is nothing. As Dworkin argues powerfully, if we can conceive of two things as 'rights', this means that they are the same category of good, and therefore both are worthy of support and protection (Dworkin, 1977).

My disquiet is at the ease with which the (liberal) requirement that rights and interests be kept in balance is glossed over in some restorative justice formulations. Established criminal justice acknowledges the built-in imbalance entailed in allotting the state with its repressive power the role of victim by elaborating a series of offenders' rights and safeguards. What is worrying about restorative justice is that it assumes a procedural model of equality between the parties in some respects— representatives of both parties, ensuring that no-one dominates proceedings—but other rules deny this equality. For example, as well as victim vetoes and rights to end meetings, in some schemes offenders are not able to include as supporters people who might approve or excuse their behaviour (Braithwaite and Daly, 1994; Morris and Gelsthorpe, 2000). While of course I do not want to promote racist, sexist or otherwise anti-social behaviour, I do think that if restorative justice is to continue very firm prioritisation of victim's rights, balanced only by vague notions such as 'respect' to offenders, then it should abandon the even-handedness which appears to be promised in its self-definitions. Instead of defining itself as a justice which offers restoration to victims *and* offenders, it should define itself more clearly as victim-centred reparative justice.

One way in which restorative justice seems to (dis)solve the equilibrium dilemma is by calling the 'measures' imposed on offenders reparation or restoration rather than punishment, importing into restorative justice the euphemistic tendency to which reformist criminal justice is unfortunately prone. A set of measures may be agreed which, in the mind of the facilitator and other participants, include some intended as retribution and some intended as reparation, but they are more accurately and honestly described as retributive and reparative *punishments*. Whether the rationale is one of treatment, or restoration and reparation, the fact of the matter is that if tasks, restrictions or deprivations are imposed on an offender in consequence of a criminal act, then this is punishment. Punishment is inflicted on offenders, and as such ought to be subject to principled limits which are to do with those offenders. The most defensible principled limit is that punishment ought to be proportionate to offenders' culpability.

Even more than by evading these problems of proportionality and offenders' rights by a terminology which denies that its impositions are punishment, restorative justice reassures through the credentials of its proponents. Most restorative justice advocates are people who have long urged abolition or reduction of punishment, and who have argued for criminal justice to be respectful and non-degrading. Nonetheless, the *contingency* of outcomes which are reasonable for offenders, upon the humanity and moderation of participants is unsatisfactory from the point of view of liberal legalism. This defect is especially problematic where innovations are proliferating in a context of ever-increasing penal severity, and is certainly a pressing concern here in the UK where restorative justice has been promoted most vigorously by a worryingly illiberal Home Secretary.[5]

My argument in this section, then, is that there is no guarantee that victim interests in adequate reparation can be equitably balanced with offender interests in impositions that do not exceed proportionality to culpability. The conventional criminal justice response is to admit the impossibility of this balancing and 'do justice' to victims and offenders in separate processes. This suggests that the way to remedy the neglect of victims by criminal justice is to first of all acknowledge that the state taking the role of the symbolic victim is not the same as restoration of actual victims, and so to provide improved victim services, including increased and more easily forthcoming compensation.

The other option *is* to move from punishment to reparation as restorative justice proponents suggest. But for the impositions to be genuinely rather than euphemistically reparation instead of punishment in another guise, they would have to be something which the offender would volunteer because of her own (revised) view of the offence. For this to be possible would entail a more even procedural balance between victims and offenders, and relinquishing in some degree the present privileging of victim perspectives, rights and interests.

IV. REDUCING CRIME

Restorative justice is held by its advocates to do more than deal fairly and constructively with victims and offenders: it makes claims to effectiveness in crime reduction. In part, its effectiveness is that of generalised deterrence, through increasing community intolerance of certain behaviours. The expressive, norm affirmation function of criminal justice can potentially be carried out at least as effectively by restorative justice as by established criminal justice, without the latter's contribution to further crime through labelling and excluding effects on offenders. Primarily, though, restorative justice's crime reduction effects are to be achieved by making the offenders involved less likely to reoffend.

The studies reviewed by Braithwaite and others make modest but worthwhile claims of greater effectiveness than penalties imposed by established criminal justice proceedings. There are, of course, difficulties in substantiating these claims, difficulties familiar from evaluation of other penal innovations. It is always hard

---

[5] Jack Straw, Home Secretary in the first New Labour administration, 1997–2001.

to be certain whether results are reflective of selection effects or programme effects: are the offenders placed on the new programme more likely to be successful than others because of factors such as fewer previous offences, readiness to admit responsibility, etc, or is the project having some direct impact independent of assignment criteria? Maxwell and Morris's recent article reports results of two restorative justice programmes which include offenders who were older and convicted of more serious offences than is often the case in restorative justice schemes, and they analyse reoffending data against matched control groups (Morris and Maxwell, 2001). They show some evidence of less reconviction, and for those who were reconvicted, less serious reoffending.

Comparisons may not, however, be measuring the effectiveness of restorative justice as such, but the effectiveness of rehabilitative as opposed to non-rehabilitative penalties. Most studies are vague about the nature of the penalty received by non-restorative justice offenders, using forms of words such as 'conventional court proceedings', without specifying the sentence. Many innovations in probation are claiming success in reducing reoffending (Raynor, 1998), and in the UK at least the current view seems to be that programme elements relevant to the causes of offending—addiction, anger management, literacy and numeracy courses, employment skills, relationship counselling—are what counts, not the setting in which or the proceedings from which these programmes are delivered (McGuire, 1995).

Braithwaite himself makes similar points in his review. Whilst he claims efficacy for reintegrative shaming in itself, he also comments on the lack of attention to rehabilitative elements in restorative justice programmes. The ideal of restorative justice is that the conference or meeting should form a 'community of care' for both victim *and* offender, and should attend to the needs of both. Rather starkly, he reports that, 'I must confess to seeing these as empty ideals in all the restorative justice programs of which I have experience' (Braithwaite, 1999: 69).

As he says, and as the evaluative literature to which I have referred makes clear, rehabilitative programmes are most likely to be effective if (i) they are felt by the offender to be relevant to his problems and if (ii) they are undertaken with at least some degree of voluntariness. Restorative justice offers the chance of delivering on both these conditions better than established criminal justice if it affords the opportunity for the careful assessment presently contained in the best probation reports, to which can be added the motivation voluntarily to agree to the programme that could be provided by recognition of the victim's perspective.

When, however, what is being considered is crime *rate* reductions rather than providing individual offenders opportunities and incentives to refrain from reoffending, the language of restorative justice is, I fear, on the same dangerous ground as much of the risk-reduction thinking which legitimates increased incarceration. Braithwaite argues that 'it is the really serious repeat offenders who are most likely eventually to be caught' and that the 'economic and protective value to the community' of reducing reoffending for that minority of offenders should not be discounted (Braithwaite, 1999: 81). This echoes the language of incapacitation theory which is based on the premise that incapacitating the highest rate offenders will bring about significant reductions in crime, and it is open to the same objections.[6]

These crime prevention claims are very risky. Restorative justice, probation and other moderate and constructive penalties cannot incapacitate as effectively as imprisonment. When tough-minded politicians say that 'prison works' they are not claiming that prison is reformative, but that it deprives offenders of the opportunity for crime (except of course against fellow offenders). Demonstrations that reoffending rates of released prisoners are worse than those after completion of non-custodial sentences are easily finessed by keeping prisoners inside for (very much) longer. Rate reduction is not the ground on which restorative justice should be selling itself, because it is a 'competition' which restorative justice is bound to lose, and because it is likely to lead to restorative justice becoming complicit in 'penal inflation', having to up the amount of incapacitative measures included in agreements, thereby distorting its original vision. In any case, because of the conflict with justice of penalising people for something which they have not done, incapacitation against the possibility of future crime is a penal principle which progressives should reject.

The way in which even the most thoughtful of restorative justice advocates slip into this incapacitative language reflects the forward-looking consequentialism in which it is rooted. Braithwaite talks of the incapacitative usefulness of 'Uncle Harry' and family and friends of offenders, making the rather startling statement that 'Uncle Harrys have a more plural range of incapacitative keys they can turn than a prison guard who can turn just one key' (Braithwaite, 1999: 67). This forward-looking is a fundamental divide between desert theorists and restorative justice theorists, and reflects the divide between their liberal and utilitarian roots. Although in theory it is argued as an either/or schism, in practice it is the dualism that is inevitable in all criminal justice. In reality all schemes must find a balance between looking backward and looking forward, between due process and crime control, finding sanctions which reflect what has already happened, and making a contribution to a better future. Retribution and reparation both look backwards and are therefore reconcilable in principle even though equilibrium may be difficult in practice for individual cases; the taken-for-granted embeddedness of the forward-looking aspect of restorative justice is the real difficulty for me.

The meshing of restorative justice and the penal-political context raises another concern for me. This is that it is putting too much responsibility onto victims and offenders, and their 'communities of care' for crime reduction, and allowing the state to divest itself of its rightful responsibilities. It is evident from my views on the structuring of choice that I believe that the opportunity structures and levels of inequality in present western societies are contributory causes of crime, and some forms of restorative justice seem to bring about a narrow focus on victims

---

[6] See Zimring and Hawkins (1995) for a robust critique of this theory and practice.

and offenders and their relationship, to the exclusion of the relationship between victims, offenders and the state. While the local community may be included, the wider state with its complicity in racist and sexist cultures, with its policies which exacerbate rather than ameliorate socio-economic inequities and lack of legitimate livelihoods, is excused its responsibilities for crime reduction. I am well aware of the argument that criminal justice cannot remedy wider social and economic inequalities, but this is not to say that the state should not bear its share of the costs and responsibilities of crime reduction.

The danger I see is that by promoting the idea that crime should be dealt with by victims and offenders in their local communities and that the state should withdraw its 'ownership' of conflicts, restorative justice colludes in perpetuating the imbalance between offenders' liabilities to punishment and the state's responsibilities to provide rehabilitative programmes. I continue to find much that is persuasive in the idea of *state-obligated rehabilitation* (Cullen and Gilbert, 1982; Carlen, 1989). This is the idea that an offender's responsibility in a crime is acknowledged by his being obliged to undertake certain rehabilitative programmes or tasks, and that the state's part in crime causation should be acknowledged in the duty to provide such programmes. Moreover, the vulnerability of offenders to sanctions for non-compliance should be matched by sanctions on the state for non-provision.

Equally, the state's role in crime should be acknowledged by the provision of services and resources to victims. Even if offenders make reparations, the state should not be absolved of its responsibilities for ensuring future safety or for providing compensation adequate to reflect its contribution to criminality. Consider the present levels of harassment and attacks on immigrants and asylum seekers in the UK—surely government discourse about 'bogus' asylum seekers; regulations which refuse them the possibility of legal, paid work; supporting them through vouchers rather than cash entitlements; dispersing them to visible centres in designated locations rather than allowing them to choose their location through supportive contacts, are contributory. Such policies certainly legitimate the victim-denying 'techniques of neutralisation' which restorative justice seeks to address. Restorative justice should not be complicit in seeing such crimes as only the result of 'wrong relationships' between offenders and victims; the wider social-political context in which these relationships are nurtured and played out must also effectively be called to account.

All restorative justice proponents call for public resources to back up the measures they recommend to reduce reoffending and to promote victim safety, and most would take a similar view to mine on recent reductions in welfare support. My point, though, is that some of the ways in which restorative justice is advocated in terms of relocating justice from the state to the community, reclaiming conflicts for victims and offenders, leaves no opening for a *right* to resources corresponding to a liability to penalties. And like the concern with the development of restorative justice in a climate of penal severity, I have an anxiety about the import of concentration on victims and offenders and their immediate communities in a context of the rolling back of the state, the so-called 'death of the social' (Rose, 1996). A very bad consequence of the spread of restorative justice would be if all the reparative, rehabilitative and reintegrative responses to crime were agreed and implemented by victims, offenders and their immediate communities, and the state was left only the extremes of either doing nothing, or delivering repressive, incapacitative and inhumane punishment and inadequate or inappropriate services for offenders and victims who were, for whatever reason deemed 'beyond restoration'.

V. CONCLUSION

It will be clear by now that what I find most appealing about restorative justice is its openness to story telling and exploration of possibilities for creative and constructive responses to offences. My preference is for *discursive justice* rather than *process justice*: I see more possibility for just outcomes in empathetic reflection on events than in application of right rules to standard cases (Ferrara, 1999).

The discursive possibilities of restorative justice offer a better possibility of substantive justice than do the rules of established justice. Established justice has quite rightly come under attack from feminists and others for the maleness and the whiteness of its perspective which represents itself as impartiality. This maleness and whiteness often prevent it from seeing either the extent of the harm done to victims or the extent of the culpability of offenders. If justice is conceived as something dispensed top-down by judges who are presumed to embody impartiality it is difficult to see how it could move beyond the ambition of distributive fairness conceived as treating everyone the same; it cannot advance towards impartially balancing the legitimate claims on justice of both real victims and real offenders.

Reflective impartialists such as Nagel see impartiality as something which has to be achieved by attending to the perspective of the 'Other', not something which the judge embodies and brings into the courtroom with her presence (Nagel, 1986, 1991). If established criminal justice aspires to do justice to offenders it must allow more discursive space for assessing culpability—it must attend to the perspective of the offender. If it aspires to be responsive to the claims of victims on the process of justice, it must allow corresponding discursive space for assessing harm—it must attend to the perspective of the flesh-and-blood victim.

If established criminal proceedings cannot do justice unless they become in some ways more like restorative justice in that they become more discursive, restorative proceedings cannot do justice unless they become more like established justice in that they become more aware of rights. In particular, restorative justice needs to think more of rights as needing to be balanced, rather than being sacrificed on one side or the other.

One thing that could undermine this potential for delivering substantive justice is too strong an orientation to crime reduction. Another is too strong an adoption of a 'rights and responsibilities' attitude rather than a 'positive and inalienable rights' stance. According to the 'rights and responsibilities' perspective of contemporary communitarianism, rights are only upheld for those citizens who behave responsibly; rights are in fact social privileges, which can be forfeit by those who behave anti-socially. This communitarian formula fits all too easily in a society with very poor elaboration of offenders' rights. Only a 'positive rights agenda', which sees all humans as having rights which do not have to be earned, cannot be forfeited, and must be respected, will yield an approach which goes beyond the zero-sum game involving victims and offenders.

REFERENCES

Braithwaite, J (1999) 'Restorative Justice: Assessing Optimistic and Pessimistic Accounts' in M Tonry (ed), *Crime and Justice: A Review of Research* (Chicago University Press, Chicago IL) vol 25, 1–127.

Braithwaite, J and Daly, K (1994) 'Masculinities, Violence and Communitarian Control' in T Newburn and E Stanko (eds), *Just Boys Doing Business?* (Routledge, London).

Carlen, P (1976) *Magistrates' Justice* (Martin Robertson, London).

——(1989) 'Crime, Inequality and Sentencing' in P Carlen and D Cook (eds), *Paying for Crime* (Open University Press, Milton Keynes).

Christie, N (1977) 'Conflicts as Property' 17 *British Journal of Criminology* 1–26.

Cullen, F and Gilbert, K (1982) *Reaffirming Rehabilitation* (Anderson, Cincinnati).

Daly, K (2000) 'Sexual Assault and Restorative Justice' forthcoming in H Strang and J Braithwaite (eds), *Restorative Justice and Family Violence* (Cambridge University Press, Cambridge).

Duff, RA (1986) *Trials and Punishment* (Cambridge University Press, Cambridge).

——(1996) 'Penal Communications: Recent work in the Philosophy of Punishment' in M Tonry (ed), *Crime and Justice: A Review of Research.*

Dworkin, R (1977) *Taking Rights Seriously* (Duckworth, London).

Farrell, S, Bannister, J and Ditton, J 'Questioning the Measurement of the 'Fear of Crime': Findings from a Major Methodological Study' (1997) 37(4) *British Journal of Criminology* 658–79.

Ferrara, A (1999) *Justice and Judgement* (Sage, London).

Finstad, L (1990) 'Sexual Offenders Out of Prison: Principles for a Realistic Utopia' 18 *International Journal of the Sociology of Law* 157.

Hudson, B (1995) 'Beyond Proportionate Punishment: Difficult Cases and the 1991 Criminal Justice Act' 22 *Crime, Law and Social Change* 59–78.

——'Punishment, Poverty and Responsibility: The Case for a Hardship Defence' (1998) 8(4) *Social and Legal Studies* 583–91.

——(2000) 'Punishing the Poor: Dilemmas of Justice and Difference' in WC Heffernan and J Kleinig (eds), *From Social Justice to Criminal Justice* (Oxford University Press, New York).

Kurki, L (2000) 'Restorative and Community Justice in the United States' in M Tonry (ed), *Crime and Justice: A Review of Research.*

McGuire, J (ed) (1995) *What Works: Reducing Offending* (Wiley, Chichester).

Maxwell, G and Morris, A 'Putting Restorative Justice into Practice for Adult Offenders' (2001) 40(1) *Howard Journal of Criminal Justice* 55–69.

Merry, S (1981) *Urban Danger: Life in a Neighbourhood of Strangers* (Temple University Press, Philadelphia).

Morris, A and Gelsthorpe, L 'Re-visioning Men's Violence against Female Partners' (2000) 39(4) *Howard Journal of Criminal Justice* 412–28.

Nagel, T (1986) *The View from Nowhere* (Oxford University Press, New York).

——(1991) *Equality and Partiality* (Oxford University Press, New York).

Raynor, P 'Attitudes, Social Problems and Reconviction in the 'STOP' Probation Experiment' (1998) 37(1) *Howard Journal of Criminal Justice* 1–15.

Rose, N 'The death of the "social"? Refiguring the territory of government' (1996) 26(4) *Economy and Society* 327–46.

Sanders, A, Hoyle, C, Morgan, R and Cape, E (2000) 'Victim Statements: Can't Work, Won't Work' June 2001 *Criminal Law Review* 437–58.

Stubbs, J (1997) 'Shame, defiance and violence against women' in S Cook and J Bessant (eds), *Women's Encounters with Violence: Australian Experiences* (Sage, London).

Tyler, W (1990) *Why People Obey the Law* (Yale University Press, New Haven, Connecticut).

von Hirsch, A and Jareborg, N (1992) 'Gauging Harm to Others: A Living Standard Analysis' in A von Hirsch and A Ashworth (eds), *Principled Sentencing* (Edinburgh University Press, Edinburgh).

Young, IM (1990) *Justice and the Politics of Difference* (Princeton University Press, Princeton).

Young, R and Goold, B (1999) 'Restorative Police Cautioning in Aylesbury—from Degrading to Reintegrative Shaming Ceremonies?' *Criminal Law Review* 126–38.

Zimring, F 'Imprisonment rates and the new politics of criminal punishment' (2001) 3(1) *Punishment and Society* 161–66.

Zimring, F and Hawkins, G (1995) *Incapacitation: Penal Confinement and the Restraint of Crime* (Oxford University Press, New York).

10

Restorative Justice and Criminal Justice: Just Responses to Crime?

Joanna Shapland

> We were struck by the widespread support for the concept of restorative justice put forward in the consultation process, not only across a wide spectrum of political opinion, but also amongst the voluntary and community groups whose views we heard. We were taken also by the sharp differences of opinion on how restorative justice should be delivered. (Review of Criminal Justice in Northern Ireland, 2000: 203)

The focus of this chapter is restorative justice in its legal and structural context and, particularly, in relation to criminal justice. This implies a focus not primarily on the philosophy behind restorative justice, or the potential for restorative justice if it were to be implemented fully, or the benefits it might bring, but a focus on the ways in which restorative justice has been implemented and is likely to be implemented, given the legal and institutional parameters of justice systems at the beginning of the third millennium. It is a grounded exploration, which needs to look at the opportunities and barriers which are fashioning the restorative justice schemes which are developing. I cannot posit an ideal society, but need to work with one which brings with it all its historical baggage and notions of justice, particularly criminal justice.

Currently, restorative justice is being portrayed as new, different and to be striven for. It has been argued that restorative justice is the fastest growing movement currently. Certainly, governments and non-governmental organisations are actively currently looking to implement schemes of different types into their existing criminal and social justice mechanisms.[1] The implication of being new and different is that restorative justice will, in practice, always be compared with 'traditional' criminal justice. This tendency has been exacerbated by evaluation designs which have compared 'new' restorative justice with previous criminal justice, such as the evaluation of RISE in Canberra (Strang et al 1999), which,

---

[1] In the United Kingdom, see for example, the recommendation of the Auld report (Auld, 2001) for 'the development and implementation of a national strategy to ensure consistent, appropriate and effective use of restorative justice techniques across England and Wales' (p 391); and the provisions in the Review of Criminal Justice in Northern Ireland (2000) for mainstreamed restorative justice conferencing for youths and young adults.

using a random assignment model, explicitly compared the experiences of victims and offenders experiencing each type of justice.

Such a comparative framework for looking at restorative justice leads to a number of questions. The first is to what extent restorative justice is different from 'traditional' criminal justice. Is it an entirely new creature, or is it rather like a new, improved brand of washing powder, with a few, important differences which are being strongly stressed by its advocates? Clearly, in order to address this I will need to bound what I am taking to be restorative justice.

The second question is to what extent restorative justice schemes are intended as replacements for 'traditional' justice. Is restorative justice intended to be used as a small part of justice, for a few offenders or offences which require different treatment on crime reductive or humanitarian grounds, like the treatment of the mentally disordered within criminal justice? Or is it to replace criminal justice, with current justice evolving into new restorative justice? Or is it to stand alongside criminal justice, as an alternative system for resolving disputes?

The third question is from whose perspective we should be considering and evaluating restorative justice and the potential for its implementation. Should it be from the perspective of the state, with its multiple aims of crime reduction and of delivering justice fairly and efficiently? Or should it be from the perspective of the individual case, so that processes and outcomes always have to meet minimum standards, as in codes of practice or human rights outcomes? Or should it be from the perspective of lay participants—defendants, victims, witnesses, local communities—who may have both processual requirements and also forward-looking problem-solving aims, more complicated than the state's simple crime reductive aim of lessening reconviction?

These three questions will necessarily complicate looking at the potential for implementation of restorative justice in its legal and social context. They must, however, be faced before we can provide any resolution to the details of the kinds of justice constraints which restorative justice needs to guarantee before it can be seen as justice. These constraints include whether the process is concerned only with the criminal incident, how advocacy is to be facilitated within restorative justice, whether legal advice or legal representation is necessary, how third parties should be dealt with and whether there are evidential constraints. They ultimately govern the relationship between restorative justice and the law. Is restorative justice to be subordinate to the law? Could criminal justice transform itself into restorative justice or will restorative justice always be perceived as a threat to criminal justice, to be dismissed, absorbed or co-opted?

I. BOUNDING RESTORATIVE JUSTICE

In order to be able to discuss the similarities and differences between restorative justice and criminal justice, we first need to bound restorative justice and to provide at least a working definition of it. This is not a simple task. As both Jim

Dignan (Dignan and Cavadino, 1996; Dignan and Lowey, 2000) and I (Shapland, 1992) have commented, restorative justice is not a unitary concept, but rather an umbrella term which has been stretched over a number of disparate practices and processes which have taken root in different countries and legal cultures. The key initiatives have been discussed in several papers, particularly that by Kurki (2001) and so I do not need to deal with them in detail. The major initiatives include:[2]

— Mediation between victim and offender, normally through a trained mediator (professional or volunteer; representing the community or not), with many schemes developing from the initial impetus provided by the VOM (Victim-Offender Mediation) and VORP (Victim/Offender Reconciliation Projects) initiatives of the Christian Mennonite movement in the US (Zehr, 1985).
— Conferences, which are characterised by being attended by supporters of the offender (and potentially victim supporters as well), as well as the victim and offender.[3] They are also facilitated by a trained co-ordinator and aim to produce a contract governing what will be done as a result of the incident provoking the calling of the conference, which may include reparation to the victim, but may not. The scope is broader than victim-offender mediation and an important element is sometimes that the conference is situated in community processes.
— Sentencing circles, developed primarily in Canada, to create a means whereby victims and their supporters, offenders and their supporters, criminal justice personnel (judges, prosecutor, defence, police) and all those in the community who have an interest in the offence come together.

The three main types of schemes have in common the key aspects of restorative justice which are represented in Marshall's (1999) definition, which is probably the most widely used: 'Restorative justice is a process whereby all the parties with a stake in a particular offence come together to resolve collectively how to deal with the aftermath of the offence and its implications for the future' (p 5).

We need to note that the major aspects of restorative justice, according to Marshall, hence involve both *process* and *outcome*. The parties must come together and must collectively resolve how to deal with the offence: the process dimension. The resolution itself provides the outcome aspect, rather than any external authority imposing a different outcome. However, this outcome is defined as necessarily having a future dimension—it should look forward to the implications that the offence has for the future—as well as dealing with the past—the aftermath of the offence.

---

[2] Another recent review of different restorative justice initiatives which takes an explicitly comparative dimension is Dignan and Lowey (2000).

[3] Examples of conferences are the Family Group Conferences of New Zealand (Maxwell and Morris, 1996), the RISE (Canberra ReIntegrative Shaming Experiments: Strang et al 1999; Strang, 2000) initiative in Australia, the other Australian police-led experiments, and the Restorative Conferences pioneered by Thames Valley Police in England.

The ways in which the umbrella has been stretched over different schemes typically seen as 'restorative justice' have included some blurring of the normal meaning of some of Marshall's concepts. It is also difficult to know whether various initiatives, normally classified as 'criminal justice', such as community service and compensation orders, are in fact restorative justice. In other words, bounding and separating 'restorative justice' and 'criminal justice' is very difficult.

A few illustrations of the blurring of restorative justice principles include indirect victim-offender mediation and some new youth justice sentences. Much victim-offender mediation in England and Wales has in practice involved not direct meetings between victim and offender, but a form of shuttle diplomacy (JUSTICE, 1998). 'Coming together' has hence sometimes been taken to be a metaphorical convergence of perspectives, rather than a physical meeting. In other schemes, 'coming together' has effectively been sacrificed to 'resolve collectively', with obtaining a final agreement on outcome between the parties being deemed to be more important than undertaking a joint process of agreeing. Equally, the term 'restorative justice' has been applied to initiatives designed to deal with young people's offending which have attempted to meld the new treatment imperatives ('dealing with offending behaviour') with reparation as an outcome, but without bringing together all relevant parties to discuss what should be done. An example is the Scottish lay panel youth justice system. Though the lay panel may well ask the offender to make an apology or pay compensation to the victim or do community service (all of which are reparative outcomes), the victim is in no way allowed to participate in the process. Indeed, the outcome has to be kept confidential from victims, because the process is seen as being for the main interests of the offender, as a young person, and so needs to be confidential (JUSTICE, 1998).

This is a good example of what van Dijk (1983), in his very useful categorisation of initiatives to help victims, has called the 'resocialisation or rehabilitation ideology': an initiative whose real aim is not, as it appears to be, to aid victims, but to understand the offender and hope for his constructive resocialisation. Restorative justice in its earlier incarnations in the US contained many of these programmes, which although supposedly aiming to undertake mediation between victim and offender, in fact concentrated upon the offender and preventing his or her reoffending (Harland, 1983). The victim was a pawn (sometimes a willing pawn) in this game.

Now that the penal pendulum has swung round again to rehabilitational or treatment strategies, particularly for young offenders, we are seeing more examples of penal outcomes and initiatives which also use the rhetoric of restorative justice, but tend to ignore the ideas of 'coming together' and 'collective resolution'. The new 'reparation order' in England and Wales under the Crime and Disorder Act 1998, may include direct work to the victim (to which the victim has to consent, but cannot be seen to be in any process of collective decision) or work for the community. However, the community is not involved in agreeing to or proposing this work. Preliminary results suggest that direct reparation is only rarely ordered because workers find it an additional and time-consuming hassle to contact and work with victims.[4] Another new initiative, the 'final warning', which has replaced a second formal caution as the last diversion alternative before a young offender is prosecuted, is also intended to allow mediation, conferencing and restorative work. However, in only 15 per cent of the pilot areas' cases where a final warning was given were victims contacted and only 4 per cent of victims had direct involvement with reparative measures (Holdaway et al 2001). Holdaway et al found that in some areas letters of apology were being required to be written routinely by offenders, but that many of these letters were not sent, it being deemed that the activity was reparative in itself (presumably only for the offender!). Some official guidance suggests that sentencers should leave the option as to whether reparative work should be for the victim or for the community for the worker to determine after sentencers, in order to reduce delays in sentencing (PA Consulting Group, 2000). In sum, youth resocialisation options which essentially sacrifice 'coming together' and 'collective resolution' to a package focusing on reducing reconviction cannot, in my view, be termed 'restorative justice'.

Compensation orders and community service orders, which are clearly reparative sentences, are, however, rather more difficult to place as restorative justice or not restorative justice. In one sense, they cannot be seen as restorative justice, because they clearly do not typically involve offenders and victims (and others) meeting together to plan what to do about the implications of the offence. Yet compensation orders do involve consultation by police with victims at an earlier stage and, in many areas, the completion of a compensation form which allows victims to state what their losses have been and whether they would wish to receive compensation. This should now be incorporated into a new 'victim personal statement', which will allow all victims to set out, if they wish, the effects of the offence on them, and which will be available to criminal justice personnel, including the sentencer (Home Office, 2001). Compensation orders, then, involve a sequential participation by victim and offender, together with criminal justice personnel. The 'coming together' is stepped, rather than being at a meeting or conference.

Criminal justice schemes such as the HALT schemes in the Netherlands come even closer to full compliance with all the restorative justice requirements. HALT (literally, 'the alternative') is a locally run set of schemes, now governed by national legislation, applicable to young offenders arrested by the police for vandalism, shop theft and letting off fireworks. If the offender admits the offence, the police, acting under the jurisdiction of the prosecutor, will forward the case to HALT.

---

[4] The evaluation of Youth Action Teams found that not all victims felt that their needs had been met by the reparation they had received and most felt that offenders' interests were seen as paramount, though they were in general pleased to have been invited to take part. Victims had in fact been contacted in only 66% of applicable cases, with only 31% of those being contacted agreeing to direct reparation. The low agreement rates are seen by the evaluators as primarily due to the inadequate means used to contact victims (an 'opt-in' letter) and the resistance of some Youth Action Team workers to working with victims. Only 19% of reparation orders actually made were to named individuals, with 63% being to the community (Holdaway et al 2001).

HALT contacts the victim and a contract is arranged between offender, victim and HALT, whereby the offender agrees to do a certain number of hours working to repair the damage caused or in the shop, as well as group sessions with HALT. HALT now deals with some 27,000 offenders annually and has to be regarded as a major criminal justice response to this kind of offending. It also clearly involves victim and offender (and offenders' parents and significant others), though there is rarely a face-to-face meeting before the contract is drawn up (obviously victim and offender meet whilst the work is being done!).

Should community service orders be regarded as restorative justice? The reparative element in community service orders is intended to be to the whole community and tends to take a communitarian view of what work should be done. Hence work, at least in England and Wales, is designed to improve the local environment (clearing footpaths etc.) or help those considered infirm or more needy (the old, the sick etc.), rather than being for the benefit of private interests. The outcome is clearly reparative work, though it is not a direct reparation of the particular harm done by the offence. The process is more difficult to categorise and I think underlines the theoretical minefield involved in placing restorative justice definitional templates onto criminal justice. The judge could be seen as the embodiment of community interests in dealing with that offending behaviour and community service as the acknowledgement of the harm done. If so, then reparative sentencing could be seen as collective resolution. Many, however, will argue that judges cannot be seen as the embodiment of the community for reparative justice. It is that tension—between state criminal justice personnel and community interests—which I think defines the essence of the difference between restorative justice and criminal justice processes and to which I turn later in the paper.

We have seen, then, that it is extremely difficult to make a clear separation between schemes which are often automatically termed 'restorative justice' and those which are normally called 'criminal justice'. It is also rare that all the elements in Marshall's definition of restorative justice are met for any particular scheme. Nor is this a matter solely of inadequate implementation. The requirement of restorative justice of participation by victim or community, as well as offender, is very difficult to achieve if that participation is to be voluntary. The ways in which 'coming together' and 'collective resolution' have been blurred or proxies used reflect the problems in making people participate if there is not a culture of individual or community resolution of offending problems. It is just those same difficulties which have led to the development of criminal justice, with its ability, where necessary, to use coercion to bring people together to resolve disputes.

II. HOW DIFFERENT IS RESTORATIVE JUSTICE
FROM CRIMINAL JUSTICE?

We need now to ask to what extent restorative justice is different from criminal justice. My argument will be that the essential differences are in fact not the ones typically adduced, such as ignoring victims, looking backwards to punishment rather than forwards to solving problems, etc. Just as restorative justice has often been caricatured, so has criminal justice. But there are some key differences. I will argue that these relate to process, rather than outcome, and that they concern the role of the state, the role of the prosecution, the role of the community, and the limiting principles posed by the current scope of human rights legislation.

1. Restorative Justice and Criminal Justice Outcomes Are Not Necessarily Different

First, I would argue that outcomes show no necessary difference between restorative justice and criminal justice. It is true that the outcomes of mediation and conferences and sentencing circles are often far more imaginative than those embodied in typical legislative sentencing provisions. However, that is due to the lack of imagination of policy makers and parliamentary drafters, compared to the contextually much more sensitive imagination of those on the ground. There is no reason why all the elements which have been produced as restorative outcomes could not be legislative sentences. We have also seen that some sentences are certainly reparative and, I would argue, embody restorative justice.

It is of course true that not all sentences are restorative or reparative. Allen (2001) has argued that we should see English and Welsh sentencing and criminal justice policy as essentially post-modern, in that it has no overarching principle or coherent philosophy, largely because the state has withdrawn from its responsibility for reducing offending.[5] Instead, criminal justice policy admits of many different elements with contrasting or even contradictory purposes. I would argue that the cafeteria tendency in sentencing (a bit of retribution, a bit of rehabilitation and perhaps a scoop of reparation) has been around for much of the modern era and has persisted into late modern or post-modern times. I would agree, however, that drawing back the frontiers of the state has made the state less able to stamp one particular philosophy onto sentencing. We are likely to see a plethora of sentences for some time to come. I would argue, therefore, that there is no necessary distinction between restorative and criminal justice in the types of potential outcomes each could admit (though not in the outcome that would be produced in an individual case).

2. The Role of the State

It is ironic, however, that at the same time as the state is trying, as Allen argues, to devolve responsibility for the outcomes of sentencing (such as reducing offending) to others (such as parents and offenders themselves), it remains so reticent

---

[5] See also Garland (1996); Jefferson and Shapland (1994).

to devolve responsibility for the process of criminal justice. Here, I think we have come up against one of the assumed, unspoken but thereby very powerful defining characteristics of criminal justice.

I have argued elsewhere that the key difference between criminal justice and civil justice is that in criminal justice the state reserves the right to control entry to and egress from the system (Shapland et al 2002). In criminal justice, cases cannot enter into the system nor leave it without the permission of the state.[6] In civil justice, though entry is controlled by the state through the issuing of (in England and Wales) a summons, writ, originating application or other instrument, cases can then stop at any point up to trial. There are barriers to the parties then trying to recommence litigation after a break, in particular, the imposition of time limits, but these forms of case management by the state are very different in principle to the requirement of criminal justice that the case must formally be ended by the state and that the defendant is in jeopardy until this happens. In criminal justice, though it may not always be clear which part of state criminal justice knows what is happening to the case,[7] it is expected that at least one part knows what is happening and is controlling it. In civil justice, the view from the state (the court) is limited. The court knows about and, through case management strategies in civil justice, is increasingly seeking to control the dispute as far as the elements which occur in the court room are concerned, but if the dispute is settled, or the plaintiff decides to withdraw, or if the case merely stops being actively pursued, this is no longer the concern of the court unless the parties try to reactivate it at court.

I would argue that many restorative justice initiatives are trying to embody civil justice procedures, rather than criminal justice procedures. Restorative justice would prefer to see the victim, offender and supporters control (with a facilitator) the timescale and outcome of the proceedings. It is loath to see the state exert its powerful mandate. However, this runs contrary to the fundamental principle of state criminal justice, which is that bringing offenders to justice requires state control over the extent and terms of entry and egress from the criminal justice process. The corollary of state control is that it is recognised to be coercive. Because it is coercive, the panoply of human rights legislation (knowing where

---

[6] In England and Wales, the police by charging, or the magistrates' court in granting a summons, determine entry into criminal justice. In other countries, there are similar provisions, though prosecutors tend to play a larger role. Where there is a right of private prosecution, this is normally (and certainly in England and Wales) subject to a decision by the court or a senior prosecutor as to whether the case should continue. Subsequently, a decision to end the case has to be taken formally by the police (not proceeding with a charge), the Crown Prosecution Service (discontinuing prosecution), or the court (discharging the defendant or convicting and sentencing him or her). Neither a lay prosecutor nor a lay defendant can formally stay the process.

[7] The problem of criminal justice is its highly atomised nature, with a large number of different agencies having a role at different points. The number of agencies has primarily arisen to provide checks and balances on state prosecutorial power and is reflected in the number of different government departments involved (separate control of police, prosecutors and judiciary/court administration), though the penchant for devolving managerial responsibility from government to executive agencies in the 1990s has added to the number.

and when you are supposed to return, knowing the charges, getting a lawyer etc.—Amnesty International, 1998) has been developed.

Restorative justice in respect of offending seems, therefore, to me to have a choice. It can either decide to exist within criminal justice or to repudiate it and be a parallel justice system (just as civil justice is a parallel system). If it exists within criminal justice, then it is ultimately subject to decisions of the state appointed agent as to whether a case is live, or has finished. Any restorative agreements or contracts will then necessarily be subject to state agreement—though they will then also be able to be enforced, if necessary, through state means. Moreover, the human rights provisions developed to protect offenders against state power, including the need for legal representation and, where necessary, advocacy, will apply, as I shall argue below.

If restorative justice decides to exist wholly outside state criminal justice as a parallel system then, if it is dealing with offending, it will potentially be in competition with state criminal justice. Many restorative justice initiatives have instead, confronted with the stark choice, decided not to challenge the state, but to take the state's leavings. They have become diversion schemes, whereby state agents have a discretion to allow cases to leave the system and to proceed to restorative justice. Most police- and prosecutor-level restorative justice is of this type. The difficulty, as has been shown with all diversion schemes of whatever type, is that state agents tend to be very loath to let many cases escape their grasp. The Canberra RISE experiments, for example, despite continuing negotiation, serious political kudos, and agreed parameters, only managed to have less than 20 per cent of eligible cases referred by the police to RISE for allocation to the random distribution between restorative justice and court (Strang, 2000). An alternative is that the state agents themselves lead the restorative justice initiative, so that if they, being present at the conference/meeting, agree with the outcome, they can let it happen because of their inherent discretionary power. The difficulty here is that the facilitator role often does not sit well with the discretionary power role (Blagg, 1997) and it is notable that the New South Wales police-led conferences Blagg criticises are now run by the Office of Juvenile Justice. One other alternative is to mainstream the restorative justice measure within criminal justice (the 'New Zealand solution') and we shall consider that below.

3. The Roles of the Prosecutor and Judge

Before considering the implications of mainstreaming, we need first, however, to look at the roles of the prosecutor and judge. The restorative justice schemes described above are not intended as a complete justice system. They all presume that the offender is the correct offender and that the offender can be expected to acknowledge that he or she was the author of the offence and to apologise or to talk about their views of the offence in that role. This is why restorative justice, in many of the papers, is being compared to philosophies of sentencing.

In sentencing, in the Anglo-American tradition or continental European tradition, the role of the prosecution is traditionally limited. The prosecutor is expected, where necessary, to acquaint the court of the 'facts' of the offence, to be responsible for providing information stemming from the prosecution side (such as details of previous convictions or written details from the victim regarding compensation), to act as guardian for the rights of third parties (so, for example, to protest if the defence were to indicate that the victim or another prosecution witness had played a more major role in the offence), to provide information about the limits of the court's sentencing powers and, in some jurisdictions (for example, the Netherlands and the US) to suggest a sentence. All of these roles are constrained to the instant offence on which sentence is to be passed.

Not uncommonly, however, in the process of sentencing, it is revealed that there is some doubt as to whether this offender has committed that offence in exactly the way suggested by the prosecution. The archetypal instance is when an unrepresented defendant who has pleaded guilty to theft says that they didn't intend to keep the goods they had picked up in the shop, but were about to put them back. If that happens, the court is bound to substitute a not guilty plea to theft and to revert to trial mode, setting aside any conviction. Alternatively, the defence and prosecution versions of events differ in some respect which will reflect in a major way on the potential severity of sentencing (for example, on the amount of drugs involved, or whether someone was kicked when assaulted, or whether there was provocation to some extent). If this is not sorted out between prosecution and defence so that the prosecution are prepared to accept the final version, then again a criminal court will tend to revert from sentencing to trial mode (this time a trial of the factual issues affecting sentence, called, for example, in England and Wales a 'Newton' trial), before the process of sentencing continues.

How are these issues dealt with in restorative justice? In restorative justice schemes, typically there is no prosecutor present, so there is no-one representing the state's interest in enforcing criminal law. Some of the roles are taken on by the co-ordinator/facilitator. Hence what might be called the 'guardian roles' of the prosecutor as officer of the court—guarding the interests of third parties and reminding the court of its powers—would typically be seen by co-ordinators as theirs. It is they who are intended to ensure that all participants are allowed to speak and that participants respect each others' human rights, as well as preventing final agreements containing illegal or overly coercive elements. It is also up to the co-ordinator to try to get all relevant participants to the meeting or to obtain necessary information (about reparative possibilities etc).

The key elements that the co-ordinator cannot take on, however, are to act as judge or take the discretionary powers of the prosecutor to accept a particular version of the offence. If the offender denies that he or she is the offender, or denies elements of the offence alleged by the victim, then typically the restorative justice meeting cannot proceed. It is of the essence of restorative justice that there should be an offence which all sides agree has occurred and which gives rise to the need for restoration. So, generally, the proceedings then revert back to the point at which they have left traditional criminal justice (police, prosecutor or court) and proceed through those channels until the offence is again clarified. Essentially, restorative justice is being backed up by traditional criminal justice. It is deliberately limiting itself to a subordinate role.

These kinds of issues over determination of the offence and of guilt have often, I feel, been swept under the carpet in restorative justice schemes. The tension is that restorative justice, by its nature, does not limit itself to discussion of the instant offence, bounded as strictly as the evidential rules of formal criminal justice would ensure. Simply because ordinary people do not see the offence as a time-limited slice of action carved from ongoing social interaction, participants at restorative justice sessions will not just discuss the offence alone. They will raise the circumstances round the offence, previous incidents, previous interaction between offender and victim and matters which have occurred since the offence. Nor, given the purposes of restorative justice, will they be wrong to do so. It is not possible to have a problem-solving, forward-looking orientation to the session and omit all these other circumstances.

In formal criminal justice, likewise, lay witnesses and people during the process between conviction and sentence, try hard to bring the surrounding circumstances into the discussion. One of the most annoying things that witnesses have to face is the instructions just to answer the questions put, rather than they being able to tell the account in their own way. One of the more attractive elements of restorative justice is that it has this more gentle attitude to lay participants.

Sentencing itself, of course, has never been as limited in its vision of events as is the trial process. Sentencers have tended to lap up and demand information about the offenders' circumstances, previous convictions, prospects for employment etc. However, details of other incidents where there has not been a conviction have not been included. I would argue that including material not related to the instant offence can carry dangers to offender and victim.

In earlier work on the construction of mitigation in magistrates' courts and the Crown Court in England, I argued that an apology in the process between conviction and sentence is in fact a very complex account, embodying stories which redefine the presentation of the offence and the character of the offender, and which are directed at all the participants present (Shapland, 1981). Legal representatives undertake this task as a proxy, sifting out material which is irrelevant, in the court's culture and perception, to sentence. They thus sift out material about other interactions between victim and offender, but leave in material about previous wrongdoing leading to convictions. In one sense, they are leaving out information which might help to solve the problem of what to do about the consequences of the offence. In another sense, they are leaving in matters which are to the offender's detriment, but which have never been proved against him or her.

The removal of the prosecutor and the judge from restorative justice has, therefore, a price. In order to facilitate problem solving and to allow people to tell their story, matters are highly likely to be raised that go beyond the instant offence. Sometimes, this will allow a more satisfactory result, which resolves not just the current offence, but other patterns of behaviour. Sometimes, the price may be that the outcome may be a judgement of the participants not just on that offence, but on all presumed offending conduct or even on the offender as a person.

The second price is that restorative justice is not set up to resolve disputes where there is no agreement on the fact of occurrence of the offence, or that that offender was the offender. Just as informal social control cannot normally cope with offenders who are strangers (Baumgartner, 1991; Shapland and Vagg, 1988), so restorative justice cannot cope with matters beyond the boundaries of the initial agreement that a particular offence has been committed.

4. The Role of the Community

Though the prosecutor and judge may be absent in restorative justice, the community is in some models far more obviously present than in traditional criminal justice. It is commonplace for community interests to be represented in the steering committees or groups who create and advise on the management of individual restorative justice meetings or conferences. Initiatives which have tapped into first nation cultural understandings often have community representatives at individual meetings and conferences as well. Moreover, restorative justice principles have been used to create means to resolve inter-communal conflict, rather than just inter-individual conflict. The clearest examples of inter-communal mechanisms to resolve conflict have been the Truth and Reconciliation Commissions and particularly that in South Africa (South African Truth and Reconciliation Commission, 1998; see also Dyzenhaus, 1998).

Advocacy of community involvement in restorative justice has often come from a communitarian philosophy, which invokes community rights as distinct from, though often assumed to be in accord with, individual rights. Cavadino and Dignan (Cavadino et al 1999; Dignan and Lowey, 2000) have argued that communitarian philosophies and associated restorative justice projects vary along a dimension from the more authoritarian, exclusionary schemes to the more inclusive ones based on reintegrative shaming. In the more exclusionary schemes, the demand is that everyone abides by the norms and culture of the assumed wishes or prejudices of the majority of the population based in that community. Dignan comments that, in a divided society, communitarianism could be used 'as a façade not only for illiberal populism but also for vigilantism and community despotism' (Dignan and Lowey, 2000: 18). Certainly, communitarianism typically wishes to proceed on the basis of a perceived consensus about the type of social order and reaction to criminality which should prevail in a particular community. Unfortunately, almost all communities and certainly all geographic communities do not have this uniform view of preferred social order. The old, the young, business people, long-term residents, incomers and representatives of state services working in that area do not have identical views about neighbourhood problems or their potential solutions (Shapland and Vagg, 1988).

Including community representatives clearly brings strengths. They are aware of and may be able to mobilise resources in that community which can contribute to problem-solving solutions. They may add perceived legitimacy to agreements through raising them from the individual level—though that legitimacy will be a function of the extent to which those bound by the agreement agree they are a member of the community and of the extent to which the process is attempting to bind participants into the community, rather than exclude them. It is one thing for traditional criminal justice to brand someone an offender and chastise them through sentencing; it is a far more damaging thing for a community to which that offender feels he or she belongs to do the same without, as Braithwaite (1989) would argue, also reintegrating them back into the community.

Adding the community, though, also effectively sets the community apart from the state. Some communitarian restorative justice itself deliberately wishes to do this, particularly where the state is regarded with suspicion and where that community does not accord all state criminal justice agencies legitimacy. At certain times, the developing 'bottom-up' restorative justice schemes in Northern Ireland have wished to be entirely separate from state agencies such as the Royal Ulster Constabulary (Auld et al 1997).

Though the community dimension to restorative justice is potentially fruitful, if restorative justice becomes enveloped in a solely communitarian jacket, then it will always have significant limitations to the cases it can take, particularly if the community definition is a geographic or affinity one. Offending is still a very local affair, with the distance to offend being an inverted J-shape (Wiles and Costello, 2000; Shapland and Vagg, 1988). Geographical and affinity communities are often very small—a housing estate, a factory, a few streets. Community restorative justice tends only to be successful on the same scale—which removes much offending from its grasp.

Moreover, the relation between state justice and community justice (often termed 'local justice') has always been an uneasy one. The history of the development of state criminal justice has largely been one of subjugating local interests and powers. Restorative justice on a community basis, or including significant community personnel, will always need backing up by a state justice system to cope with outside offending and victimisation. Yet in order to have that reach, a state justice system will need to emphasise universalistic justice values and uniformity of process and outcome. The state values are destined to come into conflict with local values. The question is whether the state can bow out, yet preserve its legitimacy.

5. Human Rights and the Role of Defence Advocacy

The legitimacy of the state is bound up with its espousal of universalistic values and dependent upon actual criminal justice processes not being shown to fall far short of these values. When there are scandals in terms of miscarriages of justice or corruption, confidence in state criminal justice can come down with a bump.[8] Scandals breed enquiries and enquiries tend to result in reforms which move towards adoption of well-known international standards of process and outcome. One of the most obvious instances of this has been the increasing adoption and promotion of international human rights standards.

I do not wish to analyse all the relevance of human rights standards to the processes of restorative justice, which is the subject of other papers. It is important here, however, to focus upon the importance of the defence lawyer and of adequate representation and advocacy in most human rights legislation. Simply because human rights legislation was the culmination of years of struggle which had focused in criminal justice upon asserting the rights of the defendant, particularly in the first half of the last century, it is framed within an image of the lone, powerless defendant confronted with the mighty power of the coercive state. Unfortunately, at the time it was being drafted, the lone, powerless victim had not yet entered the consciousness of many lawyers or policy makers. Hence, victim rights are far less developed in the more binding international documents. Human rights legislation specifically concerned with criminal justice focuses on defendants' rights and tries to ensure that the defendant has some tools and a champion to fight the state.

In international human rights documents, the champion's lance has been handed to the lawyer. When someone is accused of a criminal offence, he or she should be allowed to have legal assistance of their own choosing. If the person is penurious, then that right extends to free legal assistance provided by the state.[9] In a similar way, persons under detention should have adequate opportunity to communicate with the outside world.[10] The key aspects which the representation should afford are to ensure that information is obtained which will affect the defendant, to advise the defendant, and to allow the defendant to make representations (advocacy). They are to ensure people can understand what is going on and can say what they need to in their defence.

Restorative justice has itself recently felt the need for standards. The Restorative Justice Consortium in 1999 set out standards governing the conduct and arrangements for restorative justice meetings and conferences. They emphasise the elements which Dignan has drawn out of Marshall's original definition of restorative justice:

— The principle of inclusivity (the whole range of interests affected by offending should govern those entitled to participate)
— A balance of interests (a re-weighting of the public, state interest to give it a lower priority than in traditional criminal justice, so that victim, offender and community interests are heightened)

---

[8] Recent examples include the miscarriages of justice in England and Wales over prosecution flaws in keeping significant evidence from the defence in the 1980s and the over enthusiastic use of proactive surveillance of drug trafficking in the Netherlands, involving specialist police squads.
[9] Art 6, European Convention on Human Rights.
[10] Principle 19, Body of Principles for the Protection of all Persons under Any Form of Detention or Imprisonment.

— Non-coercive practice (participation should be voluntary)
— A problem-solving orientation (restoration of harm and forward-looking, preventive outcomes).[11]

The standards are designed to fulfil very similar aims to those in human rights legislation. They too promote understanding and the ability to contribute amongst lay participants. Both sets of standards have similar goals—but they use different means. Restorative justice is very chary of admitting lawyers as representatives, fearing either that they will 'take over' the proceedings, or that they will seek to introduce technical points-scoring. It puts its faith in procedures and scripts for meetings. Criminal justice sees the lawyer as the ultimate guarantee of the fairness of what are necessarily adversarial proceedings between defendant and state. They are necessary because of the coercive power the criminal justice state can exert.

If it is agreed that restorative justice and criminal justice can have the same outcomes, as I argued earlier, then it must be accepted that restorative justice too can wield serious coercive power over individual offenders. Conferences and mediation can be painful, transformative work. Contracts can be onerous and certainly involve work or even periods of custody. Communitarian restorative justice can include even more punitive sanctions, involving the renegotiation of relationships within the community. Offenders will of course have consented to restorative justice outcomes, but that does not remove their punitiveness.[12] Moreover, the extent to which offenders (or victims) can be said to have freely 'consented' to any justice outcome is dubious. Consenting implies the ability to walk out of the situation without prejudice. Justice processes rarely provide that opportunity.

Can then restorative justice procedures afford to ban defence lawyers? Will they not be subject to challenges under human rights legislation? In practice, restorative justice schemes have tended to compromise in this area. Offenders have always been allowed and encouraged to bring supporters. Where schemes involve the potential of producing criminal justice sentences as outcomes (as in court referrals under the New Zealand scheme), then legal supporters (termed youth advocates in the New Zealand scheme) have been allowed and, as the scheme developed, encouraged. Where schemes have been diversion schemes and do not involve potential re-entry into criminal justice, lawyers have tended to be banned.

In similar informal fora, such as the small claims court in England and Wales, lay participants have suffered without legal advice, even though they may sometimes be able to cope without legal representation (Baldwin, 1997a, 1997b).[13] He found that litigants in person found it very difficult to represent themselves without legal advice. The difficulty was not their ability to say what happened, but

---

[11] Adapted from Dignan and Lowey (2000).
[12] A similar argument applies to sentences which require the offender's consent.
[13] The small claims court deals with civil claims of relatively low value (generally up to £5,000). At the time Baldwin was observing it and interviewing those who were involved as plaintiffs or defendants, it sat in private and involved very informal procedures, where essentially each side told their story, in the same way as in restorative justice proceedings.

their ability to translate their case into evidence and to prepare and present a case. They needed advice on what was relevant and how to put it. More recently, we have observed small claims court cases and interviewed the district judges who hear them (Shapland et al 2002). We would entirely agree with Baldwin. Lay people have difficulty in preparing and presenting material which necessarily has to be contained within the contextual rules of that forum (in this case a legal, civil justice forum). Much depends upon the patience and ability of the judge to question participants and bring out relevant points.

The equivalent in restorative justice might be seen to be the preparatory sessions, in which the co-ordinator prepares victim or offender for the meeting. In terms of providing information about the meeting and trying to help the participants with what they might want to say, skilful co-ordinators may well be able to take on some of the role which traditionally defence advocates are assigned. Indeed, given some of the very worrying findings about the cursory nature of meetings between defence lawyers and defendants and the ways in which experienced defence lawyers manage the expectations of their clients (for example, McConville et al 1994; Jackson et al 1991), preparation by co-ordinators may well be better than the typical practice of defence lawyers in criminal cases.

However, co-ordinators cannot advise defendants on the choices confronting them about what to say, what to admit and what to offer for the outcome. Co-ordinators must remain true to the overall spirit of the conference and impartial between victim and offender (and community). If restorative justice conferences or meetings are likely to result in coercive outcomes for defendants, or if the defendant is still subject to criminal justice proceedings, I believe they must permit defendants to obtain legal advice.

Lawyers in restorative justice proceedings do not, however, need to mean berobed, wigged, distant, combative presences. At the 'Youth Justice in Focus' Australasian conference in 1998, where many youth advocates spoke about the way in which family group conferences had developed in New Zealand, it was remarkable to hear how they had seen their own role develop to support, rather than to challenge obstructively, restorative justice processes. Similar processes have occurred in several other areas where alternative dispute resolution has developed, such as Mental Health Review Tribunals in the UK, considering whether mentally disordered individuals should be released from detention in mental treatment facilities, or mediation in family cases. I would argue it would be advisable for restorative justice to put aside its dislike of lawyers and, instead, start to develop a new group of restorative advocates.

III. MAINSTREAM, PARALLEL OR BIT PLAYER? THE CHOICES FACING RESTORATIVE JUSTICE

In the introduction, I argued that restorative justice, which seeks to deal with offending, will necessarily be compared with traditional criminal justice. In considering the different roles in the processes of criminal and restorative justice, the question of the relation between the individual restorative justice scheme and criminal justice has constantly arisen. Is the restorative justice initiative seeing itself as mainstream, as a parallel justice process, or as a bit player? This is, for me, the key choice and challenge facing restorative justice. I would argue that, though parallel justice processes (particularly community justice schemes and neighbour dispute schemes) will continue to have their place, the future will need to lie with mainstream schemes, if restorative justice is to have an impact.

Most schemes have, as we have seen, been bit players. They have taken a subordinate role, depending for their referrals on the discretionary decisions of mainstream criminal justice actors (police, prosecutors or courts). The result, everywhere, has been a paucity of referrals and schemes struggling to achieve recognition and continued funding.[14] Those restorative justice schemes which start as bit players seem destined to continue as bit players.

An alternative is to mainstream restorative justice as part of criminal justice, normally with a separate agency housing co-ordinators. The most recent whole-sale governmental review of restorative justice has been the Review of Criminal Justice in Northern Ireland (2000).[15] This concluded that 'restorative justice should be integrated into the juvenile justice system and its philosophy in Northern Ireland, using a conference model (which we term a "youth conference") based in statute, available for all juveniles (including 17 year olds, once they come within the remit of the youth court as we recommend in the next chapter), subject to the full range of human rights safeguards' (p 205). It is envisaged that, as experience grows, restorative justice schemes for young adults (18 to 21) and adults should be piloted and introduced. All young offenders who are found guilty or plead guilty at court should be referred to this youth conferencing scheme,[16] with the youth conference producing a plan for the court which would normally become the sentence (p 207). The conference would normally include the victim and supporters of the victim, as well as the offender's family, who 'should be viewed in its broad context to include those, such as church or youth leaders, who play a significant role in the offender's life' (p 209). A defence solicitor or barrister may also be there (where this is wished by the offender or his or her guardian). Though the Report sees conferencing starting primarily as a court-based, post-conviction

---

[14] In the UK, Davis (1992), Marshall (1999), JUSTICE (1998) and Miers et al (2001), in their surveys of schemes, have showed how small and marginalised schemes have tended to be and how they had needed to twist and turn in their efforts to secure funding for co-ordinators and office expenses. In Norway, Nergard (1993) has described the work of the 89 Conflict Resolution Boards working with juvenile offenders referred by the police. In 1989, 424 young persons had their cases handled by the Boards, compared with 7,593 juveniles charged by the police.

[15] I should declare an interest as a member of this Review Team. The government response to the Review accepted restorative justice as mainstream and it is included in the Justice (Northern Ireland) Act 2002, which resulted from the Review.

[16] With the only exception being those convicted of offences triable only on indictment (for example, murder, manslaughter, rape, robbery, causing grievous bodily harm with intent to cause grievous bodily harm), where it would be discretionary to refer to the youth conference.

initiative, it also believes that, in the longer term, pre-court conferences should be developed as part of a diversionary strategy.

The Northern Ireland proposals are radical proposals, clearly designed as a major break with current youth sentencing provisions and to place restorative justice at the heart of justice for young offenders. They draw considerably on the New Zealand experience, which, together with the HALT schemes in the Netherlands, have been the major mainstream approaches. Mainstreaming is seen as key to bring restorative justice into the heart of criminal justice. Any more gradual introduction, it is feared, would lead to restorative justice being permanently a bit player, as criminal justice professionals continue to claim the territory.

A few schemes have deliberately chosen to tread the alternative path—to be parallel justice schemes. The ideology of some is to be a mechanism provided to local communities to deal with all kinds of dispute. Whether that dispute involves offending, or neighbour disputes, or housing problems, is immaterial to the way in which the scheme would handle the case. Given the fine line between these categories in many instances of neighbour problems, criminal justice authorities are often happy for disputes to be dealt with in this way, seeing their potential to prevent the development of such disputes into more major assaults or other offending as far more important than any loss of sovereignty by the criminal justice system in giving up the dispute to the neighbourhood alternative dispute resolution centre. Councils themselves are developing their own dispute resolution processes along restorative justice principles to deal with neighbour disputes in the UK, though the sovereignty aspects of using restorative justice are mitigated by the fact that the extensive legal powers backing up mediation attempts are held by the councils themselves (Dignan et al 1996). Interventions are typically quite limited, whether using formal or informal means, and costs are similar.

There has been considerably more dispute about the parallel approach adopted by, for example, the nascent community restorative justice schemes in Northern Ireland or those in South Africa. The Northern Ireland schemes, which exist on both sides of the nationalist/loyalist divide, are very local, serving tightly knit communities. They are very much community-driven. Both concern and fervent support has been expressed about their existence, structures and activities. The support stems both from the view that restorative justice has much to offer in controlling offending and reducing the risk of developing drug problems, and from the feeling that these schemes, with their roots in the community, are able to start to fill the vacuum left by some of that community's distrust of formal, state-run criminal justice mechanisms. As the Review of Criminal Justice in Northern Ireland (2000) states, 'Those communities, whether Nationalist or Unionist, which most needed a community-driven restorative justice approach were precisely those where the criminal justice agencies and the criminal justice process were distrusted most' (p 196). The concerns are primarily the fear that these schemes are trying to be a complete alternative justice system, and so may run roughshod over the need for formal trials to determine guilt, and may impose punishment through the use of violence by those associated with paramilitary groups. There is a secondary potential problem of double jeopardy, where youngsters may face proceedings both through the formal criminal justice system and through restorative justice. This has previously been a significant problem in relation to informal punishments, such as knee-capping, but the schemes themselves deny involvement in or any wish to use such punishments.

The Review of Criminal Justice in Northern Ireland (2000) has essentially taken the view that community schemes must fulfil minimum standards (including human rights standards) and also that the state has to take ultimate responsibility for dealing with criminal activity. It has, therefore, recommended that schemes should be accredited and inspected, should play no role in determining guilt or innocence, and that the police should be informed about the cases that the scheme is dealing with. Others may see this as the state attempting to control and take over schemes which will wither if they lose the confidence of their communities. It is a struggle for the power to deal with what is termed crime. It is also a struggle for legitimacy.

IV. JUSTICE CONSTRAINS, BUT JUSTICE LEGITIMATES

The original defining characteristics of restorative justice were set at the individual level. They govern the participation of individual victims and offenders and the process through which agreement is sought to be reached on the individual case. Restorative justice is clearly now a movement. My argument in this paper is that it has not yet set its boundaries and emphases as a movement. In particular it has not fixed its position in relation to traditional or formal criminal justice.

The uncertainty is mutual. Formal, state-run criminal justice has not yet decided what to do about restorative justice. The power to choose what to do has, so far, largely lain with the state. The state has the potential supply of cases, which it can decide to refer to restorative justice processes. Individuals and communities have tended to provide referrals only in rare circumstances, where there is considerable distrust of state criminal justice. In addition, the state has funding to employ co-ordinators and train volunteers. The state has the ability to fund and recognise evaluation, to measure reconviction (by, of course, the state's own criminal justice system), and to undertake cost-benefit analyses (where restorative justice is compared with the state's own processes). So far, states have generally decided to keep restorative justice at arm's length, as a bit player.

But the state has its own problems with criminal justice. Twenty to thirty years ago, in most countries, state criminal justice could bask in the approval of its people and communities. They might be concerned at individual cases; they might regard criminal justice agencies with fear rather than love; but state criminal justice was criminal justice. The courts were not challenged.

A number of factors have now conspired to sow doubts in people's regard for their state criminal justice system. Some of them are general social and economic trends expressed in the move from a modern to a late modern society.[17] They include the drawing back of the state from general service provision, which in criminal justice terms includes the move from the police being those who deal with crime, to the police being seen as, and seeing themselves as, just one partner in the fight against crime (Crawford, 1998). State control over criminal justice principles and images is relatively easy to maintain if one is considering solely the traditional criminal justice system, with its hierarchy of agencies, headed by the courts. Control is much more difficult to maintain when local government, health, education, voluntary sector groups, the private sector and the public are involved. And as those groups become involved, so they may increasingly question the legitimacy of the traditional model of delivery of criminal justice.

Another major factor has been the move to broaden the scope of the fight against crime. Crime control through criminal justice has been joined by crime reduction through crime prevention, community safety and criminality prevention. Government aims in relation to crime have broadened correspondingly. The aims of the criminal justice system in England and Wales are currently (Criminal Justice System, 2001):

— To reduce the level of actual crime and disorder
— To reduce the adverse impact of crime and disorder in people's lives
— To reduce the economic costs of crime
— To ensure just processes and just and effective outcomes
— To deal with cases throughout the criminal justice process with appropriate speed
— To meet the needs of victims, witnesses and jurors within the system
— To respect the rights of defendants and to treat them fairly
— To promote confidence in the criminal justice system.

The breadth of the aims makes it very difficult for government to promote or control one simple image of criminal justice. People's picture of criminal justice, whether from inside or outside government, is now complicated and more puzzling. Some indicators are met, others are not. Is it now possible to have one view on the legitimacy of criminal justice?

We should add to this late modern pot-pourri the increasing voice of lay people in criminal justice. It is shown in the inclusion of specific objectives to do with victims, witnesses, jurors and defendants in the criminal justice objectives above. We see it in the increasing attention paid to human rights, and in specific criminal justice initiatives, such as services for vulnerable witnesses and rights for victims. Traditional criminal justice has been measured against the needs of lay participants and found wanting—not surprisingly, given its emphasis on professional, rule-governed decision making. This too, however, has had its knock-on effects on legitimacy. Traditional criminal justice is painfully, slowly, trying to turn

---

[17] See the chapter by Bottoms.

in its tracks and admit as legitimate the needs and views of its users: victims, witnesses and defendants.

Restorative justice poses a particular problem here. Much of the spur to the development of restorative justice has come from views that the traditional criminal justice system was 'stealing conflicts', in Christie's (1977) terminology and shows up in restorative justice's emphasis on the proper treatment of victims (Strang, 2000). It is becoming very difficult for criminal justice to admit previous errors in its treatment of lay people and yet to spurn restorative justice.

Current interest from governments in developing restorative justice may not, then, be so surprising. But in the search of governments for increased legitimacy, there are significant hurdles for restorative justice. One option for criminal justice is to mainstream and absorb restorative justice. For this, restorative justice will have to acknowledge its boundaries and be prepared to produce a rapprochement with criminal justice. It will become constrained by due process needs in relation to trials, by referral paths and by human rights. Conflicts will arise, particularly between community and state, but also at the level of the individual case. Limits will be set to contracts negotiated in restorative justice meetings, because contracts will be seen as the expression of the penal mood.

Yet even if criminal justice and restorative justice decide not to engage in any such marriage—and restorative justice remains a bit player—achieving legitimacy for restorative justice will still produce constraints at the individual level. Achieving agreements, healing and participation has to be undertaken within individuals' and communities' accepted social parameters of what is fair and what is just. At present, these parameters have a very legal bent, in the decisions of human rights courts. Legitimacy implies constraint—and restorative justice is bound within a framework of justice set largely by criminal justice.

REFERENCES

Allen, C (2001) 'Parenting orders and the youth court' Seminar to Faculty of Law, University of Sheffield, April 2001.

Amnesty International (1998) *Fair trials manual* (Amnesty, London).

Auld, Rt. Hon. Lord Justice (2001) *Review of the Criminal Courts in England and Wales: Report* (The Stationery Office, London).

Auld, J, Gormally, B, McEvoy, K and Ritchie, M (1997) *Designing a system of restorative community justice in Northern Ireland: a discussion document* ('the blue book') (Published by The Authors, Belfast).

Baumgartner, MP (1991) *The moral order of a suburb* (Oxford University Press, New York).

Blagg, H (1997) 'A just measure of shame?' 37 *British Journal of Criminology* 481–301.

Braithwaite, J (1989) *Crime, shame and reintegration* (Cambridge University Press, Cambridge).

Cavadino, M and Dignan, J (1996) 'Towards a framework for conceptualising and evaluating models of criminal justice from a victim's perspective' 4 *International Review of Victimology* 153–82.

Cavadino, M, Crow, I and Dignan, J (1999) *Criminal Justice 2000* (Waterside Press, Winchester).

Christie, N (1977) 'Conflicts as property' 17 *British Journal of Criminology* 1–15.

Crawford, A (1998) *Crime Prevention and Community Safety* (Longman, London).

Criminal Justice System (2001) *Objectives of the criminal justice system in England and Wales.* Available from:
http://www.criminal-justice system.gov.uk/legal/cjs_performance_measures.htm

Davis, G (1992) *Making amends: mediation and reparation in criminal justice* (Routledge, London).

Dignan, J with Lowey, K (2000) *Restorative justice options for Northern Ireland: a comparative review*, Review of Criminal Justice in Northern Ireland Research Paper 10 (The Stationery Office, Belfast).

Dignan, J Sorsby, A and Hibbert, J (1996) *Neighbour disputes: comparing the cost-effectiveness of mediation and alternative approaches* (University of Sheffield Centre for Criminological and Legal Research, Sheffield).

Dyzenhaus, D (1998) *Judging the judges, judging ourselves: truth, reconciliation and the apartheid legal order* (Hart Publishing, Oxford).

Garland, D (1996) 'The limits of the sovereign state: strategies of crime control in contemporary society' 36 *British Journal of Criminology* 445–71.

Harland, A (1983) 'One hundred years of restitution: a review and prospectus for research' 8 (1/2) *Victimology* 195.

Holdaway, S, Davidson, N, Dignan, J, Hammersley, R, Hine, J and Marsh, P (2001) *New strategies to address youth offending: the national evaluation of the pilot youth offending teams*, Home Office Research Development Statistics Occasional Paper No 69 (Home Office, London). Available from the Home Office website on http://www.homeoffice.gov.uk (RDS publications)

Home Office (2001) *A Review of the Victim's Charter* (Home Office, London).

Jackson, J, Kilpatrick, R and Harvey, C (1991) *Called to court: a public review of criminal justice in Northern Ireland* (SLS, Belfast).

Jefferson, A and Shapland, J (1994) 'Criminal justice and the production of order and control: criminological research in the UK in the 1980s' 34 *British Journal of Criminology* 265–90.

JUSTICE (1998) *Victims in criminal justice* (JUSTICE, London).

Kurki, L (2001) 'Evaluation of restorative justice practices'. Paper for this conference.

Marshall, T (1999) *Restorative justice: an overview*, Home Office Research Development Statistics Occasional Paper (HMSO, London). Available from the Home Office website at http://www.homeoffice.gov.uk (RDS publications).

Maxwell, G and Morris, A (1996) 'Research on Family Group Conferences with young offenders in New Zealand' in J Hudson, A Morris, G Maxwell and B Galaway (eds) *Family Group Conferences: perspectives on policy and practice* (Criminal Justice Press, Monsey NY).

McConville, M, Hodgson, J, Bridges, L and Pavlovic, A (1994) *Standing accused: the organisation and practice of criminal defence lawyers in Britain* (Clarendon Press, Oxford).

Miers, D, Maguire, M, Goldie, S, Sharpe, K, Hale, C, Netten, A, Uglow, S, Doolin, K, Hallam, A, Newburn, T and Enterkin, J (2001) *Evaluation of restorative justice schemes*, Occasional paper, Research and Statistics Division (Home Office, London).

Nergard, T (1993) 'Solving conflicts outside the court system: experiences with the Conflict Resolution Boards in Norway', 33 *British Journal of Criminology* 81–94.

PA Consulting Group (2000) *Assessing the impact of reparation and action plan orders on delay*, Paper for the Youth Justice Board September 2000. Available from the Youth Justice Board website at http://www.youth-justice-board.gov.uk/

Restorative Justice Consortium (1999) *Standards for restorative justice* (National Council for Social Concern on behalf of the Restorative Justice Consortium, London).

Review of Criminal Justice in Northern Ireland (2000) *Report* (The Stationery Office, Belfast).

Shapland, J (1981) *Between conviction and sentence: the process of mitigation* (Routledge & Kegan Paul, London).

——(1992) 'Reparative justice: complexity and apple pie', Paper presented to the 3rd European Colloquium on Crime and Criminal Policy in Europe, Noordwijkerhout, The Netherlands.

Shapland, J, Sorsby, A and Hibbert, J (2002) *Finalising the civil justice audit*, Lord Chancellor's Department Research Series (Lord Chancellor's Department, London).

Shapland, J and Vagg, J (1988) *Policing by the public* (Routledge, London).

South African Truth and Reconciliation Commission (1998) *The report of the Truth and Reconciliation Commission.* Available at: http://www.truth.org.za/report/execsum.htm

Strang, H, Barnes, G, Braithwaite, J and Sherman, L (1999) *Experiments in restorative policing: a progress report to the National Police Research Unit on the Canberra Reintegrative Shaming Experiments (RISE)* (Centre for Restorative Justice, Research School of Social Sciences, Australian National University, Canberra). Available from http://www.aic.gov.au/rjustice/rise/index.html

——(2000) 'Victim participation in a restorative justice process: the Canberra Reintegrative Shaming Experiments', (unpublished PhD dissertation, Law Program, Research School of Social Sciences, Australian National University, Canberra).

van Dijk, J (1983) 'Victimologie in theorie en praktijk: een kritische reflectie op de bestaande en nog te creëren voorzieningen voor slachtoffers van delicten' 6 *Justiële Verkenningen* 5–35.

Wiles, P and Costello, A (2000) *The 'road to nowhere': the evidence for travelling criminals*, Home Office Research Study 207 (Home Office, London).

'Youth Justice in Focus' (1998) Proceedings of the conference held in Wellington, New Zealand, 27–30 Oct 1998.

Zehr, H (1985) *Retributive justice: restorative justice* (Mennonite Central Committee US, Office of Criminal Justice, Elkhart IN).

11

Mind the Gap: Restorative Justice in Theory and Practice

Kathleen Daly

I. INTRODUCTION

Mind the gap. The words crackled over a speaker in a London tube station in 1980. As an American unfamiliar with British terminology, I recall laughing at the time. The warning by a stern male voice to 'mind the gap' was repeated as my train pulled into the station and the doors opened. My initial amusement turned to concern and some anxiety. What should I be minding? What was the nature of this gap? When the doors opened, I spied the gap. It was a step up from the platform to the train floor, and there was a space to negotiate before stepping onto the train. I made it into the train with some relief.

The same year Abel (1980) was marking the death of 'gap studies' in socio-legal research. He said that like legal realists, social scientists were often 'forced to adopt a debunking posture' (p 808). The result was 'studies of impact, efficacy, the "gap"' (p 821) between ideals and practice, 'image and reality' (p 810). He proposed a shift away from an instrumentalist model of law, where

> Effectiveness [is] construed in a narrowly instrumental fashion as an examination of whether the declared goals of a law or legal institution (usually one that is new or reformed) have been attained. *Yet we know they never are.* We should ask instead: what are its inadvertent consequences or symbolic meanings? What are its costs? For whom *does* it work? What are the fundamental structural reasons why it does not work?
>
> (Abel, 1980: 828; my emphasis line 3)

Nelken (1981: 44, 60) countered Abel by saying that critiques of gap studies 'went too far' and 'were exaggerated'. 'There is nothing invalid about a focus on the discrepancy between legislative promise and performance', provided that both the claims and the evidence are treated as 'data worthy of investigation in their own right' (p 45). Abel and Nelken remind us that we should not be astonished to discover gaps in ideals and practices or in promises held out for law and its actual effects' (Nelken, 1981: 41). They invite us to 'mind the gap' in a theoretical sense, that is, not only to observe the space between the platform and the train, but also to ask why the space is there. Gaps may signal something more profound than meets the eye.

For restorative justice, one reason we should expect to see gaps in theory and practice is that most people do not fully understand the idea. By this I mean that unlike interactions with the police in the street or station, or interactions with lawyers and judges in the courtroom—for which many images are available in popular culture—most people do not have a mental map of what this justice form looks like, how they are to act in it, nor what the optimal result is. And yet, they are expected to come into a room, know what to say, and be affected by the encounter. A second reason is that restorative justice advocates assume that everyone has the requisite skills and desire to participate. However, effective participation requires a degree of moral maturity and empathetic concern that many people, especially young people, may not possess.

II. RESTORATIVE JUSTICE AND CONFERENCING IN THEORY

What then is the 'ideal' restorative justice practice? I list a set of activities and behaviours that are to occur in one practice: conferences used as a diversion from court for admitted juvenile offenders. Conferences take diverse forms and have different purposes, depending on the jurisdiction. In Australia, there are differences in the kinds of offences that can be conferenced and in the volume of cases disposed (Daly, 2001a; Daly and Hayes, 2001). This paper utilises data from the South Australia Juvenile Justice (SAJJ) project on conferencing. South Australia was the first jurisdiction to introduce a statutory-based conferencing scheme in Australia, with passage of the *Young Offenders Act* in 1993 and conferencing initiated in February 1994. It is a high-volume jurisdiction that conferences more serious kinds of cases.[1]

My analysis of the SAJJ data focuses on these conference components: the conference process, its legal context, conference outcome and compliance, and conference effects:[2]

(1) Conference process. A victim and an *admitted* offender and their supporters come together to discuss the offence, its impact, and an appropriate penalty (agreement or outcome). The discussion evokes feelings of remorse[3] in the

[1] By high volume, I mean that conferences are used routinely and frequently. In South Australia, there are 1,400 to 1,600 conferences per year, and they are 18% of youth dispositions. While some jurisdictions exclude selected offences from conferencing (eg sexual assault), South Australia does not. It has the highest maximum number of community service hours (300) and the longest period of time to complete an undertaking (12 months) than any other Australian jurisdiction.

[2] My depiction is of New Zealand model conferencing, which has two professionals present (a facilitator and police officer). This differs from the Wagga model, which has one professional present (a police officer), uses a scripted conference underpinned by reintegrative shaming theory, and is more prevalent in North America and the UK.

[3] Wagga model conferencing gives more emphasis to inducing 'shame' in offenders, drawing on Braithwaite's (1989) theory of reintegrative shaming (Harris and Burton, 1998).

offender, which leads to a genuine apology and a desire to repair the harm. All conference professionals and participants are treated fairly and with respect. Participants then discuss an appropriate penalty (or agreement or outcome). Everyone has a say, and participation by the professionals is kept to a minimum. The police officer and co-ordinator ensure that elements of the agreement are not excessive.

(2) Legal context. Young people (YPs or offenders) understand their legal entitlements, which includes an understanding of what is happening in the conference, when they can end it, and the consequences of disagreeing with the outcome.

(3) Conference outcome and compliance. The young person signs an agreement, a legally binding document, which itemises the group's outcome decision. It describes what the YP must do and completion dates. The YP completes the agreement, which may include an apology letter, work for the victim or others, or compensation. In so doing, the YP assists in 'repairing the harm' for the victim.

(4) Conference effects. From their experience attending the conference and meeting the offender, and the offender's completing the agreement, victims recover from the disabling effects of the offence. From their experience meeting victims and seeing the effects of crime on them, offenders are less inclined to commit another offence.

III. RESTORATIVE JUSTICE AND CONFERENCING IN PRACTICE

The SAJJ Project

SAJJ had two waves of data collection in 1998 and 1999 (Daly et al 1998; Daly, 2001b). In 1998, the SAJJ group observed 89 conferences in metropolitan Adelaide and two country towns. The sample was selected by offence category: eligible offences were violent crimes and property offences having personal or community victims, such as schools or housing trusts. Excluded were shoplifting cases, drug cases, and public order offences. Here are highlights of the conference sample:[4]

— 44 per cent dealt with violence (mainly assaults) and 56 per cent, property offences (mainly breaking and entering, property damage, and theft of a motor vehicle).
— In 68 per cent, the victim was a person; 20 per cent of victims were organisations, and 12 per cent, a combination.
— In 28 per cent, the victims were under 18 years of age.
— Of violence victims, nearly half required medical attention and 35 per cent needed to see a doctor.

---

[4] These are conference-based percentages, not offender-based.

— Of property victims, the total out-of-pocket expenses (that is, after insurance) ranged from none to $6,000; the mean was over $900 and the median was $400.
— In 15 per cent, there were two or more offenders at the conference.
— The number of conference participants (*excluding* the co-ordinator and the police officer) ranged from 1 to 12, with a median of 5.
— Of primary offenders, 76 per cent were male; 12 per cent, Aboriginal; and 8 per cent, members of other racial/ethnic minority groups.

For each conference, the police officer and co-ordinator completed a self-administered survey, and a SAJJ researcher completed a detailed observation instrument. When a conference had more than one YP, SAJJ observations focused on a designated primary YP. Our aim was to interview all the offenders (N = 107) and primary victims associated with the conferences (N = 89). Of the 196 offenders and victims, we interviewed 172 (or 88 per cent) in 1998; of that group, 94 per cent were again interviewed in 1999. The interview had open- and close-ended items.

1. Conference Process

1(a) Victim and Offender Come Together to Discuss an Offence

In the SAJJ sample, 74 per cent of conferences had a victim present, and an additional 6 per cent had a representative from the Victim Support Services. Figures from South Australia and New Zealand (both high-volume jurisdictions) show that victims are typically present in half of conferences (Wundersitz, 1996: 109; South Australia Office of Crime Statistics, 1999: 131; Maxwell and Morris, 1993: 118). If victimless offences are excluded, victim presence would likely increase by about 8 to 10 percentage points. Based on these figures, let us assume that in high-volume jurisdictions, victims and offenders come together no more than 60 per cent of the time.[5] This suggests a gap in ideals and practice. Can we (or should we) expect any of the claimed benefits of conferences to occur if victims are not present? Relatedly, do victims and offenders know what to do when they 'come together'?

In 1998, the 93 young people were asked to think about the time before the conference and how much they knew about the process. About half or more said they had been given 'none' or 'not much' information on what would happen (47 per cent), on possible outcomes (54 per cent), and what was expected of them (61 per cent). We asked, 'what did you think would happen at the conference?' Some 27 per cent had been to a conference before. An additional 40 per cent, who had not been to a conference before, said they had some idea, and they most frequently

---

[5] In low-volume jurisdictions such as Queensland, which emphasise victim presence, the proportion is much higher, at over 90%.

mentioned penalty outcomes: 'We thought, we knew we had to do community service' or 'Um, well, I thought it was basically going to be a way of working out how I compensate for damages' or 'That I'd have to pay a fine'. The rest (33 per cent) said they had no idea what would happen.[6] Half said they felt scared about what would happen at the conference, but it was not meeting the victim that frightened them: rather, they worried about the sanction they would receive. A telling indicator was their response to the question, 'Before the conference, did you think about what you wanted to do or to say to the victim?' Over half (53 per cent) said 'no, not at all'. These results suggest that when young offenders enter the conference room, they are concerned with what penalty they may receive. How they relate to victims is relatively less important.

For the 79 victims interviewed in 1998, a substantial share said they were given 'none' or 'not much' information on what would happen (40 per cent), what was expected of them (46 per cent), or outcomes (52 per cent). The victims' replies to 'What did you think would happen at the conference?' show that most had some idea (83 per cent), and they most often mentioned discussion of the outcome alone, or in consort with discussion of the offence impact. Therefore, like the YPs, victims are also oriented toward the sanction an offender might receive. A guiding presupposition in the literature is that victims are curious to meet the offender and to find out why the offender victimised them. But is this the case? Excluding victims who already knew the offender, and analysing the 'stranger' and 'known only by sight' cases (N = 50), 36 per cent said that they were *not at all* curious to find out what the offender was like, and 32 per cent said they were *not at all* curious to find out why the young person victimised them or their organisation.

1(b) The Conference Discussion Evokes Feelings of Remorse and Shame in the Offender

A complex sequence of actions, words, body language, and symbolic exchanges occurs in the course of a YP's 'taking responsibility for an offence', 'showing remorse', and wishing to 'repair the harm', and the victim's ability to explain the impact of the offence and to 'read' the YP's sense of contrition and the genuineness of an apology. For victims, an added complexity is that the outcome is a promise by a YP to do something; thus, repairing the harm for victims is *contingent* on whether a YP makes good on a promise.

Several gaps are evident. One is how victims and offenders interpret each other's actions and words. Another is what we expect should occur and what does occur in a conference. I focus on the second, with some attention to the first, analysing in sections *1(b)* to *1(d)* a subset of cases in 1998 (N = 53) and in 1999 (N = 47), in which victims were present at the conference and both the primary YP and victim were interviewed in that year. Although the number of cases is

---

[6] Those saying they had 'some idea' (even if their idea was inaccurate) were coded as having had some idea. Those coded as having 'no idea' said 'I had no idea', 'I didn't have a clue', and the like.

reduced, it permits comparison across three perspectives (the SAJJ researcher's, the victim's, and the primary YP's) for the same set of cases.

SAJJ observers said that 77 per cent of the YPs were actively involved in the conference,[7] 66 per cent gave a clear story of how the offence came about, 60 per cent accepted responsibility for the offence, and 53 per cent were remorseful. Three-quarters of victims were effective in describing the impact of the offence on them. Half of the YPs (53 per cent) understood the impact of the offence on the victim, whereas a lower share of victims (36 per cent) understood the YP's situation. There was positive movement, in the form of words spoken, between the victim and offender in a minority (34 per cent) of conferences.[8] Just over 40 per cent of the YP subset apologised spontaneously to the victim at the conference, but for 28 per cent, the apology had to be drawn out, and in 30 per cent, there was no apology made at the conference at all. Verbal apologies may have been made before or after the conference or an apology letter written because in almost all cases (96 per cent) the YP made an apology of some sort.

How do the YPs regard saying sorry to victims? In the 1998 interviews, 74 per cent said they felt sorry for what they had done. However, somewhat fewer said they felt sorry for the victim (56 per cent before and 47 per cent after the conference). While a substantial minority (43 per cent) said that the victim's story had an effect on them, most said that it had little or no effect. When the YPs were asked what was important for them at the conference, 'repairing the harm' to victims was less important than clearing their name and reputation or being viewed by others in a more positive light. In identifying what was most important from a list of items, three we might consider to be restorative—to make up by doing work or paying money, to apologise, and to let people know the behaviour won't happen again—were 43 per cent of responses. More often the YPs selected items concerning their own reputation and their account of events, including 'to let people know that I can be trusted', 'I don't usually do things like this', and 'to tell people what happened'. In 1999, when we asked why they decided to say sorry, 27 per cent said they didn't feel sorry but thought they would get off easier, 39 per cent said to make their family feel better, and a similar percentage said they felt pushed into it.[9] However, when asked what was the *main reason* for saying sorry, most (61 per cent) said they really were sorry.

---

[7] Unless otherwise indicated, these percentages are of the researchers' judgements that the YPs or victims 'mostly' or 'fully' did something, with the rest in the 'somewhat' or 'not at all' categories.

[8] By positive movement, I mean the expression of a mutual understanding or regard for the other, which develops over the course of the conference. To illustrate, when recording positive movement between the victim and YP, a SAJJ observer wrote: 'The victim started asking caring questions about the YP's friends and her parents and life. The YP says, "I can see why you're upset, the photos cannot be replaced". . . . The victim sees the YP as a victim of peer group pressure. The YP starts crying when the victim cried about his parents'.

[9] Of the 18 in the subset who felt pushed into saying sorry, the sources of pressure were the co-ordinator, police officer, or both (7); the 'whole situation' (7); a family member (3); and one couldn't remember.

The victim interviews in 1998 reveal that most were unmoved by the offender's story at the conference, with 36 per cent saying that it had some or a lot of impact. When asked what was most important for them at the conference, victims said they wanted to be reassured that the offender would not re-offend (32 per cent) and they wanted to tell the offender how the offence affected them (30 per cent). From the 1999 interview, we found that most victims thought that the YP's motives for apologising were not sincere. To the item, the YP was not sorry, but thought they would get off easier if they said they were, 36 per cent of victims said 'yes, definitely' and another 36 per cent said 'yes, a little'. The main reasons victims gave for why the YPs said sorry were the YP thought they would get off easier (30 per cent) and the YP was pushed into it (25 per cent). *Just 27 per cent believed that the main reason that YP apologised was because s/he really was sorry.* It is not surprising, then, that half the victims said the YP's apology did not at all help to repair the harm.

These results show a gap between the ideal and the reality of conferences. From the victims' perspectives, less than 30 per cent of offenders were perceived as making genuine apologies, although from the offenders' perspectives, just over 60 per cent said their apology was genuine. More generally, young people and victims orient themselves to the conference and what they hope to achieve in ways different than the advocacy literature imagines. The stance of empathy and openness to the 'other', the expectation of being able to speak and reflect on one's actions, and the presence of new justice norms (or language) emphasising 'repair'—all of these are novel cultural elements for most participants. These elements and expectations may be even harder to grasp for adolescent than adult participants. For the young people, repairing their reputation to others, including promises of not getting into trouble again, are what's most important to accomplish at the conference. For victims, telling the story of the offence and its impact, along with being reassured by the offender that it won't happen again, are what's most important.

1(c) Conference Participants Are Treated Fairly and with Respect

On measures of procedural justice (Tyler, 1990), offenders and victims rate the conference very highly, a result found in other research on conferencing (Daly, 2001a). Of the victim and YP subsets, 90 to 98 per cent said they were treated fairly by the co-ordinator and police officer, that the co-ordinator was impartial and seemed to treat everyone fairly, and that they were treated in a respectful manner. Some negativity was evinced by the YPs, with 28 per cent saying that other people's ideas were favoured over theirs (compared to 13 per cent of victims), and with 26 per cent saying they were pushed into things (compared to 9 per cent of victims). One-fifth of victims (21 per cent) said that when they left the conference, they were upset by what the offender or his/her supporters said.

*1(d) In Discussing the Sanction (or Agreement), Everyone—Offenders, Victims,
and their Supporters—Has a Say about What the Offender Should Do*

Two variables characterised the agreement discussion: *who proposed ideas*, and
who participated in working out the ideas in the agreement. For the conference
subset, there is an even distribution across the groups. For proposing ideas, the
average (mean) percentages were co-ordinator (22 per cent), police officer (13 per
cent), YP (19 per cent), YPs supporters (17 per cent), victim or supporters (26 per
cent), and other professionals (3 per cent). For working the ideas out, the aver-
ages were co-ordinator (27 per cent), police officer (13 per cent), YP (18 per cent),
YPs supporters (19 per cent), victim or supporters (20 per cent), and other professionals (3 per cent). A third variable described the relationship between the
police officer and YP in deciding the outcome. At a minimum, the two must agree,
although the expectation is that ideally all those in the room should agree.[10] SAJJ
observers said that agreements were reached by 'genuine consensus' in 60 per cent
of the conference subset, but for about 20 per cent each, the YP accepted the police
officer's modification as 'OK' or accepted it reluctantly.

Haines (1997) anticipates that conference dynamics will produce a 'powerless
youth in a roomful of adults'. SAJJ observers believed that this phrase did not apply
to 55 per cent of conferences, but was applicable to some or a fair degree in 41 per
cent and to a high degree in 4 per cent. Items from the YP 1998 interviews show that
'powerlessness' is variably experienced. We asked the YPs, which people were
involved in deciding the agreement? Similar proportions mentioned themselves (77
per cent) and the victim (81 per cent). Most said that *the way* the agreement was
decided was fair (81 per cent) and that they had some or a lot of *say* in it (74 per
cent). However, fewer said they had *control* in what was in the final agreement (43
per cent saying some or a lot). Most thought the agreement was about right (68 per
cent) or too easy (17 per cent); 15 per cent said it was too harsh.

Victims' perceptions were identical to those of the YPs in characterising who was
involved in the agreement (80 per cent each). High proportions said that the *way*
the agreement was decided was fair (87 per cent) and that they had some or a lot of
say in it (91 per cent). Like the YPs, the victims' sense of outcome control was relatively lower (77 per cent), although higher than that of the YPs. Victims were twice
as likely as the YPs to say that the outcome was too easy (36 per cent); 62 per cent
thought it was about right; only one victim viewed the outcome as too harsh.

These results show that conference penalty discussions are occurring as they
were imagined. The co-ordinators and police officers are stepping back, allowing
the participants room for decision-making. Young people said they were less able
to control what was in the agreement than did victims, but ultimately, few YPs felt
that the outcome was onerous.

---

[10] If the YP and police officer cannot agree, the case goes to a magistrate to 'referee' it. Most participants wrongly interpret this to mean that the 'YP's case will go to court' when, in reality, it is treated
as a conference disposition.

*1(e) The Police Officer and Co-ordinator Ensure that Elements of the Agreement
        Are Not Excessive*

Like other Australian jurisdictions, in South Australia, conferencing is the second
level in a hierarchy of responses. The first level is a police caution. The less serious
form is an informal caution, which is a warning given by an officer in the street and
is not recorded as an official police action. The more serious is a formal caution,
which is issued when an offence is 'more than trivial', the YP has already received an
informal caution, and the offence has no victim; or if there is a victim, the value of
lost or damaged property does not exceed $5,000. With a formal caution, a police
officer can require an offender to pay compensation to a victim not to exceed $5,000
(set by policy), to carry out community service not to exceed 75 hours (set by
statute), apologise to a victim, or 'do anything else that may be appropriate under
the circumstances'. The maximum length of an undertaking is three months.
Undertakings agreed to in a family conference have higher maxima: compensation
not to exceed $25,000 (set by policy) and community service not to exceed 300
hours (set by statute). The maximum length is 12 months. The third level, the Youth
Court, has the most severe array of penalties, including detention, not to exceed
three years. Compensation can exceed $25,000 (no maximum is specified in the
statute), and community service hours may not exceed 500 hours (set by statute).

The conference maxima are very loud barks compared to the bites agreed to in
conferences. Of all the YPs (N = 107), 28 per cent were to pay compensation, which
ranged from $4 to $1,089; the median was $112. Some 27 per cent were to do
community work, which ranged from six to 240 hours (median was 20 hours);
and 18 per cent, to do work for the victim, which ranged from two to 80 hours
(median was 20 hours). The most frequent agreement element was an apology,
which nearly all the YPs (93 per cent) did in some way before, during, or after the
conference. Other elements include attending counselling for anger management,
sex abuse, and the like (13 per cent); other forms of counselling (14 per cent) or
educational programmes (8 per cent), and miscellaneous other things such as
being of good behaviour, not harassing the victim, staying away from a school's
grounds, and abiding by a curfew (28 per cent). The median time to complete the
undertaking was three months; few YPs (13 per cent) had the 12 month
maximum. Contrary to concerns that conferencing will lead to greater penalties
for young people, I see little evidence of this in South Australia.

2. Legal Context

*The Process Takes Place in a Context where Young People Understand their
Legal Entitlements*

Observations of the content and quality of legal information given at the
conference, coupled with the YP interviews, show gaps in ideals and practices.

This section utilises data from all the conferences observed (N = 89) and YPs interviewed in 1998 (N = 93).

Just over 30 per cent of the YPs said that being at the conference was their own choice; 22 per cent said that they had some choice, but were under pressure, and 47 per cent said it was not their own choice. For the latter two groups (N = 64), the most frequent reasons given were that the police or their parents 'said I had to go' (63 per cent) or if they didn't go, they'd have to go to court (25 per cent). Although going to a conference was not perceived as freely chosen by most young people, they recognised it as preferable to going to court because they knew the court could impose more serious sanctions.

In the conference opening, the co-ordinator sets out the ground rules and explains people's roles and the legal context. SAJJ observers recorded their understanding of the ground rules and roles, assuming this was the first conference they had observed. Most said they understood the co-ordinator's role (80 per cent), the police officer's role (70 per cent), and what was supposed to happen (85 per cent). For legal information, in 83 per cent of conferences, the co-ordinator said the YP had a right to end the conference any time, and in about 70 per cent, that the YP had a right to seek legal advice at any time. In only half (46 per cent) was it clear what the consequences were if the young person and police officer failed to reach agreement on the outcome. Depending on the item, for 22 to 30 per cent of conferences, the legal information conveyed was inadequate.[11]

The YP 1998 interviews confirmed these observations for some variables and revealed deficits in legal knowledge for others. Some 30 per cent said they had 'no idea' how the police officer's job differed from the co-ordinator's job at the conference, and most (close to 60 per cent) wrongly believed that the co-ordinator had more power to decide what was in the agreement. This latter finding is not surprising because the co-ordinator manages the discussion. The YPs recognised this orchestration as being 'the power' in the conference more so than the police officer's ability to veto the agreement. About half (46 per cent) said they had 'no idea' what would happen if they decided not to finish the conference, and over half (56 per cent) said they had 'no idea' what would happen if they and the police officer couldn't agree on the final agreement.

These findings are in line with research on adolescents in court (O'Connor and Sweetapple, 1988) and young people's understanding of their legal rights. Ruck, Keating, Abramovitch, and Koegl (1998) suggest that young people have difficulty 'reasoning about' and 'making use of rights they have in a legal context' because they are not 'aware that they possess such . . . rights' (p 286), and that most young people 'see their rights as capable of being revoked' typically by adults in authority (p 285). Observation and interview data from SAJJ suggest that legal entitlements are what the *adults are telling young people they have*. Absorbing this knowledge is difficult for young people, in part because they do not yet see themselves as rights bearing subjects, and in part because if legal rights *are given* to the

---

[11] Some co-ordinators consistently gave legal information more accurately than others.

YPs by adults, then they can just as easily be taken away. Experience from their daily lives leads them to expect this behaviour from parents and adult authorities. The distinction between 'rights in their own lives' versus 'abstract principles' is vital, Ruck et al (1998) argue, to understanding how rights are understood from a young person's perspective.

3. Outcome and Compliance

The Young Person (Offender) Signs an Agreement. . . . In Completing the Agreement, the Offender Assists in 'Repairing the Harm' S/he Caused the Victim

Of the 107 YPs in the full sample, 6 per cent had no agreement elements to complete (they may have apologised at the conference or received a formal caution). Most (80 per cent) were officially classified has having completed all agreement elements, and another two per cent partly completed the agreement and the rest was waived. Relatively few (12 per cent) of the YPs didn't finish the agreement and were breached. [12]

While there is generally high agreement compliance by the YPs, the degree to which this is perceived by victims to be 'reparative' is moderate. One reason is that there may be no nexus between the offence and agreement elements. Another is that the agreement, though technically completed, is not perceived by victims to have been completed sincerely (eg an insincere apology letter). Of the 1999 conference victims for whom the YP had completed the agreement (N = 41),[13] 51 per cent said it helped to put the offence behind them, and 49 per cent said it helped to repair the harm ('a little' or 'definitely'). Put another way, half said that the YP's completing the agreement did not at all assist them in repairing the harm or their recovery from the offence.

4. Conference Effects

From their Experience Attending the Conference, Victims Recover from the Offence and an Offender Is Less Inclined to Commit Another Offence

For victims, I analyse the interview results for all those attending the conference (61 and 57 in 1998 and 1999, respectively); and for the YPs, I highlight results from observations and official police data for the 89 primary offenders. There are

---

[12] These percentages are similar to figures reported by the South Australia Office of Crime Statistics of 84 to 85% of YPs completing the agreement (1998: 120; 1999: 126; and 2000: 130).

[13] For the 57 conference victims interviewed in 1999, the outcomes were apology in conference or no further agreement elements (4), YP completed the agreement (41), and YP did not complete it (12). Two of 57 victims said the YP did not complete the agreement, even though it was 'officially' completed. I use the victim's view rather than the official determination here and in Section 4.

myriad conference effects that could be explored, but I restrict my analysis to victim recovery and young people's re-offending.

4(a) Effects on Victims

Over 60 per cent of the victims in 1999 said they had 'fully recovered' from the offence, that it was 'all behind me'. In cross-tabulating victim recovery by whether the YP completed the agreement, recovery was higher when YPs completed the agreement (69 per cent) than when they didn't (42 per cent). This result would seem contrary to what I reported above; however, each analysis taps different things. One asks victims whether certain things happened (recovery and repairing the harm) when YPs completed agreements, whereas the other compares victim recovery across two groups of YPs. When we asked victims what was most significant in aiding their recovery, the majority (about 60 per cent) cited the passage of time, their own resilience, and support from family and friends. Participation in the conference process, including meeting the YP and contact with the co-ordinator and police officer, were mentioned as most significant by about 30 per cent. However, when asked generally about the relative importance of the conference process and things they could do for themselves, victims were divided, with half citing their participation in the justice process as being important in getting the offence behind them. A prudent interpretation of these varied responses would be that while conferences do assist victim recovery, victims also rely on personal resources and support from others.

Conferences can have benefits in reducing victims' anger and fear. Over 75 per cent of conference victims felt angry toward the offender before the conference, but this dropped to 44 per cent after the conference and was 39 per cent a year later. Close to 40 per cent of victims were frightened of the offender before the conference, but this dropped to 25 per cent after the conference and was 18 per cent a year later.

4(b) Effects on Offenders

As others have said (Levrant, Cullen, Fulton, and Wozniak, 1999: 17–22), great faith is placed on the conference process to change offenders, when the conditions of their day to day lives, which may be conducive to getting into trouble, may not change at all. To analyse re-offending, a colleague and I asked if things that occurred in conferences could predict re-offending, over and above known predictors such as previous offending and social marginality (Hayes and Daly, 2002).

We defined offending as detected illegalities by the police, to which the YP admitted, and which were dealt with by formal caution, conference, or court. Before the offence that led to the SAJJ conference, 57 per cent of the primary YPs had offended at least once. During an 8- to 12-month window of time post-conference, 40 per cent of the YPs offended at least once. We analysed re-offending using a logistical regression analysis, where the dependent variable was dichotomous (1 = re-offended); our measure is therefore of participation, not incidence. We identified four 'control' variables: the YP's race-ethnicity (Aboriginal or non-Aboriginal), sex, whether s/he offended prior to the offence leading to the SAJJ conference, and the number of distinct addresses for the YP on the police files, a measure of the YP's residential instability and marginality. Over and above these factors, two conference variables were significant: when YPs were remorseful and when outcomes were achieved by genuine consensus, they were less likely to re-offend. The control variables were the strongest predictors of re-offending, accounting for most of the explained variation; however, the two conference variables had significant effects. The SAJJ results are remarkably similar to those of Maxwell and Morris (2001) on conferencing and re-offending in New Zealand. They found that while prior offending and negative life experiences had the strongest influences, re-offending was less likely when young people felt remorseful, were involved in the decision-making, and agreed with conference outcomes.

IV. DISCUSSION

Based on research in South Australia and other jurisdictions in the region, gaps in ideals and practice are evident in many, but not all components of the conference process. Practices are occurring as imagined in the degree of participation in the outcome (penalty) discussions, in which the professionals do not dominate; in the degree to which victims and offenders say the co-ordinators and police officers treat them fairly and with respect; and in the limits placed on penalties imposed. Gaps more often arise in areas outside the control of the co-ordinators and police officers, where organisational, cultural, and individual constraints place limits on what can be achieved. I turn now to discuss these gaps: (1) the containment of justice ideals by organisational routines, (2) new justice scripts and the legal consciousness and moral development of participants, (3) the comparative ease of achieving fairness over restorativeness, and (4) moderate positive effects and the nirvana story.

Containment of Justice Ideals by Organisational Routines

Reaching justice ideals is costly, organisationally and economically. With insufficient time to attend carefully to all cases, the justice system sieve filters out many of them. Victims want more information about their cases than justice system workers can provide. The postponement and rescheduling of cases means that defendants return to court many times before their case is disposed. Justice ideals take second place to organisational routines and professional interests. The same phenomena occur in restorative justice practices, although the bar is raised even higher. The time and labour to organise a conference is even greater than that for a court case. The co-ordinator is not only expected to identify all the relevant people who ought to be there, but also speak to each of them individually about what the conference is, what participants' roles are, and what might be achieved. It is unrealistic to reach that ideal in a high-volume jurisdiction that uses conferences as a matter of routine. Organisational shortcuts are inevitable. Not everyone can be contacted and spoken to, especially young people who are often not at home; and even if they are contacted and the conference process is explained, one cannot be sure that participants understand it. Co-ordinators are selective, giving more time to some cases than others, just as court workers do. Conference participants may have raised expectations about the quality and frequency of information they will receive that are difficult to meet in practice. If jurisdictions want to introduce conferencing as a high-volume activity, we should expect to see organisational routines, administrative efficiency, and professional interests trumping justice ideals.

New Justice Scripts and the Legal Consciousness and Moral Development of Participants

The irony in educating citizens about new justice scripts is that the conference proceeding is 'confidential': it is closed from public view and by invitation only. Compounding the problem, some co-ordinators and police officers misconstrue confidentiality, applying the term too broadly. For example, in one conference, a teacher suggested that as part of the YP's outcome, she could describe her conference experience to a group of her classmates. The co-ordinator quickly vetoed the idea, saying that the conference was confidential. In another, the co-ordinator told the YP not 'to talk about what happened here' to his friends because the conference was confidential.

In the *Young Offenders Act 1993*, confidentiality is discussed in division 4, section 13, 'Limitation on publicity', where it says that 'a person must not publish, by radio, television, newspaper or in any other way, a report of any action or proceeding taken against a youth . . . that identifies the youth . . . [or] identifies the victim'. This would *not* prohibit a young person who has been to a conference to discuss what happened to him or her. The key point is publicly naming a person, and surely, young people or victims should be free to name themselves. Invoking confidentiality, particularly, an over-broad interpretation, serves to maintain the public's ignorance about what happens and what people do.

Because there is little to go on, except their experience in a previous conference, many young people and their parents do not know what's expected of them. The potential for restorativeness is greater when participants, and especially offenders, have taken the time in advance to think about what they want to say. Yet, as we learned from the interviews, over half the YPs hadn't *at all* thought about what they'd say to the victim. While most YPs know that a conference is different from a court proceeding, they adopt a similar posture toward both: it is a place they've been made to go to because they have done something wrong. It is a place where, as the young people said, 'something would happen to us', 'an agreement would be made . . . to decide on my punishment', '[I'd] speak and answer their questions', and 'they were just going to talk to me about what happened and make me apologise and say I knew it was wrong . . . My mum told me "just be good and tell the truth" '.

Few YPs saw the conference as an opportunity to take an active role in speaking to a victim. A handful edged toward this idea, saying 'we would just sit in a room and talk about it' or 'come face to face with the victim and see what would happen'. Most YPs were not there to 'repair the harm', but rather to answer questions and hope they didn't get too many hours of community service or a good behaviour bond. Most did not think in terms of what they might *offer victims*, but rather what they would be *made to do by others*. Until the argot of restorative justice and the expected script between victim and offender in a mediation-like setting is known to a broader audience, offenders, victims, and their supporters are feeling their way through an unfamiliar justice terrain (see also Levrant et al 1999: 11–12).

The fact that all the offenders are under 18, but most victims are over 18 creates added problems in enacting this justice form. Many young people may not yet have the capacity to think empathetically, to take the role of the other (Frankenberger, 2000); they may be expected to act as if they had the moral reasoning of adults when they do not (Van Voorhis, 1995).

The Comparative Ease of Achieving Fairness over Restorativeness

Why is fairness easier to achieve than restorativeness? Fairness is largely, although not exclusively, a measure of the co-ordinators' and police officers' behaviour and words in the conference. As the professionals, they are polite, they listen, and they establish ground rules of respect for others and civility in the conference process. Whereas fairness is established in the relationship between the professionals and participants, restorativeness emerges in the relationships between victim, offender, and their supporters. Being polite is easier to do than saying you're sorry; listening to someone tell their story of victimisation is easier to do when you're not the offender. Indeed, understanding or taking on the perspective of the other may be easier if you're not the actual victim or the offender in the justice encounter. Restorativeness requires a degree of empathic concern and perspective-taking; and as measured by psychologists' scales, these qualities are more frequently evinced for adults than adolescents.

While most YPs said that they apologised because they were genuinely sorry, most victims did not think the young people's apologies were genuine. It is uncertain how to resolve these contrary views. Are victims not reading the YP's apologies correctly? Have the YPs not apologised genuinely enough (whatever this means)? Or have the victims correctly sized up a non-apologetic attitude? Whatever the answer, the gap in the perceived genuineness of the apology itself reflects problems in achieving restorativeness. Restorativeness cannot be forced or scripted in the way that fairness can. Restorativeness works with emotions and feelings, with anger and shame, with feeling harmed and feeling bad. Fairness works with established roles and procedures, and at times with deceit, as for example, when judicial officers and police officers *must appear* to be fair, polite, and respectful toward offenders, when in fact they have a low opinion of them. In short, it is easier *to pretend* to be fair and polite than it is *to pretend* to act in ways we may think of as 'restorative'.

That such high proportions of young people perceive the conference process and outcome to be fair, and at the same time, know less about its legal context or their rights, is not surprising. Being treated fairly and with respect by decision-makers, who do not seem to show favouritism toward others, is more salient to young people than is knowledge and understanding of their legal rights. For most young people, the meaning of 'fair treatment' was that decision-makers did not come down hard on them and the penalty was not onerous.

Moderate Positive Effects and the Nirvana Story

From the SAJJ project, we see that many positive things happen during and after the conference. That genuine apologies are made and accepted some of the time is a good thing, as are reductions in victims' fear toward offenders. That conferences are viewed as contributing to victims' recovery and that certain conference elements may engender law-abiding behaviour for YPs are also positives. What requires attention is, how often do such positive things need to occur before conferencing is seen as viable? Ten per cent of the time? A third of the time? More often? Conversely, what is the maximum threshold for negative things that may occur? What if we learn that victims are 're-victimised' by the conference process about 20 to 25 per cent of the time? Should this dissuade us from moving the idea forward?

The nirvana story of restorative justice helps us to imagine what is possible, but it should not be used as the benchmark for what is practical and achievable. The nirvana story assumes that people are ready and able to resolve disputes, to repair harms, to feel contrite, and perhaps to forgive others when they may not be ready and able to do any of these things at all. It holds out the promise that these things *should happen most of the time* when research suggests that these things can occur *some of the time*. How often depends on what kinds of cases (or crimes) are handled, what precisely the justice activity is and where it sits in the criminal process, and what criteria and measures are used for judgement.

V. A BRIEF CLOSING

There are limits to the idea of restorative justice, which stem in part from organisational constraints on what can be achieved, and in part, from popular understandings of what 'getting justice' means to people. It will take time for people to imagine that they can have their day in conference rather than in court. It will take time, perhaps a very long time, for people to become familiar with new justice scripts and social relations in responding to crime. Moreover, there will be variation in people's capacities to enact and read the scripts. We know that the space between the platform and the train is a gap that once we are warned of, we can traverse with ease. The spaces between older and newer understandings of justice produce gaps of an entirely different order, gaps that will be difficult to traverse. It is that knowledge we need to be most mindful of.

REFERENCES

Abel, RL (1980) 'Redirecting Social Studies of Law' 14 *Law & Society Review* 805–27.
Braithwaite, J (1989) *Crime, Shame and Reintegration* (Cambridge University Press, Cambridge).
Daly, K (2001a) 'Conferencing in Australia and New Zealand: Variations, Research Findings, and Prospects' in A Morris and G Maxwell (eds), *Restorative Justice for Juveniles: Conferencing, Mediation and Circles* (Hart Publishing, Oxford).
——(2001b) *SAJJ Technical Report No 2: Research Instruments in Year 2 (1999) and Background Notes* (School of Criminology and Criminal Justice, Griffith University, Brisbane). <http://www.gu.edu.au/school/ccj/kdaly.html>
Daly, K and Hayes, H (2001) 'Restorative Justice and Conferencing in Australia' *Trends & Issues in Crime and Criminal Justice No. 186* (Australian Institute of Criminology, Canberra). <http://www.aic.gov.au/publications/tandi/tandi186.html>
Daly, K, Venables, M, Mumford, L, McKenna, M and Christie-Johnston, J (1998) *SAJJ Technical Report No 1: Project Overview and Research Instruments* (School of Criminology and Criminal Justice, Griffith University, Brisbane). <http://www.gu.edu.au/school/ccj/kdaly.html>
Frankenberger, KD (2000) 'Adolescent Egocentrism: A Comparison among Adolescents and Adults' 23 *Journal of Adolescence* 343–54.
Gardner, J (1990) *Victims and Criminal Justice* (South Australia Office of Crime Statistics, Attorney-General's Department, Adelaide).
Haines, K (1997) 'Some Principled Objections to a Restorative Justice Approach to Working with Juvenile Offenders (Centre for Criminal Justice and Criminology, University of Wales, Swansea, unpublished ms).
Harris, N and Burton, J (1998) 'Testing the Reliability of Observational Measures of Reintegrative Shaming at Community Accountability Conferences and at Court' 31 *The Australian and New Zealand Journal of Criminology* 230–41.
Hayes, H and Daly, K (2002) 'Youth Justice Conferences and Re-offending', Australian and New Zealand Society of Criminology Conference, Melbourne, Feb 2001, revised July 2002. <http://www.gu.edu.au/school/ccj/kdaly.html>
Levrant, S, Cullen, F, Fulton, B and Wozniak JF (1999) 'Reconsidering Restorative Justice: The Corruption of Benevolence Revisited?' 45 *Crime & Delinquency* 3–27.
Maxwell, G and Morris, A (1993) *Family, Victims and Culture: Youth Justice in New Zealand* (Social Policy Agency and the Institute of Criminology, Victoria University of Wellington, Wellington).

Maxwell, G and Morris, A (2001) 'Family Group Conferences and Reoffending' in A Morris and G Maxwell (eds), *Restorative Justice for Juveniles: Conferencing, Mediation and Circles* (Hart Publishing, Oxford).

Nelken, D (1981) 'The "Gap Problem" in the Sociology of Law: A Theoretical Review' 1 *Windsor Yearbook of Access to Justice* 35–61.

O'Connor, I and Sweetapple, P (1988) *Children in Justice* (Longman Cheshire Pty, Melbourne).

Ruck, MD, Keating, DP, Abramovitch, R and Koegl, CJ (1998) 'Adolescents' and Children's Knowledge about Rights: Some Evidence for How Young People View Rights in Their Own Lives' 21 *Journal of Adolescence* 275–89.

South Australia Office of Crime Statistics (1998) *Crime and Justice in South Australia, 1997.* (Attorney-General's Department, Adelaide).

——(1999) *Crime and Justice in South Australia, 1998* (Attorney-General's Department, Adelaide).

——(2000) *Crime and Justice in South Australia, 1999* (Attorney-General's Department, Adelaide).

Tyler, TR (1990) *Why People Obey the Law* (Yale University Press, New Haven).

Van Voorhis, P (1985) 'Restitution Outcome and Probationers' Assessments of Restitution: The Effects of Moral Development' 12 *Criminal Justice and Behaviour* 159–87.

Wundersitz, J (1996) *The South Australian Juvenile Justice System: A Review of Its Operations* (South Australia Office of Crime Statistics, Attorney-General's Department, Adelaide).

12

Restorative Justice in Canada: From Sentencing Circles to Sentencing Principles

Julian V Roberts and Kent Roach

With the exceptions of Australia and New Zealand, restorative justice has evolved more rapidly and sunk deeper roots in Canada than any other jurisdiction. Canadian interest in restorative justice has spawned alternatives to criminal justice processing as well as specific statutory sentencing reforms. Canada was the site of what many regard as the first modern victim-offender reconciliation programme, as well as Aboriginal healing circles. Sentencing developments that have been influenced by restorative justice include the use of sentencing circles to assist the judge in determining the appropriate and just sanction, the statutory recognition in 1996 of reparation and acknowledgement of the harm done to victims and the community as new objectives of sentencing and the emergence of restorative justice as a 'replacement discourse' (see Dignan, this volume) to traditional penal policies tied to the use of imprisonment.

The Canadian Supreme Court has characterised the new concerns about reparation and acknowledgement of harm, as well as concerns about the offender's rehabilitation, as new restorative purposes of sentencing usually associated with the use of sanctions other than imprisonment. The Court has contrasted these goals with punitive sentencing objectives, such as denunciation and deterrence that are associated with the use of imprisonment. The Canadian experience provides an interesting and important case study in the development of restorative justice both as an alternative to criminal justice processing and as a reform idea that has influenced sentencing.

The emergence of restorative justice as an objective of sentencing provides an excellent opportunity to reflect both on the ability of the existing criminal justice system to pursue restorative means and achieve restorative outcomes and on the relation between restorative justice and more traditional sentencing purposes. This relationship between restorative and retributive justice is a question of practical as well as theoretical significance in Canada. Judges have no alternative but to consider restorative objectives of sentencing within a statutory sentencing framework which privileges retributive sentencing by defining the fundamental principle that sentences 'must be proportionate to the gravity of the offence and the degree of responsibility of the offender' (s. 718.1 of the *Criminal Code*).

The success and influence of restorative justice as a concept that has shaped sentencing reforms in Canada also raises the question of whether restorative justice will be distorted. This may be an inevitable consequence as it becomes more popular and moves beyond the periphery towards the heart of the criminal justice process. Many questions arise: To what extent can the existing tools of sentencing achieve the goals of restorative justice, especially reparation? Will restorative justice be accepted as a legitimate alternative to imprisonment? Can restorative justice be defended as a proportionate form of censure consistent with retributive justice? The danger of restorative justice being used to widen (and tighten) the net of social control is especially great if—for legitimate or illegitimate reasons—it is seen as an approach that is inappropriate for crimes that would normally merit a sentence involving imprisonment. At the same time, responding to demands that restorative approaches be seen as meaningful and even tough carries dangers as well. Some advocates of restorative justice will be uneasy with the idea that sentences accompanied with the trappings and rhetoric of restorative justice can nevertheless result in the imprisonment of the offender.

Finally, the Canadian experience with respect to restorative justice is particularly interesting because it arises from the interplay of several forces: community-based initiatives found in Aboriginal and non-Aboriginal communities; reform proposals by law reform commissions and Parliamentary committees; statutory sentencing reforms, and the intervention of the Supreme Court when asked to interpret codified sentencing provisions.

OUTLINE OF CHAPTER

The first part of the chapter will briefly describe some restorative justice initiatives that have emerged in Canada. Part II examines the development of the restorative purposes of sentencing and describes how they went from being almost totally absent from the 1987 report of the Canadian Sentencing Commission to becoming one of the codified objectives of sentencing only nine years later. This section will include a brief discussion of a hybrid sentencing tool created in 1996 which carries considerable potential to resolve some of the conflicts that arise between restorative and retributive philosophies. Part III describes the way in which Canadian courts have interpreted the restorative sentencing provisions in the *Criminal Code*. The final part (IV) of the paper explores the possibilities of reconciling restorative and retributive justice in the context of the Canadian penal and sentencing environment.

I. EXAMPLES OF RESTORATIVE JUSTICE PROGRAMMING

Restorative justice is an informal and non-adjudicative form of dispute resolution that brings offenders, victims and their supporters and other members of the community together, often in a circle, to discuss and decide what should be done with respect to a crime. Restorative justice has been described as a circle model of justice (Roach, 1999a, 1999b) and one that sees crime as a violation of a relationship involving the victim, offender and the community.

1. Origins of Victim-Offender Reconciliation Programs (VORP)

John Braithwaite (1999) has noted that '[i]nterest in restorative justice rekindled in the West from the establishment of an experimental victim-offender reconciliation programme in 1974 in Kitchener Ontario' (p 2). In an oft-recounted story, this programme began after a trial judge remanded a case of two offenders charged with vandalism in order to allow them to make restitution to the victims. With the help of a probation officer and a volunteer from a Mennonite Church group, the offenders met with the 22 victims and devised restitution agreements. In some cases these agreements involved the payment of money, while in others the offenders were obliged to perform work for the victim (Cayley, 1998: 215–17; Dittenhoffer and Ericson, 1983: 316). From this grew the first organised victim-offender reconciliation programme involving informal and voluntary 'face-to-face' meetings between offenders and victims.

There remains, however, a dearth of empirical research in Canada on restorative justice. The most comprehensive Canadian evaluation of a victim-offender mediation programme casts some doubt on its success as an alternative to imprisonment. Dittenhoffer and Ericson (1983), conducted an evaluation of a victim-offender mediation programme in an Ontario city and found that two-thirds of the victims were not individuals but business establishments, and that in 85 per cent of the cases there was no prior relationship between the offender and the victim. In many cases, the offender and the victim never met, and in one case in five, the restitution involved payments to insurance companies. Dittenhoffer and Ericson concluded that the programme 'is probably not answering the need for alternatives to incarceration and that it too has become part of the "widening net"' (p 346). This study is almost 20 years old now and it is disappointing that it remains the leading evaluation. Other studies on the Canadian experience with victim-offender mediation have focused on the incidence of agreement and the self-reported satisfaction of victims and offenders (eg Umbreit, 1996).

The absence of research data has not stopped people from both criticising and defending victim-offender reconciliation programmes in Canada. Some victims' rights organisations have opposed victim-offender mediation programmes on the grounds that their members neither need nor want to be reconciled with offenders (Roach, 1999a: 303).[1] As well, criminologists have continued to express

---

[1] The most recent review of victims' experiences with restorative programmes around the world concluded that: 'when compared to victims, whose cases were handled in the criminal justice system, there is no evidence that victims in restorative programs are any more or less satisfied' (Wemmers, 2001, p 48).

concerns that these programmes may result in net-widening (McMahon, 1992: 137–40). At the same time, restorative justice has been defended by national-law reform commissions (Canada, 1974, 1999) and Parliamentary Committees. An influential committee in 1988 defended victim-offender reconciliation programmes as a way of requiring offenders 'to "do something" for the victims and for society' and to allow offenders to 'be held accountable for their behaviour' (House of Commons Standing Committee on Justice and Solicitor General [hereafter Daubney Committee], 1988: 97). This committee relied on reports that agreements between victims and offenders were reached in 90 per cent of the 500 cases diverted to the programme with over 80 per cent of participants indicating that they would participate in mediation again if the opportunity arose (ibid: 93). These programmes have proliferated; one recent survey cites over 100 across Canada (Church Council on Corrections, 1996: p 4).

The most recent Parliamentary Committee to examine the issue of restorative justice from the perspective of the victim arrived at the following, rather guarded endorsement of restorative justice: 'The Committee believes that restorative approaches to criminal justice issues must be fostered and developed ... Although the Committee has come to this conclusion, it has done so with a sense of caution. The criticisms of restorative justice initiatives must be taken seriously and addressed directly' (Canada, 1998: pp 20–1.) The Committee recommended a comprehensive review of restorative initiatives and practices, to ensure that 'any restorative justice principles, guidelines and legislative reform proposals ... ensure respect for, and protection of, victims' interests (Canada, 1998: p 21). The relation between restorative justice and both the victims' and women's movement in Canada is somewhat uneasy (Martin, 1998; Roach, 2000).

2. Aboriginal Justice Initiatives

Canada's indigenous peoples have exercised an important influence on the restorative justice movement. The forms of Aboriginal justice are as diverse as Aboriginal peoples themselves, and should not be reduced to, or assimilated within the restorative justice paradigm. Nevertheless, Aboriginal justice remains an important source of inspiration for restorative justice in Canada. Aboriginal forms of justice, like many restorative justice initiatives, are often practised in circles, although the circle carries particular spiritual significance for many Aboriginal peoples. Some definitions of Aboriginal justice also place emphasis on formal or symbolic reparation that also plays an important role in restorative justice; others focus more on healing which has both a spiritual and a psychological dimension. In addition, concerns about the treatment of Aboriginal people in the existing system of criminal justice resulting in significant over-representation of Aboriginal people in Canada's prisons have been an important factor in official support for both Aboriginal and restorative justice in sentencing. As in New Zealand and Australia, the Canadian experience of restorative justice is tied up with both Aboriginal justice practices and concerns about the treatment of Aboriginal people in the existing criminal justice system.

A. *Hollow Water Holistic Healing Circle Project*

One significant example of Aboriginal justice is the Community Holistic Circle Healing Project in Hollow Water, an Aboriginal community in Manitoba. The programme involves an assessment team that operates a series of healing circles for offenders who admit guilt, victims of sexual abuse and for the families of both offenders and victims. In the first circle, offenders discuss the offence with the assessment team. In the second circle, victims tell offenders how the abuse has affected their life. In the third circle the larger community is involved. The last circle has at times involved over 200 people in the small community (Green, 1998: 87–9). It can take up to four months preparation for each circle (Canada, 1997). The series of circles culminates in a healing contract signed not only by the offender and victim, but a large number of people, with ceremonies being repeated at six-month intervals (Ross, 1996: 263, 36). As of June 1995, four of 52 offenders who entered the programme had completed it, with completion rates of 32 of 94 victims and 27 of 180 family members of victims (Canada, 1996: 166).

B. *Toronto Community Council Project*

The Community Council, located in Toronto, is another Aboriginal justice programme. It functions to divert offenders who admit guilt regarding a wide range of offences. The offender meets in private with volunteers from Toronto's Aboriginal community (Canada, 1996: 156). One evaluation has observed that 'the hearing resembles a family unit; council members sit in a circle with the client and try to relate to the client's past experiences' (Moyer and Axon, 1993: 65). The programme is not restricted to first offenders; many of the clients have long criminal records. Moreover, a significant number of the people diverted to the programme do not have close connections with Toronto's Aboriginal community. In this sense, the aim of the Community Council is not so much restoring but building communities (Rudin, 1998; Bottoms, this volume; Daly, this volume).

The Council makes dispositions relating to the offender's needs, including referrals to Aboriginal agencies. One evaluation found that 90 per cent of offenders had complied with, or were in the process of complying with the Council's dispositions. The focus is on the offender's rehabilitation and only about half of the cases involve victims. When there is a victim, he or she generally does not attend the Community Council hearing. Only 2 per cent of all cases included in the evaluation resulted in monetary restitution and 12 per cent in letters of apology (Moyer and Axon, 1993).

These restorative and Aboriginal justice programmes serve as an important baseline for evaluating various forms of restorative justice. They exist outside— or at the frontiers of—the criminal justice system and can be seen as a form of legal pluralism or alternative dispute resolution that is not closely tied to the adjudication of guilt and innocence in criminal trials or even traditional sentencing by trial judges. As alternative programmes, they often suffer from uncertain funding and have yet to be extensively evaluated. Nevertheless, they have been influential and have influenced attempts to bring restorative ideals into the existing justice system (Canada, 1996).

C. Circle Sentencing

The most well-known restorative justice initiative in Canada—one which has attracted considerable international attention—is circle sentencing, which began in 1992 with the much-cited case of *R v Moses*. Much of the attention to circle sentencing in Canada has focused on the successes of this form of sentencing, cases in which the circle developed a consensual solution of benefit to the victim, the offender and the community to which both parties belong (see, for example, the brief accounts of circle hearings in Church Council on Justice and Corrections, 1996). At the same time, there are important issues that need to be addressed before sentencing circles represent a restorative tool of widespread application. Limitations on space prevent a thorough exegesis of these issues (see Roberts and La Prairie, 1995; Linker, 1999, for discussion). However, some will briefly be identified. Before discussing the difficulties of accommodating circles, it is important to note some ways in which a circle may enhance the traditional mode of sentencing offenders.

While the notion of censure is central to the retributive perspective of sentencing, as a practical matter, the opportunity for the expression of legal censure is fairly limited. Most sentencing hearings last a matter of minutes, and consist of a couple of perfunctory speeches in mitigation and aggravation, followed by the imposition of a sanction with little elaboration and rarely any reference to the community, in whose name the censure is being expressed. Many offenders may well be inclined to regard the sentencing process as a punitive, 'penal tax'. In a circle hearing, however, the community is more visible, and the message of collective censure may be amplified by the presence of community members (see Pollard, 2000 for an illustration of this point in a British sentencing circle). A communication delivered in a public forum may well be more effective than a traditional sentencing court which is attended by a limited number of criminal justice professionals and few, if any, members of the public.

The professionalisation of criminal punishment runs the risk of detaching the criminal justice system from the community. By being consigned to, and punished by, the justice system, the offender may feel rejected by his society. In a circle, the presence of community members may foster a greater sense of solidarity, or at least undermine the perception of social rejection associated with a traditional sentencing hearing, particularly one which results in the incarceration of the offender. And of course, there is the question of simple numbers. Many offenders are represented by court-appointed duty counsel and appear without the support of other individuals. In a sentencing circle, the offender is supported by family members and/or friends. In short, whatever the nature of its relationship with the established sentencing process, circle sentencing represents a more communitarian response to offending.

3. Circles and the Principles of Sentencing

We agree with Kathleen Daly that restorative and retributive models are not philosophically incompatible, that 'seemingly contrary justice practices—that is of punishment and reparation—can be accommodated in philosophical arguments' (1999). In practice, however, it may be difficult for circles to co-exist within a retributive sentencing framework. Three sentencing principles are particularly important, since they were codified in Canada in 1996 as part of the statutory statement of sentencing purpose and principle:

Proportionality

No attempt is made within a sentencing circle discussion to ensure that the recommended sanction is proportionate to the gravity of the crime and the degree of responsibility of the offender as required by s 718.1 which was codified in 1996 as 'the fundamental principle' of sentencing in Canada. Concerns about proportionality can be generated both by excessively harsh or lenient sentences.

Restraint

While the sentencing judge retains the power to impose the sentence, there is a danger that a particular composition of circle participants will encourage the court to impose a sentence which violates the principle of restraint. For example, a sentence of a long term of banishment on an isolated island or a long term of intensive treatment may, depending on the circumstances, not satisfy the principle of restraint.

Equity

Circle participants are not concerned with relating the outcome of their particular circle to sentencing decisions in other, similar cases. As well, only some offenders have access to sentencing circles. Much will depend on the receptiveness of trial judges, prosecutors and defence counsel to sentencing circles, the willingness and ability of the community to participate in the circle and the resources available to implement the circle's recommendations. Sentencing circles have almost extensively been arranged for Aboriginal offenders, raising concerns about access for all offenders to sentencing circles.

The only force working to ensure that these sentencing principles will be observed is the judge who presides over the circle and who is ultimately responsible for the imposition of sentence. The sentence imposed is subject to appeal but in reality, few circle decisions are appealed (very few sentences of any kind are appealed), and the appellate courts have allowed judges great scope. In face, recent judgements from the Supreme Court have provided what can only be described as a ringing endorsement of the principle of deference to trial judge discretion. Before an appeal court can interfere with the sentence of the trial judge, there must have been an error in principle or the sentence must be 'manifestly unfit', a high standard of review which is likely to result in few sentence appeals, and even fewer successful appeals against sentence. Neither Parliament nor the Supreme Court have established national guidelines for the conduct of sentencing circles or the cases in which they may be appropriate. Some features of some sentencing circles, most notably failures to obtain the informed consent of all participants (see *R v Taylor*, 1997: para 17, for a circle conducted where the victim felt 'like I was forced to come'), ensure confidentiality and that an offender does not receive a harsher sanction if there is no agreement among the parties, may not accord with proposed United Nations principles to govern restorative justice (Van Ness, this volume). There is also an absence of evaluations of how sentencing circles affect offender recidivism and crime victims who are vulnerable to a power imbalance in the circle. Although often undertaken for Aboriginal offenders, some Aboriginal commentators have objected to sentencing circles for a variety of reasons including the power retained by the trial judge (Monture-Okanee, 1994: 226) and the danger of discrimination against Aboriginal women who have been victims of crime (Canada, 1996: 271–2).

II. THE EVOLUTION OF RESTORATIVE JUSTICE CONSIDERATIONS IN SENTENCING

The emergence of restorative justice in sentencing in Canada is a relatively recent phenomenon. The 1987 report of the Canadian Sentencing Commission contains no mention of restorative justice in the Commission's statement of the purpose and principles of sentencing, and no discussion of restorative principles within the body of the report. The only acknowledgement of restorative interests is to be found towards the end of the Commission's statement, by which judges are directed to consider 'providing for redress for the harm done to individual victims or to the community' and 'promoting a sense of responsibility on the part of offenders and providing opportunities to assist in their rehabilitation as productive and law-abiding members of society' (Canadian Sentencing Commission, 1987: 155).

A year after the release of the Sentencing Commission's report, the Parliamentary Committee chaired by David Daubney, MP, released its own report on the future of sentencing. This document contains the origin of restorative influences in sentencing. Whilst endorsing the Sentencing Commission's retributive framework, the Committee created its own statement of purpose which placed considerable emphasis on restorative objectives. Thus, the Committee proposed enacting that:

> The purpose of sentencing is to contribute to the maintenance of a just, peaceful and safe society by holding offenders accountable for their criminal conduct through the imposition of just sanctions which:
>
> (a) require, or encourage when it is not possible to require, offenders to acknowledge the harm they have done to victims and the community, and to take responsibility for the consequences of their behaviour;
> (b) take account of the steps offenders have taken, or propose to take, to make reparations to the victim and/or the community for the harm done or to otherwise demonstrate acceptance of responsibility;
> (c) facilitate victim-offender reconciliation where victims so request, or are willing to participate in such programs;
> (d) if necessary, provide offenders with opportunities which are likely to facilitate their rehabilitation or rehabilitation as productive and law-abiding members of society; and
> (e) if necessary, denounce the behaviour and/or incapacitate the offender.

In addition, the Committee's proposed principles of sentencing included the following:

> A term of imprisonment should not be imposed without canvassing the appropriateness of alternatives to incarceration through victim-offender reconciliation programs or alternative sentence planning (Daubney Committee, 1988).

Neither the Canadian Sentencing Commission nor the Daubney Committee proposals were adopted by the federal government, although clear echoes of both sets of recommendations can be found in the sentencing reforms proclaimed into law almost a decade later, in 1996. The federal government's reform Bill (C–41) represented a characteristically Canadian compromise between conflicting penal perspectives (see Roberts and Cole, 1999, for further discussion). At the heart of this reform was the creation of a statutory statement of the purpose and principles of sentencing.

The central role assigned to restorative objectives by the Daubney Committee was not adopted by the federal government. Instead, the statement of purpose identifies a list of sentencing objectives only two of which relate to restorative justice. Section 718 (e) and (f) provide for 'reparations for harm done to victims or the community' and the promotion for 'a sense of responsibility in offenders, and acknowledgement of the harm to victims and to the community'. Another codified principle (Section 718 (e)) also instructs judges to consider all available and reasonable sanctions other than imprisonment for all offenders 'with particular attention to the circumstances of aboriginal offenders'. As well, another critical element of the 1996 sentencing reforms was the creation of a new (for Canada) intermediate sanction of a conditional sentence of imprisonment, which has subsequently been interpreted as a vehicle for restorative aims.

Conditional Sentence of Imprisonment

The conditional sentence of imprisonment is a term of custody that is served in the community. This description captures the hybrid nature of the sanction: since it is a term of imprisonment, the sanction is clearly punitive; however, the fact that the offender remains in the community reflects restorative considerations. While serving the sentence in the community, the offender is required to observe certain compulsory and optional conditions, the latter being crafted to respond to the specific needs of the offender. The conditions may include community service, restitution, and court-ordered treatment. If the offender is found to have violated (without justification) one or more of the conditions, the court may commit him to custody for the unexpired sentence. The conditional sentence thus represents a new intermediate sanction with the potential to impose restorative conditions of offenders who would otherwise be sentenced to jail.

III. JUDICIAL INTERPRETATION OF THE RESTORATIVE SENTENCING PROVISIONS

The Supreme Court's intervention with respect to restorative justice emanates primarily from two leading judgments released within a year of each other. One dealt with the sentencing of an Aboriginal offender, and provided an interpretation of the codified provision that all alternative sanctions should be considered, 'with particular attention to the circumstances of aboriginal offenders' (R v Gladue, 1999). The second critical judgment was in response to six sentence appeals arising from the new conditional sentence of imprisonment (R. v Proulx, 2000). Taken together, these two judgments provide a coherent, although somewhat controversial jurisprudence of restorative justice (see Braithwaite, this volume).

In its 1999 judgement in *Gladue*[2], the Court observed that the recognition of the provision of acknowledgement and reparation of harm done to victims and the community in ss 718 (e) and (f) of the *Criminal Code* was a departure from the tradition focus on 'conflict between the interests of the state (as expressed through the aims of separation, deterrence and denunciation) and the interests of the individual offender (as expressed through the aim of rehabilitation)' (*Gladue*, 1999: para 42). The Court went on to describe restorative justice as generally involving 'some form of restitution and reintegration into the community' and not usually correlating with imprisonment (ibid: para 43). Restorative justice was described as 'an approach to remedying crime in which it is understood that all things are interrelated and that crime disrupts the harmony which existed prior

---

[2] One of the authors (Roach) represented Aboriginal Legal Services of Toronto which was granted intervenor or amicus curaie status in this case and in *R v Wells*, 2000 a companion case to *R v Proulx*, in both cases in support of the sentencing appeal by the Aboriginal accused.

to its occurrence, or at least which it is felt should exist. The appropriateness of a particular sanction is largely determined by the needs of the victims, and the community, as well as the offender. The focus in on the human beings closely affected by the crime' (ibid: para 71).

The Court related the new focus on restorative justice to the use of community sanctions rather than imprisonment. The Court also indicated that Parliament's new mandate to sentencing judges to pursue restorative purposes in sentencing should be seen as an attempt to remedy high rates of incarceration in Canada for all offenders and disproportionate rates of incarceration of Aboriginal peoples. Thus restorative justice was identified by the Court both as a penal philosophy that focused on the needs of offenders, victims and the community affected by the crime and as a penal technique that involved community sanctions and was tied to restraint regarding the use of imprisonment. The Court's focus was more on restorative outcomes, defined as alternatives to imprisonment, than restorative processes such as the use of sentencing circles or conferences.

1. Comparison with New Zealand

The Supreme Court of Canada's enthusiastic endorsement of restorative justice as a new approach to sentencing makes an interesting contrast with the response a year earlier of the New Zealand Court of Appeal. In the *Clotworthy* case, the New Zealand Court of Appeal replaced a $15,000 restitution sentence for a victim of a violent stabbing and robbery with four years imprisonment. Even though the compensation responded to the needs and desires of the victim for expensive cosmetic surgery to repair the stab wounds, the Court of Appeal concluded that 'a wider dimension must come into the sentencing exercise than simply the position as between victim and offender' including 'the public interest in consistency, integrity of the criminal justice system and deterrence of others'. Canadian courts would probably reach a similar result in a violent robbery case, nevertheless, it is clear that the Supreme Court of Canada has sounded a more receptive note to restorative justice than the New Zealand Court of Appeal in *Clotworthy*. This is somewhat ironic given that restorative justice, at least through conferencing for young offenders, is much more institutionalised in New Zealand than Canada (see Morris and Maxwell, this volume).

2. Supreme Court and Conditional Sentencing

The Supreme Court of Canada's enthusiasm for the restorative objectives of sentencing in *Gladue* was continued and carried over to cases involving non-Aboriginal offenders in the case of *Proulx*, which established unanimous guidelines for the use of conditional sentences. That decision carries a dual message for trial judges, and the criminal justice community, and created a new dichotomy between restorative and punitive purposes of sentencing while recognising that both may have a role to play in the crafting of a conditional sentence.

First, the Court made it clear that restorative justice was an important element of the sentencing process in Canada. Drawing on *Gladue*, the Court indicated that 'a restorative justice approach seeks to remedy the adverse effects of crime in a manner that addresses the needs' of offenders, victims and the community and by doing so diminish the use of incarceration and improve the effectiveness of sentencing. The restorative purposes of sentencing would be 'accomplished, in part, through the rehabilitation of the offender, reparations to the victim and to the community, and the promotion of a sense of responsibility in the offender and acknowledgement of the harm done to victims and to the community' (*Proulx*, 2000: para 18). Secondly, the Court recognised that restorative considerations were not the only purposes of sentencing: they must be balanced with the punitive purposes of sentencing which focus on deterrence and denunciation as well as the fundamental principle that sentences be proportionate to the gravity of the offence and the offender's degree of responsibility. In this way the Court acknowledged the importance of reconciling, if not integrating, the restorative and retributive perspectives.

The Court's direction to integrate restorative and retributive justice is not without challenges and potential pitfalls. One relates to the ability of trial judges at sentencing to fulfil the ambitions of restorative justice. In other words, do judges at sentencing have the tools to craft sentences that respond to the needs of victims and offenders? They can impose restitution orders on offenders after conviction that can be enforced as civil court judgements or as a condition of sentence, that if breached, can possibly result in imprisonment. These orders are, however, generally restricted to readily ascertainable pecuniary losses and the available evidence suggests that they are rarely made as part of a sentence. Judges in Canada also routinely impose victim surcharges on fines with the proceeds now being directed at funding victim services. Nevertheless, these surcharges are not 'reparation funds' nor do they represent a fundamental re-thinking of the fine (Dignan, this volume).

Voluntary restitution can also considered a mitigating factor at sentencing. The Supreme Court of Canada observed in a recent case involving an employer's conviction of assault and sexual assault of his employee, that a $10,000 payment by the offender to the victim 'weighed in favour of restorative objectives and therefore of a conditional sentence' (*R (RA)*, 2000: para 30). Although the Court ultimately found that one year of imprisonment was appropriate given the need to punish and deter the offences, this sort of payment raises concerns about equity to offenders. The offender in this case, described by the Court as a 'successful entrepreneur', had the resources to make a significant payment to the victim, but many other offenders would not. There is clearly a need to ensure that a focus on restoration is not limited to monetary restitution and that offenders have equal opportunities to fulfil the restorative objectives of sentencing. This may require state involvement so that offenders are loaned funds from victim compensation schemes to make restitution, but then have to work off the loan. If restitution is simply a matter of drawing on the private resources of offenders, a restorative approach to sentencing may be inequitable. Indeed, some elements of restorative justice may support a neo-liberal privatisation of justice functions.

To the extent that restorative justice may be more viable where the offender and the victim have a pre-existing relationship, some other principles of sentencing in Canada may inhibit the use of restorative sanctions that do not involve the use of imprisonment. The *Criminal Code* deems offences involving the abuse of the offender's child or spouse or abuse of positions of trust and authority as 'aggravating circumstances' that should result in a more severe sentence. Courts have been reluctant to impose conditional sentences in cases of domestic and sexual assault. There is also a general parity principle that sentences imposed should be similar to those imposed 'on similar offenders for similar offenders in similar circumstances'. The practical effect of this section is mitigated by substantial appellate deference to trial judges, but some advocates of restorative justice have expressed concerns that an undue concern about sentencing disparity may inhibit the development of restorative approaches to crime which, given that the immediate needs of offenders, victims and communities can differ so significantly, may result in disparate dispositions (Braithwaite and Pettit, 1990). Finally, the use of conditional sentences to achieve restorative aims is precluded whenever any mandatory minimum penalty of imprisonment is enacted, something that is occurring more frequently in Canada.

Even if judges can craft sentences that achieve restorative aims, some advocates of restorative justice may fear that the restorative approach will be polluted or corrupted by its combination with retributive approaches. In *Proulx*, the Court recognised that while conditional sentences could achieve restorative aims, they should also incorporate punitive elements. To the end of adding some degree of hard treatment that would both denounce and deter crime, the Court suggested that 'conditions such as house arrest and strict curfews should be the norm, not the exception' and that 'where an offender breaches a condition without reasonable excuse, there should be a presumption that the offender serve the remainder of his or her sentence in jail' (*Proulx*: paras 36, 39). It is not clear that house arrest and curfews can be defended as a restorative response to crime to the extent that they enforce a degree of social isolation on the offender that may be antithetical to the communitarian and relationship-affirming values of restorative justice. Some commentators have criticised the Court for co-opting and transforming a purely or primarily restorative sanction (the conditional sentence) into a hybrid disposition which contains restorative and retributive characteristics (eg Healy, 2000).

These criticisms aside, it is clear that the Court's position points the way to an accommodation between restorative and retributive perspectives in sentencing. Like any compromise, this one carries the danger of alienating both sides. By keeping the offender out of prison, the conditional sentence permits the kinds of initiatives that promote restoration of offenders into the community and makes it possible for them to earn the funds necessary to provide monetary reparation to their crime victim. At the same time, the imposition of rigorous conditions, such as house arrest, curfews and electronic monitoring, help to ensure that the sanction carries the penal equivalence of a custodial term, which is important to establish public and judicial confidence in the sanction. Finally, by modulating the number and intrusiveness of the optional conditions to the seriousness of the offence, the codified principle of proportionality can be preserved.

Advocates of restorative justice may fear that their new paradigm of justice is being swallowed within the conventional retributive framework. But at the end of the day, imprisonment is the sentencing outcome that is most retrograde to restoration. Any reform that undermines the use of imprisonment should therefore be welcomed by exponents of the restorative perspective. This, however, does not mean that there are no dangers. One is that the restorative/retributive hybrid may be used for cases that previously would have received probation; a classic case of widening the net. There appears to be some evidence from the first few years of the conditional sentence regime to believe that this has taken place (Reed and Roberts, 1999). If conditional sentences only result in net-widening, then offenders may suffer disproportionate hardships including the possibility of jail if they breach a condition imposed in the name of restorative justice. The second danger is that excessively punitive conditions will be imposed in order to make a restorative sentence consistent with the statutory framework or acceptable to a sceptical community. If this occurs, it may also trigger violations of the conditions and the subsequent incarceration of the offender for breach, perhaps for a longer period than if the offender was sentenced to prison from the outset.

IV. RECONCILING RESTORATIVE AND RETRIBUTIVE JUSTICE

Restorative justice, in Canada at least, cannot be considered in isolation from retributive theories of justice. As restorative justice gains in popularity there is a need to consider how it relates to other sentencing objectives and principles such as denunciation, deterrence and proportionality. The ability or inability to reconcile restorative and retributive justice may tell us much about how often restorative justice will be used and how it will be modified to respond to concerns informed by retributive or utilitarian theories of sentencing. In public discourse at least, restorative justice has many different faces and can be defined so as to stress its potential to rehabilitate, to prevent crime and to hold offenders to account (Braithwaite, 1999; Roach, 2000).

1. Restorative Justice as a Means of Holding Offenders Accountable

A promising means to reconcile restorative and retributive justice may be to stress the ability of restorative justice to censure offenders and hold them accountable for their actions without relying on imprisonment. Having to face the victim and others, recognise wrongdoing and make amends for a crime may in itself be seen as a sanction. Accountability for crime incorporates retributive notions of censure, but perhaps not hard treatment.[3] On one level, Canadian courts see restorative justice as a meaningful response to crime. In *Gladue* (para 72), the Supreme Court observed that 'a sentence focused on restorative justice is not necessarily a "lighter punishment" because it requires offenders to repair the wrong, and also to accept responsibility for their actions before the victim and the community'. Having to make restitution to the victim or to a fund dedicated to victim services may be more meaningful than the simple payment of fines into the public purse. Similarly, community service orders tied to restoration of victims and communities may be a more meaningful form of censure and hard treatment than 'make work' projects that are not related to the crime. Restorative sanctions may also be more meaningful than some sentences of imprisonment. The relevant comparison point should be between a restorative sentence and a short sentence of imprisonment such as 44 days (the median length of imprisonment in Canada; see Reed and Roberts, 1999). Restorative approaches to sentencing might be a significant, deserved, proportionate and just alternative to such prison sentences. As such, they could be defended as contributing to respect for the law and the maintenance of a just, peaceful and safe society while reducing courts' reliance on imprisonment.

This may, however, be an overly optimistic account of the acceptability of restorative justice as a meaningful response to more serious crime. The Supreme Court has recognised some public reluctance to see a restorative justice disposition (such as a conditional sentence) as the equivalent of a term of custody. In *Gladue* (para 72), it argued that 'the existing overemphasis on incarceration in Canada may be partly due to the perception that a restorative approach is a more lenient approach to crime and that imprisonment constitutes the ultimate punishment.' The Court's own actions both in *Gladue* and subsequent cases suggest that it still sees imprisonment as the 'ultimate punishment'. In *Gladue*, the Court affirmed a sentence of three years imprisonment as not unreasonable for an Aboriginal woman convicting of killing her spouse in a manslaughter described as a 'near murder'. In *Proulx* and subsequent conditional sentencing cases, the Court indicated that imprisonment may be particularly appropriate for crimes such as sexual assault and dangerous driving causing death where the focus is on the denunciation and deterrence of crime. The Court itself seems to have accepted the proposition that imprisonment is the 'ultimate punishment' at least for crimes that demand denunciation and deterrence.

Arguments have been made that restorative justice can itself achieve a form of accountability for even serious crime that is usually associated with retributive approaches to punishment. For example, in a written brief to the Supreme Court

---

[3] This does, however, raise difficult questions about the genuineness of the experience of accountability and apology from the perspectives of offenders, victims and others affected by the crime. (See Daly, this volume.)

in a case involving an unsuccessful appeal of a 20-month sentence for a sexual assault, one of the authors wrote that 'a healing-based community sanction can promote the difficult and painful process of denouncing unlawful conduct and promoting a sense of responsibility with respect to the offence. The accountability to self, victims and the community, which is promoted in such community-based programmes may be a proportionate response to the blameworthiness of even serious crime' (Aboriginal Legal Services of Toronto, 1999).

The Supreme Court, however, rejected the idea that a restorative sanction as recommended by a pre-sentence report and involving alcohol treatment was appropriate in the case, even in the light of a provision that requires judges to consider all reasonable alternatives to imprisonment 'with particular attention to the circumstances of aboriginal offenders.' The Court reasoned that 'the more violent and serious the offence, the more likely as a practical matter that the appropriate sentence will not differ as between aboriginal and non-aboriginal, given that in these circumstances, the goals of denunciation and deterrence are accordingly increasingly significant' (*Wells*, 2000: para 42).[4] Leaving aside the contentious issue of special regard for aboriginal offenders (compare Stenning and Roberts, 2001; Rudin and Roach, 2002), the point here is that the Supreme Court has assumed that imprisonment rather than restorative sanctions represents the optimal way to denounce and deter certain serious crimes.

To the extent that restorative approaches are not seen as a sufficient for serious crime, two main responses are possible. One is that restorative sanction will be reserved for the less serious cases, raising the danger of net-widening in the name of restorative justice. The other is that more punitive and even stigmatising elements will be added to restorative sentences in an attempt to make them acceptable for more serious crimes. It is not clear that advocates of restorative justice will be comfortable with either scenario. Either scenario, however, points to the need to adopt some version of proportionality as a limit on restorative sanctions.

2. Dangers that Restorative Sanctions Will Result in Net-Widening

If restorative justice is thought to be unable to denounce or punish serious crimes, it may exist mainly as an add-on to the existing system and one that may produce a real risk of net-widening. Onerous conditions may be imposed on offenders as part of conditional sentences or probation orders in the name of restorative justice. These conditions may attempt to respond to the rehabilitative and other needs of offenders and perhaps the monetary and other needs of victims. They may be an appropriate response to wrongdoing if restorative sanctions are considered a genuine and meaningful alternative to imprisonment, but

---

[4] This does not mean that restorative considerations may have no role to play after conviction and sentence. For an account of a Nova Scotia restorative justice programme with four entry points including parole and correction see Archibald, 1999.

they may be a form of net-widening if they are only used in less serious cases that would not usually result in the imprisonment of the offender.

A restorative conditional sentence may result in imprisonment if the offender breaches conditions designed to result in treatment or reparation. The danger of net-widening is not simply one of increased social control—some restorative advocates may be willing to accept increased social control if undertaken in a non-punitive and integrative manner. Rather, the danger of net-widening in Canada is that the offender will be imprisoned for breaching disproportionately harsh conditions for rehabilitation or reparation (Roach and Rudin, 2000: 369–72). As will be explored below, the concept of desert as a limit on punishment may be necessary to address this danger of net-widening.

3. Dangers that Restorative Sanction will be Overly Harsh

Another response to a perception that restorative justice is unable to denounce or punish more serious crimes may be to add punitive and stigmatising elements to restorative sanction to make them more acceptable for such crimes. Canada does not yet have the same experience as the United States in 'shaming' sanctions, but these may be undertaken in response to concerns that increasing the 'public humiliation' and 'degrading connotations' of restorative sanctions is necessary to 'buy political acceptability' for alternatives to imprisonment by 'transforming their social meaning' (Kahan, 1998: 704–6). Indeed, the Supreme Court of Canada has defended restorative sanctions on the basis that 'living in the community under strict conditions where fellow residents are well aware of the offender's criminal misconduct can provide ample denunciation in many cases. In certain circumstances, the shame of encountering members of the community may make it even more difficult for the offender to serve his or her sentence in the community rather than in prison' (*R v Proulx*, 2000). The Court's understanding of shame and denunciation in this passage at least does not seem to be tied to the idea of reintegration as advocated by Braithwaite (1989). A perception that restorative approaches are too soft on offenders and offences will place pressure on trial judges to add punitive and even stigmatising elements to restorative sentences.

There are some signs that restorative sanctions are being influenced by retributive concerns in Canada. Some sentencing circles have proposed substantial terms of imprisonment (18 months for a robbery and 18 months probation), terms that were themselves rejected by the courts as excessively lenient (*Morin*, 1995). As discussed above, the Supreme Court of Canada indicated that conditional sentences should generally be accompanied with punitive conditions such as house arrest and curfews that if breached will produce a presumption that the offender be imprisoned for the duration of a conditional sentence (*R v Proulx*, 2000). The Court has added these elements to conditional sentences in an attempt to make them meaningful intermediate sanctions that accord with all the purposes of sentencing, including the retributive ones. This may represent the Court's unease with the idea that a restorative sanction is in itself a meaningful response to crime that might otherwise merit imprisonment and that it must be bolstered by the addition of punitive elements to the conditional sanctions, elements that impose censure and hard treatment.

4. Proportionality as a Restraint on Restorative Sanctions

It should not be assumed that the interaction between restorative and retributive justice will always result in restorative justice being deemed excessively lenient. Restorative sanctions that widen the net for offenders who would not normally go to prison and restorative sanctions that are designed to produce stigmatising shame may be judged as too harsh by retributive theories that place a premium on restraint in the use of imprisonment, and require that sanctions be proportionate to the seriousness of the crime and the offender's degree of responsibility.

One of the important consequences of the recognition of restorative purposes of sentencing in Canada has been renewed interest in rehabilitation as a purpose of sentencing. In addition, one of the defining characteristics of conditional sentences in Canada has been their ability to impose mandatory treatment orders responding to the needs of offenders in the name of both rehabilitation and restorative justice. Retributive theories of sentencing, however, emerged as a force in the 1970s precisely in response to the dangers of punishing offenders in the name of rehabilitation. In Canada, retributive concerns—and in particular the fundamental principle of proportionality in sentencing—may have an important role to play in limiting rehabilitative and restorative sanctions. Proportionality and restraint principles may also play an important role in restraining the use of public shaming and humiliation in the name of restorative justice. The importance of the restraining role of retributive justice will be even greater if restorative sanctions result in net-widening.

Whatever the case for restorative justice in the abstract as a pure and comprehensive theory of justice, there is a need in the Canadian sentencing context to consider restorative and retributive approaches to sentencing together. In cases of some serious crimes, restorative approaches may be found excessively lenient in light of some retributive theories, but in other cases, net-widening and shaming sanctions imposed in the name of restorative justice should be restrained by retributive concepts of desert and proportionality.

REFERENCES

Aboriginal Legal Services of Toronto *Factum in James Warren Wells v The Queen* (filed with the Supreme Court of Canada, 15 Apr 1999).

Archibald, B (1999) 'A Comprehensive Canadian Approach to Restorative Justice' in D Stuart, R Delisle and A Manson (eds), *Towards a Clear and Just Criminal Law* (Carswell, Toronto).

Braithwaite, J (1999) 'Restorative Justice: Assessing Optimistic and Pessimistic Accounts' in

M Tonry (ed), *Crime and Justice: A Review of Research* (University of Chicago Press, Chicago IL) vol 25, 1–127.

Braithwaite, J and Pettit, P (1990) *Not Just Deserts: A Republican Theory of Criminal Justice* (Clarendon Press, Oxford).

——(1989) *Crime, Shame and Reintegration* (Cambridge University Press, Cambridge).

Cayley, D (1998) *The Expanding Prison* (Anansi, Toronto).

Canada (1997) *The Four Circles of Hollow Water* (Solicitor General Aboriginal Correctional Policy Unit, Ottawa).

——(1998) *Victims' Rights—A Voice, Not a Veto*. Report of the Standing Committee on Justice and Human Rights (House of Commons, Ottawa).

Canadian Sentencing Commission (1987) *Sentencing Reform: A Canadian Approach* (Supply and Services Canada, Ottawa).

Church Council on Justice and Corrections (1996) *Satisfying Justice* (The Church Council on Justice and Corrections, Ottawa).

Daly, K (1999) 'Revisiting the Relationship between Retributive and Restorative Justice' forthcoming in H Strang and J Braithwaite (eds), *Restorative Justice: From Philosophy to Practice* (Aldershot, Dartmouth).

Dittenhoffer, T and Ericson, R (1983) 'The Victim-Offender Reconciliation Program: A Message to Correctional Reformers' 33 *University of Toronto Law Journal* 315–47.

Green, RG (1998) *Justice in Aboriginal Communities Sentencing Alternatives* (Purich Publishing, Saskatoon).

Healy, P (2000) 'The Punitive Nature of the Conditional Sentence' in Department of Justice, *The Changing Face of Conditional Sentencing* (Department of Justice, Ottawa).

House of Commons Standing Committee on Justice and Solicitor General (Daubney Committee), (1998) *Taking Responsibility* (House of Commons, Ottawa).

Kahan, D (1998) 'Punishment Incommensurability' 1 *Buffalo Criminal Law Reform* 691–708.

Law Commission of Canada (1999) *From Restorative to Transformative Justice* (Law Commission of Canada, Ottawa).

Law Reform Commission of Canada (1974) *Restitution and Compensation-Fines* (Information Canada, Ottawa).

Linker, M (1999) 'Sentencing Circles and the Dilemma of Difference' 42 *Criminal Law Quarterly* 116–29.

Martin, D (1998) 'Retribution Revisited: A Reconsideration of Feminist Criminal Law Strategies' 36 *Osgoode Hall Law Journal* 151–88.

McMahon, M (1992) *Persistent Prison: Rethinking Decarceration as Penal Reform* (University of Toronto Press, Toronto).

Moyer, S and Axon, L (1993) *An Implementation Evaluation of the Native Community Council Project of Aboriginal Legal Services of Toronto* (Ontario Ministry of the Attorney General, Toronto).

Monture-Okanee, P (1994) 'Thinking about Aboriginal Justice: Myths and Revolution' in R Gosse, J Youngblood Henderson and R Carter (eds), *Continuing Poundmaker and Riel's Quest* (Purich Publishing, Saskatoon).

Pollard, C (2000) 'Victims and the Criminal Justice System: A New Vision' *Criminal Law Review* January 5–17.

Roach, K (1999a) *Due Process and Victims' Rights: The New Law and Politics of Criminal Justice* (University of Toronto, Toronto).

Roach, K (1999b) 'Four Models of the Criminal Process' 89 *Journal of Criminal Law and Criminology* 691–716.

—— (2000) 'Changing Punishment at the Turn of the Century: Restorative Justice on the Rise' 42 *Canadian Journal of Criminology* 355–88.

Roach, K and Rudin, J (2000) '*Gladue*: The Judicial and Political Reception of a Promising Decision' 42 *Canadian Journal of Criminology* 355–88.

Roberts, JV and Cole, D (eds) (1999) *Making Sense of Sentencing* (University of Toronto Press, Toronto).

Roberts, JV and La Prairie, C (1996) 'Sentencing Circles: Some Unanswered Questions' 39 *Criminal Law Quarterly* 69–83.

Roberts, JV and von Hirsch, A (1999) 'Legislating the Purpose and Principles of Sentencing' in JV Roberts and D Cole (eds), *Making Sense of Sentencing* (University of Toronto Press, Toronto).

Ross, R (1996) *Returning to the Teachings: Exploring Aboriginal Justice* (Penguin, Toronto).

Royal Commission on Aboriginal Peoples (Canada), (1996) *Bridging the Cultural Divide: A Report on Aboriginal People and Criminal Justice in Canada* (Supply and Services, Ottawa).

Rudin, J (1998) 'Alternative Sentencing' in P Healy and H Dumont (eds), *Dawn or Dusk in Sentencing* (Editions Themis, Montreal).

Rudin, J and Roach, K (2002) 'Broken Promises: A Response to Stenning and Roberts' "Empty Promises"' 65 *Saskatchewan Law Review* 3–34.

Stenning, P and Roberts, JV (2001) 'Empty Promises: Parliament, The Supreme Court, and the Sentencing of Aboriginal Offenders' 64 *Saskatchewan Law Review* 137–68.

Umbreit, M (1996) 'Restorative Justice Through Mediation: The Impact of Programs in Four Canadian Provinces' in B Galaway and J Hudson (eds), *Restorative Justice: International Perspectives* (Criminal Justice Press, Monsey NY).

Wemmers, J (2001) *Victim's Experiences with Expectations and Perceptions of Restorative Justice: A Critical Review of the Literature* (Department of Justice Canada, Ottawa).

CASES

R v Clotworthy (29 June 1998) Court of Appeal of New Zealand CA 114/98

R v Gladue (1999) 133 CCC(3d) 385 (Supreme Court of Canada)

R v Morin (1995) 101 CCC(3d) 124 (Saskatchewan Court of Appeal)

R v Moses (1992) 71 CCC(3d) 347 (Yukon Territorial Court)

R v Proulx (2000) 140 CCC(3d) 449 (Supreme Court of Canada)

R v R(R.A.) (2000) 140 CCC(3d) 523 (Supreme Court of Canada)

R v Taylor (1997) 122 CCC(3d) 376 (Saskatchewan Court of Appeal)

R v Wells (2000) 149 CCC(3d) 1 (Supreme Court of Canada)

13

Restorative Justice in New Zealand*

Allison Morris and Gabrielle Maxwell

I. INTRODUCTION

Restorative justice has become a world-wide movement (Galaway and Hudson, 1996; Hudson et al 1996; Marshall, 1999; Braithwaite, 1999; Bazemore and Schiff, 2001).[1] The Tenth UN Congress, for example, adopted a declaration which called on governments to expand their use of restorative justice.[2] New Zealand has already gone further than most countries in this direction (Consedine, 1995; Consedine and Bowen, 1999).[3] Family group conferencing, introduced in the Children, Young Persons and Their Families Act 1989, is widely seen as a case study of restorative justice within the youth justice system (McElrea, 1998; Morris and Maxwell, 1998; Morris and Maxwell, 2000) and this experience is gradually being extended to adults offenders at the discretion of individual judges (Consedine and Bowen, 1999) and through pilot programmes (Smith and Cram, 1998; Maxwell et al 1999).

This chapter draws upon research in New Zealand to describe the potential benefits to offenders and victims which can result from implementing restorative justice. It then examines the extent to which restorative processes and practices are more effective than conventional processes and practices in reducing reoffending and achieving cost savings: these are factors that are likely to

* The research reported on in this article has been funded by the Ministries of Social Development and Justice, and the Crime Prevention Unit of the Department of Prime Minister and Cabinet.

[1] In 1999, the United Nation's Economic and Social Council adopted a resolution encouraging member states to use mediation and restorative justice in appropriate cases, and called on the Commission on Crime Prevention and Criminal Justice to consider the development of guidelines on the use of those programmes. The Tenth UN Congress on the Prevention of Crime and Treatment of Offenders, held in Vienna in May 2000, included 'fairness to victims and offenders' as one of its four substantive topics and there was considerable discussion there of restorative justice.

[2] The UN's Commission on Crime Prevention and Criminal Justice, which met immediately after the Congress, approved a resolution creating an Expert Group to explore 'preliminary draft elements' of a set of Basic Principles on the Use of Restorative Justice Programmes in Criminal Matters.

[3] There is considerable support for restorative justice in New Zealand: 104 of the 113 submissions made to the discussion paper on restorative justice prepared by the Ministry of Justice in New Zealand (Ministry of Justice, 1995) were broadly supportive of a restorative approach (Ministry of Justice, 1998). On the other hand, co-existing with this is an imprisonment rate considerably higher than most comparable countries (such as Australia and England).

determine whether governments will pay heed to restorative justice (Braithwaite, 1999).[4] But, first, we describe briefly the development of restorative practices in New Zealand.

1. Family Group Conferences, Community Panels, Restorative Conferencing and Restorative Principles

Family group conferences in New Zealand share a number of features with restorative justice. They both aim to hold offenders accountable for their actions; they both involve those most affected by the offending—the offender, the victim and their communities of care—in coming to decisions, with the help of a facilitator, about how best to deal with the offending; and they both take the interests of the victim into account in reaching these decisions.

In contrast to most other jurisdictions which have introduced restorative justice, family group conferences in New Zealand are used for all medium-serious and serious offending by young people (except murder and manslaughter) and operate both as an alternative to courts (for young people who have not been charged in the Youth Court) and as a mechanism for making recommendations to judges pre-sentence (for young people who have been charged in the Youth Court).

The family group conference takes place wherever the family wishes, provided the victims agree to this. This means that conferences can take place in the family's home or on a *marae* (meeting house)—though, in practice, these are not common venues. More usual are community rooms or rooms in buildings managed by the Department of Child, Youth and Family Services. Meetings take much longer than the few minutes which judges routinely take to deal with young offenders in conventional criminal justice processes: on average one and a quarter hours (Maxwell and Morris, 1993).

The family group conference only considers cases where the young person does not deny the alleged offence(s) or, if the offence is denied, has already been found guilty in court. All the participants in family group conferences contribute to the discussions and to the decisions about the eventual outcome. One important feature is that the family and the young person are given the opportunity to discuss privately at some point how they think the offending should be dealt with. When the conference reconvenes with all the participants present, this plan is then discussed and agreement is sought or amendments are made.

---

[4] There are, of course, other reasons why governments may fail to act—for example, a concern that restorative justice may minimise the deterrent or denunciatory effect of the criminal justice system. However, restorative justice practice in New Zealand often operates alongside the criminal justice system. Also, it can be argued that restorative justice strengthens deterrence by bringing to the offender's attention the consequences of their actions in no uncertain terms and adds to denunciation by condemning the offence in front of those whom offenders most cares about.

The intended focus of the discussion and the resulting outcomes are the young person's offending and matters related directly to the circumstances of that offending. However, section 208(g) of the 1989 Act also states that, in determining outcomes, due regard should be paid to the interests of the victim(s). This invites consideration at the conference of apologies, reparation and community work. Other outcomes (or recommendations) can include donations to a charity, involvement in some kind of training programme, supervision by a social worker or community organisation, a residential placement (for a short time)[5] and, occasionally, a period in custody[6] (for more information, see Morris and Maxwell, 2000). Outcomes are limited only by the imagination of the parties though frugality (rather than proportionality) is a limiting factor.[7]

In 1995, three pilot schemes—Project Turnaround, Te Whanau Awhina and the Community Accountability Programme—were funded by the New Zealand Crime Prevention Unit in collaboration with the police and local Safer Community Councils to divert adult offenders appearing before the criminal courts. They began operating in 1996 and Project Turnaround and Te Whanau Awhina are still in operation. The Community Accountability Programme ceased operation during its first year but, as we will see shortly, it has since been resurrected. Each of these pilot schemes had elements of restorative justice.

Project Turnaround is situated in Timaru, a provincial South Island city, and it shares its offices with the Safer Community Council and the Community Police. Most of the offenders referred to it are New Zealanders of European origin. On the offender's first appearance at court, judges divert selected offenders to the scheme and, if the subsequent panel meeting is attended by the offender and if the plan agreed to there is completed, the offender makes no further court appearance and the police withdraw their evidence. The panel members in Project Turnaround are volunteers who are selected to represent the community. A police officer is normally present at most of the panel meetings and the victim is also frequently present.[8] At the panel meeting, the offender is confronted with his or her offending and its consequences. This process at Project Turnaround can be contrasted with a fully restorative process where decisions are made by those who are most directly affected by the offending rather than by appointed representatives of the community. However, the plans decided at the meetings involved making amends to the victim and the community and making arrangements of

---

[5] Supervision in a residence requires a court order. Such orders allow young people to be placed in a residence for up to three months (reduced to two months if they do not abscond or commit further offences) and the period in the residence is followed by a period of supervision of up to six months.

[6] Periods in custody (corrective training or imprisonment) require a court order, but they also require the young person to be transferred from the Youth Court to the District or High Court. Certain conditions must be met before such a transfer can occur.

[7] S 208 (f) (ii) states that any sanction should take the least restrictive form that is appropriate in the circumstances.

[8] Smith and Cram (1998) state that 70% of the meetings in their evaluation had victims present; on the other hand, Maxwell et al (1999) state that only around half of the meetings in their evaluation had victims present.

both a reintegrative and a rehabilitative nature. This focus on recompense to the victim and to the community is consistent with a restorative justice approach.

Te Whanau Awhina is situated on a *marae* (a communal centre including a meeting house and other buildings for customary activities as well as educational and training facilities) in Auckland, the largest city in New Zealand, and the community panel meetings are held in the *wharenui* (a traditional meeting house). Almost all the offenders referred to Te Whanau Awhina are Maori (the indigenous people of New Zealand). As in Project Turnaround, they are referred to the scheme by the judge at a court hearing. However, offenders who appear before a panel at Te Whanau Awhina are not necessarily diverted from further court appearances and sanctions.

At Te Whanau Awhina, the panel typically consists of three or four marae members, including one who takes the role of *kaumatua* (elder) and chairs the proceedings. In addition, the co-ordinator attends and takes the role of providing support to the offender. Other people likely to attend are the *whanau* (extended family) and friends of the offender. The police do not attend the meetings at Te Whanau Awhina, nor usually do the direct victims although those managing the conferences identify both the offender's family and the Maori community as victims. The focus of this panel meeting is first and foremost one of 'challenge': confronting offenders with the consequences of their offending for them, for their victims, for their family and whanau, and for the Maori community. The second main focus of the meeting and of the subsequent outcome is that of 'embrace': reintegrating the offender back into family/whanau and into the Maori community and finding employment. Thus, outcomes typically include plans relating to obtaining employment or job training and participation in marae-based programmes and activities as well as responses to victims. Because victims rarely attend the meetings, Te Whanau Awhina is not fully consistent with restorative processes.[9] However, the focus on reparation to victims and to the community and reintegration with family and whanau and with the Maori and the wider community is consistent with aspects of a restorative justice approach.[10]

The Community Accountability Programme was a victim-offender conferencing programme situated in Rotorua, a city in the middle of the North Island in which a significant proportion of Maori live. This programme is described by Webster (2000) as most closely approximating restorative justice practice because decisions are made by victims and offenders themselves (and their communities of care) with the aid of paid facilitators and not panel members. This programme aimed to provide greater satisfaction to victims as well as making offenders more accountable. Thus it gave victims considerable control over the meeting format

---

[9] According to Webster (2000), the victim's consent is now required for the conference to proceed. This does not seem to have been the case earlier (Smith and Cram, 1998; Maxwell et al 1999).

[10] It is also consistent with indigenous models of justice and, in particular, with Maori values and philosophy. For more information, see Jackson (1988), Consedine (1995) and the New Zealand Maori Council and Hall (1998) though contrast Tauri (1999).

and only dealt with cases where victims provided input. For a range of reasons, this pilot, as noted earlier, ceased operation, but has since begun again.

In 1998/99, three further Community Panel Diversion Schemes were funded by the Crime Prevention Unit. Two of these (in Foxton in the North Island and Rangiora in the South Island) are modelled on Project Turnaround and the third, Second Chance Programme, is a remodelled version of the original Rotorua programme. By July 2000, there were, in total, 10 programmes supported and administered by the Crime Prevention Unit (under the title 'Community Managed Restorative Justice Programmes').

A further four pilots schemes (in Auckland, Waitakere, Hamilton and Dunedin) began operation in October 2001. These court-referred restorative processes (restorative justice conferences) are administered by the Department for Courts and follow a different approach from the schemes using community panels: they are much more like family group conferences in that they rely on victims and offenders (and their support people) to come up with a plan or agreement and not panel members. However, they differ from family group conferences in that restorative justice conferences are voluntary and only take place if both the victim and offender agree to participate. Although the police, a probation officer and the offender's lawyer are usually invited to attend the conference, they may decide not to. The intention is that, at the conference, victims will have a say and offenders will take responsibility for putting things right.

The outcome of most, but not all, conferences will be an agreed plan and the conference facilitator will provide the referring judge with a copy of any such agreements (in the restorative justice report). These may contain rehabilitative or reintegrative features. However, the main purpose of the conference is to provide information to the judge who will take the conference report into account along with any other reports (for example, from a probation officer) and not to recommend a sentence. Judges will choose whether or not to incorporate all or part of any agreement reached into the sentence and sentences are expected to continue to be within the current range for 'similar' offences.

Thus these restorative conferences also differ from family group conferences in that they are less likely to have a profound impact on the eventual sentence and are more centrally and specifically victim focused. The explicit aims of these pilots are to offer better outcomes to victims and to reduce reoffending. To this extent, it is possible that sentences will also contain rehabilitative or reintegrative features.

In addition, judges throughout New Zealand have been referring offenders to conferences on an ad hoc basis. It is not possible to document the extent of this, but Consedine and Bowen (1999) present seven case histories of adult offenders who have experienced restorative conferences prior to sentencing as an aid to the judge; three of these related to sexual or physical abuse within the family. Indeed, as in the youth justice system and in contrast to schemes in other jurisdictions, restorative practices for adult offenders in New Zealand deal with relatively serious offences. Maxwell et al (1999), for example, document that the panels in Project Turnaround and Te Whanau Awhina dealt with aggravated robbery, threat to kill, driving causing death, driving with excess alcohol as well as the more 'routine' offences of wilful damage, theft and burglary. In the first year of the operation of the court-referred restorative justice pilots, all property offences with maximum penalties of two years imprisonment or more and other offences with maximum penalties of one to seven years are eligible for referral to a conference by the judge. Domestic violence offences, however, are excluded.

2. Summarising Benefits to Offenders

In 1990–1991, Maxwell and Morris (1993) carried out research on the New Zealand youth justice system.[11] They found that offenders could be involved in decisions about how best to deal with offending and that a significant proportion of offenders felt positively towards conferencing and were satisfied with the outcomes reached. In the words of one young person, 'It seemed pretty fair with people sitting around talking about things' (Maxwell and Morris, 1993: 110). Further, those young people who had experienced both conferences and courts spoke much more positively about conferences.[12] However, this research also showed that some offenders remained uninvolved in the process of decision-making and that a few were dissatisfied with the outcome: decisions had been made for and about them. Maxwell and Morris (1993) suggest that these findings resulted from poor practice rather than from any fundamental defect in restorative justice processes.

Maxwell et al (1999) obtained information from a small sample of offenders who had participated in Te Whanau Awhina and Project Turnaround about their experience. These interviews showed that most of the offenders found the experience to be positive and meaningful. They thought that the process provided an opportunity to deal with matters constructively and to avoid appearing in court or receiving court imposed sanctions. Offenders also said that, as a result of the meeting, they had an increased understanding of the impact of their offending on the victim and that they felt remorse. In the words of one offender, 'It gave me a chance to make things right—to appease my guilt and apologise' (Maxwell et al 1999: 30). Over half those interviewed said they had been involved in the decisions about how to deal with their offending. However, about one in four of those interviewed at Project Turnaround found the experience a negative one: they said they were not listened to, that decisions were coerced and that they were shamed by the process. They also commented on not feeling comfortable with the large

[11] This involved collecting data on 195 young offenders referred to a youth justice family group conference. They observed and recorded what happened during the family group conference, collected data from police and social welfare files and interviewed parents, young people, police officers, social welfare staff who were involved in the family group conference and victims.
[12] This finding is confirmed in the other research on restorative processes. See, for example, the evaluation of the Reintegrative Shaming Experiment in Canberra where offenders were randomly assigned to courts and conferences (Strang et al 1999).

number of people at the meeting or with their selection.[13] On the other hand, the small sample of offenders interviewed from the Te Whanau Awhina programme generally found that process meaningful because it happened on the marae and in the meeting house where they were in the presence of their ancestors. Despite the panel at Te Whanau Awhina often being seen as intimidating and demanding, their decisions were accepted by those interviewed. This is an important point given the mono-culturalism of conventional justice processes. The following two quotes come from offenders interviewed by Maxwell et al (1999: 31).

> It felt like I was among whanau even though it was still being dealt with through the legal system.

> It brought out emotions. I felt I was answering to my ancestors.

The majority of those interviewed in both schemes thought that the decisions reached were fair and that the plan provided help that might prevent them offending again. Looking back, 70 per cent of those interviewed said that the experience had been a good one for them either because it was constructive to be part of the process, because of the consequences of the plan or because they were able to avoid the more damaging effects of the alternatives. One interviewee summed it up as follows, 'It was a good experience. I was very anti to start but I've been won over definitely. Seeing the victims really impacts on you and opens your eyes' (Maxwell et al 1999: 37).

3. Summarising Benefits to Victims

Maxwell and Morris's (1993) research referred to above found that victims who attended the family group conference felt involved in the decisions about how best to deal with the offending against them and that a significant proportion of victims felt positively towards conferencing and were satisfied with the outcomes. In the words of one victim, 'I was impressed with it. It was a very useful exercise—very positive' (Maxwell and Morris, 1993: 118). However, this research also showed that some victims felt worse as a result of their attendance and that some victims were dissatisfied with the eventual outcomes. Maxwell and Morris (1993) suggested that these findings too resulted from poor practice rather than from any fundamental defect in restorative justice processes.

Smith and Cram (1998) examined the extent to which the 1995/6 pilot schemes responded to victims and reported the views of 20 victims who had attended panel meetings in Project Turnaround.[14] Overall, these victims said that they had had good experiences at the panel meeting and even those who were somewhat critical were nevertheless supportive of the continuance of the programme.

---

[13] This concern emphasises the significance of who the key decision-makers should be in restorative justice processes.

[14] About three-quarters of these meetings had victims present.

Victims gave a range of reasons for agreeing to attend. These included feeling that this was a better way of resolving the situation, giving offenders another chance, not wanting the case to go to court, dislike of conventional court processes, knowing the offender, wanting to have a say and to confront the offender, wanting to see the offender, the effects of the meeting on him/her and the offender's remorse, and seeking reparation. The following quotes from Smith and Cram (1998: 93–4) illustrate some of these reasons:

> It seemed a fair and just way of settling the situation.
> I wanted to give the offender another chance. I didn't want it to ruin his life.
> I think the old sick system failed, there must be a better way.
> I thought it was good to see the offender face to face—being able to confront him and have a say.
> It was satisfying to see offenders feeling sorry.

4. Benefits to the State

Irrespective of these benefits to victims and offenders, as noted earlier, governments are unlikely to pay much heed to restorative justice processes and practices unless they are more effective than conventional processes and practices in reducing reoffending and offer cost savings. The following sections set out what we know about this.

Family Group Conferences and Reoffending

Morris and Maxwell (1997) examined reconviction data on 161 of the young offenders who had been part of their 1990/91 family group conference sample.[15] The results showed that, by 1994, more than a third of their sample had not been reconvicted at all, that 14 per cent had been reconvicted only once and that only just over a quarter had been persistently reconvicted. Regression analyses using the data available to them from the 1990–1991 study highlighted a number of factors, which might explain why some young people were reconvicted and others were not. Some of these factors (for example, previous offending) were fairly predictable in terms of previous research, but other findings—the importance of the presence of victims at family group conferences and young offenders apologising to their victim(s)—were new and had important implications for current debates on restorative justice. These findings, however, could only be tentative at this stage.[16]

---

[15] Children under the age of 14 at the time they were referred to a family group conference were excluded.

[16] The regression analyses relied on the limited data Maxwell and Morris had collected in 1990–1991. They could not, therefore, take into account anything which had occurred subsequently to the young person—for example, life events like forming intimate relationships or having children; nor did they control for factors arising in the young person's early background—for example, their parents' criminal behaviour or drug and/or alcohol use.

Maxwell and Morris decided, therefore, to try and track these young people (and/or their parents) and re-interview them.[17] In all, 108 young people (67 per cent of the original sample) and 98 parents were interviewed. This meant that they were able to collect information on 72 per cent of the original sample.[18] Maxwell and Morris also updated their reconviction data so that they had a six-year follow-up period. Overall, within that time, they found that more than two-fifths of their original sample had been reconvicted only once or not at all, that over a quarter had not been reconvicted at all and that just over a quarter had been persistently reconvicted.[19]

Though precise comparisons between this sample and others are not possible because of differences in the target populations of the different systems of conferencing in different jurisdictions, these reconviction rates are certainly no worse and may be better in some respects than the closest comparisons available from within New Zealand and Australia (see, for example, Lovell and Norris, 1990; Coumarelos, 1994; Coumarelos and Weatherburn, 1995; Hayes et al 1998; Sherman et al 2000,[20] Daly and Hayes, 2001). Full details of the factors that predict reoffending are reported in Maxwell and Morris (1999). This chapter reports only the findings which are indicative of family group conference processes and, more particularly, restorative justice processes having an impact on reconviction.

First, Maxwell and Morris (1999) found that the presence of the victim, the young person making an apology, the young person feeling involved in the

---

[17] The questions asked were a mixture of fixed and open ended questions and covered a wide range of topics: for example, demographic and personal characteristics; family and early background factors; offending history including self reported offending; recollections of the family group conference which had brought them into the original sample and ongoing life circumstances. Open-ended responses were examined and a coding frame constructed to reflect key themes.

[18] Twenty-nine young people (12% of the original sample) and 41 parents were able to be contacted but refused to be interviewed. One young person was known to have died and the remainder of the young people could not be traced. There is no real way of knowing whether those young people we were able to trace were different in any major way from those we were unable to trace. Clearly, there was little difficulty in making contact with those in custody and those who had never moved from their original address. And it was easier to make contact with those who had recently been reconvicted since we had up-to-date addresses for them.

[19] Maxwell and Morris also asked the young people whether or not they had committed any undetected offences and, if so, what kind of offences they had committed. In this re-analysis, they excluded traffic and other minor infringements and personal marihuana use and, in the main, this categorisation of reoffending was confirmed. Two of those classified as 'non reconvicted' reported several undetected offences. They considered the possibility of reclassifying these two offenders. However, the interviewer suspected that one of these respondents was 'pulling his leg' when replying to the undetected offending questions and the other had also reported reconvictions of which there was no official record. They, therefore, decided that this information on self report offending was not sufficient to alter the original conviction-based classification.

[20] This study is probably the most robust since it randomly allocated four separate samples of offenders—young violent offenders under the age of 30 years, drink driving offenders, juvenile property offenders where there was a personal victim, and juvenile shoplifters—to conferences or courts. It reported one year before-after differences in offending rates rather than frequency of offending. These data indicated that there were significantly lower rates for the young violent offenders but that differences were slight or insignificant for the other three groups. These results from the RISE experiment are preliminary, but indicate that conferencing may have a different impact depending on the type of offending of the person referred.

decision and the young person agreeing with the outcome reached were all significantly related to not being reconvicted; secondly, not being made to feel a bad person or a bad parent (not feeling shamed) was significantly related to not being reconvicted; and third, the young person feeling remorse (this meant the young person remembering the conference, completing the tasks agreed to, feeling sorry for what s/he had done and feeling that s/he had made good the damage done) or the parents feeling that their son or daughter was sorry for what they had done was significantly related to not being reconvicted. Also significantly related to not being reconvicted was the young person feeling good about him- or herself and feeling optimistic about life. These young people tended to have had some education or training, to have jobs and to have positive relationships with a partner: in short, they were reintegrated with their communities. These findings on inclusion, reintegration, the encouragement of remorse and the avoidance of shaming are all endorsements of restorative justice practices.[21] Importantly, too, some of the benefits for offenders referred to earlier seem to be integrally linked to the likelihood of them reoffending. Overall, therefore, this research provides evidence that family group conferences, when they reflect restorative processes and practices, can have an impact on future offending.

Community Panel Adult Pre-Trial Diversion Programmes and Reoffending

Maxwell et al (1999) collected information on the reconvictions of 200 participants in the two pilot schemes, Project Turnaround and Te Whanau Awhina. A matched sample of the same size was obtained of offenders who had been dealt with through the courts. Each participant was randomly matched with a control subject who was convicted of the same offence (or the same most serious offence where the participant was charged with committing more than one offence) and dealt with by conventional court processes during 1995.[22] Participants and control subjects were also matched on age, sex, ethnicity, previous offending and number of charges. Convictions were used as the measure for assessing recidivism.

Data on reconvictions showed that, over the following twelve months, those participating in both schemes were significantly less likely to be reconvicted than the matched control groups. Thus, 16 per cent of the participants at Project Turnaround were reconvicted within this period compared with 30 per cent of the

---

[21] Further analyses confirmed these findings. The canonical discriminant analysis showed that the young person reporting 'not feeling shamed at the family group conference' was the fourth most important variable in the first canonical correlate discriminating between the reconviction categories and 'being remorseful' was the tenth most important. A series of path analyses attempted to explore the impact of key factors on reconviction over time. These provided further support for the hypothesis that experiences at family group conferences can moderate the patterns of the past and can contribute to the probability of reintegration into society and the prevention of reoffending.

[22] The Ministry of Justice researchers collaborating on this project took the view that the two to three year time difference between the processing of participants in 1997/8 and controls in 1995 was unlikely to confound the comparison of recidivism rates between the samples as changes in practice or patterns of offending over that period were not of a magnitude that would be likely to lead to differences in recidivism.

matched control sample; the comparable percentages for Te Whanau Awhina participants were 33 per cent and 47 per cent.[23] Clearly, not all participants and controls were 'free' to commit offences for the same length of time and so a 'survival analysis' was carried out. This takes account of the different length of follow-ups available for each offender. This too showed that both Project Turnaround and Te Whanau Awhina participants were significantly less likely to be reconvicted than their matched controls. Also, not only was there a reduction in the proportion of participants reconvicted but, for those who were reconvicted, the seriousness of the major offence (as judged by a scale of seriousness based on penalties) was not as great among participants in the schemes as it was among the matched control groups. In addition, those referred to the schemes who were seen as having successful outcomes were less likely to be reconvicted compared to those who were seen as not having successful outcomes (although the small numbers here make it difficult to be confident of this finding). The survival analysis on these sub-samples confirmed this finding.

Overall, then, the findings of this research all point in the same direction: those participating in the pilots were reconvicted less frequently and for less serious offences than matched controls who were dealt with in courts and those who successfully completed the agreements reached in the pilots were reconvicted less frequently and less seriously than those who did not. It seems clear that something in the pilots made a difference. This research cannot say definitively what this was. But the small group of participants interviewed did refer to the sorts of factors identified by the young offenders in the family group conferencing research: the importance of inclusion and the potentially negative effect of shaming.

5. Cost Savings

Restorative justice may contribute to cost savings through both its processes (less reliance on courts) and its outcomes (less reliance on custody). Maxwell et al (1999) reported on the costs of Project Turnaround and Te Whanau Awhina. Over the period reviewed (1997), the costs of the schemes per client were $462 at Project Turnaround and $1,515 at Te Whanau Awhina.[24] This difference between the schemes was largely due to the greater involvement of Te Whanau Awhina in providing programmes for participants in the scheme. At the same time, savings on correctional outcomes for 100 participants compared to the 100 matched controls were $27,811 at Project Turnaround and $168,259 at Te Whanau Awhina. This was due to a larger number of the Te Whanau Awhina controls receiving custodial penalties. There were also more savings at Project Turnaround in court

---

[23] Obviously, a greater proportion of the Te Whanau Awhina participants and their matched controls were reconvicted. This is most likely due to the fact that they were more serious and persistent offenders than the Project Turnaround participants and their matched controls.

[24] All figures quoted are in New Zealand dollars.

appearances and associated costs and these, together with the savings on correctional sentences were estimated as $85,325. Although there were no savings in court costs at Te Whanau Awhina, there were savings in the cost of programme provision: the total savings for this programme were estimated at $193,096.

It is more difficult to give precise cost savings for family group conferences in the youth justice system. However, many fewer young people are referred to the Youth Court. In 1990, only 2,587 young offenders were dealt with there: a decline to about a quarter of the previous average of 11,000 in the eight years prior to the Children, Young Persons and Their Family Act 1989 (Maxwell and Morris, 1993; Spier, 1997). The number of young people dealt with in the Youth Court rose again over the following nine years but, in 1999, it was still only just over a third (4034) of the number prior to the 1989 Act (Spier, 2000). There was, at the same time, a sharp reduction in the use of residential sentences and the number of young people given custodial sentences remained relatively stable despite increases in the number of serious offenders coming before the courts over that time. Thus, in the first 12 months of the Act's operation, 75 young people received orders which placed them in a residence—less than half the average number for the previous three years (Maxwell and Morris, 1993). This figure was recorded as having risen to 89 in 1999, but this is still a marked reduction over pre-Act years (Spier, 2000).[25] With respect to the number of young people who were sentenced to custody, the number fell in 1990 to 108 compared with 150 in 1989 (Spier, 1997). The 1999 figure was 155—about the same as the 1989 figure (Spier, 2000). This relatively low number of young people in custody has been maintained at a time when the number of adult sentenced to imprisonment increased markedly. Collectively, these changes must have resulted in significant financial savings to the state.

6. Conclusion

The data presented in this chapter point to significant benefits to offenders, victims and the state from the introduction of restorative justice processes and practices in New Zealand. The data from two different studies conducted by two different research teams examining different restorative processes demonstrated their potential to increase victims' involvement and satisfaction. These findings are consistent with those reported by researchers who have examined examples of restorative justice in other jurisdictions (see, for example, Strang, 2001; Umbreit et al 2001). The benefits reported by victims include their greater involvement in the process, the opportunity to have their say and speedier and more satisfactory outcomes. The data from two different projects also showed that offenders preferred restorative processes for reasons that are very similar to those given by

[25] Spiers (2000) noted, however, that this may be an underestimate as records do not always distinguish these cases from those in which there is an order for supervision.

victims. These findings are also consistent with research on restorative justice processes in other jurisdictions (Strang et al 1999). In addition, both offenders and victims frequently report satisfaction in being able to reach agreements that go some way to repairing the harm that was caused.

Significantly, too, the findings on reoffending (which also come from two different projects using very different methodologies) are quite consistent (and are consistent with preliminary findings from Australian studies that conferencing can have an impact on reoffending see, for example, Sherman et al 2000; Daly and Hayes, 2001). Some six years after their family group conference in 1990/91, more than two-fifths of a sample of young people were not reconvicted or were convicted once only and not much more than a quarter were classified as being persistently reconvicted. The most important finding from this research project, however, was that key factors of successful family group conferences contributed to reducing the chance of reoffending even when other important factors identified by the literature on reoffending, such as adverse early experiences and early offending, were taken into account. Similarly, adult offenders who participated in Project Turnaround and Te Whanau Awhina, both of which had restorative features, were reconvicted less frequently and of offences of less seriousness than a matched group of controls who had been dealt with in the courts. Furthermore, comparisons of the subsequent reconviction rates for those who successfully completed the schemes and those who did not suggest that those who carried out the agreements reached were less likely to be reconvicted. Taken together, therefore, the findings of these projects indicate that restorative processes and practices can impact on reconviction.

Added to this is the evidence that suggests that significant cost savings can be made from less reliance on courts, custody and residences. Although the savings that result from preventing reoffending cannot be estimated, these are undoubtedly at least as important as the financial costs that have been calculated. Incalculable, too, are the emotional or human costs of crime which restorative justice addresses. Together these findings make a strong case for the continued expansion of the use of restorative practices in both the youth justice and criminal justice systems.

REFERENCES

Bazemore, G and Schiff, M (2001) *Restorative Community Justice: Repairing Harm and Transforming Communities* (Anderson Publishing Company, Cincinnati OH).

Bowen, H and Consedine, J (eds) (1999) *Restorative Justice: Contemporary Themes and Practice* (Ploughshares Publications, Lyttleton NZ).

Braithwaite, J (1999) 'Restorative Justice: Assessing Optimistic and Pessimistic Accounts' in M Tonry (ed.), *Crime and Justice: A Review of Research* (University of Chicago Press, Chicago IL) vol 25, 1–127.

Consedine, J (1995) *Restorative Justice: Healing the Effects of Crime* (Ploughshares Publications, Lyttleton NZ).

Daly, K and Hayes, H (2001) 'Family conferencing in South Australia and Re-offending: Preliminary Results from the SAJJ Project'. Paper presented at the annual meeting of the Australian and New Zealand Society of Criminology, Melbourne, February.

Hayes, H, Prenzler T and Wortley, R (1998) *Making Amends: Final Evaluation of the Queensland Community Conferencing Pilot* (Centre for Crime Policy and Public Safety, School of Justice Administration, Griffith University, Brisbane).

Jackson, M (1988) *Maori and the Criminal Justice System Part II* (Department of Justice, Wellington).

Maxwell, GM and Morris, A (1993) *Families, Victims and Culture: Youth Justice in New Zealand* (Social Policy Agency and Institute of Criminology, Victoria University of Wellington, Wellington).

——(1999) *Understanding Reoffending* (Institute of Criminology, Wellington).

Maxwell, GM, Morris, A and Anderson, T (1999) *Community Panel Adult Pre-Trial Diversion: Supplementary evaluation* (Crime Prevention Unit Department of Prime Minister and Cabinet and Institute of Criminology Victoria University, Wellington).

McElrea, F (1998) 'The New Zealand Model of Family Group Conferences'. Paper presented at an International Symposium—Beyond Prisons: Best Practice along the Criminal Justice Process, 15–18 Mar 1998, Kingston, Ontario, Canada.

Ministry of Justice (1995) *Restorative Justice: A Discussion Paper* (Ministry of Justice, Wellington).

——(1998) *Restorative Justice: The Public Submissions* (Ministry of Justice, Wellington).

Morris, A and Maxwell, GM 'Restorative Justice In New Zealand: Family Group Conferences as a Case Study' (1998) 1(1) *Western Criminology Review* Online: http://wcr.sonoma.edu/v1n1/morris.html

Morris, A and Maxwell, G (2000) 'The Practice of Family Group Conferences in New Zealand: Assessing the Place, Potential and Pitfalls of Restorative Justice' in A Crawford, and J Goodey (eds), *Integrating a Victim Perspective within Criminal Justice* (Ashgate Publishing Group, Aldershot).

New Zealand Maori Council and Durie Hall, D (1997) 'Restorative Justice: A Maori Perspective' in H Bowen and J Consedine (eds), *Restorative Justice: Contemporary Themes and Practice* (Ploughshares Publications, Lyttelton NZ).

Sherman, L, Strang, H and Woods, DJ (2000) *Recidivism Patterns in the Canberra Reintegrative Shaming Experiment (RISE)* (Research School of Social Sciences, Australian National University). Online: http://www.aic.gov.au/rjustice

Smith, LT and Cram, F (1998) 'An Evaluation of the Community Panel Diversion Pilot Programme'. A Report to the Crime Prevention Unit, Auckland Uniservices Ltd.

Spier, P (1998) *Conviction and Sentencing of Offenders in New Zealand: 1988 to 1997* (Ministry of Justice, Wellington).

——(2000) *Conviction and Sentencing of Offenders in New Zealand: 1990 to 1999* (Ministry of Justice, Wellington).

Strang, H, Barnes, G, Braithwaite J and Sherman, L (1999) *Experiments in Restorative Policing: A Progress Report on the Canberra Reintegrative Shaming Experiments (RISE)* (Australian Federal Police and Australian National University, Canberra). Online: http://www.aic.gov.au/rjustice/rise/progress/1999.html.

Strang, H (2001) 'Justice for Victims of Young Offenders: The Centrality of Emotional Harm and Restoration' in A Morris and G Maxwell (eds), *Restoring Justice for Juveniles: Conferences, Mediation and Circles* (Hart Publishing, Oxford).

Tauri, J 'Explaining Recent Innovations in New Zealand's Criminal Justice System: Empowering Maori or Biculturalising the State?'(1999) 32(2) *Australian and New Zealand Journal of Criminology* 153–67.

Umbreit M, Coates, R and Vos, B (2001) 'Victim Impact of Meeting with Young Offenders: Two Decades of Victim Offender Mediation Practice and Research' in A Morris and G Maxwell (eds), *Restoring Justice for Juveniles: Conferences, Mediation and Circles* (Hart Publishing, Oxford).

Webster, B (2000) 'Restorative Justice Developments in New Zealand: Community Managed Restorative Justice Programmes—from Inception to Evaluation'. Paper prepared for the Australian Crime Prevention Council, 19th Biennial Conference Oct 1999 updated 25 July 2000.

14

New, Improved Police-Led Restorative Justice? Action-Research and the Thames Valley Police Initiative

Richard Young and Carolyn Hoyle

I. INTRODUCTION

This chapter presents some findings on the implementation of the Thames Valley Police initiative in restorative cautioning. These derive from a three-year research project, funded by the Joseph Rowntree Foundation, and completed in 2001. We had an action-research remit in that we were committed to assisting the police to improve their practices. The method for achieving this was to break the research project down into distinct phases so that interim findings from each could be used by the police for reshaping aspects of their initiative such as the content of training, their practice manual and so on. In phase one, interviews were carried out with restorative justice facilitators and co-ordinators across the various police areas comprising Thames Valley Police force. Three areas were chosen for more detailed study in phase two, namely Aylesbury, Banbury and Reading. Various criteria underlay this choice, amongst which were that the range of practices and problems across these three areas closely matched the range across the police service as a whole. In phase two, we observed facilitators at work, studied the surrounding administrative processes and carried out unstructured interviews with those attending cautioning sessions. Phases three and four of the research saw a shift towards the methods of formal evaluation. We collected qualitative and quantitative data through observing and tape-recording restorative processes, and also through interviews with all the participants.[1] Selected findings of these two latter phases will be used here to illuminate the developing practice of police-led restorative justice in the United Kingdom. Our focus is on the actual process of restorative justice as delivered within a policing context.

---

[1] In phase three we were assisted on a part-time basis by a D.Phil student, Shepley Orr. In phase four we appointed a full-time research officer, Roderick Hill, and part-time help was provided by our colleagues Aidan Wilcox and Martina Feilzer, and by Giselle Rosario, a D.Phil student. Our sincere thanks to them all.

The structure of the chapter is as follows. In part two we will explain the significance and scale of the Thames Valley Police initiative in restorative cautioning and examine the features of the organisational space within which this initiative is taking place. In part three we will explain why we adopted an action-research strategy and comment briefly on the extent to which our research sample is representative of Thames Valley Police practice. In the fourth part of the chapter we will present our findings on the quality of the restorative justice process achieved by the police and discuss the extent to which our research made a difference to police practice. We will also consider the relationship between the quality of process and outcomes achieved. In concluding we will reflect on the nature of our relationship with the police.

II. THE THAMES VALLEY POLICE INITIATIVE IN RESTORATIVE CAUTIONING

Following ad hoc experimentation from the mid-1990s onwards, the Thames Valley Police initiative in restorative cautioning began formally on 1 April 1998. From that date all police cautions were meant to be restorative in nature. The restorative cautioning initiative was the first step in a much larger programme of change instituted within this police service. Thus, for example, Thames Valley Police is experimenting with the use of restorative justice in predominantly non-criminal contexts such as neighbourhood disputes, conflicts within schools, and complaints by the public against the police. The restorative cautioning initiative has so far proved to be the most significant of these developments. It is on this aspect of the Thames Valley Police's programme that our research has concentrated.

David Garland (2001: vii) prefaces his recent overview of social responses to crime by noting the unavoidable tension 'between broad generalization and the specification of empirical particulars.' He notes that while such overviews are open to the charge of simplification, detailed case studies of the kind we are engaged in prompt critical questions about their significance. As he puts it: 'How does this study relate to the others that have been done, or might be done? Why should we be interested? What in the end does it tell us about the world in which we live?' He argues that the individual author cannot escape this dilemma but must instead oscillate between the 'big picture and the local detail, until alighting upon a level of analysis that seems to offer the optimum vantage point . . .'. We agree, but would add the qualification that not all case studies are of equal significance. Sometimes the local detail can reasonably be presented as something of national and international importance, as an eye-catching part of the big picture. To what extent is this true of the Thames Valley Police initiative in restorative cautioning?

1. The National Policing Context

One question that might reasonably be asked is whether the police force we are studying is sufficiently like other forces for our findings to be generalisable. Let us consider this within the national context, ie England and Wales. The area for which the Thames Valley Police service is responsible comprises the three south-ern English counties of Oxfordshire, Berkshire and Buckinghamshire. These largely rural counties contain substantial urban centres such as Oxford, Reading, Slough and Milton Keynes, but no major cities. Nonetheless, more than two million people live in the 2,200 square miles that make up the Thames Valley. The mix of offences it records each year is much the same as all other police forces in England and Wales although metropolitan police forces deal with proportionally more violent offences than do non-metropolitan ones (Povey et al 2001).

In short, Thames Valley Police is a large but otherwise reasonably typical non-metropolitan police force. Of course, whatever results Thames Valley Police has achieved with its model of restorative justice would not necessarily be straightfor-wardly replicable in major conurbations such as London or Manchester, or in areas where police-community relations are badly strained, as in Northern Ireland. But most police services in England and Wales are non-metropolitan and the majority of these are probably similar enough to Thames Valley Police in workload, outlook and organisation to make this case study of more than just local significance.

2. The Significance of Police Cautioning in England and Wales

A second question that might be asked about our case study is how important is police cautioning as a practice? If it were true, for example, that cautioning merely dealt with small numbers of trivial victimless offences in an uncontroversial manner then however restorative this practice had become, the significance of such a transformation would be slight. This is far from being the truth, however.

The police developed the practice of cautioning with remarkably little legisla-tive intervention or oversight. Under the Home Office guidelines, which governed the use of cautioning at the time our research was carried out, before a caution can be administered there must be evidence of the offender's guilt sufficient to give a realistic prospect of conviction; the offence must be admitted by the offender; and, the offender, or, in the case of a juvenile, a responsible adult, must give informed consent to the caution. These guidelines, like earlier versions, left enormous scope for discretion, and cautioning rates, policies and practices have varied widely across and between police forces and areas.

Furthermore, nationally, research has shown that in practice the pre-conditions set out in the guidelines are sometimes ignored (eg Evans, 1993: 41). Young people are particularly vulnerable to being cautioned when they should not be as they request legal advice much less frequently than do adults, relying instead on the presence of an 'appropriate adult' (usually a parent and nearly always lacking in legal knowledge) to safeguard their interests. Overall, less than half of all suspects are accompanied by a legal representative when interviewed by the police, the quality of this legal representation is often poor, and, in any case, any legal advice offered does not necessarily extend to the question of whether or not to accept a police caution (see generally Sanders and Young, 2000: 214–40).

For the most part, then, cautioning practices take place within a due process free zone. (Only five per cent of the cautioned persons we interviewed as part of our study of restorative cautioning had received legal advice relating to the caution itself.) This would be less worrying if cautions were merely brief administrative processes, but empirical research suggests that they can be demeaning and punitive. Lee (1998), for example, found that the police sometimes used a cautioning session to humiliate and stigmatise young people.[2] Thames Valley Police officers described how under the old-style police cautioning system they gave offenders a 'bollocking' with the aim of making them cry. As one told us in interview: 'Inspectors used to bang on the desk, all this bloody lark. Make them cry. They [offenders] used to go out of there thinking "Bastards!" And you could never address the victim perspective mainly because you weren't in the slightest bit interested in what the victim thought.' The officers we interviewed further explained how there had been no training on how to administer a caution, no supervision of practice, and no expectation of consistency.

Cautioning for young offenders has recently been put on a statutory basis by the Crime and Disorder Act 1998, but cautioning for adults remains governed by guidelines. After many years of Governments seeking to encourage the use of cautioning, the Home Office guidelines (Circular 18/1994), and the 1998 Act both sought to restrain the practice of multiple cautions for the same offender and the cautioning rate for indictable offences declined accordingly. Nonetheless, the fact that cautions make up one in three of all formal criminal justice disposals (ie cautions and convictions) is testimony to the continuing importance of cautioning processes in responding to crime. Indeed, just less than a quarter of a million offenders (239,000) received police cautions, reprimands or warnings in 2000 (Johnson et al 2001).

A widely held assumption about a police caution is that it amounts to no more than a 'let-off', a 'slap on the wrist' or a 'telling off'; in short that it does not result in a formal criminal record or a punishment. In fact, the distinction between police cautions and court convictions is becoming increasingly blurred. The sex offenders' register is a good example. Under the Sex Offenders Act 1997 those convicted *or* cautioned of certain sexual offences are required to notify the police of their names and addresses and any subsequent changes (Soothill et al 1997). More generally, individual police forces have long kept their own records of cautions and, as from November 1995, records of cautions have also been kept (along with convictions) on the Police National Computer. With the growing emphasis on intelligence-led policing (Maguire, 2000), caution records are increasingly likely to influence police practices such as stop-search and other forms of surveillance.

Records of cautions also influence future prosecution decisions, making court proceedings more likely. This is particularly so for young people who, under the

---

[2] The notion that these old-style cautions did not involve punishment was also undermined by the (admittedly patchy) development of so-called caution-plus schemes in the 1980s and 1990s which typically involved cautioned persons engaging in rehabilitative or reparative schemes of one kind or another (Crawford, 1996).

Crime and Disorder Act 1998, are only eligible for two cautions (at most) other than in exceptional circumstances (Leng et al 1998: 75–80). This legislation replaces the term 'caution' (for young people) with the more deterrent terminology of 'reprimands' and 'warnings'. Reprimands are reserved for first offences of a trivial nature, whereas warnings are supposed to be used for second offences or for more serious first offences. Those who initially enter the system at the warning stage cannot then receive a reprimand for a second offence, however trivial it might be, and cannot receive a second warning unless two years have elapsed since the previous warning and the offence is not regarded as serious. These complicated provisions seem likely to funnel an increasing proportion of young offenders into court in future. Whilst cautions may decline in number in future, their legal significance continues to grow.

Clearly, cautioning is a critical feature of the criminal justice process. The question is whether a shift to restorative cautioning is likely to make the system fairer and more effective.

3. Restorative Cautioning

A restorative caution aims to go much further than the delivery of the old-style caution and involves two distinct innovations. The first is that the cautioning police officer is supposed to invite all those affected by the offence, including any victim, to the cautioning session. If a victim is present, the cautioning session is termed a restorative conference, if not, a restorative caution. The second is the structuring of the session according to a script which requires the cautioning officer to put certain questions to those present according to a definite order. This script derived from the police-led model of restorative cautioning developed in Wagga Wagga, Australia. The Wagga Wagga model's main influences were the New Zealand system of family group conferences and the quite separate criminological theory developed by John Braithwaite of reintegrative shaming (Moore, 1995). The latter posits that the best way to control crime is to induce a sense of shame in offenders for their actions whilst maintaining respect for them as people (as to condemn them as bad people might push them towards deviant identities, commitments or sub-cultures). It further posits that this kind of reintegrative shaming is best achieved not by the police or the courts but rather by exposing offenders to the emotionally-charged opinions of those who they most care about, such as parents, partners and friends.

The primary aim in the scripted model is to encourage the offender to take responsibility for repairing the harm caused by the offence. Structured discussion between offenders and those affected by their actions is seen as central to this endeavour. According to the script, the officer first sets a reintegrative focus for the meeting by emphasising that participants are not there to judge whether the offender is a good or bad person, but, rather, to discuss the harmful effects of the offending behaviour and to work towards repairing that harm. This is intended to guard against any open-ended stigmatic shaming of the offender. The facilitator then asks the offenders present to describe their thoughts and feelings at the time of the offence and subsequently. The other participants are then invited to talk about the harm the offence caused. In a restorative caution the views of any absent victims are meant to have been sought by the police and should be conveyed at this stage in the process. Offenders are then asked if there is anything they wish to say in response, and this sometimes prompts apologies or other reparative gestures. The participants are then encouraged to explore the issue of repair further. Sometimes any oral commitments made are reflected in a written (non-enforceable) reparation agreement drawn up by the facilitator. Whilst the discussion about the offence and its implications is meant to induce a sense of shame in the offender, the apology and reparation stage is designed to foster a sense of reintegration.

Officers can facilitate restorative cautions and conferences only if they have first received specialist training. During this training they are provided with a practice manual which includes modules on the underlying theories, practice standards, and the script. Once trained, they are allocated cases by local co-ordinators who also endeavour to monitor whether the practice standards are adhered to. In addition, a team of officers at police headquarters, known as the Restorative Justice Consultancy, oversees all aspects of the initiative and maintains a database of all restorative cautions and conferences. The restorative cautioning initiative can thus be portrayed as seeking to engineer a shift away from low visibility, idiosyncratic, sometimes overtly stigmatic, police behaviour towards more consistent practice under conditions of greater visibility and accountability according to definite aims and standards.

One important point that this discussion should have made clear is that the extent to which restorative cautioning can be truly reintegrative is currently limited by the legal and political context within which it takes place. As we have seen, the law now encourages prosecution at an earlier stage of an offender's criminal career and in any case the keeping and use of caution records (as with other forms of police record such as fingerprints, DNA and photographs) might preclude any sense of full reintegration. Thus, in response to concern we expressed that a particular young offender might have felt uncomfortable being observed during the conference, the facilitator replied:

> I don't think [the cautioned person] was bothered either way. I think [she] just thought 'well yeah', you know, I mean I suppose when you think that she's gone through fingerprints, photo, and all that, and she'd have been up the police station with hundreds of policemen milling about, and you get the sense then that everybody knows what you've done. I think perhaps for her one more wouldn't make any difference.

Furthermore, we witnessed many restorative cautions that concluded with the facilitator saying something similar to the following example taken from a transcript:

What happens with a caution, basically, is it is recorded for five years. After the five years, if you haven't committed any further offences, then the record is wiped off. If, however, you do get into further trouble in the next five years, what will happen is, you won't get the chance of another caution. Because, in this area, it's one caution, unless there are exceptional circumstances. One caution, and then if that hasn't sunk in, well, you know, you obviously haven't taken it seriously, then you might as well go to court. Um, and, if that does happen, then this matter will be brought up as well, because the caution is declared to be void.

Although this facilitator misrepresents the legal position by suggesting that a caution is voidable, the deterrent thinking behind the claim and the language employed nonetheless echoes core themes in government policy and legislation. This tension between reintegrative and restorative intent and deterrent legal form and practice cannot be wished away. It can, however, either be minimised or maximised depending on the orientation and behaviour of the specific facilitator.

4. The Importance of the Restorative Cautioning Initiative

We have shown in the preceding two sub-sections that police cautioning is a practice of major sociological significance. What remains to be demonstrated, in the light of Garland's concerns, is that the restorative cautioning initiative of Thames Valley Police is of other than just of marginal or local interest.

The National and International Significance of the Scripted Model

Whilst there is a great diversity of police-led conferencing schemes in operation across the world, it is the scripted model that has so far proved the most influential. It provides the basis for the protocols underpinning various high-profile schemes, including Bethlehem, Pennsylvania; Canberra, Australia; the Royal Canadian Mounted Police, as well as that in the Thames Valley. All of these schemes are playing a major role in shaping thinking and policy in this area (Young, 2001).

The Thames Valley initiative has been the focus of extensive media coverage. The police force has encouraged such publicity and has actively sought to market the idea of restorative justice through organising national and international conferences and presentations, and by providing training to other police forces as well as to schools, prisons, probation services and so on. The initiative has attracted intense interest from national and international policy-makers, practitioners and others, scores of whom have sat in on restorative conferences as observers. Thames Valley's then Chief Constable, Sir Charles Pollard, was a founder member of the Youth Justice Board and has done much to promote restorative justice within the new framework governing youth justice in the U.K.[3] In 1999–2000, the Youth

---

[3] For a discussion of this new framework, see Dignan and Marsh (2001).

Justice Board paid for Thames Valley Police (in partnership with two other police forces) to deliver training in conference facilitation to several hundred youth justice practitioners across England and Wales. The Wagga Wagga model has also informed the training of several thousand practitioners carried out by the international organisation 'Real Justice'. Thus it can be argued that research findings relating to this model are likely to be of direct interest to criminal justice practitioners throughout England and Wales, and to restorative justice practitioners in many other countries.

The Range of Criminal Behaviour and Criminal Offenders Covered

Many restorative justice initiatives target a fairly limited range of offenders or offences. Some, for example, exclude institutional victims, thus removing the vast number of thefts from shops from their ambit. Others focus on young offenders only, or exclude certain types of offence because they are seen as inappropriate for restorative justice, such as public order matters, racially motivated offences and domestic violence. By contrast, the Thames Valley Police have adopted the default position that any matter to be disposed of by a caution should be handled in a restorative manner. It is true that they are wary of using restorative justice for some issues, particularly domestic violence and sexual assaults, but even here there is no absolute prohibition on exploring the possibilities of a restorative response.

The upshot is that the Thames Valley initiative covers a wide range of offences and offenders, ranging from the very trivial to matters so serious that if they had gone to court the defendant would have faced the possibility of life imprisonment. Whilst respectable arguments can be put forward for excluding particular offences or offenders from restorative justice programmes, there are counter-arguments in all cases (see chapters by Dignan and Hudson, this volume). What is urgently needed is better empirical data on how restorative justice practices might need tailoring according to context and circumstances. One of the reasons why the Thames Valley Police initiative is so important is that it is allowing researchers to find out much more about these matters.

Scale

Many restorative justice initiatives deal with very small numbers and are marginal to mainstream criminal justice. They tend to act as supplements rather than as alternatives, and existing practices are left largely undisturbed. Often the lip service paid to restorative justice ideals masks a distinctly unimpressive underlying reality. For example, the Youth Justice Board of England and Wales is currently funding some 46 restorative justice schemes which target young offenders at various points within the criminal justice system. Together with our colleague, Aidan Wilcox, we are acting as national evaluators to this programme. We have been sent information on 30 of these schemes from their respective local evalua-

Table 1: Thames Valley Police restorative cautioning—first three years

Year	Instant Caution	Restorative Caution	Restorative Conference	Total Cautions	% of caution based on the restorative justice script
1998–1999	3,123	2,815	652	6,590	53%
1999–2000	1,177	4,388	626	6,191	81%
2000–2001	1,715	4,862	637	7,214	76%
Total	6,015	12,065	1,915	19,995	70%

Source: Restorative Consultancy Database.

tors covering (roughly) their first year of operation. Some 2,101 'restorative interventions' have taken place, which means, on average, 70 per scheme. The impression given by the Board is that these interventions involve bringing offenders and victims together, either in a conference of some sort, or through smaller-scale victim-offender mediation. In fact there have been only 142 such face-to-face encounters, amounting to seven per cent of the total interventions, or less than five per scheme per year. The three biggest categories of 'restorative activities' reported to date include 'general victim awareness sessions' for the young offender (20 per cent of the total), indirect reparation to the community (20 per cent) and letters written by young offenders to their victims but not sent (nine per cent). In a further 25 per cent of cases all we know about the restorative intervention is that no contact at all took place between the scheme and the victim (Wilcox, Hoyle and Young, 2001: 30).

This low level of victim involvement can be compared with the first three years of the Thames Valley Police restorative cautioning initiative as set out in Table 1. In the year ending 31 March 2001 the police conducted 4,862 restorative cautions and 637 restorative conferences. Hence, over three-quarters of its cautioning activity was restorative. Table 1 also reveals that not all police cautions since the initiative formally began have been carried out according to restorative principles. Some Thames Valley Police cautions are termed 'instant' in recognition of the fact that a victim's participation was not secured or their views not sought, or that there was no direct victim *and* the caution was dealt with in a perfunctory non-scripted manner (as is usually the case when a custody sergeant decides to offer a caution shortly after someone's arrest and detention in the police station). The discouragement of such cautions by the Restorative Justice Consultancy is reflected in the sharp decline in the number carried out after the first year of the initiative.

It can be seen that the Thames Valley Police appear to have transformed their cautioning practices to a substantial degree. About three-quarters of all cautions are now taking the form of a scripted session, and over 600 a year (about 10 per cent of all cautions) involve offenders coming face-to-face with victims. In short, the sheer scale and intensity of the restorative cautioning initiative in the Thames Valley has created an excellent opportunity to study the value of introducing restorative justice principles and methods within criminal justice.

II. THE ACTION-RESEARCH PROJECT

1. On Minding the Gap

As Kathy Daly (this volume) notes, it would be a naïve researcher who did not expect to find a gap between a programme's ideals and its achievements. Indeed, many criminal justice programmes fail not because of the weakness of the underlying ideas but because of weak implementation (Hollin, 1995; Bennett, 1996). One possible response to the 1970s slogan 'Nothing Works' was that little had been properly tried. Thus, when Thames Valley Police opened a discussion with us early in 1997 concerning the design of an independent study of its restorative cautioning initiative, our advice was that a formal evaluation should only be attempted following a period of action-research in which we helped the police implement its model as planned.

For several reasons we fully expected there to be a large initial gap between the blueprint for restorative cautioning (as established through training manuals and programmes, and the facilitator's script) and the actual practice of police officers when facilitating cautioning sessions. First, all initiatives tend to suffer from teething difficulties. Secondly, an exploratory study conducted in the Thames Valley in 1997 by Young and Goold (1999) had highlighted the likelihood of such a gap. Thirdly, and more fundamentally, we expected a wide gap because we conceived of restorative cautioning not as a stand-alone new practice capable of being evaluated in isolation but rather as an attempt to transform a long-existing policing practice. In other words restorative cautioning would necessarily involve some accommodation and conflict between two sets of philosophies and practices, the first, restorative justice, the second, established policing. The difficulties of changing entrenched policing practices are too well known to merit reiteration here (see eg Chan, 1996). It suffices to say that we expected to find that established policing culture, structures and patterns of behaviour would shape and often distort the supposedly restorative nature of cautioning sessions. It made sense, therefore, to evaluate restorative cautioning as something embedded within wider policing structures and understandings. Our overall aims were to measure the gap between theory and practice, understand its causes and effects and test whether it was possible for the police to close this gap once these matters had been documented through research. This would also allow us, we hoped, to test the impact of police-led restorative justice, as opposed to police-led cautioning sessions masquerading as such.

We thus built in a 'before and after' component to the action-research. Systematic 'before' measurements were made in phase three (the interim study) between January and April 1999. The resulting interim study (confidential) report produced in October 1999 was based on our observations of 23 cautioning sessions, all but one of which were tape-recorded, and on the 135 interviews relating to these cases. The report included 81 recommendations designed to close (or at least narrow) the gap we detected between the programme's protocols and the behaviour of the 11 facilitators (nine police officers and two social workers) we observed. All of these recommendations were accepted by the police. After a pause to allow for their implementation, which included issuing a modified script and top-up training for facilitators, in phase four (the full evaluation), between January and April 2000, we collected our 'after' data by observing a further 56 cases and by conducting 483 interviews with the 242 participants observed in these cases.

2. The Representative Nature of the Study

Following careful analysis we have concluded that the samples we drew were reasonably representative in both the interim study and the full evaluation, thus allowing us to make meaningful comparisons between these two periods of data collection *and* to make inferences about the Thames Valley initiative as a whole (Hoyle, Young and Hill, 2002: appendix 2). For example, the offenders we saw were neither the worst risks nor the best risks but rather were typical of those who experienced restorative cautioning. Their previous criminal records, their gender, and their age were all in line with those of the total population cautioned. We determined, however, that our sample could not be said to be sufficiently representative of any of the three individual police areas we studied. We have therefore refrained from making judgements about practice in any particular area.

Once we had been notified of a case our method was to introduce ourselves to the participants as they arrived at the cautioning session venue and to seek permission to observe and tape-record the process. Out of 82 sets of participants we approached, only three refused permission to observe, with a further two refusing permission to tape-record. Our presence as observers during the process did not appear to have any major effect on participants. When we carried out in-depth interviews with them about their experience of the process, very few participants mentioned that they had been distracted or otherwise affected by our presence in the meeting.

On the other hand, as Daly and Kitcher (1999) found in their study of restorative conferences in South Australia, the presence of observers did seem to make facilitators more self-conscious and more concerned to do and say 'the right thing'. This was no doubt particularly so in our full evaluation (some facilitators told us as much) as by then facilitators had been given the opportunity to digest the critical remarks we had made in the interim study report about some aspects of their handling of cases. To some extent, then, our presence put facilitators on their best behaviour, and this strengthens our sense that our research represents police-led restorative justice under optimal conditions, in other words, a best case scenario.

III. IMPROVING THE QUALITY OF RESTORATIVE JUSTICE

In this section we explore the extent to which facilitation practice improved over the lifetime of our research project, taking the interim study data as the baseline.

1. Baseline Data: Interim Study Findings on the Quality of the Facilitation

In the interim study our main conclusion was that only two of the 23 cases we observed merited the label of restorative justice in that they adhered closely to the Thames Valley model and were therefore restorative in nature. Each of the other cases involved major deviations from the Thames Valley Police model. In particular, facilitators tended to dominate the exchanges which took place (accounting, on average, for half of all the words spoken) and some participants, notably offenders' supporters, were side-lined. However, the practices we observed were in most cases significantly different from old-style cautioning in that they included at least some commitment to broader community involvement, procedural fairness, and the use of a coherent criminological theory.

When police officers dominated the substantive discussion itself the influence of wider policing understandings and processes could plainly be seen. In the worst cases, more fully documented elsewhere (Young, 2001), we saw instances of facilitators re-investigating the offence, seeking admissions to prior offending and asking questions that appeared to be attempts to gather useful criminal intelligence. In one case the facilitator even encouraged a young offender to act as a low-level police informant in future. More generally, and more frequently observed, was the tendency for the facilitator to behave as if the offender had to account to him or her personally with the other participants reduced to little more than passive observers. In such instances the script was often abandoned and replaced by detailed investigation of the minutiae of the offence, as in the following exchange:

> F: So you took something, you took this [item stolen], whereabouts did you put it?
> O: Erm . . .
> F: Where did you hide it?
> O: In my waist.
> F: What inside your coat, or your . . .
> O: Yeah.
> F: What were you wearing at the time?
> O: I was wearing this white jacket . . .
> F: Yeah.
> O: . . . I dunno, and my Nike trousers I think, I don't remember.

F: Mmm, so you just hid it in your waist, is it an elasticated waist or something?
O: Yeah.
F: Yeah, so that kept it in place did it?

And so it continued. It was not clear why some facilitators were so keen to find out exactly how offenders had 'secreted' stolen items on their person, or exactly when criminal intent was formed, and who shared in it. We have no evidence to suggest that these facilitators were seeking to gather information that might be passed on to fellow officers (although it might look that way to the participants) and we think it more likely that the questioning style was partly a matter of habit (the style was that of a standard police interview) and partly an attempt to understand or categorise an offender's behaviour. However, regardless of intent, the experience for the cautioned person could not have been reintegrative.

Some facilitators' questions took the form of judgmental statements or moral lectures—and these occasionally carried the implication that the offender was perceived to be someone persistently offending or at risk of becoming such a person. Here are two examples, the first taken from a case involving an offender receiving a second caution:

F: I'm surprised that you've got another caution. This is a different kind of offence, and it's some ten months later that it's been committed. But nevertheless it's two offences in the space of a year. It just seems such a shame if you're going to put your future in jeopardy. So that's really why you're here and not in court for this offence. I do have to say in the strongest terms really that it can't go on like this. And that a caution for a third time won't happen. Alright. So you really do need to stop and think. Whether . . . is there any kind of reason there as to why you did it?
O: I don't know why.

Later in the caution the facilitator admitted that he suspected that the offender had committed many previous offences. The second example is drawn from a case involving someone detected for a criminal offence for the first time. The point in the conference reached is half way through the facilitator's questioning of the offender, and the facilitator's frustration at the offender's reluctance to give a fuller account of the offence is evident:

Whatever you say to me today, the end result is gonna be the same, you're gonna get a caution . . . unless obviously we stop it and go to court. So . . . regardless of what your thinking was . . . I mean it's done now . . . you've done it now . . . what we want to do at the end of this is put it behind you, so that when you go out there it's dealt with, and it's finished. I'm not trying to catch you out, or anything like that, or, get you to say 'oh yeah, we've done it loads of time before.' That's not the issue. The issue is, what you did on that day, was out of order, and, you know, I wouldn't be doing my job if I didn't make sure that at least I had an inkling that you weren't gonna do it again. That's what I'm asking you. I'm not asking you . . . you know there's no trick to it. You know I don't wanna catch you out. . . . But all I will say is that, you know, obviously if you're gonna try and be honest with yourself . . . what I'm asking you to do really is to be honest with yourselves about why you did it . . .

Finally, we saw many instances of facilitators over-stepping the remit of their position by extracting apologies from offenders in a fairly coercive way and, more generally, by pursuing their own reparative agenda rather than enabling a discussion by the key participants.

The interim study report fully documented all these problems and more in the space of some 200 pages. We hoped that this would leave the police in no doubt as to the scale and nature of the deviations from the script and in this we were not disappointed. Our 81 recommendations for change (all accepted) were designed above all else to encourage those running cautioning sessions to adopt a more even-handed and genuinely facilitative stance. In other words, we urged facilitators to be more neutral in their facilitation, rather than to align themselves with either the offender or the victim, or, of even more concern, the police organisation. Facilitators were also urged to set a clearer focus for these sessions and to adopt a reintegrative rather than deterrent approach to their work. Some facilitators read the report in its entirety, whereas others attended presentations at which the findings were summarised. All of those we observed in the full evaluation had received top-up training designed to reinforce the impact of the interim report and had also been issued with a reworded script which explicitly exhorted them not to pursue a policing agenda within the cautioning session. The question is, did any of this make a difference to police practice?

2. Measuring Improvement: The Full Evaluation Findings on the Quality of Facilitation

In some respects the full evaluation data suggested that facilitators remained the dominant figures that the interim study had showed them to be. As in the interim study, there were many instances of offenders, victims and their respective supporters saying proportionately very little, with facilitators contributing, on average, half of all the words spoken during a restorative session. However, closer analysis demonstrated some significant improvements in facilitation practice. Table 2 presents some direct comparisons between the interim study and the full evaluation in terms of non-compliance by facilitators with selected aspects of the script.

As can be seen, there generally was a much greater degree of fidelity to the script in the full evaluation. On the other hand, progress has clearly been patchy and there remains substantial room for improvement in facilitation practice. For example, the fact that 38 per cent of victims in the full evaluation were not asked what they would like to see come out of the restorative conference is a significant failing, even if it does represent a considerable improvement over the interim study.

We devised an overall measure of the quality of facilitation. This was based on allocating a score to six different aspects of facilitator behaviour, with the minimum overall score being six and the maximum 18. Facilitation scoring

Table 2: **Non-compliance with selected aspects of the script**

	Interim study	Full evaluation*
SETTING THE CONFERENCE FOCUS		
Failure by the facilitator to . . .		
. . . explain that the meeting will focus on the act and harm done	39%	20%
. . . say that 'we're not here to decide if [o] is a bad person	61%	31%
. . . check whether participants want to ask questions or clarify anything	83%	60%
FACILITATING THE OFFENDER'S STORY		
Failure by the facilitator to . . .		
. . . cue in story by saying 'it will help us to understand who's been affected'	74%	52%
. . . refrain from irrelevant or improper questioning	57%	26%
. . . refrain from improperly referring to the police version of the incident	43%	17%
FACILITATING REPARATION AND RESOLUTION		
Unjustified failure by the facilitator to ask the . . .		
. . . victim what they want to see come out of the conference	61%	38%**
. . . offender's supporter(s) what they want to see come out of the conference	59%	34%**

* Excludes one case where a minor tape recorder malfunction prevented definite judgements.

** Also excludes one case which was aborted (due to a denial of the offence by the 'offender').

between six and 10 was deemed to be least restorative, between 11 and 14 mid-restorative and between 15 and 18 most restorative (Hoyle, Young and Hill, 2002: appendix 3). As Table 3 shows, there was a substantial improvement in the quality of facilitation from the baseline established by the interim study. Thus, for example, 70 per cent of the interim study cases were adjudged least restorative as compared with 39 per cent of the full evaluation cases.

As noted earlier, there has undoubtedly been a research effect here. Following the publication of the interim study report we know that some facilitators became more wary of our presence and went through the motions in order to avoid further criticism. A few of the facilitators hinted at this or bluntly told us that 'when you've finished collecting your cases you should come and see how I really do them.'

Our comments on the performance of facilitators in the interim study created particular strains in our relationship with one of our three research areas. Facilitators at this site felt angry that their behaviours, although anonymised, had been described critically in our interim report. It was only following a tense meeting

Table 3: Improvements in quality of facilitation

Quality of facilitation	Interim study (n = 23)	Full evaluation (n = 54*)
Most Restorative	9%	35%
Mid Restorative	22%	26%
Least Restorative	70%	39%

* Two of the 56 cases in the full evaluation have been excluded from this table, one because it was aborted early on in the process and the other because it involved an informal cautioning session.

involving us, them, their line managers and the head of the Restorative Justice Consultancy that they consented to the research proceeding. However, it was not only in this area that we detected that some facilitators would be less inclined to follow force policy once we had left the field.

This is not to say that facilitators had not genuinely tried to change their behaviour because of our interim report, as we have evidence that some had. Furthermore, a couple of facilitators who were recruited in the period between our interim study and full evaluation were explicit in their appreciation of our research, in particular of the interim report, as one explained:

> Yeah. I re-read it [the report] . . . because I've come in straight, that's my little bible at the moment and I go away with that, read it, and [think] 'oh, I could try something like that'. It's helpful. . . . When I heard about the job, I came down here, had a look, what do I need to know, basically. 'Oh, you've got to know about the script, and here's a report on it.' So I took one away and I was flicking through. I read it once before the interview. . . . And then I re-read it because I knew you were coming today, and after my course it made a lot more sense then, and I've no doubt that in six months it will make even more sense. 'Oh yeah, I can see that now.' It's brilliant that you can pick it up. Like I'll come back with fears of what happened in a process . . . and then I'll feel better after reading the report. It's just a guide really. Nothing else I've been given goes into nearly as much depth, so yeah I'd definitely use that.

Overall, we helped Thames Valley Police, in the aggregate, to change facilitators' behaviour in the desired direction. The force cannot, however, assume that all of its facilitators have continued to behave in the way we observed them to do in the full evaluation. Rather, it could be assumed that some of them have not, and that the gap between theory and practice has widened since we finished collecting our cases.

We tested whether cases that run according to script are associated with more positive outcomes than those where facilitators run the session more in line with their own instinctive feel for what is appropriate. We found that the better outcomes tended to result from the cases where the facilitator adhered reasonably closely to the script (Hoyle, Young and Hill: 2002). For example, Table 4 shows that whilst the majority of participants we interviewed felt that the meetings had been

Table 4: Interview based analysis on the relationship between quality process and positive outcomes

Outcome variable	Proportion of interviewees from the *most restorative* cautions saying yes	Proportion of interviewees from the *least restorative* cautions saying yes
Did the meeting help the offender to understand the effects of his behaviour?	80%	56%
Did participants think that the meeting was facilitated well?	71%	54%

run well and had achieved one of their main aims, they were more likely to feel positive if they had experienced one of the most restorative meetings as compared to the least.

The results of this study have thus provided a new incentive for Thames Valley Police to intensify the process of securing proper implementation of its model. If the police continue to facilitate restorative justice sessions, greater use of the scripted approach must be secured. Whilst following a script without a decent grasp of the restorative model can result in problems when deviations from the script are necessary, unnecessary deviations from the script are the greater evil. The script is not just a collection of ritualistic phrases, but rather expresses restorative justice thinking on how to structure an encounter between the stakeholders to an offence so that the chances of a restorative process and outcome are maximised. When used wisely it tends to reinforce a facilitator's understanding of restorative justice and his or her confidence in the model's effectiveness. When abandoned in favour of a more ad lib approach, a policing agenda can quickly come to the fore and threaten the legitimacy of the process.

IV. CONCLUSION

Police-led restorative justice has some clear advantages over other types of initiatives. Thames Valley Police have not had to face the all too typical struggle of stand-alone initiatives *for* referrals and funding and *against* marginalisation. As we have argued, restorative cautioning is part of mainstream criminal justice and a transformation of cautioning practices has been effected which is remarkable in its scope and intensity. On the down side a stand-alone initiative would have faced far fewer problems of facilitators bringing their existing professional baggage to their restorative work. Nor would it have had to manage the tension created by role conflict of the kind now evident in Thames Valley Police. Police officers are still responsible for enforcing the law through procedures that often stigmatise, and they frequently engage in practices which infringe the rights of suspects or inflict social discipline upon them (Sanders and Young, 2000: chs 2–6). To expect the police against this backdrop to be able to facilitate a restorative encounter in a fair, neutral and effective manner is to ask a lot.

The argument could be made that the expectation is simply unrealistic until the nature of policing itself is reformed. But this comes dangerously close to saying that we cannot change anything until we have changed everything. Our own position is that it is necessary to recognise the enormity of the task the police have undertaken and to argue the case for keeping in focus the need for wider structural reforms of policing. Thames Valley Police itself quite explicitly intended that its restorative cautioning initiative would have a beneficial impact on its organisational culture. Moreover, it has recognised that it would be hypocritical to introduce restorative justice processes as a way of encouraging offenders to take responsibility for harm caused whilst not encouraging its officers to do likewise when well-founded complaints are made against them by suspects, fellow officers and members of the public. Thus it is now seeking to move its complaints and discipline procedures in a restorative direction.

The relationship between ourselves and Thames Valley Police remains a productive one. It is not an easy relationship and nor should it be. This police service is at the forefront of attempts to introduce restorative justice values throughout the criminal justice system and beyond. Research findings that are less than glowing are bound to make life awkward for the police when operating on the political stage. But Thames Valley Police officers have indicated repeatedly that they understand that our findings (whether positive or negative) would not be credible if we were seen as having lost our independence or critical edge. Perhaps the best evidence we have of the determination of this police service to learn from research and improve its practice is that it has welcomed a new two year study by us of its use of restorative justice in the police complaints and discipline system.

For our part, we would have been unwilling to invest so much of our professional lives in working with Thames Valley Police were it not for the fact that we are broadly sympathetic to restorative values. Research projects are not all equally attractive. A research officer we know was engaged recently in a study of drug testing which involved him standing outside of a police station toilet collecting samples from suspects. Whilst we might be cajoled into evaluating such a programme we could not be persuaded to try to help the police improve their practices of extracting urine from suspects. The action-research design of our existing research thus reveals us to be closet supporters of restorative justice values. That design also, of course, betokens a degree of scepticism about the ability of the police to implement restorative justice successfully. We think they need the assistance of academics in this difficult endeavour but that this help has to take a critical form and cannot be expected to be entirely effective. We have thus thought it right here to enter a word of caution, or 8,869 words of caution to be precise.

REFERENCES

Bennett, T (1996) 'Problem-Solving Policing and Crime Prevention: an assessment of the role of the police in preventing crime' in T Bennett (ed), *Preventing Crime and Disorder: Targeting Strategies and Responsibilities* (Cambridge, The Institute of Criminology, University of Cambridge).

Chan, J 'Changing Police Culture' (1996) 36(1) *British Journal of Criminology* 109–34.

Crawford, A (1996) 'Alternatives to Prosecution: Access to, or Exits from, Criminal Justice?' in R Young and D Wall (eds), *Access to Criminal Justice* (Blackstone Press, London).

Daly, K and Kitcher, J 'The R(evolution) of Restorative Justice through Researcher-Practitioner Partnerships' (1998) 2(1) *Ethics and Justice*. Online:www.ethics-justice.org/v2n1

Dignan, J and Marsh, P (2001) 'Restorative Justice and Family Group Conferences in England: current state and future prospects' in A Morris and G Maxwell (eds), *Restorative Justice for Juveniles* (Hart Publishing, Oxford).

Evans, R (1993) *The Conduct of Police Interviews with Juveniles*, Royal Commission on Criminal Justice Research Study No 8 (HMSO, London).

Garland, D (2001) *The Culture of Control* (Oxford University Press, Oxford).

Hollin, C (1995) 'The Meaning and Implications of "Programme Integrity"', in J McGuire (ed), *What Works: Reducing Reoffending* (John Wiley, Chichester).

Hoyle, C, Young, R, and Hill, R (2002) *Proceed with Caution: An Evaluation of the Thames Valley Police Initiative in Restorative Cautioning* (Joseph Rowntree Foundation, York).

Johnson, K et al (2001) *Cautions, Court Proceedings and Sentencing, England and Wales, 2000* (Home Office, London).

Lee, M (1998) *Youth, Crime, and Police Work* (Macmillan, Basingstoke).

Leng, R, Taylor, R, and Wasik, M (1998) *Blackstone's Guide to the Crime and Disorder Act 1998* (Blackstone Press, London).

Maguire, M 'Policing by Risks and Targets: Some Dimensions and Indications of Intelligence-Led Crime Control' (2000) 9(4) *Policing and Society* 315–36.

Moore, D with Forsythe, L (1995) *A New Approach to Juvenile Justice: An Evaluation of Family Conferencing in Wagga Wagga* (Centre for Rural Social Research, Charles Sturt University).

Povey, D et al (2001) *Recorded Crime, England and Wales, 12 Months to September 2000*, Statistical Bulletin 1/01 (Home Office, London).

Sanders, A and Young, R (2000) *Criminal Justice* 2nd edn (Butterworths, London).

Soothill, K, Francis, B and Sanderson, B (1997) 'A Cautionary Tale: The Sex Offenders Act 1997, The Police and Cautions' *Criminal Law Review* 482.

Wilcox, A, Hoyle, C, and Young, R (2001) *Interim Report for the Youth Justice Board on the National Evaluation of Restorative Justice Projects*, unpublished report (Centre for Criminological Research, Oxford).

Young, R (2001) 'Just Cops doing 'Shameful' Business?: Police-led Restorative Justice and the Lessons of Research' in A Morris and G Maxwell (eds), *Restorative Justice for Juveniles* (Hart Publishing, Oxford).

Young, R and Goold, B (1999) 'Restorative Police Cautioning in Aylesbury—From Degrading to Reintegrative Shaming Ceremonies?' *Criminal Law Review* 126.

15

Evaluating Restorative Justice Practices

Leena Kurki

Restorative justice responses to crime promote inclusive dialogue, acceptance of responsibility, repair of harm, and the rebuilding of relations among victims, offenders, and communities. Restorative practices have evolved from victim-offender mediation to family group conferencing, circle processes, and various types of citizen panels. They all share a common element: the transfer of some decision-making authority from government to victims and offenders, their family, friends, and other supporters, and community members.

A recent development has been in thinking about the role of local residents and communities. It is increasingly common to identify community participation as an essential element of restorative justice (eg Bazemore, 1997; Pranis, 1997). The premise is that communities are strengthened when people have more opportunities to interact, to create personalised relationships, to establish support networks, and to exercise informal social control (eg Bazemore, 2000, 2001).

Research shows that restorative justice practices are, by a number of important criteria, successful. Participants tend to be pleased with processes and outcomes, agreements on offenders' responsibilities are often reached, and reparation plans are carried out by offenders. However, there are definite limits upon the scope, quality, and results of existing research. Although we know that face-to-face meetings are more humane and emotionally intensive than trials dominated by legal professionals (Sherman et al 1998; Strang et al 1999), there is still little evidence that the experience yields any long-term effects on offenders or communities. Evaluations so far have focused on individual-level outcomes and have often used measures that are typical in analysing results of conventional criminal justice programmes. Short-term satisfaction issues have dominated evaluation efforts and it has proved difficult to develop more innovative measures that would better capture the values and goals of restorative justice.

It is too early to promise that restorative justice initiatives reduce crime, prevent offending, or build better communities. However, the limited results to date probably reflect more on the inadequacies in implementation and evaluation research than the non-feasibility of restorative justice principles and goals.

This chapter discusses only those restorative justice practices that respond to crime. Restorative approaches are increasingly used in other than crime-related conflicts, for example, problems in schools (bullying, truancy), in work (management, labour disputes, sexual harassment), and within families (child welfare, family violence). Also excluded are practices lacking the essential criteria for restorative justice: inclusive dialogue in face-to-face meetings, consensus decision-making, agreement on offenders' responsibilities, and commitment to restorative values. Thus, this chapter does not discuss restitution, community service, or other intermediate sanctions as such, since they are typically ordered by a court. Neither will I discuss many community-based responses that are often grouped under 'community justice'. These typically redefine the role and operations of criminal justice agencies, but do not give decision-making authority to those directly affected by crime (see Kurki, 2000 for the distinction between community justice and restorative justice).

This chapter is organised in the following way. Section I describes what we currently know about the outcomes of restorative justice practices. Section II identifies new areas for research. Section III introduces the concept of social capital and discusses community-level outcomes. Section IV presents brief concluding remarks.

I. WHAT WE KNOW NOW

Current evaluations on restorative justice practices address the following general issues: participant satisfaction, procedural justice, 'restorativeness' (restorative quality), and outcomes. Participant satisfaction typically includes general measures of being satisfied with the whole restorative programme experience (eg overall satisfaction, recommending the process to others, choosing to participate again). Procedural justice measures tend to be more detailed and refer to different aspects of fairness: respectful and fair treatment by others, fairness of the agreement, impartiality of the facilitator, and the like. Measures of restorativeness are beginning to emerge and include genuine remorse, consensus, apology, expression of feelings, and sense of reintegration. Outcome measures so far have focused on the effects on victims and offenders—reduced anger and fear regarding the victim and reduced offending or improved quality of life for the offender. Community-level outcomes are yet to be defined and measured.

Most evaluations concern victim-offender mediation and family-group conferencing, which will also be the main focus of this chapter. The literature on circle processes and citizen panels is today still descriptive and provides only anecdotal accounts of their success.

A. Victim-Offender Mediation

Victim-offender mediation is the most common form of restorative practices. Crime victims and offenders meet with trained mediators to develop a reparative plan, although reaching an agreement is often seen as secondary to emotional healing and growth. Victims consistently report that the most important element of mediation is to be able to talk to the offender and to express their feelings. Similarly, offenders report that being able to explain what happened is often more important than the restitution agreement (eg Umbreit, 1994; Umbreit, 1995; Umbreit and Warner Roberts, 1996).

If cases are mediated, there is no question about short-term success: most victims and offenders are satisfied with the process and outcomes, an agreement is reached in practically all cases, and the vast majority of restorative plans are completed by offenders. This is true for earlier as well as more recent studies, both juvenile and adult programmes, and in US and international evaluations. Satisfaction, agreement, and completion rates typically vary between 75 and 100 per cent. For example, according to a phone survey of 116 victim-offender mediation programmes in the United States, on average, 87 per cent of cases resulted in an agreement and 99 per cent of agreements were completed (Umbreit and Greenwood, 2000). A meta-analysis of 35 restorative justice initiatives (mostly victim-offender mediation) revealed that they effectively increased both victim and offender satisfaction (Latimer, Dowden and Muise, 2001).

Several studies show that mediation can significantly reduce victims' anger, anxiety, fear of re-victimisation by the same offender, and fear of crime in general. For example, a combined evaluation of four Canadian programmes found that 11 per cent of victims feared re-victimisation by the same offender after mediation, compared with 31 per cent of victims who were referred but did not participate in mediation (Umbreit, 1995). Similarly, 16 per cent of victims were afraid of further victimisation in two English mediation programmes (compared with 33 per cent of victims who did not participate) (Umbreit and Warner Roberts, 1996). In four US juvenile programmes, 67 per cent of victims were upset about crime before and 49 per cent after mediation; 23 per cent were afraid of re-victimisation before and 10 per cent after mediation (Umbreit and Coates, 1993; Umbreit, 1994). Davis, Tichane, and Grayson (1980) report that victims in the mediation group were less likely to fear revenge (21 per cent) than victims in a randomly-assigned control group (40 per cent). They were also less angry at the offenders (23 per cent vs 48 per cent).

Recently, mediation programmes' effects on recidivism have received increased attention. While many agree that the results still are inconclusive and do not necessarily show reductions in reoffending (eg Miers et al 2001; Umbreit, Coates and Vos, 2001a, 2001b), others disagree (eg Braithwaite, 2002; Latimer, Dowden and Muise, 2001; Nugent et al 2001). It seems that evaluations on individual programmes seldom find statistically significant decreases in recidivism. However, when original data from individual studies are combined (Nugent et al 2001) or statistical meta-analyses conducted (Latimer, Dowden and Muise, 2001), results show significant decline in future offending.

The following evaluations failed to detect significant effects on reoffending. Davis, Tichane and Grayson (1980) employed random sampling in their evaluation of the Brooklyn Dispute Resolution Center (only crimes against acquaintances were mediated, most cases were felonies, and most cases involved immediate family members or lovers). During a four-month follow-up period, hostility levels and the number of conflicts between disputants declined, but there was no difference between the mediation and the court group. Police were called to resolve new conflicts in 12 per cent of mediation cases and 13 per cent of court cases. New arrests were equally unlikely in both groups (four per cent).

Roy (1993) compared mediation to court-ordered restitution, and found that in both programmes recidivism rates were about 27 per cent for first-time juvenile offenders and 42 per cent for repeat juvenile offenders during a two-year follow-up period. Niemeyer and Shichor (1996) report that 28 per cent of the mediation group and 24 per cent of the control group (juveniles who were referred to mediation but did not participate) committed new crimes within two years. Umbreit's (1994; Umbreit and Coates, 1993) original analysis of four US juvenile programmes did not reveal significant differences in reoffending between the mediation and the control group within one year (18 per cent vs 27 per cent). A recent evaluation of six English restorative justice schemes (Miers et al 2001) found that one of them had effects on future offending. In an adult programme that handled also serious crimes, 44 per cent of participants were convicted within two years, compared with 56 per cent of the control group. While the risk categories of participants became higher, differences in recidivism rates became smaller. The programme participants had also fewer reconvictions per offender and for less serious crimes.

Evaluations by Nugent and Paddock (1995, 1996) and Wiinamaki (1997, cited in Nugent et al 2001) are exceptional not only because they found reductions in recidivism, but also because they controlled for many factors that correlate with crime, such as age, gender, prior offences, family structure, and number of siblings. While Wiinamaki's goal was to replicate Nugent and Paddock's study, findings in both were similar: participation in juvenile mediation reduced reoffending by 38 per cent within one-year follow-up period.

Latimer, Dowden and Muise (2001) conducted a meta-analysis of 27 victim-offender mediation programmes and 8 family group conferencing programmes (10 published and 12 unpublished sources). Recidivism was measured in 32 of the 35 initiatives. According to the meta-analysis, more than two-thirds of the programmes had a positive effect size, meaning that they were able to lower reoffending. The 32 programmes together reduced offender recidivism by 7 per cent. However, the analysis did not control for any individual characteristics of offenders.

Nugent et al (2001) combined data from four victim-offender mediation studies—two of which had reported significant reductions in reoffending (Nugent and Paddock, 1996; Wiinamaki, 1997) while two had not (Umbreit, 1994; Niemeyer and Shichor, 1996). In the combined sample of 1,298 juveniles, the recidivism rate was 19 per cent for those who participated in mediation and 28 per cent for those who went through the traditional juvenile justice process. The juveniles who participated in mediation were 40 per cent less likely to reoffend than the other juveniles. Again, the combined analysis did not control for individual characteristics of offenders.

Most of the studies on the effects of victim-offender mediation share similar methodological problems. First, positive outcomes may be the result of self-selection effects. If control groups are used in the study design, they are usually matched comparison groups and only rarely are based on random assignments. It is not uncommon to find that 40 to 50 per cent of cases that are initially referred to programmes are never mediated because the victim or the offender refused to participate or they could not be contacted (eg Gehm, 1990; Niemeyer and Shichor, 1996; Umbreit, 1995). Therefore, it is possible that only those cases were mediated in which both the victim and the offender had a positive attitude toward mediation prior to their participation. Secondly, self-selection biases are even worse when control groups are composed of those who were referred to victim-offender mediation but did not participate. Thirdly, it is often unclear what the evaluated programme was supposed to do and whether this happened in practice. Cases or programmes where the victim and offender never actually met personally are sometimes included in studies.

Fourthly, evaluations seldom discuss outcome differences that may be based on demographic characteristics, for example, gender, race, and ethnic origin. Neither do they control for other characteristics that might explain findings, such as age, criminal history, seriousness of the offence, socio-economic status, or family structure in the case of reoffending.

Finally, there is no knowledge of the quality of restorative justice in victim-offender mediation programmes or how the restorative quality may be related to outcomes. The vast majority of evaluations are based on self-administered questionnaires or interviews. There have been no structured observations on the essential elements of restorative justice: genuine remorse, apology, consensus, expression of feelings, better understanding of each other, and the like.

B. Family Group Conferencing

Compared to victim-offender mediation, family group conferencing involves a broader range of people, and family members and other supporters may take collective responsibility over the offender to ensure the fulfilment of his or her agreement. Conferencing relies more on official agencies, and police, probation, or social officers often organise and facilitate conferences.

1. Background

Family group conferencing was introduced in 1989 in New Zealand as part of a new juvenile justice model that shares basic principles with restorative justice. By the mid-1990s, family group conferences were adopted in every state and territory of Australia. Theoretical frameworks, objectives, bureaucratic positioning, and severity of offences vary by jurisdiction. In New Zealand and Western Australia, cultural sensitivity and involvement of Maori and Aboriginal people were important concerns (Maxwell and Morris, 1993); in South Australia, conferencing is used statewide as a component of the juvenile justice system (Wundersitz, 1994); in Wagga Wagga, New South Wales, conferences were originally part of a police diversion programme and organised and facilitated by police officers (Moore and O'Connell, 1994); and in Canberra (Australian Capital Territory), the Australian federal police set up a conferencing programme based on the Wagga Wagga model (Sherman et al 1998). The original Wagga Wagga and later the Canberra police conferencing model have strongly influenced family group conferencing in the United States, Canada, and England (Umbreit and Zehr, 1996; Jackson, 1998; Young and Hoyle, in this volume).

2. Satisfaction

The initial evaluation of family group conferencing in New Zealand raised concerns about the satisfaction and involvement of the victims and juveniles (Maxwell and Morris, 1993). Victims participated in 41 per cent of meetings; 51 per cent of victims who participated were pleased with the process and agreement, one-third felt better after conferencing, one-third felt worse; 34 per cent of juveniles felt involved in the conferencing process and only 9 per cent thought they were able to influence outcomes. Yet almost all juveniles and their parents (over 80 per cent) were satisfied with the outcomes. Since then, there have been changes in legislation, practices, and priorities that seek to increase rates of victim participation.

Evaluations of practices elsewhere show very high satisfaction rates for all conferencing participants. A study of the Wagga Wagga conferencing (police facilitated) reports that victim participation exceeded 90 percent, participants felt involved in the process and satisfied with the outcomes, and an agreement was reached in 95 per cent of conferences and then completed in 95 per cent of cases (Moore, 1995). In twelve Minnesota sites (police facilitated), over 90 per cent of victims, juveniles, and support persons were satisfied with the facilitator, progress, and outcomes (Fercello and Umbreit, 1998). In four Queensland pilot sites (not facilitated by police), more than 97 per cent of participants were pleased with conference agreements, felt that they had had a voice in the conference, and had *not* been pushed into things (Hayes, Prenzler and Wortley, 1998). Similar results were found in New South Wales (Trimboli, 2000) and Western Australia (Cant and Downie, 1998) (not facilitated by police).

The following sections discuss in more detail four major research projects on family group conferencing. They all were exceptional in using advanced research methods or innovative measures.

3. Bethlehem, Pennsylvania Police Family Group Conferencing

Evaluation of this police-facilitated conferencing was the first completed study to employ random assignment and to measure recidivism (McCold and Wachtel,

1998). Eligibility was limited to first-time juvenile offenders who were arrested for misdemeanour or summary offences. Since participation in conferencing was voluntary, three different groups of juveniles emerged: those randomly assigned to formal adjudication, those randomly assigned to conferencing who participated, and those randomly assigned to conferencing who refused to participate. Conferences were conducted only in 42 per cent of the referred cases because offenders or victims declined to participate. Therefore, random assignment did not eliminate the problem of selection bias.

The Bethlehem study reports that over 90 per cent of victims, offenders, and offenders' parents would recommend conferencing to others, would choose conferencing again, found meeting with the other parties helpful, felt they were treated fairly, and thought that the tone of the conference was friendly. Victims felt their opinion was adequately considered (94 per cent), offenders developed a positive attitude toward the victim (80 per cent), had a better understanding of how their behaviour had affected the victim (94 per cent), and found conferencing a more humane response to crime (92 per cent) (McCold and Wachtel, 1998).

The Bethlehem study followed recidivism for a twelve-month period from the arrest that led to adjudication or conferencing. Like the majority of victim-offender mediation evaluations, it concluded that conferencing had no independent influence on reoffending. The difference in recidivism between the conference group and control groups was more a function of the offender's positive attitude toward conferencing than conferencing itself (McCold and Wachtel, 1998). The study reports that typical American police officers were able to conduct conferences in conformity with restorative justice and due process principles, if given adequate training and supervision. However, the exposure of a few officers to restorative justice principles and community involvement did not change overall police attitudes, organisational culture, or role perceptions in the Bethlehem police department.

4. Indianapolis Juvenile Restorative Justice Experiment

An evaluation of restorative conferencing in Indianapolis found both high satisfaction levels and lower offending rates (McGarrell et al 2000). The project accepts very young juveniles (14 years or younger) who have no prior convictions or arrests for serious violent crime. Juveniles were randomly assigned to restorative conferencing (N = 232) or to other court-ordered diversion programmes (including victim-offender mediation, N = 226). Most cases involved shoplifting (36 per cent), followed by criminal mischief (26 per cent), assault (25 per cent), theft (16 per cent), and disorderly conduct (14 per cent). Conferences were facilitated by police officers, prosecutors, restorative justice co-ordinator, or civilian volunteers.

Results showed that victims were the most satisfied with conferencing. More than 95 per cent would have recommended conferencing to others, were involved in the conference, and felt treated with respect. The same indicators were relatively high for the young persons and their parents, ranging from little less than

80 per cent to little over 90 per cent. While no victim felt pushed around in the conference, 20 per cent of the juveniles and 15 per cent of their parents felt this way (McGarrell et al 2000).

The Indianapolis study generated findings that are rare for restorative justice evaluations—a reduction in reoffending and a strong sense of reintegration at the conference. For those who successfully completed the assigned programme, recidivism rates at six months (measured as new arrests) were 12.3 per cent for the restorative conference group and 22.7 per cent for the control group (a statistically significant 46 per cent reduction). At twelve months, the difference had declined and recidivism rates were higher: 30.8 per cent for the conference group and 41.2 per cent for the control group (a statistically significant 25 per cent reduction).

Fifteen trained observers attended 182 Indianapolis conferences. They reported that about 75 per cent of the young offenders expressed remorse and in 80 per cent of the conferences the victim appeared to forgive them. While all participants displayed respect toward the young offenders, almost 35 per cent of the offenders were neutral or disrespectful toward the victim. Observers believed that in more than 75 per cent of the conferences there was a strong sense of reintegration (McGarrell et al 2000). This finding is exceptional. For example, less than 10 per cent of observed conferences in an English police-facilitated initiative were reported to be restorative (see Young and Hoyle in this volume.)

5. South Australia Juvenile Justice (SAJJ) Conferencing

Evaluation of SAJJ (not facilitated by police) included several data collection methods: observations of 89 conferences in 1998, surveys for the conference co-ordinators and police officers, and interviews with victims and offenders in 1998 and 1999 (Daly, 1998, 2001). Since the results are discussed in detail elsewhere (see Daly in this volume), only some general remarks are made here.

In short, SAJJ achieved high rates of victim participation and strong sense of procedural justice among participants, but lower understanding of the conferencing process and the role of different people and less evidence of the restorative nature of the process. Victims participated in 74 per cent of conferences. More than 90 per cent of victims and offenders felt that they had been treated fairly by the co-ordinator and the police officer, that they had been treated in a respectful manner in general, and that the co-ordinator had been impartial and fair to everyone. At the same time, 40 to 60 per cent of victims and offenders said they did not have information about what was expected from them or what would happen at the conference. Also, only about 30 per cent of the young persons said that it was their own choice to participate in the conference, while 43 per cent said it was not. Observers reported positive communication between the victim and offender in 34 per cent of conferences, a spontaneous apology by 40 per cent of offenders, and genuine consensus on the agreement in 60 per cent of conferences (Daly, in this volume).

Despite the shortcomings on the restorative quality, SAJJ found positive effects on victims and offenders. In the 1999 interviews, over 60 per cent of victims said they had put the offence behind them and fully recovered. The proportion of victims who felt angry toward the offender decreased from 75 per cent before the conference to 44 per cent immediately after the conference to 39 per cent a year later. Similarly, the proportion of victims who were afraid of the offender dropped from 40 per cent to 25 per cent and to 18 per cent a year later (Daly, in this volume).

Almost 60 per cent of the juveniles who participated in SAJJ had a criminal history. In the eight to twelve months that followed the conference, 40 per cent of the young persons had committed one or more offences. Having controlled for the influence of several predictors of reoffending, two restorative aspects of conferences remained significantly related to reduced recidivism. If the young people expressed remorse in the conference and if the agreement was reached by genuine consensus, they were less likely to reoffend. Other restorative aspects, such as having the victim present or the expression of emotions, did not have similar effects (see Hayes and Daly, 2002).

A similar relationship between 'restorativeness' and reoffending was found by Maxwell and Morris (1999). In 1996–1997, they interviewed juveniles and their parents who had participated in New Zealand conferences during 1990–1991. Questions focused on the young person's early childhood experience, the conference experience, and life events after the conference. Several conference features were related to reduced reoffending: victim presence, an apology by the young person, involvement of the young person in decision-making, expression of remorse, and agreement of the conference outcome.

6. Canberra Reintegrative Shaming Experiments (RISE)

RISE evaluates family group conferencing ('diversionary conferencing') by the Australian federal police in Canberra (police-facilitated). The research team expects the RISE project to work better than the current criminal justice system in three different ways: conferences treat victims and offenders more fairly than courts, conferences lower recidivism rates, and conferences cost less money. Findings relating to the fairness of conferencing (Sherman et al 1998; Strang et al 1999) and recidivism (Sherman, Strang and Woods, 2000) are available, but statistics concerning costs have yet to be compiled.

Fairness and client satisfaction were assessed by systematic observation and interviews with participants. The analysis consists of four different groups of cases: 'drunk driving' (any age), juvenile property crime with an individual victim (under eighteen years; 'property crime'), juvenile shoplifting from stores (under eighteen years; 'shoplifting'), and 'violent crime' (under thirty years). Offenders in each group were randomly assigned to conferencing or courts (Sherman et al 1998). Only brief summaries of some of the results are possible here.

RISE highlights the fundamental difference between restorative justice and traditional criminal justice approaches: face-to-face meetings in a setting where everyone has equal freedom to talk are more humane and emotionally intensive than structured court sessions dominated by legal professionals. Systematic observations showed that emotions or any kind of shaming, whether reintegrative or stigmatising, are rare in court where legal professionals are the main players. In conferences lay participants are the main actors, and the atmosphere is quite different.

In general, victims and offenders were pleased with conferencing and its outcomes (Strang et al 1999). However, there were clear differences between the four categories of crime. For example, victims of violent crime (89.7 per cent present at conference) were less satisfied with conferencing than were victims of property crime (72.9 per cent present at conference). About 97 per cent of property crime victims and 77 per cent of violent crime victims thought that the conference had been fair. Few property crime victims felt too intimidated to speak, but 16 per cent of violent crime victims reported they felt agitated. While 91 per cent of property crime victims thought that conferences took account of their opinions in the decision, only 69 per cent of violent crime victims thought so. However, all victims were less angry with the offender after conferences; the percentage of victims being angry fell from 60 to 23 per cent in the property crime group and from 69 to 31 per cent in the violent crime group (Strang et al 1999).

The drunk-driving group composed primarily of adults was the most satisfied (generally over 90 per cent) and the juvenile property offender group the least satisfied with conferencing. Only 56 per cent of these juveniles thought they had had some control over the outcome, 31 per cent felt too intimidated to speak, and only two out of 25 procedural justice measures were significantly higher in the conference group than in the court group. It is also worrying that about one-third of the violent offenders thought they had been coerced by others in conferences and about one quarter felt they had been compelled to do things they did not agree with. Unfortunately, we do not know more about the offenders who felt intimidated or powerless in Canberra conferences. Although the evaluation provides details regarding victims and offenders (for example, by gender, ethnic origin, place of birth, marital status, and employment) none of these variables are reported with the results (Strang et al 1999).

The RISE project found that perceptions of consistency and equal treatment were higher in the conferencing groups than in the court groups regardless of the type of offender. For example, 71 per cent of juvenile property offenders thought that 'offenders with same offence were treated the same' in conferencing. About 50 per cent thought that this was the case in court (see Strang et al 1999: p 80).

Second-wave interviews with offenders two years after they entered the RISE study investigated the long-term effects. The measures included 19 life events such as school attendance or graduation, unemployment, homelessness, divorce, financial problems, or serious troubles with others. Results showed few differences between the conference groups and court groups. None of the measures was statistically significant for juvenile property offenders. Two measures were significant in the impaired driving group ('dropped out of school' and 'laid off from work') and shoplifting group ('financial pressure' and 'trouble with others') and one in the violent crime group ('changed jobs') (Strang et al 1999).

Recidivism was measured for each conference and court group before and after participation, for a twelve-month period from assignment to the programme (Sherman, Strang and Woods, 2000). Conferencing reduced recidivism rates for one category of offenders, juveniles who committed violent crimes. The rate of reoffending fell by 49 per cent for the conferencing group and by 11 per cent for the court group, a net reduction of 38 per cent. However, this difference was reported as statistically significant at a higher error-level (0.16) than is conventional. There were no differences in offending rates for the property crime and shoplifting groups, while the rate actually increased very slightly for the drunk drivers who participated in conferencing, by 4 offences per 100 offenders per year (again, not statistically significant as reported at the 0.13 level). No other controlled factors, such as race, gender, number of prior offences, length of criminal career, or time at risk after RISE, explained the differences.

Clearly, the evaluation of conferences is a complex issue and results vary by and within individual programmes. Some initiatives show success in achieving restorative quality while others do not. Certain offenders do not commit further crimes while others do. Young offenders may feel that they were coerced to participate or did not have input on the agreement, yet may still be satisfied with the overall experience. There is a fundamental problem in drawing general conclusions from individual evaluations: programmes understand restorative justice in different ways, deal with different types of crimes, implement different interventions, and spend more or less time for preparing participants for the conference (see Latimer, Dowden and Moise, 2001; Miers et al 2001).

C. Circles

Circles take many forms and are used in various settings ranging from schools and workplaces to the criminal justice system. As a response to crime, sentencing circles involve the victim and the offender and their supporters, but also key community members, and are open to everyone in the community. While the immediate goal is to give voice to community members and to reach an agreement, the larger goal is to create trust and relationships that in the long run build and empower communities.

However, to date, there is no evidence whether these broader goals can be attained. Besides descriptive literature and anecdotal examples of success, there have been very few attempts to evaluate circle processes. One of them includes interviews with individuals who participated in the Milaca and Princeton (Minnesota) sentencing circles (Campbell, 1999). Five out of six offenders were in general satisfied with the experience. Community members helped them in many concrete ways and trusted them. However, some offenders felt that they could not express themselves freely or question the fairness of the circle. Experience from the Milaca and Princeton circles suggests that the positive effects may be much stronger on community members than on offenders. When community members were interviewed, many reported that the greatest impact of the circle process had been on themselves. They believed that their personal benefit and development far exceeded the effects on offenders (Campbell, 1999: p 18).

A qualitative analysis of South Saint Paul (Minnesota) circles describes their implementation in the community, in two elementary schools, and in a junior high school (Coates, Umbreit and Vos, 2000). The community circles handled four criminal cases in 1997–1998, 21 cases in 1999, and eight cases in 2000 through June. Of the 29 cases in 1999 and 2000, one was a post-court felony, one was a probation revocation, two were pre-charge felonies, and the rest were pre-charge misdemeanours. The circles involved 57 offenders (6 adult, 51 juveniles), 84 victims (36 participating directly in circles), and 60 community members. Volunteer hours by community members were estimated as 840 in circles and 260 hours outside circles providing support and accountability for offenders.

Interviews with offenders and their family members (15), and victims and their family members (15) showed that more than two-thirds felt uneasy and nervous going into the circle. However, over three-quarters reported feeling comfortable speaking in the circle. All victims thought that the circle process had been fair, and only one victim thought that the outcome had been too lenient. All offenders thought that the process and the outcome had been fair, but some thought that the parents should not be required to take time off to participate in the process. Victims and offenders alike said that the feature they liked the most was the connection with people in the circle. The feature they liked the least was the time-consuming nature of the circle. All victims and offenders were ready to recommend the circle process for others (Coates, Umbreit and Vos, 2000).

Circle keepers participated in circles because they wanted to help people change and to improve their communities. They also found circles personally rewarding and satisfying. Not surprisingly, representatives of the criminal justice system were more reserved. Although they supported circles in general, there were doubts about the practicalities: time and labour required, criteria for eligibility, fairness, and equal treatment (Coates, Umbreit and Vos, 2000). One can only repeat what has been said time and again before: there is critical need for quality research on sentencing circles and their effects on individuals and communities (see Roberts and Roach, this volume for discussion of sentencing circles in the Canadian context).

D. Citizen Panels

Various types of citizen boards or panels are used in the United States and Canada to devise dispositions in minor criminal cases. Adult citizen panels adjudicate non-violent crimes in many US juvenile court jurisdictions (eg in

Denver, Colorado; Austin, Texas; Philadelphia, Pennsylvania); offenders appear before a small panel of fellow community members in several Canadian Aboriginal and non-Aboriginal communities (Clairmont, 1996; Green, 1997); local neighbourhoods have organised their own citizen conferencing in many US cities (eg Minneapolis, Minnesota) (Knapp, 1999); and reparative boards in Vermont develop conditions for probation (Sinkinson and Broderick, 1997; Walther and Perry, 1997).

Citizen panel initiatives often rely on both community justice and restorative justice rhetoric and principles. In fact, programmes may mostly handle victimless crimes that community residents feel are decreasing the quality of life in their neighbourhood, such as public urination and drinking, graffiti and prostitution. Naturally then, there are no direct victims present at panel meetings. However, victim participation rates tend to be low in other cases, too, and victims seldom attend meetings.

In Vermont, citizen boards are part of reparative probation in which a judge sentences the offender to probation with a suspended sentence, volunteer board members meet with the offender and the victim, and together they agree on a contract, which the offender agrees to carry out. Fulfilment of the contract is the only condition of probation. In 1998, reparative boards handled 1,200 criminal cases, more than one-third of the targeted probation caseload. By August 1999, 46 boards had processed more than 4,000 cases since the programme's inception in 1995. Currently, over 300 trained volunteers participate as board members or in assistant roles (victim liaison, community work service development, administrative assistant). Volunteers in assistant roles alone provided nearly 7,300 hours in 1998 (Karp and Walther, 2001).

About half of the offenders successfully completed reparative probation in 1998 and provided almost 12,000 community service hours. At the same time, only 15 per cent of victims (62 out of 424) participated in board meetings. A recidivism study of 157 offenders that completed reparative probation in 1996 showed a 8.2 per cent re-conviction rate in a six month period following probation termination. The rate was 11.6 per cent for comparable probationers who completed regular probation (Karp and Walther, 2001).

Karp (2002) observed and videotaped 53 reparative board hearings in 1998–1999. He analysed the role of community members in three main areas: creating common ground in the beginning of meetings, affirming the shared community norms, and confronting denial of responsibility by the offender. The study did not directly analyse the restorative quality of reparative probation, however, some remarks reveal that reparative boards may not achieve restorative justice in practice. According to Karp, offenders tend to passively accept any terms of agreement suggested by board members, since they recognise that any disagreement might be seen as uncooperative. 'It is generally in their interest to be polite and agree with board members at every turn' (Karp, 2002: p 76). Although the practices of boards vary, some have adopted the role of a citizen court where the offender is excused while the board negotiates appropriate conditions for an agreement.

Community conferencing in four Minneapolis neighbourhoods is another example of citizen panels. Conferences address 'quality of life' crimes, such as soliciting prostitution, public urination, or public consumption of alcohol. On average, conferences have eight participants: three community members, two facilitators, the offender, the offender supporter, and the victim or an interpreter. Knapp (1999) reports that over 90 per cent of participants were pleased with the facilitator, process, and outcome. However, offenders completed only 20 of the total 160 evaluation forms, and more than half of offenders did not take part in the evaluation. Community members reported that they felt more connected to the community after conferencing and were more aware of problem behaviours in their neighbourhood. But they did not think that crime rates had been reduced because of the programme, and nor did they establish relationships with offenders or see them after conferencing (see Knapp, 1999).

The restorative resolutions project in Manitoba, Canada is a community-based alternative to incarceration in which offenders, staff, and victims work together to develop sentencing recommendations for judges (Bonta, Rooney and Wallace-Capretta, 1998). The average sentence is probation of 28.5 months, supplemented with specified requirements of sentencing plans, which are more likely than regular probation to include restitution (56.4 per cent vs 24.9 per cent) and community service (96 per cent vs 13.8 per cent). Two major problems emerged during implementation, though. First, although the project staff managed to contact almost 85 per cent of victims, only 10 per cent of them (25) actually met with the offender. However, roughly 80 per cent of victims provided written impact statements and 79 victims received personal or written apologies. Second, nearly 20 per cent of offenders received a custodial sentence *before* the placement to the project—a net-widening problem found in other diversion programmes as well.

In order to measure recidivism, Bonta, Rooney and Wallace-Capretta (1998) created matched control groups of male prison inmates, female and male probationers, and female and male probationers who had either restitution or community service as a condition of probation. Compared with male prison inmates, the male offenders in restorative resolutions had significantly fewer violations (16.7 per cent vs 37 per cent) and slightly fewer convictions (6.7 per cent vs 16.7 per cent; this difference was not statistically significant). They also had significantly fewer supervision violations than probationers in general (16.7 per cent vs 48.6 per cent) or probationers with community service or restitution (14.1 per cent vs 56.3 per cent). According to the authors, the restorative resolutions project can be expected to reduce overall recidivism by 13 per cent (the inmate group) to 22 per cent (probationers with community service or restitution).

We know very little about the effects of citizen panels on individuals or communities. Initiatives typically identify both community justice and restorative justice as their underlying theories or philosophies. In practice, community justice aspects might prevail, and it is unclear how true these types of initiatives are to restorative justice values.

II. DIRECTIONS FOR FURTURE RESEARCH

It seems more and more important to focus resources and research on the restorative quality of initiatives. To what extent are restorative elements achieved? What are the restorative strengths and weaknesses of different types of initiatives? How is restorative quality related to positive outcomes and what are the specific elements that make the difference? Restorative quality may be critical for achieving long-term effects on offenders. There is also a danger that the current popularity of restorative justice will undermine the core values and principles. Many things are labelled 'restorative justice' and programmes that in their beginning were true to restorative justice values may lapse, over time, into mechanical sanctioning processes. This is another reason why evaluation on the restorative quality of programmes becomes increasingly important.

Variation in philosophy, eligibility, and practices among restorative initiatives complicates evaluation. It is difficult to compare results or to draw general conclusions from individual studies. Routines and treatment vary often even within the same programme. There has been little attention to these problems, which also question the value of conducting meta-analyses of restorative justice initiatives. In fact, more detailed research is needed—evaluations that take into account differences in offender characteristics, types of cases, programme components, and treatment of participants.

Restorative justice practices do not provide procedural safeguards that would be comparable to those provided in criminal trials. Offenders may have lawyers present in some initiatives, but typically the only right is to withdraw from the programme and instead to choose the regular criminal justice process. There are legitimate concerns about power-imbalances in face-to-face meetings—young offenders, for example, are more vulnerable, less equipped to represent themselves, and often lack good communication skills. Several studies demonstrate that young offenders can feel too intimidated to speak, may have little input on agreements, or do not willingly participate in the first place. We need more information on these juveniles and the dynamics of conferences.

Strict guidelines or protocols would contradict the essence of restorative justice—tailoring reparative agreements to the situation of the offender and the victim. However, some argue that the lack of guidelines leaves too much room for unequal or disproportionate outcomes. Although participants may perceive restorative justice practices as being fair, equal, and consistent (eg Strang et al 1999), it does not mean that this is true in reality. Sceptics of restorative justice are especially concerned about these issues, which have yet to be addressed in evaluation research.

It is increasingly common to find restorative justice programmes that are initiated and run by criminal justice agencies, whether by police, prosecution, or corrections. Restorative justice values have also been added to juvenile justice legislation in many countries. However, there has been little interest in examining whether the increased restorative justice activity has had any effect on the operational culture of the agencies or the role perceptions of individual officers.

Finally, we know too little about the critical question of whether restorative justice creates safer or better communities. When long-term community building and empowerment were introduced as new goals of restorative justice, research did not follow. Community-level issues are discussed in more detail below.

III. COMMUNITY-LEVEL OUTCOMES

Many restorative justice initiatives are based on volunteerism and significant numbers of community members participate in their operation. Similarly, an increasing number of ordinary people participate as victims and offenders, their family members, and other supporters. Many restorative justice advocates believe that when community members in these different roles are brought together, they develop new relationships. These relationships then continue to evolve and create other relationships and even whole networks, which then generate new activities or action with respect to other community matters. At the same time, individuals feel more connected to and care about their community (eg Bazemore, 2000, 2001; Pranis, 1997).

It is a challenge to conceptualise measures for this type of community change. Personal connections, support networks, collective monitoring, socialisation to shared values, and other processes through which community effects might operate are hard to define, identify, and document (see Presser and Van Voorhis, 2002). It may be useful to borrow concepts from other fields and state that restorative justice builds *social capital* among participants and within communities.

Social capital can be defined as the good embodied in the structure of relations and shared values among people, and is distinctive from human capital (individual skills, knowledge) and physical capital (material improvements) (eg Coleman, 1994; Portes, 1998; Putnam, 2000). When a community has social capital, people tend to do favours for each other. Social capital provides support through relationships, but also creates *informal social control.* Informal social control can be defined as residents' willingness to interfere and take action when community norms are violated. The promise of social capital and informal social control is rooted in connections that arise naturally and internally within the communities—in networks of relationships, which help to create, understand, and monitor community norms and values (Sampson, 1999).

Research has established the connection between collective social organisation and crime (eg Elliott et al 1996; Sampson, 1997; Sampson, Raudenbush and Earls, 1997; Sampson, Morenoff and Earls, 1999), but has been unable to answer the critical question: how to create and increase positive interaction, social capital and support, and informal control in neighbourhoods? Perhaps restorative justice can do this, although the experience in other fields has not been particularly promising.

Various community crime prevention initiatives have shown little or no success in mobilising communities: 'Much of the effort to alter the structure of communities in order to reduce crime has not been noticeably successful or sustainable' (Hope, 1995). Obstacles to community building have been hard to overcome, and include: neighbourhood infrastructures that obstruct civic participation; residents' frustration with short-lived programmes that swiftly come and go; conflicts among different residential groups; poor relations between governmental agencies and residents; agency culture and hierarchical organisation; and bureaucratic boundaries between city, county, and state departments that prohibit true partnerships among them (eg Sadd and Grinc, 1996). Success is often achieved when least needed. 'Community responses to crime are easiest to generate in exactly those areas where they are least needed and hardest to establish in those where the need is the greatest' (Crawford, 1998: p 159).

Experience with community policing shows that benefits often go to white and better-educated residents of target communities (eg Skogan, 1990). Critics argue that aggressive law enforcement is actually weakening community bonds and social capacity in inner-city neighbourhoods (Guarino-Ghezzi and Klein, 1999). Despite sincere efforts, such outcomes as empowerment of local residents, collaboration among police, residents, and governmental agencies, or resolution of social problems are seldom achieved (eg Skogan and Hartnett, 1997).

Results in the field of community development have not been much better. It seems that efforts to generate strong, close relationships among neighbours seldom succeed (Sampson, 1999). Typically, community development corporations are more successful in representing residents' interests than in involving them directly in key decisions (Briggs, Mueller and Sullivan, 1997).

However, there are many reasons to expect that restorative practices will work better than do most other community building efforts. First, restorative justice processes are based on direct participation and transfer decision-making authority from criminal justice agencies to ordinary people. Secondly, restorative justice processes are based on dialogue and consensus decision-making. Thirdly, restorative justice processes seek concrete solutions to concrete problems. As such, they are more likely to engage people than general community meetings that discuss broader social or safety matters in a particular community. Fourthly, although restorative justice processes follow from a specific crime, they do not limit discussions to narrow incident-related topics. Participants often want to talk about other social problems in their community. Fifthly, restorative justice processes offer personal and tangible support for victims and offenders. Sixthly, restorative justice processes reduce the distance between different groups of people—victims, offenders, their families, community members, and criminal justice professionals. Conversations based on equal voice, personal stories, and mutual respect are a natural and spontaneous way to create new relationships (DeLeon-Granados, 1999: p 11).

IV. CONCLUSION

Findings from research to date demonstrate two general trends. First, participant satisfaction, procedural justice, and victim outcomes are achieved in most restorative justice initiatives. Second, restorative quality and offender outcomes are achieved sometimes for some offenders in some initiatives. And there seems to be a relationship between restorativeness and offender outcomes. Most initiatives that have achieved very high levels of satisfaction and procedural justice have not been able to demonstrate reductions in recidivism or other positive changes in the offender's life. However, initiatives that have reported high-observed restorativeness have also achieved significant decreases in reoffending. Victim presence, genuine apology and remorse by the offender, equal participation in decision-making, and consensus on decisions are reported as factors that are related to lower rates of recidivism.

Restorative justice processes carry a great potential to turn negative incidents of crime into positive opportunities of creating new relationships, building communities, and strengthening grass roots democracy. The potential is as yet unrecognised by most criminal justice agencies and researches, and as a result, largely unrealised and unstudied.

REFERENCES

Bazemore, G (1997) 'The "Community" in Community Justice: Issues, Themes, and Questions for the New Neighborhood Sanctioning Models' 19 *Justice System Journal* 193–228.

—— (2000) 'Community Justice and a Vision of Collective Efficacy: The Case of Restorative Conferencing' in J Horney, R Peterson, D Mackenzie, J Martin and D Rosenbaum *Criminal Justice 2000: Policies, Processes, and Decisions of the Criminal Justice System* (US Department of Justice, Office of Justice Programs, Washington DC).

—— (2001) 'The Offender/Community Encounter: Stakeholder Involvement in the Vermont Community Reparative Boards' in DR Karp and TR Clear (eds), *What Is Community Justice?* (Sage, Thousand Oaks CA).

Bonta, J, Rooney, J and Wallace-Capretta, S (1998) *Restorative Justice: An Evaluation of the Restorative Resolutions Project* (Solicitor General Canada, Ottawa).

Braithwaite, J (2002) *Restorative Justice & Responsive Regulation* (Oxford University Press, New York).

Briggs, X, Mueller, EJ and Sullivan, ML (1997) *From Neighborhood to Community: Evidence on the Social Effects of Community Development* (New School for Social Research, Community Development Center, New York).

Cant, R and Downie, R (1998) *Evaluation of the Young Offenders Act (1944) and the Juvenile Justice Teams* (Social Systems and Evaluation, Perth).

Campbell, J (1999) 'Milaca and Princeton Community Justice Circles. First Year Evaluation Report.' Unpublished manuscript.

Clairmont, D (1996) 'Alternative Justice Issues for Aboriginal Justice' 36 *Journal of Legal Pluralism and Unofficial Justice* 125–57.

Coates, RB, Umbreit, M and Vos, B (2000) *Restorative Justice Circles in South Saint Paul, Minnesota* (University of Minnesota, The Center for Restorative Justice and Peacemaking, St. Paul MN).

Coleman, JS (1994) [1990] *Foundations of Social Theory* (Harvard University Press, Cambridge MA).

Crawford, A (1998) *Crime Prevention and Community Safety: Politics, Policies and Practices* (Longman, Dorchester MA).

Daly, K (1998) *South Australia Juvenile Justice (SAJJ) Research on Conferencing. Technical Report No. 1: Project Overview and Research Instruments* (School of Criminology and Criminal Justice, Griffith University, Brisbane, Queensland).

——(2001) *South Australia Juvenile Justice (SAJJ) Research on Conferencing. Technical Report No. 2: Research Instruments in Year 2 (1999) and Background Notes* (School of Criminology and Criminal Justice, Griffith University, Brisbane, Queensland).

——(this volume) 'Mind the Gap: Restorative Justice in Theory and Practice'

Davis, RC, Tichane, M and Grayson, D (1980) *Mediation and Arbitration as Alternatives to Prosecution in Felony Arrest Cases: An Evaluation of the Brooklyn Dispute Resolution Center* (Vera Institute of Justice, New York).

DeLeon-Granados, W (1999) *Travels Through Crime and Place: Community Building as Crime Control* (Northeastern University Press, Boston MA).

Elliott, DS, Wilson, WJ, Huizinga, D, Sampson, RJ, Elliott, A and Rankin, B (1996) 'The Effects of Neighborhood Disadvantage on Adolescent Development' 33 *Journal of Research in Crime and Delinquency* 389–426.

Fercello, C and Umbreit, M (1998) *Client Evaluation of Family Group Conferencing in 12 Sites in 1st Judicial District of Minnesota* (University of Minnesota, The Center for Restorative Justice and Mediation, St Paul MN).

Gehm, J (1990) 'Mediated Victim-Offender Restitution Agreements: An Explanatory Analysis of Factors Related to Victim Participation' in B Galaway and J Hudson (eds), *Criminal Justice, Restitution, and Reconciliation* (Criminal Justice Press, Monsey NY).

Green, RG (1997) 'Aboriginal Community Sentencing and Mediation: Within and Without the Circle' 25 *Manitoba Law Journal* 77–125.

Guarino-Ghezzi, S and Klein, A (1999) 'Protecting Community: The Public Safety Role in a Restorative Juvenile Justice' in G Bazemore and L Walgrave (eds), *Restorative Juvenile Justice: Repairing the Harm of Youth Crime* (Criminal Justice Press, Monsey NY).

Hayes, H and Daly, K (2002) 'Youth Justice Conferencing and Reoffending'. A revised paper presented at the Australian and New Zealand Society of Criminology annual meeting, Melbourne, Feb 2001.

Hayes, H, Prenzler, T and Wortley, R (1998) *Making Amends: Final Evaluation of the Queensland Community Conferencing Pilot* (Queensland Department of Justice, Brisbane).

Hope, T (1995) 'Community Crime Prevention' in M Tonry and DP Farrington (eds), *Building a Safer Society: Strategic Approaches to Crime Prevention* (University of Chicago Press, Chicago IL).

Jackson, SE (1998) 'Family Group Conferences in Youth Justice: The Issues for Implementation in England and Wales' 37 *Howard Journal of Criminal Justice* 34–51.

Karp, DR (2002) 'The Offender/Community Encounter: Stakeholder Involvement in the Vermont Community Reparative Boards' in DR Karp and TR Clear (eds), *What Is Community Justice?* (Sage, Thousand Oaks CA).

Karp, DR and Walther, L (2001) 'Community Reparative Boards: Theory and Practice' in

G Bazemore and M Schiff (eds), *Restorative Community Justice: Repairing Harms and Transforming Communities* (Anderson Publishing, Cincinnati OH).

Knapp, KA (1999) 'An Evaluation of Community Conferencing: The Central City Neighborhoods Partnership Restorative Justice Program'. Unpublished manuscript.

Kurki, L (2000) 'Restorative and Community Justice in the United States' in M Tonry (ed), *Crime and Justice: A Review of Research* (University of Chicago Press, Chicago IL) vol 26, 235.

Latimer, J, Dowden, C and Muise, D (2001) *The Effectiveness of Restorative Justice Practices: A Meta-Analysis* (Department of Justice, Ottawa).

Maxwell, G and Morris, A (1993) *Family, Victims and Culture: Youth Justice in New Zealand* (Victoria University of Wellington, Social Policy Agency and Institute of Criminology, Wellington, New Zealand).

—— (1999) *Understanding Reoffending* (Victoria University of Wellington, Institute of Criminology, Wellington, New Zealand).

McCold, P and Wachtel, B (1998) *Restorative Policing Experiment: The Bethlehem Pennsylvania Police Family Group Conferencing Project* (Community Service Foundation, Pipersville PA).

McGarrell, EF, Olivares, K, Crawford, K and Kroovand, N (2000) *Returning Justice to the Community: The Indianapolis Juvenile Restorative Justice Experiment* (Hudson Institute, Indianapolis).

Miers, D, Maguire, M, Goldie, S, Sharpe, K, Hale, C, Netten, A, Uglow, S, Doolin, K, Hallam, A, Enterkin, J and Newburn, T (2001) *An Exploratory Evaluation of Restorative Justice Schemes* (Home Office, London).

Moore, D (1995) *A New Approach to Juvenile Justice: An Evaluation of Family Conferencing in Wagga Wagga* (Charles Sturt University, Wagga Wagga, New South Wales, Australia).

Moore, D and O'Connell, T (1994) 'Family Conferencing in Wagga Wagga: A Communitarian Model of Justice' in C Alder and J Wundersitz (eds), *Family Conferencing and Juvenile Justice: The Way Forward or Misplaced Optimism* (Australian Institute of Criminology, Canberra).

Niemeyer, M and Shichor, D (1996) 'A Preliminary Study of a Large Victim/Offender Reconciliation Program' 60 *Federal Probation* 30–4.

Nugent, WR and Paddock, JB (1995) 'The Effect of Victim-Offender Mediation on Severity of Reoffense' 12 *Mediation Quarterly* 353–67.

—— (1996) 'Evaluating the Effects of a Victim-Offender Reconciliation Program on Reoffense' 6 *Research on Social Work Practice* 155–78.

Nugent, WR, Umbreit, MS, Wiinamaki, L and Paddock, J (2001) 'Participation in Victim-Offender Mediation and Reoffense: Successful Replications?' 11 *Research on Social Work Practice* 5–23.

Portes, A (1998) 'Social Capital: Its Origins and Applications in Modern Society' 24 *Annual Review of Sociology* 1–24.

Pranis, K 'Rethinking Community Corrections: Restorative Values and an Expanded Role for the Community' (1997) 8(1) *The International Community Corrections Association (ICCA) Journal on Community Corrections* 36–9, 43.

Presser, L and Van Voorhis, P (2002) 'Values and Evaluation: Assessing Processes and Outcomes of Restorative Justice Programs' 48 *Crime and Delinquency* 162–88.

Putnam, RD (2000) *Bowling Alone* (Simon & Schuster, New York).

Roberts, JV and Roach, K (this volume) 'Restorative Justice in Canada: From Sentencing Circles to Sentencing Principles'.

Roy, S 'Two Types of Juvenile Restitution Programs in Two Midwestern Counties: A Comparative Study' (1998) 57(4) *Federal Probation* 48–53.

Sadd, S and Grinc, R (1996) *Implementation Challenges in Community Policing: Innovative Neighborhood-Oriented Policing in Eight Cities* (US Department of Justice, National Institute of Justice, Washington DC).

Sampson, RJ (1997) 'Collective Regulation of Adolescent Misbehavior: Validation Results from Eighty Chicago Neighborhoods' 12 *Journal of Adolescent Research* 227–44.

—— (1999) 'What "Community" Supplies?' in RF Ferguson and WT Dickens (eds), *Urban Problems and Community Development* (Brookings Institution Press, Washington DC).

Sampson, RJ, Morenoff, JD and Earls, F (1999) 'Beyond Social Capital: Spatial Dynamics of Collective Efficacy for Children' 64 *American Sociological Review* 633–60.

Sampson, RJ, Raudenbush, SW and Earls, F (1997) 'Neighborhoods and Violent Crime: A Multilevel Study of Collective Efficacy' 277 *Science* 918–24.

Sherman, LW, Strang, H, Barnes, GC, Braithwaite, J, Ipken, N and The, MM (1998) *Experiments in Restorative Policing: A Progress Report to the National Police Research Unit on the Canberra Reintegrative Shaming Experiments (RISE)* (Australian Federal Police and Australian National University, Canberra).

Sherman, LW, Strang, H and Woods, DJ (2000) *Recidivism Patterns in the Canberra Reintegrative Shaming Experiments (RISE)* (Australian National University, Canberra).

Sinkinson, H and Broderick, J 'Restorative Justice in Vermont—Citizen's Reparative Boards' (1997) 8(4): 1 *Overcrowded Times* 12–13, 20.

Skogan, WG (1990) *Disorder and Decline: Crime and the Spiral of Decay in America Neighborhoods* (Free Press, New York).

—— and Hartnett, SM (1997) *Community Policing, Chicago Style* (Oxford University Press, New York).

Strang, H, Barnes, GS, Braithwaite, J and Sherman, LW (1999) *Experiments in Restorative Policing: A Progress Report on the Canberra Reintegrative Shaming Experiments (RISE)* (Australian Federal Police and Australian National University, Canberra).

Trimboli, L (2000) *An Evaluation of the NSW Youth Justice Conferencing Scheme* (New South Wales Bureau of Crime Statistics and Research, Sydney).

Umbreit, MS (1994) *Victim Meets the Offender: The Impact of Restorative Justice and Mediation* (Criminal Justice Press, Monsey NY).

—— (1995) *Mediation of Criminal Conflict: An Assessment of Programs in Four Canadian Provinces* (The Center for Restorative Justice and Mediation, University of Minnesota, St Paul MN).

Umbreit, MS and Coates, RB (1993) 'Cross-Site Analysis of Victim-Offender Mediation in Four States' 39 *Crime and Delinquency* 565–85.

Umbreit, MS, Coates, RB and Vos, B 'The Impact of Victim-Offender Mediation: Two Decades of Research' (2001a) 65(3) *Federal Probation* 29–35.

—— (2001b) *Juvenile Victim Offender Mediation.* A Final Report submitted to the Oregon Dispute Resolution Commission.

Umbreit, M and Greenwood, J (2000) *National Survey of Victim-Offender Mediation Programs in the United States* (US Department of Justice, Office of Justice Programs, Washington DC).

Umbreit, MS and Warner Roberts, A, (1996) *Mediation of Criminal Conflict in England: An Assessment of Services in Coventry and Leeds* (University of Minnesota, The Center for Restorative Justice and Mediation, St Paul MN).

Umbreit, MS and Zehr, H 'Restorative Family Group Conferences: Differing Models and Guidelines for Practice' (1996) 60(3) *Federal Probation* 24–9.

Walther, L and Perry, J 'The Vermont Reparative Probation Program' (1997) 8(2) *The International Community Corrections Association (ICCA) Journal on Community Corrections* 26–34.

Wundersitz, J (1994) 'Family Conferencing and Juvenile Justice Reform in South Australia' in C Adler and J Wundersitz (eds), *Family Conferencing and Juvenile Justice: The Way Forward or Misplaced Optimism?* (Australian Institute of Criminology, Canberra).

Young, R and Hoyle, C (this volume) 'New, Improved Police-Led Restorative Justice? Action Research and the Themes Valley Police Initiative'.

16

Models, Challenges and The Promise of Restorative Conferencing Strategies

Mara Schiff

I. INTRODUCTION

Restorative justice is a philosophy for reforming criminal and juvenile justice intervention strategies based on principles of repairing harm, involving key stakeholders and creating community/government partnerships in the justice process (Van Ness and Strong, 1998; Bazemore and Umbreit, 2001). According to Zehr (1990), traditional approaches focus on three attributes of the criminal process: identifying culpability and assigning blame (who did it?), determining what legal contract was violated (what laws were broken?), and determining the offender's resulting obligation to the state (what should be done to punish or treat the offender?). Restorative justice, on the other hand, asks: What is the *nature of the harm* resulting from the offence (as differentiated from the legal wrong, eg Duff, this volume)? What needs to be done to *repair the harm*, or 'make it right'? *Who is responsible* for repairing this harm? (Zehr, 1990) Unlike traditional justice strategies which stress censure punishment and procedural uniformity (eg von Hirsch, 1975, 1998; Duff, 2001), restorative justice decision-making focuses primarily on values of encounter, reparation, reintegration and participation (Van Ness and Strong, 1997; Van Ness and Schiff, 2001; Stuart, 2001).

Restorative justice has been applied in a variety of contexts, under a multitude of conditions and including a number of different stakeholders. In most parts of the world, however, restorative justice has been implemented as a series of ad hoc programmatic initiatives rather than as a systemic approach to justice intervention. The primary exceptions to this have been in Australia and New Zealand where national legislation has led to countrywide juvenile justice system implementation (Morris and Maxwell, 2001; Daly, 2001). There is also evidence of increasing interest in promoting conferencing as a diversionary tool for adults in those countries as well (Daly, 2001). In addition, there has been movement towards such nationalised strategies in the Netherlands and Northern Ireland (Shapland, this volume), Norway and Slovenia (Miers, 2001). In the United States, the closest attempts to implement restorative justice systemically have been through institutional mandates in individual states' Departments' of Corrections or Divisions of Juvenile Justice (eg in Minnesota, Vermont and Florida).

The purpose of this chapter is threefold. First, to generically describe the most common restorative models (focusing predominantly on those in use in the US), where and how they are being implemented and the evidence, if any, for their effectiveness.[1] Secondly, to examine some of the key obstacles to effective implementation and to obtaining reliable research data on those processes. Thirdly, to consider what promise, if any, restorative processes hold for the future. Although the models herein described are being implemented around the world, in this chapter I will concentrate predominantly (though not exclusively) on those currently being employed in the United States due to limitations in time, space.

II. TYPES OF RESTORATIVE PROGRAMMES

Restorative justice encompasses a number of different strategies for identifying and repairing the harm caused by a criminal offence. These processes have been generically referred to as *restorative conferencing* and are designed to bring the affected parties together in a non-adversarial, face-to-face meeting to talk about what happened and what should be done about it (Bazemore and Umbreit, 2001; Schiff, Erbe and Bazemore, 2001). Such strategies are designed to hold offenders accountable for their actions while simultaneously giving victims and other affected community members the opportunity to discuss the impact of the crime *directly* with the person responsible for causing it (Bazemore and Umbreit, 2001; Bazemore and Schiff, 2002). Once the impact of the crime has been communicated to the victim, offender(s) and their supporters, parties can then collectively determine an appropriate response to the wrongdoing (Bazemore and Griffiths, 1997; Umbreit, 1999). In this way, the offender can make amends directly to the persons harmed, rather than to 'the state', an abstract, formal and impersonal entity that has little meaning for most offenders or victims. Restorative justice has been said to 'humanise' the justice process and make it less formal by including victims and community members in its processes, planning and implementation (Umbreit, 1999; Miers, 2001).

There are a number of innovative programmes currently being implemented around the world designed to address the needs of crime victims, offenders, their respective families and other community members who are affected by criminal events. These processes are designed to intervene in the context of the community in which the event has taken place rather than in the formal and frequently intimidating atmosphere of the courtroom. Such restorative conferencing processes are gaining acceptance in both communities and courts and, while not without problems, are increasingly becoming recognised as effective strategies for dealing with the challenges and opportunities that both adult and youthful

---

[1] For a more detailed look at the outcome research on restorative justice, see Kurki, this volume.

offending presents (Bazemore and Schiff, 2001; Kurki, 2000; Umbreit and Coates, 1992, 1993; Morris and Maxwell, 2001; Pranis, 1998). Current estimates suggest that there are about 750 such programmes operating in the United States alone (Schiff, Erbe and Bazemore, 2001).[2] Some of these approaches, such as Victim-Offender Mediation/Dialogue, have been operating for decades and research has documented their effectiveness on a number of dimensions; other, more recent innovations such as Family Group Conferencing and Peacemaking Circles, are presently being implemented and evaluated around the world.

Restorative conferencing processes can be broadly organised into four primary categories. These categories do not represent *all* the possible variations in restorative conferencing practices, rather they are intended to synthesise and clarify the primary restorative decision-making models for purposes of this discussion. These models include:

— Victim Offender Mediation/Dialogue
— Family Group Conferencing/Community Conferencing
— Peacemaking, Sentencing and Community Circles
— Community Boards and Panels

Each of these models has been implemented in a variety of jurisdictions and under a variety of conditions (eg urban/suburban; economically advantaged/disadvantaged; culturally homo-/heterogeneous). Some of these processes have been subjected to rigorous outcome evaluation while others are still too new to have been adequately assessed. What follows is a brief description of each model, including its process, history and primary components, and an overview of the evidence (if available) for its effectiveness. It is appropriate to note that the practical distinctions between many different restorative processes are tending to fade as programmes are moving towards a more 'multi-method' approach. Such approaches tend to utilise elements of different processes that best fit the individual circumstances of the event and the parties involved (Umbreit, 2001). Moreover, it is also important to consider that by the time this is published, advances in both research and practice may outdate some of this information. The pace at which restorative practices are evolving far exceeds the ability of researchers and scholars to write about them.

1. Victim Offender Mediation/Dialogue

Overview

Victim-Offender Mediation and Dialogue (VOM/D) has been operating in the United States, Canada and Europe for over 20 years, the longest of any restorative

---

[2] This figure is based on an extensive search including telephone interviews, Internet-based information and a national survey of restorative conferencing programmes conducted during August through December 2000 by Schiff, Bazemore and Erbe at Florida Atlantic University. This figure is based on self-reported data, however, and has not been verified for accuracy or objective measures of actual programme 'restorativeness.'

intervention strategy. VOM/D has moved steadily from its beginnings as a marginal, predominantly faith-based justice process (known as VORP—Victim-Offender Reconciliation Programs) to a staple justice system resource in most jurisdictions around the world (Umbreit, 2001). Currently, estimates suggest that are over 1,300 VOM/D programmes operating around the world (including 302 in the United States, 450 in Germany and 175 in Finland, and 159 in France) (Umbreit, 2001). The majority of cases handled by VOM/D involve property offences and less serious violent offences committed by youthful offenders, although the process is also being used in cases of severe violence involving both adults and juveniles (Bazemore and Umbreit, 2001; Umbreit, 2001).

Process

VOM/D is designed to bring victims and offenders together face-to-face in a safe, structured, facilitated dialogue that typically occurs in a community-based setting. After holding separate pre-conference meetings with both the victim and the offender to explain and assess the individual's readiness for the process, a trained mediator assists the victim in communicating the physical, emotional and financial impact of the crime to the offender. In addition, the meeting enables the offender to take responsibility for his/her part in the event, and the victim to receive answers from the offender about why and how the crime occurred (Umbreit, 2001). Following this sharing of stories, the victim and the offender together determine an appropriate plan to repair the harm to the victim, which may include material and/or non-material compensation.

Cases may be referred to VOM/D by judges, probation officers, victim advocates, prosecutors, defence attorneys, police, and sometimes even the parties themselves. Cases may be referred as a diversion from prosecution or as post-conviction/adjudication sentencing alternatives; in the latter instances, VOM/D may be a condition of disposition. Recent research in the US suggests that VOM/D programmes are typically housed in community-based organisations and that about 62 per cent of their cases are referred prior to the court process (Schiff and Bazemore, 2002). The purpose of VOM/D is to give victims the opportunity to express their feelings and discuss the material and non-material impact of the crime; allow offenders to hear the impact of their crime(s) and take responsibility for their behaviour; bring the parties together to determine an appropriate reparative plan to address the harm caused by the crime (Bazemore and Umbreit, 2000).

Research Findings in Brief[3]

There is more, and more reliable, research on VOM/D than on any other restorative process. Research from the US, Canada and Europe has shown that both

---

[3] Please remember that this is intended to be only a brief summary of main research findings; for a more comprehensive and critical review of research, see Kurki, this volume.

victims and offenders who participated in VOM/D were more likely to be satisfied with both the process and the outcome than were comparably matched (though not randomly assigned) groups experiencing traditional court processes (Umbreit and Roberts, 1996; Umbreit and Coates, 1992, 1998; Umbreit, 2001; Miers, 2001; Miers et al 2001). Research also suggests that victims who met their offenders were less likely to fear revictimisation and to receive restitution (Umbreit, 1995; 1998), although some were initially fearful of meeting 'their' offender in person (Miers, 2001). Offenders who completed VOM/D were more likely to complete their restitution obligations and were less likely to recidivate than were comparable offenders processed by the court (Carr, 1998; Roberts, 1998; Nugent and Paddock, 1995). Among those who did reoffend, their subsequent crimes were likely to be less severe than those who did not participate in VOM/D (Nugent and Paddock, 1995; Nugent et al 1999; Miers, 2001). Overall, research on VOM/D has typically shown more positive outcomes on a number of dimensions when compared to offenders processed through traditional mechanisms; where positive outcomes have not been found, the research has generally shown outcomes *no worse* than those experienced by court processed offenders.

2. Family Group Conferencing and Community Conferencing

Overview

Family Group Conferencing (FGC) is based on ancient practices originated by the Maoris of New Zealand, although its present day applications often diverge from traditional Maori methods (Zellerer and Cunneen, 2001; Daly, 2001). National legislation mandating FGC for youthful offenders was adopted in New Zealand in 1989, making New Zealand the first country to officially adopt a restorative justice mandate, and making FGC the most systematically utilised practice in any country. FGC was also begun in South Australia in the early 1990s as a means by which police could divert youths from the formal juvenile justice system. FGC is becoming increasingly widespread in the United States, and is currently practised in Minnesota, Pennsylvania, Montana, Vermont, Colorado and several other states (an estimated 94 such programmes were operating in the US as of about June 2001; Schiff and Bazemore, 2002). There are two primary models of FGC: (1) the New Zealand model in which all but the most serious and violent youthful offenders are diverted from the court whenever possible; (2) the original Australian model where police and/or school officials facilitate meetings between the parties and their families (Alder and Wundersitz, 1994; Maxwell and Morris, 1993; Morris and Maxwell, 2001; McCold and Wachtel, 1998). Australia practices both police and court-based FGC and has expanded use to include court diversion cases for adults as well (Daly, 2001). The police-based strategy is the predominant method used in the US, although the court-referred New Zealand model is also practised in some states (eg Minnesota, Colorado). FGC is used in a variety of types of cases, including assault, theft, arson, drug offences and child welfare cases (Bazemore and Umbreit, 2001; Pennell and Burford, 2000; Burford and Hudson, 2000). FGC has predominantly been used in lower severity level cases in most applications, although it is used for severe and repeat crimes in New Zealand.

Community Conferencing (CC) is a variation of the FGC model that recognises the community as a victim of crime and empowers affected citizens to have a role in determining the outcome of incidents that impact the community at large. Community Conferencing is based in the understanding that communities, as well as victims and offenders are significantly affected by crime, and should be a part of determining the outcomes of crimes that occur in their neighbourhoods. Community conferencing may address harms that have affected individuals directly (eg theft, assault) or indirectly (eg vandalism, graffiti, prostitution).

Process

Both FGC and CC bring together the victim, the offender, members of their respective families and any supporters the key parties wish to have present (eg a grandparent, a best friend, a teacher, a counsellor). Like VOM/D, FGC meetings typically occur following separate face-to-face meetings with the victim and the offender (which may include their respective families and supporters). In CC, members of the community who feel they were affected by the event are also invited to participate, including local residents, business owners, shopkeepers, property managers, school officials and other community stakeholders.

Similar to VOM/D, FGC and CC enable the parties to share their stories, identify the impacts of the crime on those present, and to collectively determine an appropriate resolution. Many US practitioners were trained in methods following the Wagga-Wagga approach which uses a script and encourages the offender to speak first by recounting the incident. The victim speaks next and describes the impact of the event in their lives, followed by other participants. Sometimes, the victim may begin speaking first or may be offered the choice of who they would like to hear from first. The object of the conference is to enable the offender to see the impact of his/her actions on the victim(s) and others, and to allow the victim to ask questions, express feelings and talk about the incident. Following discussion of the impacts, the victim may be asked to identify his/her desired outcome (which some programmes have already asked the victim to begin thinking about in pre-conference interviews) and then be invited to participate in shaping a reparative agreement. All participants contribute to the problem-solving process.

Conferences are complete when the agreement is signed by all present; refreshments are then typically served, allowing time for more casual conversation and connection. FGC and CC are designed to directly involve the victim in discussing and shaping the reparative agreement; hold the offender accountable, increase awareness of the impacts of his/her behaviour and provide an opportunity to take responsibility for that behaviour; involve both the victim's and the offender's support system in shaping both the process and the final agreement. In addition, the conference may help empower communities to establish and be responsible for normative standards of behaviour and enhance the overall well being and connectedness of its members (Bazemore and Umbreit, 2001).

Research Findings in Brief

There have been studies of FGC in New Zealand (Maxwell and Morris, 1993; Morris and Maxwell, 1998), the United States (McCold and Wachtell, 1998; Fercello and Umbreit, 1999; McGarrell, 2001), the United Kingdom (Roberts and Masters, 1999; Young and Hoyle, this volume), Canada (Bonta, Rooney and Wallace-Capretta, 1998) and Australia (Sherman et al 2000; Daly, 2000; Trimboli, 2000). In New Zealand, where FGC is utilised as the primary dispositional approach for all juvenile cases (excluding murder, rape and aggravated assault), research suggests that youthful offenders who participate in FGC are more frequently and actively involved in the justice process than are offenders who do not participate (Maxwell and Morris, 1993; Morris and Maxwell, 1998). In addition, participant satisfaction rates are generally higher for FGC participants than for court-processed youth and their victims (Morris and Maxwell, 2001). In the United States, research also suggests high levels of participant satisfaction as well as high levels of offender compliance with agreements (Fercello and Umbreit, 1999; McCold and Wachtel, 1998). Preliminary results from Australia indicate that re-offence rates decreased for violent offenders, and young offenders who participated in conferences were more likely to say they would obey the law in the future than were offenders processed through the court (Sherman and Strang, 1997; 2000). Victims also reported feeling better served by the conference process than by 'court' and offenders felt fairly treated by the process as well (Sherman, et al 2000; Daly, forthcoming). Finally, a decrease in the juvenile incarceration rate in New Zealand has been attributed to increased use of FGC although this is anecdotal and not empirically documented (McElrae, 1998).

There is virtually no research available on the impacts of community conferencing, although given the similarities in process, many of the lessons learned from FGC are applicable to community conferencing. An informal 1999 uncontrolled study of the effectiveness of one community conferencing programme conducted in Minneapolis, Minnesota found that 91 per cent of conference participants reported satisfaction with the experience and that 98 per cent of participants felt they were treated fairly (Knapp, 1999). Community members reported feeling more connected as a result of the programme and 84 per cent of participating offenders completed their agreements and did not recidivate (Knapp, 1999).

3. Peacemaking, Sentencing and Community Circles

Overview

Circles derive from traditional Native American and Canadian First Nations dispute resolution processes (Stuart, 2001; Melton, 1995). These processes are alternatively referred to as Sentencing Circles, Peacemaking Circles and

Community Circles, which all serve slightly different purposes. Circles were res-urrected in 1991 by judges and community workers in the Yukon Territories and other communities in Canada.[4] Their use spread to the US in 1995 when a pilot project was initiated in Minnesota. Circles are used in both juvenile and adult cases in the US and currently operate in Alaska, Minnesota, Oregon, Texas, Mass-achusetts and Colorado. There is no evidence that circles are being used outside of North America. Circles have been used in response to serious crimes, commu-nity disputes, in school settings where suspension or expulsion might otherwise have occurred, and in child protection cases; some suggest that their labour and emotionally intensive nature may be best suited to more serious cases (eg Coates, Umbreit and Vos, 2001).

Process

Circles are designed to address the needs of victims, communities and offenders in a holistic, reintegrative process. Participants in circles include the victim, his/her family and supporters, the offender, his/her family and supporters, and any other member of the community who feels they were affected by the event and wishes to participate. The goal is to collectively share experiences about the event and its impact in an effort to search for understanding and healing. The process is more complicated and time consuming than most other restora-tive decision-making processes and typically involves five key steps: (1) an appli-cation circle held in response to an the offender's request to participate in the circle; (2) a healing circle for the victim; (3) a healing circle for the offender; (4) a sentencing circle to develop consensus on what happened and what should be done to repair the harm; (5) a series of follow-up circles to monitor compli-ance with agreement and support the offender in completing the agreement. All of these events are labour intensive and demand a considerable amount of commitment to the process by participants. Circles often include an explicitly spiritual component based on Native American (or in Canada, First Nations) tra-dition, although this is not required and many circles have adapted the process with local culture. Goals of the process include promoting healing for all affected parties; offering the offender an opportunity to make amends; empowering victims and community members to speak from their hearts and to share in fash-ioning a constructive agreement; and building a sense of community and devel-oping members own capacity to resolve conflict (Bazemore and Umbreit, 2001; Stuart, 2001).

Research Findings in Brief

There has been very little systematic research performed on circle processes. One anecdotal report from the Yukon Territories suggests that recidivism was less

---

⁴ For a more detailed examination of Circles in Canada, see Roberts and Roach, this volume.

likely among offenders who participated in circle than among court processed youth, however this is not based on comprehensive and rigorous research (Stuart, 1996). Perhaps the most comprehensive qualitative report on the circle process comes from South Saint Paul, Minnesota which found that holding the offender accountable and allowing him/her an opportunity to accept responsibility, developing future relationships between former antagonists, expressing feelings and developing awareness and support from the community were most important to participants. Drawbacks included the length of the process and occasionally longwinded participants (Coates, Umbreit and Vos, 2000). This study was not controlled and did not examine recidivism or compliance rates.

4. Community Reparative Boards and Neighbourhood Panels

Overview

Community Boards and Panels have been in use in the US since as far back as the 1920s as mechanisms for community involvement in youth sanctioning and have been known under a variety of names, including youth panels, community diversion boards, and neighbourhood boards. More recently, contemporary versions include Reparative Boards in Vermont, Neighborhood Accountability Boards in San Jose, California, Community Panels for Youth in Chicago, Illinois and Community Accountability Boards in Denver, Colorado. Boards may be located in a variety of, typically public, organisations, for example, Vermont's Reparative Probation Program began in 1995 under the jurisdiction of the Vermont Department of Corrections. In San Jose, California's Neighborhood Accountability Board programme began in 1999 as part of the Restorative Justice Project, an initiative of the Santa Clara County Probation Department. In Denver, the Community Accountability Boards are run out of the prosecutor's office, although referrals are generally made by probation and police, rather than prosecutors. These boards enable community members to become involved in determining what should happen in cases of youthful offending and to help enhance perceptions of neighbourhood safety. Boards have not been intensively studied and hence there is relatively little research available about their implementation and effectiveness.

Process

Community Boards are generally composed of small groups of citizen members who come together to determine what should happen primarily in instances of relatively low level, non-violent offending and property offending. Board members meet with offenders in a face-to-face encounter to discuss the nature of the offence, its implications and what reparative action is appropriate. Board members typically determine the outcome, but seek to involve the offender whenever possible; victims are not usually present although they may be consulted and asked for input prior to the Board meeting. Board members will discuss the conditions of the agreement with the offender until a suitable arrangement and time frame for completion is generated. Progress will be monitored, and upon completion of the conditions a report may be filed with the probation department, court, or other official body to document conclusion of the case. This process is designed to: promote citizen involvement and ownership of the justice process; offer the offender and the community a chance to come together constructively to deal with the crime and its consequences; offer offenders the opportunity to take responsibility for their actions and to be held accountable for the harm caused; generate community-government partnerships to respond to neighbourhood crime and delinquency, thereby reducing reliance of formal, government resources and formal system intervention (Bazemore and Umbreit, 2001).

Research Findings in Brief

There has been limited research conducted on Boards to date. Research on the Vermont Reparative Boards suggests that recidivism may be slightly lower for defendants who participate in Boards rather than the court process (Karp and Walther, 2001). There is, however, very little empirical data on participation rates, levels of satisfaction or completion of reparative agreements among offenders involved with boards as compared with regular probation or other court-imposed sanctions. Victim participation in reparative boards is low (about 15 per cent) (Karp and Walther, 2001), in part due to the low-level nature of most of the offences. Most offenders in a recent Vermont study were required to do community service work as part of their agreement (63 per cent) (Karp and Walther, 2001). A Canadian study showed decreased recidivism among offenders experiencing 'restorative resolutions' (roughly equivalent to Boards in the US) when compared to offenders sent to prison or traditional probation (Bonta, Rooney, Wallace-Capretta, 1998).

II. OBSTACLES TO EFFECTIVE RESTORATIVE CONFERENCING

As with any new or innovative justice intervention, there are considerable challenges to implementing and evaluating restorative processes. Some obstacles to implementation include potential rights violations and procedural safeguards (Delgado, 2000; Levrant, 1999; Polk, 2001; Zellerer and Cunneen, 2001), the ambiguity of community (Crawford and Clear, 2001; Crawford, 1997) and the identification of appropriate stakeholders and their level of involvement (Crawford and Clear, 2001; Lindner, 1996; Achilles and Zehr, 2001; Bazemore and Griffiths, 1997; Bazemore and Schiff, 1996). Others obstacles include developing and conducting rigorous process and outcome evaluations, and identifying and relating restorative goals to outcomes (Schiff, 1998, 1999; Bazemore, 2000). This is not meant to be an exhaustive list of obstacles; rather, it is intended to elucidate some of the primary concerns that have been expressed in the literature about restorative justice processes.

1. Obstacles to Implementation

Potential Violations of Rights and Procedural Inequities

Restorative processes have been accused of paying insufficient attention to the rights of both victims and offenders by limiting the involvement of lawyers and legal procedural safeguards in the restorative processes (Delgado, 2000; Levrant et al 1999; Polk, 2001). For example, Delgado (2000) argues that restorative justice (formulated simply as VOM) fails to provide the uniformity in process and outcome borne of having regular actors consistently carrying out regular duties. Moreover, he argues that victims are given too much power in the process as they are required to perform a sentencing function with only limited information about the offender, the system and its alternatives; offenders, on the other hand, are treated as 'objects' to be 'managed, shamed, and conditioned' (p 765). At the same time, the state is given too much control over offenders whose cases might otherwise be dismissed or who might receive minimal treatment (see also Levrant et al 1999). Delgado suggests that middle-class VOM mediators and victims are insensitive to the antecedent conditions that may have spawned the lower class offender's behaviour and hence to the plight of socially disadvantaged offenders. 'In most cases,' Delgado argues, 'a vengeful victim and a middle-class mediator will gang up on a young, minority offender . . .' (p 764).

Delgado (2000) raises some important concerns, although he fails to adequately substantiate them. Delgado sees VOM as the primary restorative practice on which his conclusions are based. As suggested by this chapter and considerable other literature (eg Morris and Maxwell, 1992, 1993; Bazemore and Griffiths, 1997; Bazemore and Umbreit, 2001; Bazemore and Schiff, 2001; Umbreit, 2001; Galaway and Hudson, 1996; Alder and Wundersitz, 1994; Bazemore and Walgrave, 1999; McCold and Wachtel, 1998; Stuart, 1996, 2001; Umbreit, Coates and Vos, 2000; Karp and Walther, 2001) restorative justice consists of a number of processes in addition to VOM, including Family Group Conferencing, Community Conferencing, Circle Sentencing and Reparative Boards. While it is true that the majority of research has been performed on VOM and there is thus more information on that practice than others, the data do not support the contention that the majority of offenders feel unfairly treated by either VOM or other restorative processes (eg Umbreit, 2001; Daly, 2001). In fact, to the contrary, research shows that both victims and offenders who participate in VOM feel more fairly treated than comparable offenders processed through the courts (Umbreit and Coates, 1992; Umbreit, Coates and Roberts, 1998; Umbreit, 1995, 1999, 2001; Umbreit and Bradshaw, 1997; Fercello and Umbreit, 1999).

Delgado (2000) posits that uniformity of actors will ensure procedural equity. Restorative justice undoubtedly can and often does result in inconsistent outcomes, but there is little evidence that the lack of consistent actors in the process is to blame or that such concerns are absent from traditional court processes. The court process has been shown to result in outcomes that discriminate against blacks (Tonry, 1998; Walker, Spohn and DeLone, 1996; Petersilia, 1985) women (Albonetti, 1986; Zellerer, 1999; Bumiller 1990; Frohman, 1991), indigenous populations (Zellerer and Cunneen, 2001; Cunneen, 2000; Zellerer, 1996, 1999) and the poor (Levin, 1972; Holmes et al 1996). It is, in fact, more likely that the complex procedural and managerial issues that consume most criminal justice system workers will have them more concerned with caseload management, conviction rates and workplace relationships than repairing harm, procedural consistency or offender (and victim) interests (eg Fleming, Nardulli and Eisenstein, 1992; Klinger, 1997; Bazemore, 2000).

The concern of race and class disparity between mediators, victims and offenders is an important and valid one. Indeed, significant concerns have been raised about about the potential for restorative justice to represent the interests of a white majority at the expense of indigenous and other peoples of colour, particularly in Canada and Australia (Zellerer and Cunneen, 2001; Cunneen, 1997; La Prairie, 1995). In the US, many restorative programmes draw both their cases and their volunteers from the same neighbourhoods. For example, circles in North Minneapolis and Saint Paul, Minnesota operate and draw their membership from primarily African-American communities. In San Jose, California, Neighborhood Accountability Board members and the offenders with whom they interact (NABs) are drawn from local communities comprised of Latino, White and Asian communities (Bazemore and Schiff, 2002). In Woodbury, Minnesota, a police-based family group conferencing programme primarily deals with offenders and their families from a predominantly white, middle class suburban area; the police facilitators in that programme typically have similar backgrounds (Hines, 2000). In recent years, restorative processes have become considerably broader and more far-reaching, and while research lags behind practice, there is little, if any, empirical evidence that facilitators, victims and offenders drawn from disparate socio-economic classes, diminishes equitable outcomes in the US. Recent research from South Australia suggests that offenders find the process *more* procedurally equitable than do victims (Daly, 2001).

The absence of unyielding devotion to principle guiding restorative justice policy and practice may result in justice processes no more equitable or effective than those currently dominating justice systems around the world (Schiff and Bazemore, 2001; Stuart, 2001; Crawford and Clear, 2001; Achilles and Zehr, 2001). While the dangers of discrimination and inequity are present, they arise not from the disparate backgrounds of mediators and victims in contrast to offenders, but rather from poorly conceived and implemented programmes (Morris and Maxwell, 1998). Some concern has been raised that restorative conferencing processes have been improperly imposed on indigenous, youthful and female populations in Australia and Canada (Zellerer and Cunneen, 2001; Polk, 2001) and that such processes have been insensitive to or failed to adequately include victims and their needs in the process (Achilles and Zehr, 2001; Stuart, 2001; Bargen, 1995). However, in contrast to the overwhelming evidence of minority overrepresentation in juvenile and adult court systems and the historical lack of attention to victims needs in those same processes (eg Walker et al 1996; Tonry, 1998; Cunneen, 1997; Weed, 1995; Young, 1997), it is difficult to criticise restorative processes for being unable to resolve justice system dysfunctions most would agree existed long before even minimal experimentation with restorative practices. Other reforms, such as just desserts policies, case management in community corrections, the 'what works', or effective correctional treatment movements have, quite frankly, had considerably more time and resources with which to cause the harm implicitly attributed to restorative justice or, alternatively, to make things better (Bazemore and Schiff, 2001). The critical question is not whether restorative justice has resolved inequity in the justice process, but rather the degree to which actual and potential abuses engendered by restorative justice compare with those now and historically perpetuated by current systems.

Stakeholder Identification and Involvement

Restorative justice is premised on including and engaging stakeholders who have not traditionally been privy to justice decision-making processes, such as victims and communities. Identifying the interests of such stakeholders in the process and the outcome, how and where their participation should be encouraged as well as limited, and how to protect rights while encouraging involvement has not adequately been considered by justice system decision-makers. Several important concerns have been raised in the literature.

First, restorative justice presumes that once educated about the potential benefits of the process, public apprehension will diminish and victims and community members will choose to participate. Research suggests several limitations on the degree to which such stakeholders may choose to participate in restorative processes: the type of crime involved (Niemayer and Sichor, 1996), the relationship between the victim and the offender (Lindner, 1996), and the extent to which they are contacted, invited to participate and apprised of upcoming meetings (Morris and Maxwell, 1998). While there is evidence that community members are interested in opportunities to contribute to justice decision-making (Doble and Associates, 1994), the extent of this desire and how to stimulate it remain ambiguous. There are many victims who would rather not face their offenders (Lindner, 1996), and many community members who prefer to 'leave it to the professionals.' In fact, after over 50 years of being systematically and intentionally excluded from justice decision-making, it is hardly surprising that most citizens consider themselves neither capable of, nor responsible for, directly responding to criminal harm (Bazemore and Griffiths, 1997). Concomitantly, justice system professionals have long been encouraged to exclude lay citizens from justice processes and to take sole responsibility for responding to criminal events. It is therefore to be expected that engaging non-traditional stakeholders in the justice process would, at a minimum, be problematic.

Secondly, even in a well-designed and implemented restorative intervention, the primacy of the victim and the offender may inadvertently be diluted by involving and giving power to unrepresentative community members who are neither educated about the process nor subject to any accountability restrictions (Crawford and Clear, 2001; Bazemore and Griffiths, 1997). To the extent that these members self-identify as 'experts', the problem is exacerbated as 'in' groups of volunteers may come to dominate what are supposed to be inclusive processes, and potentially co-opt participatory processes to serve individual and exclusive ends. In addition to the legal and ethical challenges of such exclusion, this might diminish others' feelings of being valued and welcomed, further weakening the possibility of 'community' as representative, inclusive and a viable participant in restorative processes.

Thirdly, victim advocates and others have suggested that victims' interests may not be served by processes idealising reparation and healing when such outcomes may neither be possible nor desired by victims (Bargen, 1995). Moreover, by stressing the reintegrative or other needs of the offender, conferencing may inadvertently leave the victim in a secondary role (Daly, 2001). Insincere apologies proffered for the benefit of decreasing the severity of the offender's sanction, incomplete restitution agreements, or processes that leave victims feeling that they are expected to support the offender's problems and/or recovery may be more damaging than restorative and may do little to improve on current practices (Lavery and Achilles, 1999).

As suggested above, research tends to support that both victims and offenders who participate in restorative conferencing processes feel generally more satisfied than do others who experience traditional court alternatives. In Australia and New Zealand, the leading examples of institutionalised restorative conferencing, research has consistently found high level of satisfaction among victims and offenders who participated in restorative conferencing processes (Maxwell and Morris, 1993, 1996; Morris and Maxwell, 1998, 2001; Palk, 1998; Trimboli, 2000) as well as perceptions of fairness of the process (Palk, 1998; Trimboli, 2001; Cant and Downie, 1998; Strang, 1999; Daly, 2001). Research from the United States and Canada reports similar findings (Umbreit and Coates, 1998; Umbreit, 2001; McCold and Wachtel, 1998). However, irrespective of evidence indicating satisfaction, fairness or other participant outcome measures, it remains important that restorative justice continue to examine precisely what is meant by 'stakeholder' and how such participants should be identified, included and their experiences measured (Crawford and Clear, 2001). That some critical characteristics of what constitutes a 'stakeholder' are, at present, rather ill-defined has implications for clarifying exactly who should be included in restorative processes and at what stage their input should be solicited.

The Ambiguity of Community

Consistent with the above discussion concerning stakeholder involvement, community is difficult to define in most western societies today and its meaning varies with place, context and culture. In Europe, for example, the term 'community' may imply something significantly different from the United States, making cross-cultural conversations problematic (Walgrave, 2000). Crawford and Clear (2001) point out that in most discussions about community, a common definition is presumed, as is agreement about the boundaries and characteristics of 'community.' Clear and Karp (2000) further suggest that community may be defined by geographic, organisational, professional or other boundaries. There are few, if any, 'essential characteristics' which define and characterise all communities. Given the intention of restorative justice to involve 'the community' and to develop outcomes measuring the degree to which 'community' goals have been met, concerns about the precise meaning and value of the term in the context of justice system intervention are warranted. If community cannot be clearly defined or identified, government efforts to devolve justice to the community level may be undermined (Schiff and Bazemore, 2001).

Given the dubious nature and identity of the community, it follows that questions of resources, cohesion, power relationships and equality within such environments limit the extent to which restorative processes can, on their own, be effective in involving, engaging and empowering communities. Public policy literature is rife with examples of different 'communities' or 'publics' that coalesce around particular policy problems and which represent different interests, problems, needs and demands (Clemons and McBeth, 2001). The term 'communities of care' has been used to distinguish those that might unite around a restorative conferencing event (Braithwaite and Roche, 2001). It is possible that the notion of unified communities that may come together through the restorative process may be naive, and may fail to recognise that members of one group may benefit from restorative justice processes at the expense of others that are less powerful, less well-off or less organised.

However restorative justice, like any other justice intervention, must obviously be implemented in existing conditions and these harbour inherent inequities. Another way to approach the concern may be to ask not whether the absence of a cohesive and definite community precludes restorative processes, but rather *at what stage of development* is the community and how can restorative interventions strengthen and enhance existing resources? Understanding, identifying and measuring these stages may be central to the future of restorative justice. Some environments may be better suited to restorative intervention than others; recognising and working within this constraint may be most appropriate at this stage of development. In essence, it seems that rather than denying the possibilities of restorative justice, these concerns highlight the need to further discuss and distinguish who and what falls under the umbrella of 'community' and how and to what degree such entities can be powerfully incorporated into the justice process.

2. Research Obstacles

Before assessing if restorative justice is effective, it is first important to ask some fundamental questions about how 'success' and 'failure' of restorative justice programmes is, or should be, measured. The real question may not be 'what works?' but rather 'what works, for whom, when, and how often?' (Schiff, 1998; Bazemore, 1999a; Van Ness and Schiff, 2001). If the intention of evaluation research is to assess whether outcomes achieved are consistent with intended goals (Anderson, 1994; Langbein, 1980; Welsh and Harris, 1998) it is appropriate to design research strategies that first distinguish the goals of an intervention, and then determine if these goals have been met. Restorative justice is a multidimensional process that seeks multidimensional outcomes, which complicates matters for researchers.

As a justice strategy, restorative justice is concerned with much more than simply what is done to or with offenders, and as such it is a much more ambitious justice response that either retribution, deterrence, rehabilitation or incapacitation, all of which have far more modest, offender-centred goals. If restorative justice seeks to improve the status of victims and communities *as well as* offenders, its measures must reflect the needs and interests of each of these groups. Specifically, principle-based restorative justice strategies are concerned with repairing harm, involving key stakeholders and developing powerful government-community partnerships (Van Ness and Strong, 2001; Clear and Karp, 2000; Bazemore and Schiff, 2002). Offender outcomes such as ensuring accountability and reducing recidivism are also important, but not as exclusive, perhaps even dominant goals. Assessing the effectiveness of restorative justice depends on measures that reflect such multidimensional, principle-based goals. To simply measure whether the offender has been either controlled or fixed would be inconsistent with both the intent and the philosophy of restorative justice.

Van Ness has developed a model to examine the effectiveness of restorative interventions based on a continuum of outcomes reflecting 'degrees of restorativeness' (Van Ness, 2000; 2001). In this model, Van Ness suggests that restorative strategies should be measured based not on simple dichotomous measures (eg Was the victim repaired? Did the offender recidivate? Was the victim satisfied?), but rather on the *degree* to which a number of important outcomes occurred or not; achieving 'more' of these key characteristics would represent greater restorativeness, and less of one attribute may be offset by more of another. The model considers a multitude of dimensions pertaining to victim, offender and community that are grounded in restorative values of encounter, amends, reintegration and inclusion (see also Van Ness and Strong, 2001). The model thus makes it possible to distinguish between a minimally, moderately and a fully restorative system based the extent to which outcomes representing these key values have been achieved. Whether or not Van Ness has precisely identified the exact dimensions by which to measure the effectiveness of restorative initiatives is, at this point, less important than is the inherent strength of a model that seeks to incorporate multiple outcomes for multiple parties and then examines the degree to which these goals have been achieved. This multidimensional structure for evaluating the effectiveness of restorative interventions is critical to understanding and evaluating the effectiveness of restorative justice strategies.

When considering the viability of restorative processes for improving the justice system response to crime, the first question must be 'in comparison to what?' In virtually all cases, the response must be 'in comparison to current practice' and research must be able to measure the relative costs and benefits of both strategies on dimensions that reflect the multitudinous goals of an effective justice system. It is unrealistic to expect that restorative, or any other, justice strategy will reliably meet *all* goals *all* the time. It is appropriate, however, to identify what goals are most important to whom, and then to examine the how well restorative justice is doing in meeting them. From here it is possible to develop evaluation measures that adequately reflect the complex nature of restorative interventions. This question, as well as the answers, must be relative—is restorative justice better, worse or equally effective as present strategies? While there are, as Kurki (this volume) suggests, considerable gaps in restorative justice evaluation to date, research has yet to offer conclusive evidence that restorative justice models are intrinsically any *worse* than current practices at meeting either the needs of its participants or those of the broader society.

III. CONCLUSION: THE PROMISE OF RESTORATIVE CONFERENCING

Many restorative justice practices and initiatives are, at best, fledgling efforts to experiment with new ways of preventing and responding to crime. Moreover, the theory on which such interventions are based is also evolving. Relatively speaking, modern experimentation with restorative justice has had a comparatively short history. In this context, critics should be cautious about concluding at this stage that restorative justice policies have 'failed.' It is one thing to point out that after ten years of partial implementation, restorative justice has failed to resolve pervasive justice system problems of insensitivity to minority cultures, legal coercion or inadequate attention to due process, for example. It is quite another to *blame* such longstanding problems on restorative justice (Schiff and Bazemore, 2001).

The majority of research on restorative conferencing to date has been positive, indifferent or has been methodologically inadequate (eg failing to use adequate control groups, using insufficient or incorrect measures). Rarely has research found effects that are *more* negative than current practices. In the end, the value and promise of restorative justice must depend on demonstrated effectiveness based on rigorous empirical assessment. However, with the exception of victim-offender mediation in many countries and FGC in Australia and New Zealand, most restorative programmes have barely been implemented, let alone evaluated. Even in Australia and New Zealand, results from the first comprehensive studies are just now being published (ie the RISE programme in Canberra and the SAJJ programme in South Australia). In addition, most research conducted to date has not been consistently linked to programme aims, and multiple measures that adequately reflect restorative principles have not been adequately developed. It is therefore inappropriate to conclude that such processes, which have barely been implemented, have either succeeded *or* failed. It seems more appropriate to suggest that before such conclusions can be drawn, results must be generated from reliable and methodologically sound research. Then, upon consideration of the results, will it be appropriate to assess whether restorative justice has succeeded or failed, and whether continued experimentation is warranted.

At this point, there is no empirical basis on which *not* to do restorative justice. While the evidence that restorative justice produces *better* outcomes is inconclusive, this does not yet warrant the repudiation of restorative practices. If restorative interventions do no harm, cost less, produce outcomes that are no worse than current practices, then there appears no good reason *not* to do them. While admittedly there are important concerns surrounding the implementation of restorative practices as suggested earlier in this (and other) chapter(s), these tend to imply greater, not less attention to such processes. At the Toronto conference preceding publication of this volume, Richard Young suggested that perhaps we have evolved from the first generation of basic, and relatively unsophisticated research in restorative justice to the second or even third generation, wherein restorative justice researchers are becoming increasingly adept at developing and testing rigorous, principle-based evaluation strategies. Such strategies can, far more comprehensively, help identify the benefits and costs of restorative interventions.

Thus, the promise of restorative justice lies in three areas: (1) increasing the quality and quantity of research documenting the development, implementation and outcomes of restorative initiatives; (2) continuing to generate and refine the theoretical basis on which such initiatives are premised and increasing the consistency with which restorative practice reflects theory; (3) expanding the dialogue between researchers, policymakers and practitioners such that restorative justice policy and practice reflects integrated and informed strategies; and, (4) continuing the discourse in conferences and volumes such as these where advocates of different perspectives may together reflect on the benefits and drawbacks of their respective approaches in a comprehensive effort to enhance the overall quality of the justice system response to crime.

REFERENCES

Achilles, M and Zehr, H (2001) 'Restorative Justice for Crime Victims: The Promise, The Challenge' in G Bazemore and M Schiff, *Restorative Community Justice: Repairing Harm and Transforming Communities* (Anderson Publishing Company, Cincinnati).
Adler, C and Wundersitz, J (1994) *Family Group Conferencing and Juvenile Justice: The Way Forward or Misplaced Optimism?* (Australia Institute of Criminology, Canberra ACT).

Albonetti, CA 'Criminality, Prosecutorial Screening and Uncertainty: Toward a Theory of Discretionary Decision Making in Felony Case Proceedings' (1986) 24(4) *Criminology* 623–43.

Bargen, J (1995) 'A Critical View of Conferencing' *The Australian and New Zealand Journal of Criminology* Special Supplementary Issue 100–3.

Bazemore, G (1999a) 'The Fork in the Road to Juvenile Court Reform' 564 *The Annals of the American Academy of Political and Social Science* 81–108.

——(2000) *Community Justice and a Vision of Collective Efficacy: The Case of Restorative Conferencing* (Department of Justice, Washington DC).

Bazemore, G and Griffiths, C 'Conferences, Circles, Boards, and Mediations: The "New Wave" of Community Justice Decision-Making' (1997) LXI (II) *Federal Probation* 25–37.

Bazemore, G and Schiff, M 'Community Justice/Restorative Justice: Prospects for a New Social Ecology for Community Corrections' (1996) 20(1) *International Journal of Comparative and Applied Criminal Justice* 311–35.

——(2001) 'What and Why Now: Understanding Restorative Justice' in G Bazemore and M Schiff (eds), *Restorative Community Justice: Repairing Harm and Transforming Communities* (Anderson Publishing Co, Cincinnati OH).

Bazemore, G and Umbreit, M (2001) 'A Comparison of Four Restorative Conferencing Models' (Feb) *Juvenile Justice Bulletin* (Office of Juvenile Justice and Delinquency Prevention, Washington DC).

Bazemore, G and Walgrave, L (1999) 'Restorative Juvenile Justice: In Search of Fundamentals and an Outline for Systemic Reform' in G Bazemore and L Walgrave (eds), *Restorative Juvenile Justice: Repairing the Harm of Youth Crime* (Criminal Justice Press, Monsey NY).

Bonta, J, Rooney, J and Wallace-Capretta, S (1998) *Restorative Justice: An Evaluation of the Restorative Resolutions Project.* User Report 1998–05 (Solicitor General Canada, Ottawa).

Braithwaite, J and Roche, D (2001) 'Responsibility and Restorative Justice' in G Bazemore and M Schiff (eds), *Restorative Community Justice: Repairing Harm and Transforming Communities* (Anderson Publishing Company, Cincinnati OH).

Bumiller, K (1990) 'Fallen angels: the representation of violence against women in legal culture' 18 *International Journal of the Sociology of Law* 125–42.

Burford, G and Hudson, J (eds) (2000) *Family Group Conferencing: New Directions in Community Centered Child and Family Practice* (Aldine Gruyters, New York).

Cant, R and Downie, R (1998) *Evaluation of the Young Offenders Act (1994) and the Juvenile Justice Teams* (Social Systems and Evaluation, Perth).

Carr, C (1998) VORS Program Evaluation Report.

Coates, R, Umbreit, M and Vos, B (2000) *Restorative Justice Circles in South Saint Paul, Minnesota* (Center for Restorative Justice and Peacemaking, School of Social Work, University of Minnesota).

Crawford, A and Clear, T (2001) 'Community Justice: Transforming Communities Through Restorative Justice? in G Bazemore and M Schiff (eds), *Restorative Community Justice: Repairing Harm and Transforming Communities* (Anderson Publishing Company, Cincinnati OH).

Crawford, A (1997) *The Local Governance of Crime: Appeals to Community and Partnerships* (Clarendon Press, Oxford).

Clear, T and Karp, D (2000) *The Community Justice Ideal* (Westview Press, Boulder CO).

Cunneen, C 'Community Conferencing and the Fiction of Indigenous Control' (1997) 30(3) *Austria and New Zealand Journal of Criminology* 292–311.

Cunneen, C 'Community Conferencing and the Fiction of Indigenous Control' (2000) *Policing Indigenous Communities* (Allen and Unwin, Sydney).

Daly, K (2000) 'Ideals meet reality: Research results on youth justice conferences in South Australia'. Paper prepared for the Fourth International Conference on Restorative Justice for Juveniles (Tübingen Germany).

——(2001) 'Restorative justice in Australia and New Zealand: variations, research findings, and prospects' in A Morris and G Maxwell (eds), *Restoring Justice for Juveniles: Conferencing, Mediation and Circles* (Hart Publishing, Oxford).

Delgado, R (2000) 'Prosecuting Violence: A Colloquy on Race, Community, and Justice. Goodbye to Hammurabi: Analyzing the Atavistic Appeal of Restorative Justice' 52 *Stanford Law Review* 751–75.

Duff, A (2001) *Punishment, Communication and Community* (Oxford University Press, New York).

Elias, R (1993) *Victims Still: The Political Manipulation of Crime Victims.* (Sage, Newbury Park CA).

Feld, B (1999) 'Rehabilitation, Retribution and Restorative Justice: Alternative conceptions of Juvenile Justice' in G Bazemore and L Walgrave (eds), *Restorative Juvenile Justice: Repairing the Harm of Youth Crime* (Criminal Justice Press, Monsey NY).

Fercello, C and Umbreit, M (1999) *Client Evaluation of Family Group Conferencing* (The Center for Restorative Justice and Mediation, St. Paul MN).

Flaten, C (1996) 'Victim Offender Mediation: Application with Serious Offences Committed by Juveniles,' in B Galaway and J Hudson (eds), *Restorative Justice: International Perspectives* (Criminal Justice Press, Monsey, NY).

Flemming, RB, Nardulli, PF and Eisenstein, J (1992) *The Craft of Justice* (University of Pennsylvania Press, Philadelphia PA).

Frohmann, L 'Discrediting victims' allegations of sexual assault: prosecutorial accounts of case rejections' (1991) 38(2) *Social Problems* 213–26.

Galaway, B and Hudson, J (1996) *Restorative Justice: International Perspectives* (Criminal Justice Press, Monsey NY).

Hines, D (2000) Personal communication to the author.

Holmes, M, Hosch, HM, Daudistel, HC, Perez, DA and Graves JB 'Ethnicity, Legal Resources, and Felony Dispositions in Two Southwestern States' (1996) 13(1) *Justice Quarterly* 11–30.

Karmen, A (2000) *Crime Victims* (Wadworth, Belmont CA).

Karp, D and Walther, L (2001) 'Community reparative boards: Theory and practice' in G Bazemore and M Schiff (eds), *Restorative Community Justice: Repairing Harm and Transforming Communities* (Anderson Publishing Company, Cincinnati OH).

Knapp, K (1999) 'An Evaluation of Community Conferencing: Central City Neighborhood Partnership (CCNP)' Internal Review, Minneapolis MN.

Kurki, L (2000) 'Restorative and Community Justice in the United States' in M Tonry (ed), *Crime and Justice: A Review of Research* (University of Chicago Press, Chicago IL) vol. 27, 235–304.

Lavery, C and Achilles, M (1999) 'Apologies: Balancing the Needs of Victims and Offenders' *Office of Victim Assistance Newsletter* (Office of Victim Assistance, Pennsylvania). http://sites.state.pa.us/PA_Exec/ova/ovapubs.htm

Levin, M (1972) 'Urban Politics and Policy Outcomes: The Criminal Courts' in GF Cole, *Criminal Justice: Law and Politics* (Duxbury Press, North Scituate MA).

Levrant, S, Cullen, FT, Fulton, B and Wozniak, JF 'Reconsidering Restorative Justice: The Corruption of Benevolence Revisited?' (1999) 45(1) *Crime and Delinquency* 3–27.

Lindner, C (1996) 'VORP: Unproven Fringe Movement' 20 *Perspectives* 15–7.

Maxwell, G and Morris, A (1996) 'Research on Family Group Conferences with Young Offenders in New Zealand' in J Hudson, A Morris, F Maxwell and B Galaway (eds), *Family Group Conferences: Perspectives on Policy and Practice* (Leichhardt AUS and Criminal Justice Press, Monsey NY).

——(1993) *Family Participation, Cultural Diversity and Victim Involvement in Youth Justice: A New Zealand Experiment* (Victoria University, Wellington NZ).

McCold, P and Watchel, B (1998) *Restorative Policing Experiment: The Bethlehem, Pennsylvania, Police Family Group Conferencing Project* (Community Service Foundation, Pipersville PA).

McGarrell, EF (2001) *Restorative Justice Conferences as an Early Response to Young Offenders* (Office of Juvenile Justice and Delinquency Prevention, Washington DC).

Melton, A 'Indigenous Justice Systems and Tribal Society' (1995) 70(3) *Judicature* 126–33.

Miers, D (2001) *An International Review of Restorative Justice*, Crime Reduction Research Series Paper 10 (Home Office, London).

Miers, D, Maguire, M, Goldie, S, Sharpe, K, Hale, C, Netten, A, Uglow, A, Doolin, K, Hallam, A, Enterkin, J and Newburn, T (2001) *An Exploratory Evaluation of Restorative Justice Schemes*, Crime Reduction Research Series Paper 9 (Home Office, London).

Morris, A and Maxwell, GM (1992) 'Juvenile Justice in New Zealand: A New Paradigm' 26 *Australian Journal of Criminology* 72–90.

——'Restorative Justice in New Zealand: Family Group Conferences as a Case Study' (1998) 1(1) *Western Criminological Review*. Online: http://wcr.sonoma.edu/v1n1/morris.html

——(2001) 'Restorative Conferencing' in G Bazemore and M Schiff (eds), *Restorative Community Justice: Repairing Harm and Transforming Communities* (Anderson Publishing Company, Cincinnati OH).

Niemeyer, M and Shichor, D (1996) 'A Preliminary Study of a Large Victim/Offender Reconciliation Program' 60 *Federal Probation* 30–4.

Nugent, WR and Paddock, JB 'The Effect of Victim-Offender Mediation on Severity of Reoffense' (1995) 12(4) *Mediation Quarterly* 353–67.

Nugent, W, Umbreit, M, Wiinamaki, L and Paddock, J 'Participation in Victim-Offender Mediation and Severity of Subsequent Delinquent Behavior: Successful Replications?' (2000) 11(1) *Journal of Research in Social Work Practice* 5–23.

Palk, G, Hayes, H and Prenzler, T 'Restorative and Community Conferencing: Summary of Findings from a Pilot Study' (1998) 10(2) *Current Issues in Criminal Justice* 138–55.

Pennell, J and Burford G (2000) 'Family Group Decision Making and Family Violence' in G Burford and J Hudson (eds), *Family Group Conferencing: New Directions in Community Centered Child and Family Practice* (Aldine Gruyters, New York).

Polk, K (2001) 'Positive Youth Development, Restorative Justice, and the Crisis of Abandoned Youth' in G Bazemore and M Schiff (eds), *Restorative Community Justice: Repairing Harm and Transforming Communities* (Anderson Publishing Company, Cincinnati OH).

Pranis, K (2001) 'Restorative Justice, Social Justice, and the Empowerment of Marginalized Populations' in G Bazemore and M Schiff (eds), *Restorative Community Justice: Repairing Harm and Transforming Communities* (Anderson Publishing Company, Cincinnati OH).

Roberts, L (1998) *Victim Offender Mediation: An Evaluation of the Pima County Juvenile Court Center's Victim Offender Mediation Program (VOMP)*. Available from Frasier Area Community Justice Initiative in Langley, British Columbia.

Roberts, AW and Masters, G (1999) *Group Conferencing: Restorative Justice in Practice* (The Center for Restorative Justice and Mediation, St. Paul MN).

S Roy 'Two Types of Juvenile Restitution Programs in Two Midwestern Counties: A Comparative Study' (1993) 57(4) *Federal Probation* 48–53.

Schiff, M and Bazemore, G (2001) 'Dangers and Opportunities of Restorative Justice: A Response to Critics' in G Bazemore and M Schiff (eds), *Restorative Community Justice: Repairing Harm and Transforming Communities* (Anderson Publishing Company, Cincinnati OH).

Schiff, M and Bazemore, G (2002) *Emerging Grounded Theory in Restorative Justice Decision-making: A Qualitative Case Study of Juvenile Justice Conferencing Programs*. Final Report to the National Institute of Justice and the Robert Wood Johnson Foundation, Unpublished Manuscript.

Schiff, M, Bazemore, G and Erbe, C (2001) 'Understanding Restorative Justice: A Study of Youth Conferencing Models in the United States'. Updated Paper presented at the Annual Meeting of the American Society of Criminology (San Francisco, CA).

Schiff, M 'Restorative Justice Interventions for Juvenile Offenders: A Research Agenda for the Next Decade' (1998) 1(1) *Western Criminology Review*. Online: http://wcr.sonoma.edu/v1n1/schiff.html.

Sherman, L, Strang, H and Woods, D (2000) 'Captains of Restorative Justice: Experience, Legitimacy and Recidivism by Type of Offense.' Paper presented at the Fourth Annual International Conference on Restorative Justice for Juveniles (Tübingen, Germany).

Stone, S, Helms, W and Edgeworth, P (1998) *Cobb County Juvenile Court Mediation Program Evaluation*. Final report for project funded by grants from the Children and Youth Co-ordinating Council and the State University of West Georgia (State University of West Georgia, Carollton GA).

Stuart, B (2001) 'Guiding Principles for Designing Peacemaking Circles' in G Bazemore and M Schiff (eds), *Restorative Community Justice: Repairing Harm and Transforming Communities* (Anderson Publishing Company, Cincinnati OH).

——(1996) 'Circle Sentencing: Turning swords into ploughshares' in B Galaway and J Hudson (eds), *Restorative Justice: International Perspectives* (Criminal Justice Press, Monsey NY).

Tonry, M (1998) 'Racial Politics, Racial Disparities and the War on Crime' in GF Cole and MG Gertz (eds), *The Criminal Justice System: Politics and Policies* 7th Edn (Wadsworth Publishing Company, Belmont CA).

Trimboli, L (2000) *An Evaluation of the NSW Youth Justice Conferencing Scheme* (New South Wales Bureau of Crime Statistics and Research, Sydney).

Umbreit, M (1988) 'Mediation of Victim Offender Conflict' *Journal of Dispute Resolution* 85–105.

——(1989) 'Violent Offenders and Their Victims' in M Wright and B Galaway (eds), *Mediation and Criminal Justice* (Sage, London).

——, 'Crime Victims Seeking Fairness, Not Revenge: Toward Restorative Justice' (1989) 53(3) *Federal Probation* 52–7.

——, 'Holding Juvenile Offenders Accountable: A Restorative Justice Perspective' (1995) 46(2) *Juvenile and Family Court Journal* 31–42.

——(1996) 'Restorative Justice Through Mediation: The Impact of Programs in Four

Canadian Provinces' in B Galaway and J Hudson (eds), *Restorative Justice: International Perspectives* (Criminal Justice Press, Monsey NY).

——(1997) 'Restorative Justice Through Victim Offender Mediation' in L Walgrave and G Bazemore (eds), *Restoring Juvenile Justice: An Exploration of the Restorative Justice Paradigm for Juvenile Offenders* (Kugler Publications, Amsterdam).

——, 'Restorative Justice Through Victim-Offender Mediation: A Multi-Site Assessment' (1998) 1(1) *Western Criminology Review*. Online: http://wcr.sonoma.edu/v1n1/umbreit.html

——(1999) 'Avoiding the Marginalization and McDonaldization of Victim-Offender Mediation: A Case Study in Moving Toward the Mainstream' in G Bazemore and L Walgrave (eds), *Restoring Juvenile Justice: Repairing the Harm of Youth Crime* (Criminal Justice Press, Monsey NY).

——(2001) *The Handbook of Victim-Offender Mediation* (Jossey-Bass, San Francisco CA).

Umbreit, M and Bradshaw, W 'Crime Victims Meet Juvenile Offenders: Contributing Factors to Victim Satisfaction with Mediated Dialogue in Minneapolis' (1998) 49(3) *Juvenile and Family Court Journal* 17–25.

Umbreit, M and Coates, R (1992) *Victim Offender Mediation: An Analysis of Programs in Four States of the US* (The Center for Restorative Justice and Mediation, St. Paul MN).

Umbreit, M, Coates, R and Roberts, A 'Impact of Victim-Offender Mediation in Canada, England and the United States' (1998) 1(6) *The Crime Victims Report* 83, 90–2.

Umbreit, M and Fercello, C 'Family Group Conferencing Program Results in Client Satisfaction' (1998) 3(6) *Juvenile Justice Update* 3–13.

Umbreit, M and Roberts, A (1996) *Mediation of Criminal Conflict in England: An Assessment of Services in Coventry and Leeds* (The Center for Restorative Justice and Mediation, St. Paul MN).

Van Ness, D (2000) 'The Shape of Things to Come: A Framework for Thinking about A Restorative Justice System'. Paper presented at the Fourth International Conference on Restorative Justice for Juveniles, Oct 1–4 2000 at Tübingen, Germany and the Balanced and Restorative Justice 'Train the Trainers' Seminar 19 May 2001, Jupiter, Florida.

Van Ness, D and Schiff, M (2001) 'Satisfaction Guaranteed? The Meaning of Satisfaction in Restorative Justice' in G Bazemore and M Schiff (eds), *Restorative Community Justice: Repairing Harm and Transforming Communities* (Anderson Publishing Company, Cincinnati OH).

Van Ness, D and Strong, K (1997) *Restoring Justice* (Anderson Publishing Company, Cincinnati OH).

Walgrave, L 'Restorative Justice: Just a Technique or a Fully-Fledged Alternative?' (1995) 34(3) *Howard Journal of Criminal Justice* 228–49.

Walker, S, Spohn, C and DeLone, M (1996) *The Color of Justice: Race, Ethnicity and Crime in America* (Wadworth Publishing Company, Belmont CA).

Warner, S (1992) *Making Amends: Justice for Victims and Offenders* (Avebury, Aldershot).

Wiinamaki, K (1997) Doctoral Dissertation (School of Social Work, University of Tennessee).

Zehr, H (1990) *Changing Lenses: A New Focus for Crime and Justice* (Herald Press, Scottdale PA).

Zellerer, E 'Community-Based Justice and Violence Against Women: Issues of Gender and Race' (1996) 20(2) *International Journal of Comparative and Applied Criminal Justice* 235–44.

Zellerer, E 'Community-Based Justice and Violence Against Women: Issues of Gender and Race', 'Restorative Justice in Indigenous Communities: Critical Issues in Confronting Violence against Women' (1999) 6(4) *International Review of Victimology* 345–58.

Zellerer, E and Cunneen, C (2001) 'Restorative Justice, Indigenous Justice, and Human Rights' in G Bazemore and M Schiff (eds), *Restorative Community Justice: Repairing Harm and Transforming Communities* (Anderson Publishing Company, Cincinnati OH).

Index